Diving the World

**A guide to the world's
most popular dive sites**

Beth and Shaun Tierney

Contents

Introduction

Maldives

Indonesia

Egypt

Thailand

Philippines

East Africa

Malaysia

Micronesia

Solomons

Galápagos

Grenada

Australia

Fiji

Mexico

Resources

Papua New Guinea

Central America

Front cover image:
Giant Pacific manta ray at San Benedicto Island, Mexico
Inside front:
Green turtle off the Borneo coast
Introduction page:
Table corals in the Banda Sea

It's lunchtime on Monday. There's no complaining about being back at work after the weekend as we round a pinnacle of rock, passing through a thick mass of redtail triggerfish. We rise up and over a ledge in the reef and there she is... a giant Pacific manta ray hovering effortlessly in the blue and – truly – waiting for us to approach.

We forget to breathe, freezing in our tracks for fear she will go away. But she doesn't. She approaches us and looks deep into our eyes. A gentle wing flap and she glides away, then comes back to us. Again and again.

We've been diving for 20 years but we have never experienced anything like this. Our memories are rich, but just when we think we have done it all, the oceans manage to surprise us. In this last year we have seen more sharks than we thought were left in the ocean, more turtles than we ever dreamed of. We have squinted at a whole new species of pygmy seahorse and seen the biggest Spanish Dancer on the planet. We are still deeply, utterly addicted.

Introduction

About this book

Times change. There is no doubt about it, but even in the sea, nothing stays the same for very long. If anything, our oceans are even more transient in this era where climate change is the topic on so many people's minds.

As the world adapts, so does the dive travel industry. A destination that was *the* hot place one year, quietly takes a back seat the next as somewhere new suddenly hits the diver radar. It is what makes it all so exciting: adventurous sorts opening up new realms for us to visit and see what lies below.

The divers' hit-list

For the first edition of *Diving the World* we sent out questionnaires to as many people as we could asking what destinations they had been to and where they wanted to go for their next diving holiday. The results became a hit-list of worldwide where-to-dive destinations. Three years later, many of those destinations remain on the list (we know because we bothered all those dive buddies once again) but what was even more interesting for us was what happened when Diving the World hit the stores. Complete strangers emailed us. "Why didn't you include Zanzibar?" and "what about Socorro?" or "you left out my favourite." So after a bit more research, we dived some of these areas and they are now included. Our thanks to those who took the time to share their experiences with us.

This guide still aims to cover what is most popular with travelling divers, the places they dream about and aspire to reach. All new areas have been visited and reviewed; all old ones have been updated and a few have even been revisited. However, in this edition, the four Asian countries have been assigned shorter chapters. This is still the world's most biodiverse region – and it seems the most visited – so if you are hoping to head that way, we'd suggest you get your hands on a copy of **Diving Southeast Asia**.

Every diver has their own personal hit-list of sites so how do you decide which one to visit first, which becomes the number one priority and which dream will have to wait for yet another year? Read on – our hope is that you find inspiration in these pages rather than definitive answers. The world is a small place these days, and the seas cover most of it. Explore, dream, discover.

About the authors

Our love of all things underwater first developed whilst snorkelling in Mexico during a round the world trip in the late 1980s. By the time we reached Indonesia we were completely hooked by what we were seeing beneath the surface.

As soon as we returned to London, we gained our BSAC qualifications and headed off to do our first open water dives in the Maldives. It was a heart-stopping moment when we came face-to-face with a whitetip reef shark and the start of a love affair that has influenced our lives ever since. As a photo-journalist team, we went off around the world again in the 1990s, this time specifically to dive. During this incredible year we explored many of the exotic locations that are now in this guide and in *Diving Southeast Asia*.

Since then we have become increasingly involved in the dive industry, and have been lucky enough to have revisited, photographed and written about many of the best dive destinations in the world.

Author image © Cindi LaRaia

Using this book

It's not our intention to claim this is the 'absolute' in dive guides, rather we hope to give divers and divers-to-be enough information to feel secure about choosing and booking that all-important trip.

Everything in this guide has been based on our personal experiences. Over the years, we have dived each and every one of the sites listed: some dives were a few years back but we have managed to revisit most. Sometimes, we would ascend thinking we had been there before so it was a case of working back through our old log books to check. Where we couldn't visit a new destination, we have asked those that have for their personal views: check these tales from others, they are great for making comparisons.

When it came to deciding which destinations to include, we asked both dive professionals and ordinary divers for their opinions, listening to their often very emotional responses. We've mentioned up-and-coming places for those who like to be more adventurous and have done our best to ensure that information is up-to-date, unbiased and, more importantly, first hand.

However, things change in a heartbeat so regard what is written in these pages as reference rather than gospel. And more than anything, bear in mind that If you go at a different time of year, chances are your experiences will be very different to ours. And that, of course, is the fun of dive travel.

66 99 Our hope is that you find inspiration here rather than definitive answers. The world is a small place these days, and the seas cover most of it. Explore, dream, discover.

Country rankings These are a simple way to compare the benefits of each country and were judged on a factual basis. For example, those with 5 stars against diving have high biodiversity and a broad variety of dive styles – reefs, wrecks, big animals and small. Likewise, a wide range of accommodation standards pushes up the number of stars; few dive centres or liveaboards in a destination takes the facilities star rating back down.

Dive logs Descriptions of dives are as we found them when we did them. Names for sites vary as do modes of transport: many sites can be reached both by day boat and liveaboard. More than anything else conditions change season by season. These logs are not definitive, nor are the descriptions: after all, fish swim away.

↘8 Roca Partida - South		The name of the site when we went
🜄 Depth	39 m	Our depth, not necessarily recommended
🜨 Visibility	good	Visibility on the day and season dependant
🜂 Currents	moderate but variable	Currents on the day and tide dependant
🜁 Dive type	liveaboard	How we travelled to the site

Images The photos used in each chapter – and against the dives – are what we saw on the day we were there. We have not taken images in Mozambique and used them in the Maldives. If a dive site is famous for manta rays but we haven't shown one, it's because we missed out. And that, as we all know, is the way of things when you play in the sea.

Maps Dive area maps are not to scale and are only intended to be an indication of a site's location in comparison to the nearest landmass and dives nearby. Sea depth and drop-offs are indicated by colour changes to give a loose indication of reef locations and surrounding sea conditions.

Drying out At the end of each chapter are some ideas on things do to when you are not diving along with contact details for dive centres, resorts, liveaboards and so on. Listings that have a full descriptive review are those we have first-hand experience of; any businesses with just a very short description or listed under *Other options* may have been recommended by friends and colleagues, or when someone we have worked with in the past has moved on or perhaps started their own operation.

Resorts and liveaboards To the best of our knowledge all operators listed hold PADI, BSAC, SSI, NAUI or similar affiliations, but always check, especially if you're taking a course.

Sleeping and eating What makes some people happy will not be to someone else's taste. We target hotels in the three star range as these are more likely to be comfortable, safe for you and secure for all your expensive dive kit. However, star ratings don't exist everywhere and some remote destinations have only minimal or basic accommodation options. These are noted on the Drying out pages along with a few up-market hotels, ideal for special events or honeymoons. Meal costs are subjective, but will give a general idea of how much cash to take out.

Marine species names When it comes to naming creatures, there are many and often conflicting common names. In general, we have used what seems to be most frequent. Likewise, the spelling of common names varies considerably so we chose to set a standard based on some well trusted, scientific sources as listed under Resources on page 355.

Planning a trip

Inspiration for the ultimate dive trip can come from this book, magazine articles or tales from friends. Wherever you plan to go, specific details of getting there, and what to do once you've arrived, are covered in the respective chapters. But before you rush into booking, take a look at the bigger picture. Does your dive destination have all the elements that you're looking for?

It's not enough to know that someone else had fun – if you don't get what you personally want, you'll be disappointed. To solve this, define your requirements before you start the booking process. Think about what time of year you can go and the prevailing weather conditions; how much you can afford, including the cost of the trip itself plus the cost of any extras; and most importantly, what type of diving you want to do and what you want to see.

On land or by sea

First, ask yourself, do you want to be on a liveaboard or on land? Being on land is perfect for people who are happy with fewer dives, have a non-diver or family with them or want to enjoy the local culture. There's more flexibility to go where you want, when you want but there is usually a limit to the number of dives you can do. In some countries, two dives will be cramped together into a single morning trip, in others they will take a more relaxing whole day but that leaves no time for other activities. Liveaboards, in comparison, are perfect for serious divers who like to do as many dives as possible in their time away, or those who just like floating about an idyllic location with no need to do more than eat, sleep and dive. You will have access to more remote, uncrowded areas with fewer divers and often better reefs.

Weather and seasons

For any dive holiday, this is the next consideration. Are you going at the best time of year or the cheapest? If you go in low season and save some money don't be surprised if it rains or the seas are choppy. That's why it's the low season. Marine life is seasonal too: be aware that even if a destination is promoted as year round, its most famous attraction may not be. Pelagic species in particular move great distances and can often only be seen for a few months. Also consider if you want to combine diving with land-based attractions. A cultural experience or rainforest trek may be ruined by rain while underwater it's not such an issue.

❝ ❞ Diving holidays are not like other holidays. They are not about lazing around in the blistering sun, waving at a passing cocktail waiter and spending hours over a three-course lunch. They are instead a series of all-action, adrenaline-rush days interspersed with balmy nights, waiting for dawn. Just so you can go and do it all again.

On land or by sea

Consider these options before making a final decision:

Land-based diving
- ▸▸ Hotel standard: luxury versus rustic, lively or quiet
- ▸▸ Hotel location: near a beach, restaurants, bars and shops
- ▸▸ Is the dive centre on site or will you need to travel there each day; if so, will they pick you up?
- ▸▸ Is the dive centre PADI, NAUI, SSI or BSAC regulated?
- ▸▸ Check scheduling: 2-tank morning dives or full day?
- ▸▸ Distance to the dive sites – is it shore or day boat diving?
- ▸▸ How many divers and guides will be on the boat?
- ▸▸ Are you expected to dive as a group or in buddy pairs? Will you have to abort your dives if others run out of air?
- ▸▸ Check for specific needs like nitrox or course availability
- ▸▸ Camera facilities on the boat
- ▸▸ Other activities for the kids, a non-diving partner and drying out days

Liveaboard diving
- ▸▸ Boat standard: luxury versus budget
- ▸▸ Cabins: en suite or shared bathrooms, air-con or fan?
- ▸▸ Meals are always included but ask if special diets can be catered for and what drinks are included
- ▸▸ Maximum number of passengers
- ▸▸ How many dives in a day?
- ▸▸ Is nitrox available if you want it?
- ▸▸ Boat policy on buddy pairs, solo or group diving
- ▸▸ Are land visits scheduled?
- ▸▸ If you are travelling with a non-diver, are sites suitable for snorkelling and are there other activities available?
- ▸▸ Camera and computer facilities, battery charging stations, specific rinse tanks for non-dive equipment
- ▸▸ On bad weather days can the boat shelter or be re-routed?
- ▸▸ Boats rarely accept children but you may want to check

More Knowledge
Modern educational system with interative media

More Safety
Professional SSI Centres with experienced, fully trained staff

More Diving
Qualification through training and experience

More Adventure
International Training Agency with Dive Centres, Dive Schools and Resorts all over the world

More Fun
Experience the underwater world together with your buddy. Enjoy. Relax. Feel free.

'Start today'.

SSI as one of the best training agencies worldwide will help you to make this dream come true. With SSI the adventure of diving is safe and easy for everybody.

www.diveSSI.com

serious diving. serious fun.

Costs

There is no doubt that diving is an expensive sport. As a rule of thumb, a land-based diving day worldwide averages at around US$120, which includes transport to the site, two dives with tanks, weights and a light lunch, although this will vary depending on local staff costs and expenses. Training courses average in a similar way with a PADI Open Water course costing around US$375. Liveaboard rates vary more as they reflect both the location of the vessel and its calibre in much the same way as a hotel may be two-star or four.

When you are budgeting for your trip look at all the angles to see if you are getting good value for money. Many people reject liveaboards as the initial price can seem prohibitive, yet as this often includes unlimited diving and extras like soft drinks, the cost in real terms may not be as high as it seems.

To work out a value-for-money comparison, try looking at the cost per dive. Choose your destination, then add the cost of your flights, accommodation, dive packs and any extras you can think of (marine park fees or visas) together and divide by the number of dives you expect to have. Use this as a benchmark to see if your trip will be good value. In the comparison below, both packages are available for the same period and include flights and transfers. However, the liveaboard includes all meals and soft drinks while the hotel package only includes breakfast. Essentially, you are getting free meals and double the dives on that option. Of course, this scenario won't always come down in favour of the liveaboard and much depends on the cost of flights, time of year and what you want out of your holiday.

Thailand liveaboard	
Deluxe 10 day trip with four dives per day	US$3,900.00
Cost per dive (3,900 ÷ 40 dives)	*US$97.50*
Thailand resort	
10 days/3 star resort with two dives a day	US$2,018.00
Cost per dive (2,018 ÷ 20 dives)	*US$100.90*

Budgets

So how long is a piece of string? When it comes to guessing how much cash to take for extras, it makes sense to consider the cost of living in the country you are going to. Naturally, westernised countries like Australia and American-run Micronesia will cost far more than Asian countries. What might be more surprising is that even some poorer countries can be quite pricey for travellers, particulary ones where you are obliged to buy drinking water – an absolute necessity for divers. Water, soft drinks and that post-dive cocktail can add a lot to your overall costs. Here are some basic price comparisons, correct at the time of writing:

Prices in US$	Litre of water	soft drink	330ml beer		Litre of water	soft drink	330ml beer
Australia	1.80	2.90	4.25	Maldives	2.50	2.75	5.00
Belize	1.10	0.75	2.00	Mexico	2.00	2.20	3.75
Egypt	1.30	2.00	2.45	Micronesia	2.10	1.50	3.50
Fiji	1.20	1.00	2.00	Mozambique	3.00	2.30	2.50
Galapagos	0.75	0.70	1.50	Palau	1.80	1.30	3.50
Grenada	2.40	2.20	1.90	Papua New Guinea	2.00	1.75	3.75
Honduras	0.26	0.65	1.05	Philippines	0.44	0.30	0.75
Indonesia	0.25	0.15	1.00	Solomons	1.65	1.50	2.90
Kenya	2.00	2.00	2.75	Tanzania	2.25	1.50	2.75
Malaysia	0.30	0.50	1.50	Thailand	0.35	0.40	1.50

Fees, taxes and surcharges

When you are planning and budgeting for your trip, allow a 'slush fund' for all those little extras you never quite know about until you arrive. These can be marine park fees, diver taxes that are ostensibly intended to support local recompression chambers or rescue services. Fuel surcharges are becoming ever more common. Individually, these costs are quite low but can add up.

Nautilus Explorer at Guadalupe Island; Kapalai dive resort in Sabah, Borneo

Currency

It has become a worldwide standard for US dollars to be the currency of choice with dive operators although more and more are quoting and accepting Euros. All rates in this book are US$. Travelling with currency is much the same: US dollars are easy to exchange no matter where you go, in fact many resorts accept them rather than local currencies.

Depending on current world politics, you may find it advantageous to have some cash in a second currency as well. Travellers' cheques are secure but can be hard to exchange. An option is to take your bank cash card with you. Most countries have cash machines and although your bank may charge a fee, it's not going to be far different from that of a foreign purchase. Hotels always charge a premium to change money so it pays to know the going rate in advance. Check rates inside your arrival airport. These may be slightly lower than with a local exchange office but the airport is more secure and less hassle.

In the end though, you cannot beat having a credit card with you. Although some countries add ridiculous surcharges to your bill for using them, they are still accepted and will give you automatic insurance on purchases from flight tickets to souvenirs.

Insurance

Travel insurance is an absolute necessity. Don't ever consider trying to save a few bucks by not covering yourself properly. You need a policy that will cover travel and flight delays, cancellations, baggage and diving equipment, money, cameras and other valuables and, most importantly, medical emergencies. Ensure

that any policy you take out covers repatriation home or to the closest recompression chamber. Note that even some dive specific policies have a depth limit. DAN (The Divers Alert Network) has thorough dive accident insurance but they do not automatically cover travel related issues (diversalertnetwork.org). Other worldwide insurers offer policies that may suit personal needs just as well. Check diveassure.com, scubasure.com, diveinsure.co.uk and divinginsuranceuk.com. A special note is to check any other insurance you may have. Many life insurance policies, for example, specifically exclude scuba diving as a high-risk sport.

Paperwork and disclaimers

There you are, just arrived and settling in to your room or cabin, and along comes a whole raft of paperwork. You feel like you are signing your life away: first, acknowledge that your operator is in no way liable for any harm that might come your way. Second, promise that if anything does go wrong, and it was someone else's fault, you won't take action against them. Third, accept that even if there is a complete blunder, you will only ever blame yourself... then sign the papers regardless as you know, deep down, there is no choice. And in reality there isn't.

If you question a disclaimer, or refuse to sign it, it's likely you won't be able to dive. Where disclaimers may once have been a declaration of fitness and training levels, they have since become a reflection of a society inclined to sue at the drop of a hat. There is nothing the average diver can do about this, except ensure that you choose reputable operations that will take all the necessary precautions to guarantee your safety.

✪ Reasons to be insured

Apart from the obvious one for divers, a diving accident, there are many other reasons to ensure you are completely insured. Loss of baggage, missed flights, camera flooding, getting pregnant and so on. We are well and truly covered for all that and any other eventuality – or so we thought – until recently when we got caught out. Yes, even travel writers blow it occasionally.

We had booked flights on a low-cost carrier that went bankrupt two days before our due departure. Thank heavens for insurance we thought! Until we rang up and the fine-print was quoted: not covered for bankruptcy of any provider used in the formation of the trip. The lesson to be learned: pay by credit card. Although rules vary by country, generally a card issuer is liable for your purchase and with sufficient evidence, will refund your cost. This will apply to nearly all purchases made using a credit card, but not a debit or cash card. Many companies charge a premium if you pay by credit card, but really, it is worth it.

Another warm welcome in Indonesia

Tipping

It's hard to be definitive about such a sensitive subject. Individual attitudes to tipping depend very much on where you grew up. In America it's an accepted way of life to tip generously for every service as staff rely on their tips to make a living wage. In Europe, the attitude is more likely to be a considered sum for good service while in Australia and Singapore people tip less, if at all, as these countries have higher minimum wage structures.

When it comes to tipping your dive crew, consider how much work they do behind the scenes, whether their actions ensured your trip went smoothly – or better than smoothly – and what their likely wage is. Although they will have been paid in line with local standards, a tip will reward those who often work very long hours for meagre salaries. Liveaboard crews, in particular, are often on call 24 hours a day to cater to your every whim. And always remember that these are the people who ensure you come back safely from every dive.

There is no magic formula but for land-based diving, a starting point could be US$5 per day. If you did three days shore diving and had a guide and driver looking after you, consider US$15. If you are a couple, US$25 might suffice. However, if you are on a liveaboard where a crew of 15 saw to your every need for 10 days, US$50 would be far too low. In these circumstances, $10 per day would be a better starting point. Bear in mind too, that over-tipping in certain countries can be an insult. If you need advice, ask your cruise director or resort manager.

There is a growing trend among higher-end liveaboard operations to formally request that guests leave 10% of the trip cost as a tip. At US$3,000 a trip that would be US$300 – which may well be appropriate, but many divers find this approach offensive, regarding it as an extra charge. In the end, only you can decide what the service was worth but always remember that it was worth something and being generous is a good thing.

Hard working crew on *Bilikiki* in the Solomons

☯ Booking a trip

Although this is probably the first thing on your mind, it should be the last thing you do. Once you are confident that you know what you want, you can either contact a specialist dive travel agent or book the trip yourself.

Agents With access to information and systems not available to the public, these can be a mine of information. A dedicated dive travel specialist will not only understand divers' needs but also be incredibly knowledgeable of the regions they promote. They will have suggestions, up-to-date information on local situations and often first-hand experience. They will also take the flack if things go wrong – very important these days – rearrange flights when schedules change or re-book you to another destination if there is a political or natural disaster. In some countries, they are also bonded or registered with government backed bodies. This may not always be a failsafe but it really can help.

DIY Becoming ever more popular as the internet continues to spread its web, booking your own trip can have advantages: you might find a product that is not available in your home country and direct rates are sometimes discounted. However, if you book direct you assume complete responsibility for your own trip. You have to ask all the right questions, ensure you have the right papers and coordinate every aspect involved – flights, accommodation, transfers, diving, meals, sightseeing. It can be a hefty job but if you like a sense of adventure it can also give you the flexibility to make on-the-spot changes.

There are many specialist dive travel agents around the world. Everyone will have their favourites, just as we do. The following are ones we can personally recommend:

▸ **Dive Discovery**, divediscovery.com. Based in San Francisco. Personally tailor-made diving holidays; organizes group tours and can issue flight tickets for unusual regions. Also owns Africa Discovery, africa-discovery.com, for safaris.

▸ **dive-the-world**, dive-the-world.com. Knowledgeable and informative European-run booking service; impartial advice on diving in all areas of Southeast Asia, Australia, the Red Sea, Maldives, and Fiji.

▸ **Dive Worldwide**, diveworldwide.com. Based in Hampshire, UK, this full-service company promotes a broad range of destinations and has very knowledgeable staff.

And for speakers of other languages, a wide range of worldwide dive trips can be arranged through:

▸ **Dive Advice Travel**, diveadvice.com. Based in Valbonne, southern France.

▸ **Ultima Frontera**, ultima-frontera.com. Office located in Madrid, Spain.

Diving Grenada

where nature meets art

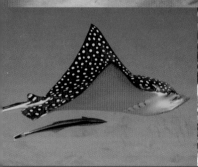

Scuba Diving in Grenada has never been so good: stunning reefs, awesome wrecks and the Underwater Sculpture Park all within 10 minutes of our strategically based dive center on beautiful Grand Anse Beach.

For more information on diving with us and our dive-and-stay packages, email info@divegrenada.com

Dive Grenada
Scuba Centre

Air travel

That saying 'getting there is half the fun' was obviously coined by someone who had never spent 18 hours in the rear economy class cabin of a jumbo – with two screaming kids behind and the person in front's seat resting on their nose. Nothing will ever convince most people that flying is a good way to spend time, but it is a means to an end. The trick is to minimise the difficulties and discomforts.

Airlines

Delays, overbooking, stray luggage – airlines seem like a law unto themselves. Some treat their passengers as honoured guests while others bring a new meaning to the term 'cattle class'. Some airlines are so much better than others that paying a little extra really can make the difference between a miserable long haul flight and a pleasant one. Ask yourself if you really want to save US$75 on a 12-hour flight and not have seat-back TVs with on-tap entertainment and free drinks?

If you have a choice of airline, go to **skytrax.com** for reviews: generally, Asian and Middle Eastern airlines have the best service with drinks and entertainment included in the ticket price, while American based airlines are least likely to include drinks and meals can be grim.

The ever expanding number of low-cost carriers is making this type of comparison even more obvious. Try booking a cheap flight with one of those and half way through the booking process you realise that the bargain of the year has just skyrocketed. Do you want a meal (click, $10 extra), to book the seat beside your partner (click, $10). Do you want to check your bags into the hold (click)? Are you overweight (excuse me? click, more money). The only positive result from this is at least it's clear what you are paying for. Until you get on board and it's, 'Headphones?' $10. Plus the plane is freezing, so you ask for a blanket, and guess what? Finally, once you have booked, look at **seatguru.com** which has advice on what seats are best so you can request your favourite.

Baggage

All divers bemoan their lot when it comes to airline baggage allowances. It can be very hard to pack your dive kit plus the usual holiday necessities and remain under the limit. The good news is that most scheduled airlines will waive a couple of kilos. However, that does mean a couple, not ten or twelve! It is now internationally accepted that all bags must weigh under 32 kilos for health and safety reasons.

In general, airlines flying to or from Europe, Australasia and Africa allow 20 kilos in economy, while US airlines will sometimes (but not always) allow two bags of up to 23 kilos each. If you know you will be over this, call in advance for current excess rates but whoever you fly with, if you exceed the limit be prepared to be charged. If you are faced with having to pay at check-in, keep cool and try to negotiate based on being a sports person. Bear in mind that the standard complaint that 'golfers can take their clubs for free' is rarely true. Nor can surfers take their boards. Instead they both get a dispensation to take oddly shaped items. The few airlines that do allow free golf clubs also allow free dive kit so beware – if you use this type of complaint at the desk, you are likely to get less sympathy as they have heard it all before. Charter and low-cost airlines allow less and are quite strict but have introduced clearer and more affordable excess rates.

With heightened security across the world, **hand luggage** is coming under more frequent scrutiny. Be sure to check your allowance before you head to the airport.

Another item of note, always lock your bags. There is a trend of not doing so because "if security wants to check, they'll break the lock". This is true, but it is better than having a stranger sneak a look at the contents of your bags if you leave them in your hotel reception say, on check out. There have been several high profile cases of people being arrested for drugs offences after leaving unlocked bags in hotel foyers and airports. Carry spare miniature padlocks or use plastic cable ties to secure your luggage, or if you are travelling from or via the USA, you can get special padlocks that can be opened by security at the airport.

Air travel Mozambique-style; hanging around at London Heathrow

Packing

Unfortunately one of the biggest problems for most divers is that they have non-travel-friendly dive kit. No one ever considers the weight of an item before they buy it and if you hope to do a lot of travelling, you should. Simply compare the weight of two pairs of fins. They can range from half a kilo per fin to well over a kilo. That extra weight per item really adds up. If your current kit is heavy, consider having a second travel-friendly set and before you get negative on the additional purchase cost, remember that excess charges at check-in can be as much as 1½% of a full economy fare. To Bali that might be as much as $900.

▸ Reduce the weight of your luggage. A hard case can weigh as much as five kilos more than a soft bag, which is much the same as your BCD.
▸ Reduce the weight of your kit by buying travel BCD's (or at least ones without integrated weights) lightweight regulators and fins.
▸ Buy a safety sausage rather than a reeled SMB. Invest in small, lightweight torches; get a small multipurpose knife.
▸ Do not take scuba toys – or other toys – away with you unless they serve a purpose.
▸ Do not take doubles of major items. Any dive centre that's worth diving with will have a spare if yours breaks down.
▸ Take a small repair kit for minor emergencies. Include duct tape, superglue, a multi-tool, strong cord, plastic cable ties and a spare mask strap.
▸ If you only intend diving for a few days consider hiring your equipment, but book it in advance.
▸ Get out what clothes you think you need and halve them. Then halve it all again. Really, no one cares if you wear the same t-shirt every other day.
▸ Reduce toiletries by getting mini-bottles, take medicines out of packets and write instructions down.

Watching the bags get loaded; ready to dive on Medjumbe

✪ Trouble-free travel

▸▸ Make sure your passport has at least one free page and six months to run after your departure date
▸▸ Check visa requirements well in advance
▸▸ Take out travel insurance that specifically covers diving as well as transport problems but check the fine print for depth limitations
▸▸ Take a copy or record of your passport numbers, travel insurance, qualification card, credit cards and any documents; pack separately to the originals
▸▸ Tell someone at home where you are going to be and when you are due back
▸▸ Take copies of booking forms and correspondence from your agent, hotel or dive centre
▸▸ Research your destination; check health requirements and updates on government advisory sites
▸▸ Ensure your dive gear is working and you have the appropriate kit for your intended location
▸▸ When you arrive obey the law and respect local customs and traditions

Equipment

We are all taught how important it is to be familiar and comfortable with our diving equipment so are encouraged to buy our own. This is a highly valid standpoint, but in light of recent airline restrictions, may need to become a more considered decision.

A full set of gear – BCD, regulator with octopus, fins, mask and snorkel, wetsuit and dive computer – can weigh 12 or 15 kilos, which at 65% of your total allowance means you need to think carefully about what you can take and what you have to leave behind. As you buy any new items, compare the weights of different brands alongside what you need them to do. You may for example, need to have a lightweight, warm-water regulator for trips abroad as well as a sturdier model for diving at home.

Rental equipment

There is another resolution – consider renting some of your equipment if you are travelling abroad. For some people this simply won't work: if you are over two metres tall, you will never get an off-the-rack wetsuit; if you are a very petite lady, it's unlikely you will find a BCD small enough. However, it may be worth renting fins, which average 1½-2 kilos a pair, or a regulator with octopus, which may be 2-3 kilos. Email in advance to find out what is available. Many dive operators offer complete kit packages purely for this reason. Remember that any operator that is worth diving with will maintain their kit well. On the same note, never take spares of bulky items like regulators with you. If you trust this operator to find you floating in an ocean after a dive, it's fair to assume you can trust them to supply you with a decent regulator.

Well-maintained rental kit at Carriacou Silver Diving

" On our last research trip we decided not to take our own trusted dive equipment and instead, rented from four different operations. Three had fantastic kit that was almost new. At one, things were a little less than perfect but still completely usable after a few swaps were made. It was a reminder, though, to ensure we double-checked everything we were given.

Wetsuits

Most countries covered by this book have similar, tropical climates with water temperatures averaging 26-28°C. For these conditions you should only need a 3 mm full wetsuit. However, a hood, rash vest or fleecy-lined skin is worth poking into a corner of your bag and will allow some layering up. You may appreciate this on the fourth dive of the day, where there are known thermoclines or if you stay still for long periods like photographers do. However, some will shiver in a 3 mm suit while others swelter. It's a personal issue that only time and experience will resolve.

Exceptions to the above are the waters of the Galápagos, Baja California in Mexico and Egypt. If you are going to these areas, especially in their winter months, you will need a 5 mm suit. For the Galápagos, some people even suggest a dry suit.

Other equipment

When it comes to smaller items of dive equipment you need to weigh the pros and cons of safety versus enjoyment. Torches, for example, are useful for night dives and dark spots on wrecks, but keep them small, so they fit in your pocket, and lightweight: huge ones are heavy and annoy other divers at night. Likewise, you must have an SMB (safety sausage) but a simple tube that rolls up in your pocket is as good as one with a reel.

Rechargeable items mean you don't have to carry as many batteries and that is also better for the environment. As you buy items, aim to get all one battery type – AAs are the most common – then look for a single recharger that is small and light. However, you will need to ensure you bring the right power adaptors: common types are in the table below and referenced in the Fact files at the beginning of each chapter.

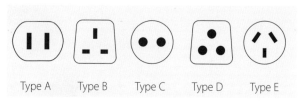

| Type A | Type B | Type C | Type D | Type E |

Egypt

Fairies at the end of the garden: if any one fish defines the Red Sea, it is the fairy basslet, *Pseudanthias species.* *Elphinstone Reef, Egypt*

Mediterranean Sea

Alexandria ●

ISRAEL

JORDAN

CAIRO ✈

Eilat ● ● Aqaba

Sinai
Peninsula

SAUDI ARAB

EGYPT

Sharm el Sheik ● ✈ ⬎1

El Gouna ●

Hurghada ● ✈

⬎2

Safaga ●

Red Sea

Nile

El Quesir ●

⬎3

Broth
Islar

Marsa Alam ● ✈

⬎4

Aswan ●

Hamata ●

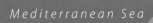

⬎1 Sinai Peninsula ▶▶ p26

Sinai Peninsula

Straits
of Tiran

⬎3

⬎2

Na'ama Bay ●
Sharm el Sheik ● ⬎1

Tiran

⬎5

Ras Mohammed

⬎4

⬎1	The Tower
⬎2	Ras Nasrani
⬎3	Woodhouse Reef
⬎4	Ras Mohammed
⬎5	The Thistlegorm

⬎2 South coast ▶▶ p29

Hurghada ●

Big Giftun
Little Giftun

⬎6

⬎6	Little Giftun
⬎7	Tobia Arba
⬎8	Panorama
⬎9	The Salem Express

⬎8

Safaga ● ⬎7

⬎9

Introduction

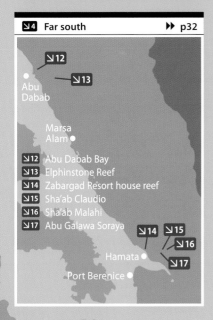

↘3 Brothers Islands ▶▶ p31

Big Brother

↘10

↘10 Little Brother
↘11 Big Brother

Little Brother

↘11

↘4 Far south ▶▶ p32

↘12

↘13

Abu Dabab

Marsa Alam

↘12 Abu Dabab Bay
↘13 Elphinstone Reef
↘14 Zabargad Resort house reef
↘15 Sha'ab Claudio
↘16 Sha'ab Malahi
↘17 Abu Galawa Soraya

↘14 ↘15

↘16

Hamata

↘17

Port Berenice

70 km

The lands surrounding the Red Sea are steeped in legend and ancient history. According to the story from Exodus, it was here that the waters parted to save the Israelites from the Egyptian army. Across the following centuries, great races populated both the intensely dry deserts and lush Nile Valley, all the time building unrivalled monuments and developing new technologies we still rely on thousands of years later.

The name, Red Sea, is something of an enigma. The most favoured explanation is that every now and then, a seasonal bloom of red algae turns the sea a pink hue, but ask an Egyptian about it and you will get a quizzical look. Whatever the reason, this sea is far from red: intense blue waters mask the rich coral reefs of the world's most northern tropical sea. It is also an exceptionally saline sea and combined, these unique features earn it a special ranking in the diving world.

Seven nations border this narrow ribbon of water but Egypt grabs the lion's share of diver attention. Yet the land of the Pharaohs may not be what you expected. Coastal resorts are highly developed and ancient monuments are a long way away. Not that this appears to matter to the million or more divers who descend on the ever-growing resort areas year after year.

Egypt rating

Diving
★★★

Dive facilities
★★★★

Accommodation
★★★

Down time
★★

Value for money
★★★★

Essentials

Getting there and around

If you live anywhere in Europe, you will already know that getting a charter flight to any Egyptian coastal resort is as easy as grabbing a dive magazine and booking a package. You could make your life a little more complex and try to fly scheduled – and you would be more comfortable – but as it's only a few hours on the plane, most people take the cheaper charter option.

However, if you're coming from further afield you will need to do some research. Many European airlines fly to Cairo, routing through their home base. Choose a flight based on if you would like a stopover: for London try British Airways, Alitalia for Rome and KLM for Amsterdam, to name just a few. From Australasia, Singapore Airlines and many Middle Eastern airlines such as Emirates, fly to Cairo where you can swap to an Egypt Air (egyptair.com) internal flight, or fly Egypt Air all the way. Their extensive network allows a stop in Cairo.

Once you have arrived at the Red Sea coast, you will be collected by your dive operator, assuming you have booked a package, or at least a night, in advance. As these resorts can get horribly busy, arriving without a booking isn't recommended.

Getting around during the day is easy enough in most resort areas. There are taxis but a price should be agreed in advance. Mini-buses provide shuttles between hotels and restaurants for a nominal sum and there are public buses and ferries that cover longer distances.

Local laws and customs

Egypt is principally a Muslim country so there are a few things to be aware of if you travel inland from the coast. Red Sea resorts are highly Westernized and tourist savvy but what you can get away with on the coast may be frowned upon in Cairo. Both sexes should dress modestly and avoid displays of affection in public. If you are with local people remember to eat with your right hand only and try to never show the soles of your feet (which is obviously a little difficult while you're diving). Women should be prepared to cover all bare skin and expect to be spoken to through their male partner or dive buddies.

Safety

In Cairo, as in any other city, be aware of what is going on around you. Personal safety is no more of an issue here than any major capital but be sensible about where you go and at what time of day. Women, especially those who are fair or redheaded, may feel uncomfortable with the amount of attention they receive. This is rarely malicious but can be disturbing.

However, the Red Sea coast is a whole different kettle of fish and tourists are nearly always treated as welcome guests. Although resorts are modern and feel perfectly safe, recent terrorist activity will no doubt discourage some. Be assured that security services are highly vigilant in all dive areas.

Egypt	
Location	27°00'N, 30°00'E
Capital	Cairo
Population	83,082,869
Land area in km²	995,450
Coastline in km	2,450

Homeward bound along Safaga Beach

Language

From the ancient days of hieroglyphics through to the modern day, language in Egypt has changed many times. However, once Islam took hold, Arabic became official. Local dialects are spoken across the region with Egyptian Arabic differing even between the north and south. God's Will, *inshaalha*, and never mind, *maalish*, are two phrases you will hear constantly. Dive crews seem to enjoy teaching a few words here and there:

hello	*salam alekom*	thank you	*shukran*
goodbye	*maasalaama*	excuse me	*ismahlee*
yes	*naam*	how much is this?	*kum hada?*
no	*la*	water	*moya*
please	*men fadlak*	good	*kowiees*

Health

Tutankhamen's Two-step, Pharaoh's Revenge... you guessed it, euphemisms for a classic case of Egyptian stomach upset. You would be lucky to get there and back without a minor dose, which is surprising as hotel kitchens seem spotless. But meals are often specifically targeted at tourist taste buds and it is this that appears to cause problems. Local-style cooking is often fresher but can be hard to find. If a place looks clean and well patronized, especially by Egyptians, it's a good sign. Be sure to keep up your fluid levels; it's a great way to combat tummy troubles. For other health issues, chemists or pharmacists are well trained. Hotels hold details of English-speaking doctors. And beware of the sun – midsummer temperatures can reach over 50°C. Factor eight sunscreen is close to useless in this environment. Get 30 plus.

Costs

A week-long package including flights, room and diving can be exceptional value at as little as US$900, but it is harder to judge costs for hotels if you travel independently. However, eating out is something you can quantify. In busier regions there are many restaurants in many styles. A burger and chips may be as little as EGP£30 but in the far south, where you are limited to your resort, that same meal may be EGP£50. Likewise, a beer could be as much as EGP£22 which is tipping the scales at European prices: some resorts now charge for extras in Euros which may have encouraged price increases. If you can get to a supermarket for incidentals like mineral water, you will keep costs down.

Tipping – or baksheesh – is a way of life in Egypt. Salaries are low, especially in the service industries, so 'donate' an Egyptian pound or two to everyone, from cab drivers to the chap who watches your shoes when you a visit a mosque. On restaurant bills, consider 10%. For dive crews see page 12.

Tourist information → The government website can be found at egypt.travel. For extra diving information visit goredsea.com and click on their Red Sea magazine link.

Fact file

International flights	Alitalia, British Airways, Egypt Air, Emirates, KLM
Departure tax	Usually included in your ticket
Entry	Visas usually issued on entry. The fee varies from US$20-60 depending on your nationality
Internal flights	Egypt Air
Ground transport	Countrywide buses, trains, taxis, mini-buses
Money	US$1 = 5.5 Egyptian pounds (EGP)
Language	Arabic and English
Electricity	220v, plug type C (see page 16)
Time zone	Time zone GMT +2
Religion	Muslim, small Coptic Christian minority
Phone	Country code +20; IDD code 00; Police 0

Soft corals and anthias on Elphinstone Reef

Dive brief

Diving

At 2,240 kilometres long, 380 wide and up to 2,150 metres deep the Red Sea is a lifeline for the countries that border her shores. The northern end is enclosed – or was until the building of the Suez Canal – while the southern opening into the Indian Ocean is extremely shallow, preventing deep ocean currents from entering the gulf.

The surrounding deserts and extreme temperatures create the highest salinity in any open sea, yet despite this, it sustains one of the world's more prolific marine systems. Being isolated from both the Indian Ocean and the Mediterranean Sea (originally) means this most northern tropical sea has an unrivalled biological set-up. Almost 10% of her species are endemic: they might look a bit like something you've seen somewhere else but chances are they're a unique form. Crustaceans, cephalopods, molluscs – they're all there along with schools of reef and pelagic fish. Sharks swoop past in the current and dolphins play in the bow wave on an almost daily basis.

However, whether you've headed for the Sinai or the south or somewhere on a boat out in the middle, the appearance of these dives will be fairly similar. Seasonal variations can be marked though. The summer months are exceptionally hot and when it's windy you will know all about it. Winters can be surprisingly cold and surface conditions can be very choppy. Beneath the water, the marine life seen from one season to another differs substantially. Plankton blooms are linked to temperature changes and can occur at any time, as can a change in the currents.

Snorkelling

There are many beach-side reefs but even if you don't dive it's worth heading out on a boat with the divers as many of Egypt's offshore reefs can be snorkelled. The only issue for snorkellers will be the weather. Be very aware of how harsh the sun can be. As the water here is cool, you may not realize that you are burning. Conversely, when it's winter you may need a wetsuit as the water temperature drops sharply.

Marine life

The majority of divers who dive the Red Sea do so regularly and tend to see much the same things: anthias, butterflyfish, rays and morays. But you can be surprised by anything from a tiger shark or manta ray to tiny seagrass ghost pipefish.

Egypt
animal
encounters

Sinai	Napoleon wrasse
Hurghada	mantas and morays
The Brothers	sharks
Marsa Alam	green turtles

One of Abu Dabab Bay's resident green turtles

When we learnt to dive, the swimming pool in central London made our training dives in Cyprus look exotic. In turn, those dives meant our first trip to the Red Sea took on the status of a pilgrimage. After several trips there we got a hankering to go further. We spread our wings and spent the '90s traversing one continent after another. We've been back to Egypt since and it's good to be reminded that this is one of the world's better coral reef systems. Catch it at the right time of year in the right part of the sea, with the right operation, and you will find some great diving. But you do have to remember that because this is such an easily accessible destination, it's also one of the busiest and most crowded places you will ever dive.

Making the big decision

The Red Sea is only a stone's throw from southern Europe and though you can dive much of it, Egypt is by far the easiest country to reach. It has a highly diver-focussed infrastructure, it is reasonably priced (especially for Europeans) and is perhaps the least politically sensitive country (for those coming from further afield). Choosing a specific destination inside the country is only difficult in that there is little difference between the resort areas – a little bigger or smaller, a lot busier or a little quieter – there's not much in it as long as you accept that wherever you go, there will be many others with you.

Pristine hard coral bowl on Abu Galawa Soraya in the Fury Shoals

Dive data

Seasons	All year: July-August is extremely hot, December-January can be very cool especially at night
Visibility	10-40 metres
Temperatures	Air 20-30°C; water 20-28°C
Wet suit	Summer: 3 mm full body suit; winter: 5 mm+
Training	Courses available in most resorts, standards vary
Nitrox	Available everywhere
Deco chambers	Sharm el Sheikh, Hurghada, El Gouna, Marsa Alam

Bottom time

Sinai Peninsula	Birthplace of the Egyptian dive industry, once sleepy fishing villages have now grown almost beyond recognition with ever more resorts spreading both north and south along the Sinai Peninsula.
Sharm El Sheikh ⏵ p26	The much-loved dive sites cover famous reefs like Ras Mohammed and even more famous wrecks like the Thistlegorm.
South coast	Across the Straits of Gubal is this continually expanding resort region. Small ports and coastal towns are now marketed as the Red Sea Riviera.
Hurghada and Safaga ⏵ p29	Popular but less prolific inshore reefs that still maintain the potential to surprise.
Brothers Islands ⏵ p31	Six hours' sail from the coast, these distant islands have potentially breathtaking diving in a pristine environment.
Far south	Egypt's final dive frontiers are the areas almost on the Sudanese border.
Marsa Alam and Abu Dabab ⏵ p32	Some unusual sites and pelagic species make this an increasingly popular destination.
Hamata and Fury Shoals ⏵ p34	How diving in the Red Sea used to be – quiet, peaceful and comparatively unexplored.

Diversity   reef area 3,800km²

HARD CORALS	57
FISH SPECIES	746
ENDEMIC FISH SPECIES	1
FISH UNDER THREAT	32
PROTECTED REEFS/MARINE PARKS	9

All diversity figures are approximate

Dive log

Sinai Peninsula

Sharm el Sheik

Diving in the Sinai is legendary. This area is definitely one of those 'must do' places: home to Ras Mohammed, Egypt's first marine park, the Straits of Tiran and the Straits of Gubal. To the west is the entrance to the Suez Canal where many a wreck is found. And despite the large numbers of boats, operators and divers, this is an area of distinctive beauty.

Dive tourism was born in a tiny fishing village which grew out of all recognition to become the upscale resort of Sharm el Sheikh. There are hotels and dive centres, restaurants and more hotels. At its heart is Na'ama Bay, a crescent shaped cove that somehow manages to retain a little of the town's early charm. It's a lively place, with lots to do. There's golf and camel riding, you can arrange a trip into the desert with a Bedouin guide or head off on a tour to a medieval site but the focus remains pretty much dive, dive, dive – and party. Bars and restaurants abound.

On either side of Na'ama, the resorts in Shark Bay and Old Sharm (Sharm El Maya)

are good for those who like it a little less frenetic. Facilities are just as good and you are only a short taxi ride away from the activities and nightlife in the centre.

Development continues to spread right up the coast towards Israel. In Dahab, a smaller number of hotels with dive centres are better for those who like an even quieter life. Numbers of visitors, both on land and in the water, are fewer here, yet the diving is still impressive. Nearby are St Catherine's Monastery and Mount Sinai, said to be where Moses received the Ten Commandments.

If you are a novice and want to gain experience there are plenty of dives to practise on: shallow wrecks, pretty reefs, drifts and caves – it's all there. For more experienced divers, there's all of that plus some deeper wrecks and more exposed conditions. The downside, though, is the numbers. You will never be the only boat moored at any site. Sometimes there are so many you need both hands, and a toe or two, to count them.

⚓1 The Tower	
⏱ **Depth**	20 m
◑ **Visibility**	good
〰 **Currents**	slight to medium
〰 **Dive type**	shore

This shore dive is popular both day and night. The entry over the reef can be a little tricky at low tide so most divers take a spectacular short-cut through a small cave. The mouth is part way across the reef top and as you swim down it opens into a wider passage then exits on the reef wall. You could drop as deep as 40 metres, and may encounter a whitetip or two, but the most interesting parts of the dive are under 20 metres. The marine life is a microcosm of all things Red Sea –masses of anthias flitting in and out of soft corals, moray eels, butterflies, lionfish and plenty of crustaceans. At night every surface is alive with shrimp and decorator crabs, which are attracted by the moonlight shining through the opening.

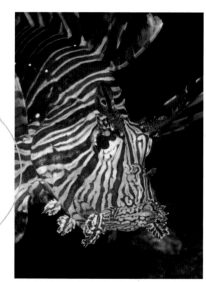
Nosy lionfish on Ras Nasrani

⊠2 Ras Nasrani

🧭 **Depth**	24 m
◐ **Visibility**	good
🌊 **Currents**	can be strong
⬤ **Dive type**	day boat

This name means Christian Headland and, like everywhere in the Sinai, the location leads to more than one dive. The wall below the tip of the point is quite steep and at its base there is a good covering of soft corals and gorgonians. In the shallows is a healthy background of hard corals, which harbour scorpionfish and anemones with clownfish. Glassfish shoals hover in small caves while in open water there are fusiliers, jacks and surgeons. Moving south from the point you come to another dive site called White Knights. It's an equally good dive but what's more interesting is that mantas sometimes flap lazily to and fro between these sites.

⊠3 Woodhouse Reef

🧭 **Depth**	24 m
◐ **Visibility**	good
🌊 **Currents**	can be strong
⬤ **Dive type**	day boat

Heading east from Sharm are the Straits of Tiran where a series of reefs are great dives yet troublesome for boat navigation. As you approach, you will see a couple of partially submerged, wrecked hulls that came to an early demise here. Woodhouse is one of the reefs, sitting between Jackson and Gordon and a little sheltered by them. However, this long narrow reef is nearly always swept by currents, making it a drift dive. The top is quite shallow but it drops steeply on both sides. Divers get dropped on the east and drift along the wall. Coral cover is pretty good all the way along and you can spot many animals such as morays sheltering in amongst them. Because of the current, there are jacks, tuna, snapper and occasionally turtles in the blue. Up in the shallows are creatures such as pipefish and bluespotted rays.

⊠4 Ras Mohammed

🧭 **Depth**	20 m
◐ **Visibility**	good
🌊 **Currents**	can be very strong
⬤ **Dive type**	day boat

Off the very southern tip of Ras Mohammed are several dives loosely known as 'Ras'. The actual sites mostly referred to are the twin peaks of Shark Reef and Jolanda. Their joint status derives from dives starting on one and finishing on the other. A submerged sea mound is separated from the mainland by a shallow channel and rising from it are the two peaks, themselves linked by a saddle. The dive starts off as a drift at Shark Reef where a wall drops dramatically into the blue. You float past swarming orange and blue anthias and over colourful soft corals feeding in the current. Reef sharks (black and whitetips) are often seen; less often are hammerheads. Next you pass over the saddle, then it's on to the coral gardens at Jolanda. You may spot a few cargo remains from the freighter of the same name but the wreck itself dropped into the deep during a storm in the 80s. The dive finally ends in the shallows beyond.

Various types of grouper, clownfish and Napoleon wrasse live all over the Sinai

Fish tales

In the Northern Red Sea, on a point called Beacon Rock, lies the *Dunraven*. Built in 1873, she was a sail and steam hybrid, utilizing sail when conditions permitted. This ship came to an untimely end on the 25th April, 1876. According to records she ran aground due to a navigation error. However, our dive guide told a different tale. The Captain caught the Master of the ship below decks with his wife. The two men fought a great battle and in the heat of the fight, the distracted crew did not notice the approaching rocks. Whether this has any truth, or is an apocryphal tale, only goes to make this a more interesting dive.

Descending the buoy line to the stern of the ship, we found the wreck lying upside down at 30 metres. A large intact propeller was encrusted in coral and below that was an opening. We entered into relative darkness but soon become accustomed to the gloom. Rows of portholes let light through to create a mysterious atmosphere. Slowly, working single file forwards, we came across two large boilers surrounded by glassy sweepers and the odd overfed lionfish. Then, leaving the interior, we explored the bow. There were Napoleon wrasse and giant morays amongst the ever-present anthias.

Finally, we headed over to the adjacent reef, which was a nice end to the dive and it was here that my buddy and I were joined by a lone dolphin. We are both photographers and were a way behind the main group. I turned to see 'our' dolphin close by. With the camera stuck in front of my face and a smile so wide that my reg nearly fell out, I was amazed to watch this inquisitive fellow almost touch noses with my buddy. We spent some 20 minutes with him until my air was so low I had to come up. I have dived this wreck a few times and, to be honest, it is far from the best in this region, but that experience made the *Dunraven* a memory to be cherished forever.

Sean Keen, Bexhill-on-Sea, UK

⬇5 The Thistlegorm	
🕐 **Depth**	25 m
◑ **Visibility**	fair
🌊 **Currents**	can be strong
🌊 **Dive type**	day boat/liveaboard

The Straits of Gubal, the stretch of water that leads to the Suez Canal, are a shipping graveyard. One of the most renowned dives here is the *HMS Thistlegorm*, a British cargo vessel bombed during the Second World War en route to resupply troops. Now she is like a deserted shop, with holds full of motorbikes, engines and even toilets that never reached their destination. Conditions here are highly variable – when it's calm it's an easy dive but if the wind and waves pick up, it 's not a place for novices. The hull is lying almost upright at 30 metres and is pretty much intact. Descent is down a line tied to the forward section from where you can swim into a few of the holds then down towards the stern. This took the brunt of the bomb blast but you can see the propeller, crew quarters and some anti-aircraft guns. The wreck is well colonized with corals and fish life and just off to one side, if you can tear yourself away, is a locomotive engine.

Descending on the *Thistlegorm*

South coast

Hurghada and Safaga

Opposite Sharm, but on the other side of the Straits of Gubal, lies Hurghada. This was a small Bedouin encampment but after the airport was built the town quickly expanded into a major resort. In a few short years, all the small towns in this area were targeted for tourism and, like their Sinai neighbours, have grown up to become sophisticated resorts.

Hurghada is Egypt's biggest beach resort stretching for many kilometres north and south of downtown Dahar. The whole coastline is connected by the Corniche, a single road lined with resorts, restaurants, shops, dive centres and facilities for a range of sports, from golf to windsurfing. Dahar itself is a working town, busy, messy and typically Egyptian.

Offshore, the reefs once suffered from misuse and over-diving. However, in 1992 operators formed a conservation group, organizing mooring buoys and protective schemes. The reefs are now safeguarded under the same rules as Ras Mohammed

and regenerating well, although those closer to shore are not as profuse as you might hope. Day boats head out to better reefs and you can book special fast boats to reach the wrecks in Gubal. Hurghada is also the starting point for many liveaboards that travel all over the southern Red Sea.

A short drive north of Hurghada, is El Gouna, a custom-built resort area. Fancy landscaping turned the desert into a maze of palm tree- and hotel-studded islands surrounded by lagoons. There's a small, insignificant 'downtown', a full complement of dive and other activities and a certain sense of seclusion not found in Hurghada. As it is closer to Gubal, day trips head up there as well as to the offshore reefs.

The shipping port of Safaga, an hour south of Hurghada, has lent its name to another resort. Few tourists see the small port town as it lies a few kilometers away from the tourist zone. There are a handful of hotels with on-site dive centres and as it is less busy, local reefs here are in fairly good condition.

Surface conditions can be rougher as Safaga is also a highly favoured destination for windsurfers and has hosted world-championship competitions.

☑6	Little Giftun	
🌀	**Depth**	28 m
◐	**Visibility**	fair to good
〰	**Currents**	slight to medium
🌊	**Dive type**	day boat/liveaboard

A short sail offshore from Hurghada are Big and Little Giftun islands. These are popular sites for novices and trainees so the corals are not at their best, especially in the shallower areas. However, the wall on Little Giftun is an exception. Entering the water opposite the lighthouse, you drop in to find a current that will carry you on a drift through a forest of pink and yellow fans. Longnose hawkfish hide in these and scrawled filefish try to do the same. There are a lot of schooling fish and giant morays that free swim along the wall.

Swimming through a bait ball; flounder in the sand; masked butterflyfish on Little Giftun

---

↘7 Tobia Arba	
Depth	19 m
Visibility	good
Currents	mild
Dive type	liveaboard

Although named the Seven Pillars there only seem to be five – well at least that's all you have time to find on an average dive. The pillars rise from a flat seabed and are marked by interesting hard coral shapes. Small caves are full of glassy sweepers, overhangs protect butterflyfish couples and corals and anthias cover the walls. You can swim through small tunnels and find moorish idols nosing around. On the sand there are seagrass ghost pipefish and, at night, Spanish Dancers.

Conservation

Back in the late 80s a group of four dive companies in Hurghada got together to discuss the state of the reefs. They had realised that if someone somewhere didn't do something, they would soon be looking at the demise of the local marine environment. Over fished, over dived, the area was in trouble. They banded together and started making things happen.

From such small beginnings, the Hurghada Environmental Protection and Conservation Association was born and has done a world of good for local reefs – and much of Egypt's marine environment. This non-governmental association works to get mooring buoys positioned on reefs – and wrecks like the *Thistlegorm* – and educates school children and boat crews. They also spearhead politically motivated campaigns, helping to reverse decisions on projects that could cause damage to the marine environment: Giftun Island will not become a tourist development and, with any luck, there won't be any drilling for oil allowed in Egyptian waters.

When you think there are now over 300 dive centres and boat operators just in the Hurghada area, you realise just how vital their work is.

↘8 Panorama	
Depth	33 m
Visibility	good
Currents	none to mild
Dive type	liveaboard

Regarded as one of Hurghada's most impressive reefs, this long coral mound can be dived from several points. On all sides, gentle slopes lead down to 25 metres or so then there is a sudden drop-off, falling to unreachable depths. The northwest corner is lacking in soft coral growth but there are plenty of overhangs along the walls. Turtles and morays hide amongst the craggy rocks formed by a good cover of hard corals. If you move to the opposite corner, it's a little more colourful with some fans brightening the view; whitetip sharks are regular visitors and there are a surprising number of bottom dwellers like crocodilefish and blue spotted rays. Masked pufferfish huddle down inside sponges while scorpion and stonefish blend perfectly into the background.

↘9 The Salem Express	
Depth	22 m
Visibility	good
Currents	mild to medium
Dive type	liveaboard

A controversial addition to the dive list is the wreck of the *Salem Express*. In 1991, this passenger ferry was heavily loaded with pilgrims returning from Mecca. She was only a few hours short of Safaga when she hit the reef at Sha'ab Shear and sank with a huge loss of life. Many operators feel that she should be left in peace and will not dive here. However, many others will and you will be briefed on treating the wreck with the respect it deserves. Suffice it to say that any trophy hunting would be exceptionally bad form. The *Salem* is majestic in her demise, lying on her side at just 32 metres. There are many signs of the people who were on board at the time, like suitcases and life rafts rotting quietly on the sea floor. She appears peaceful and is succumbing to the elements, which are taking her back in the usual cycle of life. Small corals are forming across the hull, pipefish and octopus hide in crevices and puffers hover like silent sentinels.

Hard corals plaster the sides of a local reef walls; the *Salem Express*

Brothers Islands

El-Akhawein, better known as the Brothers Islands, staked their place in diver folklore after the surrounding marine park was reopened a few years ago. The islands consist of two harsh rocks that rise steeply from the sea bed.

Big and Little Brother are a six-hour sail from Hurghada and the crossing can be rough but once you are there you will find a flawless reef system, reminiscent of the Red Sea of past decades. Corals are still pristine – get your buoyancy right – and as the only reefs for miles, they attract a large number of pelagic fish. It is said that you can also see sharks – oceanic whitetips, hammerheads and threshers. These only appear when the currents are running so night diving is banned. Less experienced divers may find the going tough. Moorings are limited and tucked away on the calmer sides of these tiny islands. The authorities are supposed to restrict the number of permits given to liveaboards but appear to over-supply them. Don't be surprised if your promised four days at the Brothers ends up being less than two because your captain can't find a vacant spot.

⑩ Little Brother	
Depth	38 m
Visibility	infinity
Currents	mild to strong
Dive type	liveaboard

Opinions on currents are relative to what you have done but a truly strong current will threaten to rip the mask from your face. Fortunately, at Little Brother the pace can be fairly easy going at times – it all depends on what season you are here to dive. Entering at the northern point of the island a tongue-shaped section of reef leads seawards. This section is usually a faster, drift dive where thresher sharks, greys or hammerheads pass by at depth. On the southern side, amazing soft corals carpet a steep wall that looks like a manic modern painting. At its base, there is a forest of huge fan corals. Small caves and overhangs are thick with rabbitfish, surgeonfish, butterflies and moorish idols while bright orange anthias constantly flash in and out of the reef wall.

⑪ Big Brother	
Depth	36 m
Visibility	infinity
Currents	mild to strong
Dive type	liveaboard

This northern island is marked by a stone lighthouse, which is manned by the military, and dominates the otherwise pancake-flat vista. There are two diveable wrecks: the first is a large freighter named the Namibia and the other a supply boat, the Aida II. Both are splendid, if very short dives due to their depth, and they can get crowded. The Aida lies on an extremely steep slope with her bow resting at 25 metres or so. Her propeller isn't reachable within normal sport diving limits so all you will manage is a quick glimpse unless you go into deco, which is frowned upon due to the remoteness of the islands. Along the southern side of the island the reef catches some strong currents so there are plenty of fabulous corals and a huge variety of marine life.

Bannerfish on patrol; the wall at Little Brother

Far south

Marsa Alam and Abu Dabab

In long distant times, the village of Marsa Alam marked the junction with the Red Sea's coastal road and a lone road that led inland to Edfu on the Nile. More recently, it became the site of a small military airport, which then led to the region's expansion as a tourist destination.

Ancient records reveal some interesting history although you are unlikely to see it. Ptolemy II built that road as a trade route between the Nile Valley and the Red Sea; the ancient Egyptians mined much of their gold here and Pharoah Seti I built a temple. Later, the Romans mined for precious gems and much prized marble. Fortunes changed after the airport was rebuilt. Now flights land from all over Europe and the focus on tourism is intense. There is a new and relatively classy marina at Port Ghaleb but the main draw is still diving, although there isn't anywhere near the number of dive resorts as in Sharm or Hurghada. Yet.

Heading south the coast road is sporadically bordered by clusters of hotels, followed by long stretches of nothing but desert until you encounter another cluster of potential resorts. These get smaller, and the open stretches longer, the further you go. There are resorts both north and south of Marsa Alam town, then some ring the beautiful bay at **Abu Dabab.**

The coast from here to Hamata is also unique in that much of it is protected. There are mangroves and seagrass areas, unusual to see against the stark sand of the desert opposite. And the diving is still comparatively uncrowded, so you will see some of the best corals in Egypt. Hard corals are particularly splendid and in almost perfect condition.

⊠12 Abu Dabab Bay	
🕐 **Depth**	14 m
◉ **Visibility**	fair
〰 **Currents**	none
◗ **Dive type**	shore

This horseshoe-shaped bay makes a deep indentation in the coastline. Enclosed by a lovely beach, the bay remains shallow a long way out from shore with the seabed almost completely covered in seagrass. It is this habitat that has made Abu Dabab famous for its permanent residents. One is a male dugong: he is one of seven known to live in the area; the others evidently have havens further along the coast. The bay is also home to 10 green turtles: nine females and a male. Visiting these amazing creatures involves a long swim at less than two metres. The bay gradually slopes until eventually you find a ridge at about 12 metres. The seagrass beds end and turn into silty dunes punctuated by patches of vegetation. It's at this point that you are more-or-less guaranteed to see the turtles and you would be very unlucky to see less than half of them. They are unphased by divers approaching, even to within a few inches, and just keep chomping away at the grass, eating around 40 kilos a day. Watching these giants eat, ascend to breathe and descend again is unforgettable.

Sadly, the dugong is far more elusive: he can be seen all day at certain times, and at others not seen for days on end.

The remainder of the bay can be quite interesting – it's not just about these large animals. On one side lies a small section of patchy, flat corals and some rocks, which harbour blue spot rays, lionfish and nudibranchs. Jacks and snapper hover over the grassy seabed and black and white seasnakes wind their way through it. Schools of squid seem to be another permanent feature although they are wary of diver bubbles. The outer edges of the bay have small walls and caves and divers can be dropped off in a RIB, swimming back to shore.

Abu Dabab's resident turtles sport the hugest remoras; a bluespotted ray

13 Elphinstone Reef

> **" "** Beyond anything else, this reef is all about colour. Mad, crazy splashes of the most vibrant tones but painted by Nature. Jackson Pollock, eat your heart out.

⊘	**Depth**	32 m
◐	**Visibility**	stunning
≋	**Currents**	can be ripping
⊜	**Dive type**	day boat

This long, oval-shaped reef is another Red Sea legend: a dive with a well deserved reputation even though that reputation was partly built on how little you can get to dive it. If the currents are wrong or too strong, you are out of luck; if the wind is up you may not even get from shore to the reef. But if you are there when the conditions are just so, you may see some of the pelagics that make it famous. And if not – who cares? There is so much life in this one small place that only a grand cynic would fail to be impressed.

Dives start over a low plateau at the north end. It's about 30 metres down to the top but then drops a long way beyond. Divers wait here to see if there are any large animals and are usually rewarded by dancing schools of chevron barracuda and glimpses of various reef sharks. Oceanic whitetips are mostly seen in winter when conditions are least cooperative. You then ascend to one side or the other, depending on the day, and onto the most magnificent wall of soft corals and black corals. There are a lot of fish too, not just the obligatory anthias, but masses of coral trout, some pipefish, jacks in the blue, butterflies and angels and tangs. You could list fish for ages, but suffice to say, it is all very, very lively. By the time you reach about 15 metres the scenery changes to a cover of perfect hard corals and there are schools of snapper and free swimming morays.

Hamata and Fury Shoals

Almost as far south as you can go whilst still remaining in Egypt is the tiny town of Hamata. Blink and you could miss it, but not for long as development is rife here too. There is even talk of another airport at Port Berenice just to the south.

After spending over two hours driving down the coast road, during which all signs of civilisation gradually reduce to nothing at all, the first glimpse of shiny new dive boats moored at Hamata is quite a surprise. There are only two hotels, no shops, no town, nowhere to go. This is purely and simply a dive destination although some guests at one of the resorts also go in for windsurfing. Why though, when the Fury Shoals are just there, less than eight miles from shore, is anybody's guess.

Currently regarded as the last frontier, the Fury Shoals are a collection of offshore reefs, all built by hard corals of the most exceptional calibre, which sit on the top rim of an undersea shelf. This also the gateway to Zabargad Island and St John's, reached by liveaboard only. The next stop south is Sudan.

N14 Zabargad Resort house reef

🧭 **Depth**	24 m
🌓 **Visibility**	good
〰 **Currents**	none to mild
🌊 **Dive type**	day boat

At the front of the resort is a rickety old jetty that extends out over the sea. The leap in can be a big one, depending on the tides, but the drop below is about 16 metres. The first thing you see is an amazing conglomeration of struts and metal posts: nothing is symmetrical but every surface is either sprouting small corals or has a fish perched on it. There are more hawkfish than you can count and masses of schooling two bar sea bream just hanging around. A sandy shelf leads away from the jetty and reef wall, and hovering over it are some monster-sized grouper that come to greet divers. Further along the sandy bed are nicely decorated bommies, coated in soft corals and anthias. A lone barracuda patrols the wall and an octopus pokes his eyes out from a hole. A small table coral shelters eight young batfish that are unbelievably curious, coming right up to a camera or mask if they can see their reflections.

N15 Sha'ab Claudio

🧭 **Depth**	16 m
🌓 **Visibility**	good
〰 **Currents**	mild to strong
🌊 **Dive type**	day boat

From the surface it's hard to judge what this dive is going to be like: the brief of 'enter over the dark path and go into the cave' only really makes sense once you are in. Beneath what appears to be a solid reef top is a warren of narrow crevices that lead to a cathedral-like cave. Well lit by sun rays that pierce parts of the reef, there are tunnels between sections, openings to the outer edge and all sorts of nooks and crannies filled with snappers and copper sweepers. The floor of the main chamber is sandy with a shelf-like rock embedded in it. Beneath it lives a coral banded shrimp and a blue-spotted ray moves between the sand to the shelf, parking himself in front of the shrimp. On the outer edge there are swathes of stunning hard corals that mask the entrances and at times, some current. But you can easily find your way back inside by following the many free swimming morays as they go.

Beneath the jetty at Zabargad Resort; free swimming moray at Sha'ab Claudio

⏚16 Sha'ab Malahi

⏱	**Depth**	16 m
◐	**Visibility**	good
≋	**Currents**	mild to strong
⬙	**Dive type**	day boat

Fondly named the Crystal Maze by the local divemaster, this reef is as stunning a dive as Sha'ab Claudio. There are several sections to the site, so potentially more than one dive, but the best bit is the 'maze' of tunnels on the southern side. Entering the water on the outer reef edge you are faced with too many choices of which way to enter, but once inside there are a multitude of twists and turns between bommies and pinnacles. It's great fun swimming through the large tunnels spotting more copper sweepers and squirrelfish as you go. Some of the corals inside the tunnels are a little damaged but there are fabulous shapes in the rocks and at the far, northern, end of the site you can exit onto a section of the most brilliant, pristine hard corals. Returning south to the boat by going around the edge, a pinnacle stands to the side like a sentinel and is home to some clownfish in their anemone hosts.

⏚17 Abu Galawa Soraya

⏱	**Depth**	18 m
◐	**Visibility**	good
≋	**Currents**	mild to strong
⬙	**Dive type**	day boat

This reef is split into sections. Off one end lies the wreck of an American sailing boat that went down in the 80s. Lying on her side, the 17-metre long hull is completely intact, with the insides full of glassfish, coral banded shrimp and pipefish. The outsides are nicely coated with corals but the metal railings are still quite shiny in places, so the overall shape is easy to see. Swimming around the outside of the reef you encounter more fabulous hard coral outcrops and also some current. A channel leads to a lagoon-like depression in the reef top, which is full to bursting with the most amazing hard coral formations.

🔅 Up close and personal

I had dived the more famous northern Red Sea many times from both day boats and the shore with the diving ranging from very average to truly spectacular, so now it was time for something different – a Southern Red Sea liveaboard.

The problem was that I'd become very used to the excellent standards and service of the high-end South East Asia liveaboards so how was a more basic Red Sea boat going to hold up? I need not have worried; the superb 40 metre Grand Sea Serpent delivered everything I was hoping for and more. This very well laid out, spacious, clean and well run boat was a pleasure to spend a week on, obviously helped by an attentive crew, great chef and a pair of unassuming, helpful and knowledgeable dive guides. Of course, all that was a bonus but how was the diving going to hold up against a good day on Ras Mohammed or in the Straits of Tiran? Again I need not have worried.

It was going to be a busy itinerary, starting from Port Ghalib near Marsa Alam working our way down past world-famous Elphinstone Reef – which was amazing to dive but a little disappointing in that we missed the schooling hammerheads by just 30 minutes – then it was on to the truly amazing Daedalus Reef.

I have a list of ten things I want to see in my diving lifetime and I've been lucky enough to already have seen the first six. What I didn't expect was to see numbers seven to nine in an hour on Daedalus but sure enough: dolphins up close, thresher sharks and then 20 minutes of serious up close and personal encounters with Oceanic whitetip sharks. That dive on its own would have been worth the cost of the trip.

More exciting diving followed as we made our way down to Rocky Island and the reefs at St. Johns where we saw dugongs, grey reef sharks, dozens of turtles and fantastic cave systems along with pristine hard and soft corals . Every log book entry was a chapter and not just a sentence. The Red Sea is getting busy but on the right day on the right boat it can still deliver world class diving by anybody's standards.

Andrew Perkins, manager, retail superstore, Telford, UK

The Crystal Maze and the remains of a yacht

Drying out

While the Egyptian Red Sea coast has untold accommodation options and diving facilities, it does have less than its fair share of ancient sights or cultural attractions. Drying out time is mostly focussed on other sports or daytime relaxation and night-time partying.

Sinai Peninsula

Dive centres

The majority of divers will arrive on pre-booked packages, which do not offer a choice of dive centres. However, any independent travellers will find a good selection professionally run by Europeans.
Red Sea College, Na'ama Bay, T+20 (0)69 360 0145, redseacollege.com. One of the original operators; a variety of programmes including a Diamond Service which buys upgraded services for experienced divers.
Sinai Divers, T+20 (0)69 360 0697, sinaidivers.com. Another of the pioneers. In Na'ama Bay, plus Dahab and Taba to the north. Packages include variety of dive options and all levels of courses.

Sleeping

Virtually all hotels in the Sinai (and across all Egyptian coastal areas) tend to be large resort complexes. Choose a higher level of hotel as 3-star in Egypt is less impressive than elsewhere.
$$$-$$ Hilton Hotels, hilton.com. In Sharm El Maya, Na'ama Bay and Shark Bay. All are modern hotels with good facilities.
$ Camel Dive Club and Hotel, T+20 (0)69 360 0700, cameldive.com. Smaller, diver-orientated hotel in Na'ama Bay. The Camel Bar, up top, is good for sunset views and light meals. A popular divers' haunt.

Eating

$$ Dananeer Opposite the Movenpick Hotel, western fare, steaks and seafood.
$ Sinai Star A proper Egyptian restaurant. No menus, just fabulous catch-of-the-day seafood served with rice, salad and dips. Located in Old Sharm in the market; don't be put off by the lack of fancy decoration.

Hurghada, El Gouna and Safaga

In the south, as in Sharm, you are unlikely to get a choice of dive centre. The coastal area is rather sprawling so use the dive centre in your hotel or the one next door.

Dive centres

Divers Lodge, T+20 (0)65 346 5100, divers-lodge.com. Located between the Hilton and Intercontinental resorts. Used by both hotels, well run outfit with friendly crews.
Dive Tribe, T+20 (0)65 358 0120, divetribe.com. At the El Gouna Mövenpick Resort but accepts divers from any hotel.

Sleeping

$$$ Hilton Hurghada Resort, T+20 (0)65 3465036, hilton.com. Big complex that feels quite small and located on a good section of beach.
$$ Hotel Shams Safaga and Diving Centre, shams-dive.com. Medium size resort on a lovely bay with a decent house reef and on-site dive centre.
$$ Sultan Bey, T+20 (0)65 3545600, optima-hotels .com. Bedouin-style hotel in El Gouna. Balconies overlook nice gardens.

> 66 99 As authors, we are sad to say that we have never been on a Red Sea liveaboard that we would recommend to our friends. Of course, there are some good ones out there and standards are definitely on the up. But in this sense, Egypt is a victim of its own success. The sheer numbers of divers wanting ever cheaper trips mixed with operators all undercutting each other equals a drop in standards. Complaints include air-con that doesn't work, poor food or not enough of it, dives limited, low safety standards... Then there's high-profile tales of boats hitting reefs at night and even leaving divers behind. (Heaven help us all). There is just one thing to say about this, you get what you pay for. Go cheap, ask for a deal, but don't expect a full service boat if you do.

🛏	**Sleeping**	$$$ US$150+ double room per night		$$ US$75-150	$ under US$75
🍴	**Eating**	$$$ US$40+ 2-course meal, excluding drinks		$$ US$20-40	$ under US$20

Eating

$ Felfela, Sheraton Rd, Hurghada, T+20 (0)65 344 2411 This Egyptian restaurant is justifiably famous. Amazingly good food is served on terraces that catch a cool breeze from the Red Sea. No booze though.

Far south

With tourism still in its infancy, there are comparatively few dive centres and hotels.

Dive centres

Orca Dive Clubs, T+20 (0)10 646 6632 orca-diveclub.com. Pioneering dive centres in both Abu Dabab and Hamata, but also throughout Egypt. High levels of service and standards across the group.

Sleeping

$ Abu Dabab Diving Lodge, T+20 (0)12 6650240. Small resort with an old world feel, rather like how dive clubs used to be. Affiliated to Orca Dive Clubs whose spacious and well set up centre is across the road and right on Abu Dabab bay.

$ Zarbagad Dive Resort, T+20 (0)10 646 6632. Newly built hotel on the beach just north of Hamata. Pool, bar and restaurant on site and – happily – nothing much else in any direction yet. Orca Dive Clubs run the diving here too, and there is the excellent option of shore diving.

Sunset at Orca in Hamata

Sinai Peninsula

Ras Mohammed National Park Contrary to popular belief, at least in diver brains, Ras isn't just about diving. Landside there are some fantastic, 'other world' landscapes to admire plus rare mammals, thousands of birds and some unusual flora species. About US$50 for a guided day trip.

St Catherine's Monastery Dating back to AD 300, this religious site is worth a visit for its varied history. Now owned by the Greek Orthodox Church, there is a collection of illuminated manuscripts, works of art and of course, the site of Moses' Burning Bush. About US$50 for a guided day trip.

Mount Sinai This is where Moses is said to have received the Ten Commandments. To reach the top it's either 4000 steps or a 3-hour walk along a winding path, but many make the pilgrimage. About US$50 for a guided day trip.

South coast

There isn't a huge amount to do heading out from either Hurghada, Safaga or El Gouna but you could arrange to visit a couple of ruined, ancient Roman sites. There's Mons Porphyrites, where the Romans mined a stone called Imperial Porphyry (a purple and white crystalline rock) and left behind temples, shrines and fortresses. Mons Claudianus was a Roman settlement in the 1st and 2nd centuries AD and the base for mining a grey granite that was sent to Rome. The ruins include a Pantheon, Hadrian's Villa and an unfinished temple. Day trips are around US$50.

Likewise, cultural excursions and day trips are non-existent in the area around Marsa Alam and Hamata. There are ruins of an old emerald mine, but no emeralds; the temple of Seti I, but you can't go in and the remains of an extensive Ottoman fort at El Quesir – but no tours. You get the picture... come to this area and dive, although that's bound to change soon.

Cairo

Egypt's capital is a shock to the system. Hot, completely manic, it's a non-stop pulsating, gyrating, merry-go-round of people. There are close on 16 million in the capital and mostly you will feel that they are right in your face. But to go to Egypt and not see the pyramids? A day in the city will give you a chance to sample her incredible history.

Head out to the Giza, admire the Sphinx, then, unless you are horribly claustrophobic, stretch your calf muscles by walking down the 45 degree ladders inside the great pyramid of Cheops at Giza. You can even take a camel or horse ride a short way into the Sahara and look back at the pyramids. With a little imagination you can almost see what they would have been like all those centuries ago.

Afterwards head back into the centre and visit the Egyptian Museum. Gaze on the face of god-king Tutankhamen (if you can get close enough – the museum is always crowded) before heading to one of the city's many bazaars for a little retail therapy. This is definitely best undertaken with an Egyptian guide or you will find the hassle-factor overwhelming. Finally, at sunset take a Nile dinner cruise, terribly touristy but at least you can say you've done it. Day tours run from US$30-100 depending on content and distances.

$$ Intercontinental Citystars, Omar Ibn El Khattab St, Cairo, T+20 (0)2 480 0100, ichotelsgroup.com. Classy city centre hotel, only a few minutes from the airport.

$$ Sophitel Le Sphinx, 1 Alexandria Rd, Giza, T+20 (0)2 383 7444, sofitel.com. Lovely, modern hotel right beside the pyramids.

East Africa

Forever friends: two giant frogfish
compete to see who can blend into
the background best.
Sandbanks, Mnemba Atoll

NAIROBI

KENYA

Serengeti
National Park

Ngorongoro
Crater

Kilimanjaro

Tsavo National Park

Arusha

● Malindi

⬊1

● Mombasa

⬊2 Pemba

Zanzibar

⬊3

Stone Town ●

DAR ES SALAAM ●

UNITED REPUBLIC
OF TANZANIA

Selous Game Reserve

Quirimb
Archipela

⬊4

Pemba ●

MOZAMBIQUE

⬊1 Kenya   ▶▶ p46

Malindi ●

Turtle Bay ●   ⬊1
          ⬊3 ⬊2

Mombasa ●

Shimoni ●   ⬊4

          ⬊5

Pemba

⬊1 The Canyon
⬊2 Deep Place
⬊3 Red Firefish Reef
⬊4 Galu
⬊5 Nyeli Reef

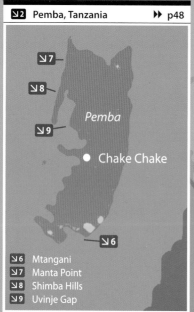

⬊2 Pemba, Tanzania   ▶▶ p48

⬊7

⬊8

Pemba

⬊9

● Chake Chake

⬊6

⬊6 Mtangani
⬊7 Manta Point
⬊8 Shimba Hills
⬊9 Uvinje Gap

110 km

↘3 Zanzibar, Tanzania ⏩ **p50**

Mnemba Atoll

↘14 ↘10
↘13 ↘11
↘12

Zanzibar

↘20
↘19
↘18 ↘17
Paje ↘16
↘15

Stone Town

↘10 Jackfish Spot
↘11 Coral Gardens
↘12 Sand Banks
↘13 Kichwani
↘14 Aquarium to Grouper Rock
↘15 Shindano
↘16 Cuipis Garden
↘17 Ukwele
↘18 The Lagoon
↘19 Point 8
↘20 Cave 20

↘4 Mozambique ⏩ **p56**

↘26 ↘25
↘27 Medjumbe
↘28

Ibo

Quirimbas
Archipelago

↘21 The Gap
↘22 The Ranch
↘23 Playground
↘24 Sailfish Tree and Rivermouth
↘25 Edge of Reason
↘26 Sambi-Sambi
↘27 The Restaurant
↘28 Joe's Ridge

↘24
↘23
↘22 ↘21

Pemba

Introduction

East Africa

Wide open plains baking in the African sun, ancient tribes facing up to the realities of modern life, herds of exotic animals roaming wild and free. At least once in your life you have to come face-to-face with the big five. It's a heart-stopping, spine-tingling moment when a male lion walks straight up to you – just inches from your open Land Rover – and looks deep into your eyes.

If you're a diver, however, it might seem hard to give up peaceful days floating in warm waters for a close encounter with nature on dry land. But you don't have to. East Africa is an alluring dive destination simply because you can do it all.

While inland landscapes are baked to exquisite shades of gold and terracotta, the coastal waters are cooler tones of deep indigo and pale turquoise. Sitting on the fringe of the Indian Ocean, the world's warmest, the vista changes to one lush with coconut palms, spice trees and mangroves. Under perfect blue skies, tiny dhows float over little-known fringing reefs which meander gently along the shoreline. They protect the flat coastal regions that lie behind while creating nursery grounds for rainbow-hued reef fish. And although larger animals are mostly to be found on land, the marine life is still exciting enough to justify a visit.

East Africa rating

Diving
★★★

Dive facilities
★★★

Accommodation
★★★★

Down time
★★★★★

Value for money
★★★

Essentials

Getting there and around

For travellers living in Europe, getting to Kenya and Tanzania is a cinch. But if you're coming from any other continent – or want to add northern Mozambique to the trip – you'll probably need to route through a European hub or the Middle East. Nairobi is the easiest place to get to and there are good onward connections. Kenya Airways (kenya-airways.com) has the most wide-ranging schedules, with flights to Nairobi and then on to Dar es Salaam and regional destinations. Other carriers include British Airways and Emirates or you could fly on KLM's route to Kilimanjaro, should you feel you need to climb a mountain before submerging. There are also many European-based charter flights which head to the Kenya coast but these mostly require you to book a package holiday.

To reach Northern Mozambique there are flights from either Nairobi or Dar es Salaam to Pemba on the coast. The only airline that flies this route is the national carrier, Linhas Aéreas de Moçambique (lam.co.mz), with a twice weekly schedule that connects both capitals to Pemba. They also have flights from Lisbon to capital Maputo with easy connections up to Pemba. From Pemba transfers to the Quirimbas Archipelago are on scenic light aircraft and arranged by your resort.

If you intend going on safari, it makes a lot of sense to do that first: a substantial network of small airlines connect the cities, national parks and coastal areas. Kenya Airlines (kenya-airways.com) and Precision Air (precisionairtz.com) are the main ones, but there are many more like ZanAir (zanair.com) and Coastal (coastal.cc).

If all of this seems complex, make it easier by choosing your ideal safari (see page 63) or dive location, then turning over the arrangements to a specialist company. They will advise on current schedules, make the relevant bookings and organize transfers for you.

For days out rely on your dive centre or hotel for advice and assistance. Although some areas are tourist friendly, and local transport is available, in cities and bigger towns independent travel is not highly recommended.

Local laws and customs

The people of both Kenya and Tanzania are an almost equal mix of Christian, Muslim and tribal religions, while in Mozambique about half the population are Catholic and about 20% are Muslim. Be sensitive to local practices. Common sense goes a long way – don't walk around half dressed in a Muslim coastal town, for instance – but generally the people in all these countries are friendly and outgoing.

Kenya
Location
1°00'N 38°00'E

Capital	Nairobi
Population	37,953,838
Land area in km²	458
Coastline in km	1,519

Tanzania
Location
6°00's, 35°00'E

Capital	Dar es Salaam
Population	40,213,162
Land area in km²	702
Coastline in km	6,112

Mozambique
Location
15°00'N, 86°30'W

Capital	Maputo
Population	7,639,327
Land area in km²	111,890
Coastline in km	820

Medjumbe at full moon

Safety

Government advisories recommend that travellers are cautious in East Africa but most advice relates to what happens in the major cities (Nairobi's nickname is 'Nai-robbery'). Most crime is petty but avoid political rallies, stay out of city centres at night but if you are out and about after dark, catch a cab and carry as little as possible. Lone female travellers should be extra cautious if only because you will appear vulnerable. Now that the bad news is over, here's the good news. Dive regions tend to be well away from hubs of political sensitivity and your dive centre will collect you from wherever you are. Safari parks are well policed, hotels employ security guards and locals just love tourists, who they see as generous and friendly. If you do get hassled by touts, a few firm 'no thank yous' work wonders or, if you want to go anywhere unusual, ask your hotel reception for an escort. A few dollars will buy a lot of peace of mind.

Language

With a couple of hundred tribal groups across the region, the language that links most people – apart from English – is Swahili. It's a language that has influenced many others – safari, meaning journey, is now a universal term. Here are some basic words:

hello	*jambo*	sorry!	*pole!*
goodbye	*kwaheri*	how much is ...	*ngapi ...*
yes	*ndiyo*	great dive!	*adhimu mbizi!*
no	*hapana*	no problem	*hakuna matata*
thank you	*asante sana*	one beer	*mojo bia*

However, in Mozambique the lingua franca is Portuguese as Portugal was the colonial power in days gone by. While some hotel managers and divemasters will have good English, most others will appreciate a few of these words:

hello	*Olá*	sorry!	*desculpe!*
goodbye	*adeus*	how much is ...	*quanto é ...*
yes	*sim*	great dive!	*grande mergulho!*
no	*não*	no problem	*nenhum problema*
thank you	*obrigado*	one beer	*uma cerveja*

Health

East Africa requires most of the standard jabs and malaria is a risk but these potential dangers are easy to protect against (see page 342). Health facilities are not great so if you do get ill, chances are you will be airlifted to Johannesburg or straight home. HIV is a bigger problem right across Africa. As the Kenyan beach strip is known to be an area where the world's 'oldest trade' is plied, not only would you risk AIDS but, if caught, the local will be jailed.

Tourist information → Government websites can be found at Mozambique: mozambiquehc.org.uk/tourism; Kenya: magicalkenya.com; Tanzania: tanzaniatouristboard.com.

Fact file

International flights	Kenya Airways for Kenya and Tanzania; Linhas Aéreas de Moçambique (LAM) for Mozambique
Departure tax	US$30, if not included in your ticket
Entry	Visas are required for all Tanzania, US$50 and Mozambique, US$30
Internal flights	Kenya Airlines, Precision Air, ZanAir,
Ground transport	Countrywide bus connections
Money	US$1 = 80 Kenyan shillings (KES) US$1 = 1,350 Tanzania shillings (TZS) US$1 = 26,500 Mozambique meticals (MZM)
Language	Swahili officially but English is common
Electricity	220-240v, plug types B,C,D (see page 16)
Time zone	GMT +3
Religion	Christian, Muslim, animist and tribal variations
Phone	Country codes: Kenya +254; Tanzania +255; Mozambique +258; IDD code 00; Police 0

Costs

Value for money almost becomes irrelevant once you've spent your day sitting beside a new-born zebra or making eye-contact with a lion. However, it must be said that East Africa is not a cheap destination. Most coastal resorts and island hotels are self-contained complexes where your package will include breakfast and dinner. However, extras can be pricey: a large beer averages out to around US$3 and a soft drink is not much less. A lunch can easily cost over $10 per dish. It's unusual to be able to walk somewhere else for a snack unless it's to the hotel next door. In most places you will sign for everything so while tipping is the norm, it may be hard to do. Some operations will leave a box on reception or you can add a gratuity when you pay your final bill: 10% for meals and so on, but for guides on a safari consider 5-15% of the trip cost. For divemasters and crews, see page 12.

Porcelain crab sitting on a seapen

Dive brief

Diving

While seeing animals on land in East Africa is a given, life in the marine realm is less well known. The defining geography both on land and underwater is the incredibly flat topography. The continental shelf is generally less than 20 kilometres wide from the centre of Kenya to the top of Mozambique. Even the islands that emerge from it are small and equally flat.

The mainland and island coastlines are bordered by long fringing reefs which are often completely exposed at low tide. These protect the shores, but take a pounding from constant wave action and the effects of the sun when the tide is out. Every day as the sea recedes, the reef top is revealed and the lagoons behind become so shallow that snorkelling and swimming are often out of the question. Diving is restricted to times when there is enough water for boats to navigate over the reef.

Another set of conditions are created by the constant movement of water over the shallow seabed which, combined with several massive river deltas and mangrove regions, means that visibility in most areas is less than you would like for substantial periods of the year. The entire Indian Ocean has consistently warm sea temperatures.

This means that hard corals – especially in the shallower sections – are not as prolific as in other oceans. The El Niño phenomena took its toll a few years back as well. All the same, once you are out over the reef edge, or off one of the nearby islands, and get below about 10 metres, the marine life can be lively.

Snorkelling

Conditions for snorkellers are better than the above comments would lead you to believe. Floating over a very shallow reef at low tide is less of an issue with no tank on your back. Most hotels run snorkelling trips to just outside the reef, but watch the time – at extreme low tide you may have to walk back over the fragile exposed reef, which won't do it any good at all.

Marine life

Although the reef structures here are not particularly lush, animals like turtles and morays are frequently seen. The migratory patterns for both mantas and whalesharks traverse this stretch of coast. They are occasionally spotted by divers, but less often than the operators would care to have you think. If you get out in the blue, there are plenty of pelagic fish.

East Africa
animal
encounters

Kenya	all types of morays
Tanzania	Djibouti Spanish Dancer
Mozambique	goliath groupers

Incredible hard corals near Medjumbe island; skunk clownfish and host anemone

“ When we first started travelling, an African safari was right at the top of our hit list and we were not disappointed. The Masai Mara, Ngorongoro Crater, the Serengeti... these places are burnt into our memories, and every now and then remind us that there is more to life than diving. While East Africa's warm waters and the iridescent colours of her marine realm are delightful, the quality and variety of diving may not be quite enough for hardened tank-suckers. But put it together with a safari and this becomes a holiday that can't be rivalled.

Making the big decision

Choosing a dive destination in East Africa will be dictated by where else you want to go, if anywhere. If you want a relaxing break with a couple of morning dives and a few afternoons out, the Kenya coast is for you. The diving will be pleasant and you will have access to day trips into the coastal game parks. If you want to get off the beaten track, Tanzania's islands are the place to head for. Their waters have more prolific marine life influenced by the open ocean beyond the continental shelf. Tanzania's safari regions are also bigger and wilder. However, for lovers of simple luxuries and blissful island destinations, there can be no better choice than the comparatively new tourist destination of the Quirimbas Archipelago in Mozambique.

Spinner dolphins in the bow wave

Dive data

Seasons	Rainy seasons vary but run between December and May depending on location. Visibility can be reduced due to river run-off. Islands may be affected by wind patterns from April to May
Visibility	10-40 metres
Temperatures	Air 25-34°C; Water 25-29°C
Wet suit	3 mm shorty or full body suit
Training	Courses available in most hotels, standards vary; look for PADI/SSI schools
Nitrox	Not easily available
Deco chambers	Mombasa, Zanzibar, Durban

Bottom time

Kenya	**A multitude of resort hotels dotted along pretty white sand beaches with easy access to both reefs and nearby wildlife parks.**
Kenya Coast ►► p46	On the north coast, Turtle Bay sits inside the protected Watamu Marine Park, while further south, gently shelving reef systems run from popular Diani Beach to the Kisite-Mpunguti Park.
Tanzania	**Deservedly famous wildlife parks and the promise of exciting, offshore diving.**
Pemba island ►► p48	Deep water dives in the Indian Ocean contrast with the calmer waters in the Pemba Channel.
Zanzibar ►► p50	Gentle sloping reefs and reefs that reflect the long steps of rice terraces.
Mozambique	**The latest destination to hit the diver wish-list is this peaceful, post civil-war country.**
Pemba ►► p50	Reef and muck diving around the edges of one of the world's largest natural bays.
Medjumbe ►► p59	At the heart of the Quirimbas Archipelago, sharp walls to the north and flat reefs to the south.

Diversity   combined reef area 6,070 km²

	Kenya | Tanzania | Mozambique
HARD CORALS	54 | 57 | 49
FISH SPECIES	734 | 973 | 1,556
ENDEMIC FISH SPECIES	11 | 25 | 11
FISH UNDER THREAT	84 | 148 | 60
PROTECTED REEFS/MARINE PARKS	14 | 9 | 3

All diversity figures are approximate

Dive log

Kenya

The coast that stretches north and south from Mombasa is paralleled by low-lying coral reefs. Its basic structure is of hard corals which form small drop-offs and gentle sloping banks. The corals tend to be slower-growing, hardier varieties that survive pounding Indian Ocean swells.

Due to the substantial tidal range, diving is only possible for part of the day. Currents can be strong, although rarely unbearable, and visibility is never crystal clear. Below the waves, the reef scenery is consistent, so choose a destination by excluding the less appropriate ones. For example, the beaches close to Mombasa town suffer from its industrialized nature so can easily be ruled out. Likewise Malindi, to the north, is affected by the run-off from the Sabiki River. Despite being a national marine park, diving here is limited to between May and December. However, there are three small areas which promise better all-round conditions. The very pretty Turtle Bay sits in Watamu Marine Park and although this area is still tidal, the formation of the bay means it is possible to swim and dive for longer periods of the day.

Heading south from Mombasa, the section of white-sand coast known as Diani Beach is highly developed, with large resort hotels reaching towards the Tanzanian border. The good news is that they are well spaced out with decent landscaping, so you are unlikely to notice the extent of the development. Virtually all have dive centres on site. Just a few kilometres from the Tanzanian border is the Kisite-Mpunguti Marine National Park. The only access to this area, apart from the day trips Diani hotels offer, is via the town of Shimoni where there is a lone dive-orientated hotel. The park borders the deeper waters of the Pemba Channel so the diving is a little more adventurous and less limited by tidal changes.

⬛1 **The Canyon**	
Depth	20 m
Visibility	fair
Currents	can be strong
Dive type	day boat

This classic Kenyan dive site is just a short boat ride to outside the main reef at Turtle Bay, then a descent to the reef top at about 10 metres. The reef structure is hard coral with some small soft corals for colour. Over the edge is an archway where you can sometimes find resting turtles. If the current is running, and it often is, whitetips will spin past in the blue. The divemasters say this is one of the best places to spot passing whalesharks, but you are more likely to spot lobsters, lionfish, butterflies and nudibranchs.

⬛2 **Deep Place, Turtle Bay**	
Depth	25 m
Visibility	fair
Currents	can be strong
Dive type	day boat

Just along the outer reef from The Canyon, this is a rather nice wall that can sometimes be a drift dive. It's not all that deep and you can investigate the sandy bottom where some interesting smaller creatures like lionfish hang out. Moray eels poke their noses out of the wall at passing divers and plenty of colourful fish hang around, such as anthias, butterflies, angels and so on. There are often sightings of turtles and large Napoleon wrasse around this reef.

Regal angelfish are seen frequently in Kenya

⌖ Red Firefish Reef

Depth	20 m
Visibility	good
Currents	can be strong
Dive type	day boat

Heading out past the inner reef for about 15 minutes brings you to this sloping site. The top of the reef sits at about 15 metres and the bottom is around 25. The corals are quite pretty but sparse and patchy, which makes for a lot of hidey-holes for the marine life. The divemasters promote a large resident grey stingray who usually obliges with an appearance fairly soon after divers enter the water. There are also bluespotted rays on the sand, lobsters in small caverns and some sweetlips hanging on the mini-wall. Smaller fish include clowns in anemones and fire dart gobies.

⌖ Galu, Diani Beach

Depth	20 m
Visibility	fair to good
Currents	none to strong
Dive type	day boat

At the right time of day – usually early in the morning – this can be a very pretty dive and is often used for training up new divers as conditions are easy. There are plenty of fish to see with butterflies and wrasse all over the reef. Lobsters, octopus and small rays hang around in the cracks and crevices of the hard corals and turtles are frequent visitors. Later in the day the current can lift, which makes the dive a bit more of a challenge for the inexperienced.

Nudibranchs are common in Turtle Bay

⌖ Nyuli Reef

Depth	20 m
Visibility	good
Currents	mild to strong
Dive type	day boat

Not far from Shimoni, a set of reefs ring the small islands of the Kisite-Mpunguti Marine Park. There are a reasonable variety of dive sites. Some have suffered damage in the past, both from natural and man-made causes, but a few reefs are very impressive and the deeper waters attract schools of fish. Nyuli Reef starts at about 20 metres then drops sharply to over 40. Shoals of pelagics like barracuda have been seen and reef sharks are common visitors, although you are unlikely to get close.

⊙ What could be better?

It was eight o'clock, the sky was nice and blue, the sea calm and it was already getting hot. I was about to dive Verena, a site just a few minutes' boat ride from Turtle Bay Beach Club.

As we descended towards the bottom of a shallow canyon, a large Napoleon wrasse watched our approach. We explored nooks and crannies until our dive leader pointed out a honeycomb moray – it was about as long as I'm tall and as thick as my thigh, with those characteristic honeycomb markings. We swam over the sandy bottom and disturbed a stingray about five feet across. A whitetip reef shark swam lazily towards a small coral outcrop just where the canyon narrows. As we approached the outcrop, a manta ray, as large as my living room (3.5 metres), appeared from behind us. We dropped to the bottom so we didn't scare it off and it looped up towards the surface and back down, its left wing passing right over my head. So majestic, so serene and with a deceptive turn of speed for something so graceful. It swam off, turning back the way it came and was gone.

We finished the dive and climbed back on the boat, thinking to ourselves "what could be better?" when our dive leader shouted, "whaleshark". We grabbed masks and fins and jumped back in. It was passing right by us and we saw its profile with those distinctive white spots and the ridges along its side. We all tried to follow but the whaleshark just carried on its way, probably not even noticing the four irrelevant objects trying unsuccessfully to keep up.

Two years later, I returned with my girlfriend. We went on a safari that covered most of Kenya. We saw loads of wildlife including all the big five and have stories to tell about those adventures! Then we went to Watamu for a week. However, this time no mantas, no sharks – all the big animals had been and gone. It was disappointing but life can be like that. The only creature worth mentioning this time was a honeycomb moray. I wonder if it was the same one?

Roy Calverley, IT specialist, Redhill, UK

Tanzania

Unlike Kenya, Tanzania's diving is based around the small islands lying off her coastline rather than off the coast itself. Pemba and Zanzibar are the best known. Both have good facilities but Pemba is more dive focused, while Zanzibar is more of an all-round holiday destination.

Pemba island

So close to the Kenyan coast it's actually easiest to get there from Shimoni, Pemba is just a 30-minute speed boat ride away. There are two distinct styles of diving; the east side is exposed to the open ocean so the diving is mostly big blue. Rough seas and strong currents can sometimes bring in schools of sharks. Hammerhead sightings are said to be common, but even if they were, the sharks are generally deeper than sport diving depth limits will allow. To the south, the channel that separates Pemba from Zanzibar has similar conditions.

For more classic reef diving, Pemba's western side has shallow walls, sloping reefs and a surprising number of unusual critters. The geography, like Kenya, is always liable to the vagaries of time and tide. The reefs are a little way offshore and the inner lagoons extremely shallow. Currents are an every-dive occurrence, although they are not as strong as on the east and there are many small islands to shelter behind.

↘6 Mtangani	
🕐 **Depth**	35 m
🔵 **Visibility**	excellent
〰 **Currents**	ripping at times
🌊 **Dive type**	liveaboard

When they say the currents that run off Pemba's east coast can be strong, it's no exaggeration. This water races, and less experienced divers may find the challenge hardly worthwhile unless, of course, the hammerheads come past. The issue is that when they do, they are often deeper than you can sensibly go to look at them. Instead, dives are spent pretending to fly through unbelievably clear water watching out for them, whitetips or even some Napoleon wrasse. It's still quite an adrenaline rush.

↘7 Manta Point	
🕐 **Depth**	22 m
🔵 **Visibility**	fair
〰 **Currents**	slight to medium
🌊 **Dive type**	day boat

As soon as someone sees a manta on a dive site, it gets named in honour of the event. So what are the chances of actually seeing a manta at Manta Point? Opinion varies – and the operators do tend to wax lyrical – but that doesn't spoil what is a very good reef dive. As this site is tucked in amongst the protective islands off the west coast, currents are less aggressive and the pace is easy. Visibility isn't that impressive but there are plenty of animals. There are always schools of snapper about and when the currents lift a little, bigger animals appear. Turtles often pass by, as do barracuda and jacks – and, of course, the mantas. If you are lucky. Otherwise, it's angels, triggerfish and Napoleon wrasse. There are plenty of animals in the rubble areas between the coral heads and you can spot frogfish and blue ribbon eels.

Mantis shrimp, seagrass ghost pipefish, slipper lobsters and the ornate ghost pipefish are all easy to spot in Pemba waters

N8 Shimba Hills

🌀	**Depth**	20 m
◐	**Visibility**	fair
🌊	**Currents**	slight to medium
🌓	**Dive type**	day boat

Many of the shallower reefs in this region are affected by their position. The warm, shallow waters make it difficult for the hard corals: they struggle to survive, especially as the reefs are exposed at low tide. This reef off the north of the island shows a fair bit of damage because of this and constant wave action, yet somehow manages to be a very interesting dive regardless. A gentle wall drops down to a rubble-strewn sea bed. There are some tubastrea coral trees with anthias flitting about them and along the wall, a series of caverns and overhangs protect angelfish, snappers and coral grouper. It's worth taking some time to inspect the smaller cracks and crevices as they reveal all sorts of interesting animals. These include many types of shrimp, several different coloured leaffish and even small lobster.

N9 Uvinje Gap

🌀	**Depth**	22 m
◐	**Visibility**	fair
🌊	**Currents**	slight to medium
🌓	**Dive type**	day boat

The string of small islands that borders Pemba's west coast separate it from the channel and distant mainland. At the bottom of this string are Uvinje and Kokota islands and surrounding both are a series of good dives, including a surprising one in the gap between the two.

During the day, divers head for the walls on the outer sides at Uvinje Gap, North or South. In places, these two quite similar sites drop to as much as 40 metres deep, but dives are mostly around 25 metres. Along the walls are small caverns and overhangs which are inevitably full of masses of shiny glassfish. The hard corals are in pretty good condition with the currents feeding the table, lettuce, and tubastrea species. Along the wall there are morays, nudibranchs and all the usual suspects in terms of colourful fish life. This

is also regarded as a very good site for spotting turtles and – very occasionally – passing by in the blue will be schools of barracuda. The top of Uvinje's southern wall comes up to about six metres so it's a good snorkelling site as well.

After exploring these sections, another dive will involve dropping right between the two islands. Sitting midway, a section of sandy seabed at about 20 metres is a surprisingly good critter-hunt dive, with the type of macro animal life that is reminiscent of far distant countries.

There is plenty to see during daylight hours, including swimming crabs and tiny imperial shrimp living on sea cucumbers, shrimps in anemones, gobies and the rare seagrass ghost pipefish. At night the dive becomes even more exciting as you can spot an incredible number of species: octopus, morays and masses of decorator crabs come out to hunt. Cowries and mantis shrimp seem to appear from nowhere while the sandy seabed comes alive with sprouting seapens, all revealing their resident porcelain crabs.

Barracuda passing through Uvinje gap

Zanzibar is just south of Pemba and has a unique mix of history, culture and natural beauty. The marine life is similar to Pemba, although the underwater topography is perhaps a little less varied due to the shallow reef system. From the coast of Tanzania to nigh on three miles offshore where the continental shelf drops, the seabed is rarely more than 40 metres below the surface. Consequently, the water is rarely gin clear.

There are dive sites all the way around Zanzibar, from the tiny islands opposite World Heritage, Stone Town to the channels in the far south, but the majority of divers head to either Mnemba Atoll, off the northern point, or to the delightful east coast beaches.

These two areas attract quite different sorts of visitors. The village of Matemwe opposite Mnemba has traditionally catered for backpackers and travellers who have been up Kilimanjaro or across the Serengeti and are looking for some cool, relaxing waters. Mnemba island is only tiny, but sits to the side of a pear-shaped atoll that measures around 15 square kilometres. It is also regarded as a conservation zone and, while some would question that (see page 339), there is no doubt that it is a charming spot with some impressive marine life. Day trip boats that travel across to explore the lagoon and its fringing reefs usually include both divers and snorkellers. It's all very much a fun, social thing but the reef's popularity can make it feel a little crowded at times. However, the diving is easy, currents are avoidable and the visibility is good.

Divers in search of less busy reefs go southwards to the holiday resort region east of the Jozani Forest and near the village of near Paje. Because these reefs are only easily accessible to those staying nearby, it's unlikely you will meet any other divers apart from your buddies. The tides recede daily across the fringing reef – as they do right around Zanzibar – so dives are arranged to work around that, often with access across the coastal lagoon made by driving along to a deeper bay before boarding a dhoni. On the outer edge of these reefs, the underwater terrain is almost perfectly flat. A shelf will extend for some way at about 15-18 metres, then there is a sudden drop over a short wall. This leads down to another flat reef at 25-28 metres, which again descends almost imperceptibly until it finally crashes to depth from a sharp ridge at about 50 metres. Beyond that are adrenaline rush sites for advanced divers only.

⛴ 10	Jackfish Spot	
🧭	**Depth**	36 m
◑	**Visibility**	good
🌀	**Currents**	can be strong
🌊	**Dive Type**	day boat

This dive site lies on the eastern side of Mnemba island where the wall comes in closest to the lagoon area. Descent is into the blue and you drop down rapidly to over 30 metres to find a sharp, perfectly vertical wall. This then drops down around another 10 metres or so and leads to an even deeper plateau. The wall has a lot of caverns along its front that are full of colourful corals and fish but you don't get much chance to look in them before the most stupendous school of batfish starts buzzing you. There must be hundreds that whizz in quickly, around and up, off then back. They don't stay all that long but it's quite an overwhelming sight. After that, it's likely to be time to head up and as you ascend, you pass through some schools of snapper and the jacks. The shallows are perfect for gassing off, but the life seems less interesting after the huge schools of fish. All the same, there are lots of small creatures, such as anemones, imperial angels, pufferfish and scorpionfish.

Batfish in the hundreds at Jackfish Spot

ⓈⒻⓇⓇ Coral Gardens

⬢	**Depth**	20 m
◐	**Visibility**	good
➿	**Currents**	slight
⬭	**Dive Type**	day boat

One of Mnemba's signature dives, Coral Garden is also on the eastern edge of the lagoon but in shallower water. Lots of hard coral bommies are dotted about a lovely white sand seabed so divers can hop from one to the next, hunting out the resident creatures. Discovering all the smaller animals is a non-stop adventure: one minute it's a giant puffer, the next an unusual zebra moray. Under another coral head are clusters of lionfish, then passing by them, you stumble over an enormous Spanish Dancer, the *Hexabranchus Djibouti*, which is the largest known nudibranch. Usually nocturnal, these are wandering across the sand in broad daylight. They also measure around 50 centimetres long and even have imperial shrimp in the gills. There are octopus too but it's time to ascend into the shallower hard coral gardens where there are loads of small and colourful fish.

ⓈⒻⓇⓇ Sand Banks

⬢	**Depth**	20 m
◐	**Visibility**	good
➿	**Currents**	slight
⬭	**Dive Type**	day boat

Creating the southern rim of the lagoon, the profile is of a small wall that drops to a sandy shelf. Due to its location, it can get some slightly stronger currents and a very surprising and chilly thermocline! Staying close to the edge of the small wall there are some good patches of coral where lionfish are out and feeding – another slightly puzzling activity as they usually feed at night too. A little further along, you might be lucky to find your overexcited divemaster has just spotted the resident giant frogfish that are often seen sitting together on a sponge.

ⓈⒻⓇⓇ Kichwani

⬢	**Depth**	20 m
◐	**Visibility**	good
➿	**Currents**	can be very strong
⬭	**Dive Type**	day boat

Sitting a little further west around the bottom edge of Mnemba, Kichwani can be done as a very deep drift dive but the divemasters bypass that idea by casually mentioning a resident dragon moray eel, who lives in just four metres of water on a hard coral bommie. These rarely seen morays must be the most beautiful ones in the species group with their bizarre patterns, colours and horns. They are also said to be quite aggressive, yet the local chap is living just where expected and is nestled in a hole between hard corals with a small brown moray as companion. After exploring this shallow bommie, which reveals plenty of other morays but just this one dragon, the dive moves down the slope to a small drop-off, which is being mobbed by loads of schooling fish. The water has turned golden with many yellow-toned species including the ever-present striped snappers, fiesty sargeant majors guarding their eggs and prolific moorish idols. There are also large numbers of silver cornetfish flitting above the hard corals on the wall, which are in very good condition.

Zebra moray eel; dragon moray and friend; the Djibouti Spanish Dancer

14 Aquarium to Grouper Rock

Depth	28 m
Visibility	good
Currents	none to mild
Dive type	day boat

The section of reef closest to Mnemba island is where most newcomers get taken for their first dive, yet there are so many levels to explore that you end up wanting to go back time and again. From just a few metres deep to way down to 30, there is surprise after surprise. Entry is over a slope covered in powdery white sand and interspersed with small outcrops of rock. These would have once been coral, which has died back in the past but is now regenerating, the healthy regrowth showing clearly. Travelling along the Aquarium towards Grouper Rock – these sites are close enough together that you can do them on the same dive – there are stands of thick lettuce leaf corals. Many fish hover above them: striped snapper, rainbow runners, rabbitfish, moorish idols, anthias, sweetlips and angels. There are

jacks hanging off the reef edge in the blue water and several really big grouper lurk about but will never let divers get close.

Down on the sand though is where the real action is. It's a non-stop treasure hunt with playful but naughty mantis shrimp, pink, beige and white leaffish, lionfish and blue-spotted rays who nestle in every nook and cranny. Scorpionfish sit inside matching sponges pretending to be non-existent.

At the bottom of the sloping wall near the drop-off, an encounter with a turtle is almost guaranteed. By the time you head back to the shallows you will have seen five or six. They are quite small and curious with beautifully patterned clean shells.

66 99 **Careful! Mantis shrimp retaliate if they think you are getting too close with a camera.**

↘15 Shindano	
Depth	25 m
Visibility	good
Currents	mild
Dive Type	day boat

↘16 Ciupis Garden	
Depth	18 m
Visibility	good
Currents	mild
Dive Type	day boat

Travelling down the east coast of Zanzibar, the dive sites take on a different slant: long, straight fringing reefs parallel the shore, creating, at low tide, a shallow inner lagoon. Beyond, the topography is reminiscent of a series of rice terraces. The level seabed is clad in low-lying corals that extend out towards the ocean then suddenly drop a few metres in a perfectly vertical wall. Broken by mini caves, these small walls end on another terrace, which then extends further and drops again. On Shindano, one tiny ledge of about a metre deep is full of glassfish and all around are leaffish and scorpions. There are cleaning stations and even a titan triggerfish sits inside a hole to be spruced up. Shrimp are everywhere: hingebeak, coral banded, Durban dancing shrimps and a Saron shrimp.

Ciupis, which means Y-fronts (don't ask), is a little further north and a local favourite as it is a multi-level dive. The topography is more or less the same as Shindano so it can be dived by starting deeper and then moving up to the shallows, or just on one level at a time. Either way, the reef terraces are home to a substantial array of fish life. There are angelfish, their wildly patterned juveniles hiding wherever they can. Small clusters of sweetlips shelter under hard corals while powderblue surgeonfish hover above. On the shallower level, there are several curious octopus, who pop in and out of holes to watch the divers, a free-swimming whitemouth moray and the gorgeous juvenile rockmover wrasse. Carpet anemones house pairs of white-patched anemone shrimps.

Coral banded shrimp; juvenile rockmover wrasse

☺ Unforgettable

The surface was like glass, the viz was so good we could see the reef below (at 30 metres) from the boat, and we were about to dive my favourite site, Cave 20, which once again didn't disappoint!

With five guests, we descended through the gin-clear liquid. Gently making our way along the small ledge, we encountered such creatures as pink whip rays, garden eels, ribbon eels, lionfish, and a pair of cobia lying in the sand. Upon reaching the overhang for which the site is given its name, massive schools of snapper and surgeons hung around above, with groupers and trevally mixed in between. I was surrounded by glassies, and motioned for divers to join me, one by one, under the ledge. Those with cameras snapped away at the assortment of shrimps and nudibranchs, and I could see the disappointment as I motioned for them to move out so everyone could get their turn. What seemed like mere seconds later, I poked my head out of the cave. We only had two minutes until deco, so with much reluctance, I motioned for the group to ascend, and amongst signals of tears and kisses (directed at the reef), we started up.

Hanging at our safety stop, more than happy with the dive, I watched as the three minutes on my dive computer changed to two, and then two to one. I caught a glimpse of something out the corner of my eye, and thinking it was a diver, I casually turned to look. There, not more than arm's length away, was a three-metre sailfish. I frantically searched for my signaling device to alert the rest of the group, but fumbled around till at last they looked my way to see what the commotion was and I could just point in the direction of the magnificent animal. We watched in amazement as it swam a half circle around us and moved off in the opposite direction. We gave chase, but in vain. Needless to say, no-one had their cameras on at the safety stop. And people have to ask why I chose diving as my profession!

Gabriel Frankel, Dive Instructor, Zanzibar, Tanzania

⬎17 Ukwele

🜨	**Depth**	34 m
◑	**Visibility**	good
🌊	**Currents**	mild
🌅	**Dive Type**	day boat

Dives on the deeper, outer sections of this stretch of reef require a blue-water entry. The boat waits above the reef rim for divers to roll in then descend through blue water until the top of the reef appears. It sits at about 25 metres or so. Depending on the time of the month, there can be some current along these outer edges that attracts some pelagics. Even when there is no current, you can be lucky and drop straight into a massive school of chevron barracuda. This isn't a common occurrence and even the divemasters are surprised when it happens. Down on the reef rim, there is another small wall that hides a tiny cavern which is full to bursting with copper coloured glassfish. Investigating inside, there are white leaffish and marbled dragonets that skitter around the sand. Several cleaning stations are busy with clients and nearby there are a group of porcelain crabs on an anemone.

⬎18 The Lagoon

🜨	**Depth**	8 m
◑	**Visibility**	low
🌊	**Currents**	mild
🌅	**Dive Type**	day boat

The perfect spot for novices to do their open water training dives, this calm and protected lagoon is also known for its population of pipefish. The water can be murky and silty, but the horseshoe shaped reef has a rim of hard corals that are in good condition. At their base there are seagrass beds and that's where most of the pipefish are hiding, although some are also crawling around the corals. There are also large lobsters, plenty of feisty damsels and an anemone with two porcelain crabs sitting together.

⬎19 Point 8

🜨	**Depth**	18 m
◑	**Visibility**	good
🌊	**Currents**	can be very strong
🌅	**Dive Type**	day boat

Although Point 8 is found on one of the flatter sections of reef, the terrain here is a little more interesting than on some of the terraces. The sloping reef drops gradually from around eight metres down to about 20, but it's unlikely you will get beyond the shallow section as you keep stopping to investigate the life in the coral mounds that rise up from the flat seabed. It seems that everywhere you pause you find another creature. Blue ribbon eels are the stars of the dive, lurching up from their tunnels to demand your attention, especially if you stop near one to look at something else. There are nudibranchs and a few whitemouth morays then, hidden deep in porites coral, is a gold spot scorpionfish and a coral crab. Another mound is host to the prolific glassfish found on almost every dive, plus copper sweepers, juvenile tobies and fluttering, juvenile oriental sweetlips.

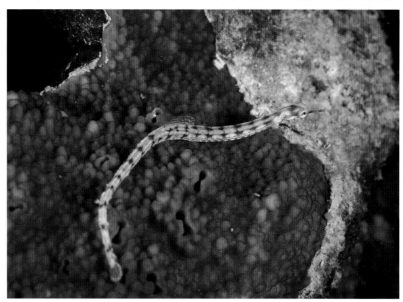

Blue ribbon eel on Point 8; porcelain crabs and pipefish are found in the Lagoon

⊠20	**Cave 20**	
🕐	**Depth**	42 m
◑	**Visibility**	good
≋	**Currents**	none
◒	**Dive Type**	day boat

For more experienced divers, this is quite probably the best site in the area – some are deeper and can be more exciting but are also a bit hit and miss. However, this has a reputation of being both a serious adrenaline rush and reliably good for pelagic creatures. Most divers enjoy it so much they ask to go straight back.

Entry is out past the reef edge and down through the blue water column until you land on a flat section of seabed at about 25 metres. This is covered in seagrass and drops very gradually, leading past an area thick with garden eels. The next patch of sand is covered by masses of resting bluespotted rays who are disturbed by the passing divers and take off rapidly. Eventually you reach a small lip in the reef where there are a few caverns and the most enormous numbers of both pelagic and reef fish. There is a cobia on the sand: this torpedo-shaped fish has a long, depressed head with small eyes and, from a distance, can be mistaken for a reef shark. It takes off just as quickly too, revealing the tail of a huge marbled ray which is hiding under one on the caverns. The ray is almost impossible to see – and too hard to shoot – as the cave is masked by phenomenal numbers of glassfish, but you can spot banded pipefish, mantis and cleaner shrimp and marbled dragonets inside. Around the cave's edges and all over the reef rim above are schools of striped snapper, small pink cardinals, untold numbers of rabbitfish and some unicornfish that have commensal remoras. In the blue are jacks, striped trevally and much more.

Swamped by glassfish in Cave 20

Mozambique

Once a Portuguese colony, Mozambique has only recently started to appear on the diver radar. For many years, the coastal reefs were explored by South Africans, who could simply hop over the border from their own country to dive along the neighbouring shores.

While the southern region is slowly becoming more popular, attracting divers from right around the world, the northern and central coasts remain unexplored. This is virgin dive territory.

⑤21 The Gap	
🕐 Depth	40 m
◑ Visibility	fair
🌀 Currents	mild
🌊 Dive Type	day boat

One of the few deep dives in the area, the Gap is a short distance from Wimbe Beach heading towards Ponta Maunhane, the point on the southern side of the bay. This is where the continental shelf comes closest to shore. Entry is over a plateau of hard corals at around 15 metres which leads to an almost sheer drop that ends at over 100. After an overnight storm the visibility is low so the dive takes on dark and mysterious overtones. A small tunnel opens up beneath a shelf at about 35 metres and then exits on the other side of the wall at 40. Just beneath and around the cave mouth are clusters of big fans. There are plenty of fish, including a small gang of batfish.

Pemba

This, the most northern coastal city, is something of a surprise. Located on the edge of the world's third largest bay (local residents claim only Sydney harbour and Rio are larger), Pemba has a deep-water harbour, an international airport and is a fairly neat town despite also being the major port for the region. Tourism is still in its infancy, with just a couple of top calibre hotels and a few small ones.

The diving can only be described as unexpected. Prolific hard coral reefs run around the outer edges of the massive bay and are backed by lush mangroves and beautiful white sand beaches. Most dives are shallow, but there are a variety of sites and marine life, including some incredible muck diving. However, the visibility tends to be quite low, especially in the rainy season as several rivers dump freshwater and sediment into the bay. The rainy season runs from November to April, but this is also the best dive season. After that, the winds pick up and can make being out on a boat unpleasant.

⊠22 The Ranch

🌀	**Depth**	12 m
◐	**Visibility**	fair
🌊	**Currents**	slight
⬤	**Dive type**	day boat

Heading inside Pemba bay and towards the main shipping docks takes you past the fishing village to an area of pea green water. It's hard to believe that this is going to be an outstanding dive site although the water does clear a little once you are past the jetty. The brief for this dive is to follow the divemaster and do not kick up the silt as this is a classic muck dive. It's also the place to encounter seahorses and you certainly will see them. Dropping down to just five metres you pass some very unusual starfish, then descending further over the slope you see there are almost no landmarks, not even any bits of rubbish; however, every tiny hollow or dip in the sand has a critter in it. These include prolific numbers of seahorses, which are thought to be the Reunion Seahorses, although that has not been confirmed. There are lots of spiky urchins with tiny cardinalfish sheltering in the spines, live sand dollars (these spiny critters are related to urchins), filefish, lots of tiny hogfish, dwarf zebra lions, cuttlefish, small moray eels hiding in holes and octopus in shells. Perhaps the most exciting find is a juvenile flying gurnard barely five centimetres long.

Introducing some of the residents of The Ranch, clockwise: pretending to be a rope, a scrawled filefish; the Reunion seahorse; an unusual nudibranch; juvenile flying gurnard; cuttlefish muscling in on the rope; octopus in hiding; juvenile cardinals taking advantage of an urchin; the smallest of dwarf lionfish

◉N23 Playground

◉	**Depth**	15 m
◉	**Visibility**	fair
◈	**Currents**	mild
◉	**Dive Type**	day boat

On the opposite side of Pemba bay, and on the outer edge of Ponta Saide Ali peninsula, the winding coastal wall is defined by rocky cliffs with sharp undercuts created by wave and surge action. The underwater terrain reflects that above, with lots of small ins and outs and some overhanging shelves. Dropping down to the base of the small wall, the seabed is well covered with healthy hard corals and swathes of anemones. Most of these have fantastic orange-coloured skirts and are hosting masses of damselfish with their tiny black juveniles. Outcrops of rock are plastered with razorclams and vase sponges. Finning along the wall, you find first a white leaffish (called paperfish here) and then a bit further on, a yellow one. The fish species include lizardfish, lionfish, juvenile sweetlips, anthias and tobies. The critter life includes commensal shrimp and goby pairs, starfish, flatworms and some tiny nudibranchs. In one elbow in the wall, a cavern is full of long whip corals then a second cavern reveals schools of copper sweepers, glassfish and coral banded shrimp, cleaner shrimp and pipefish. The dives along this stretch can only be done in calm waters due to the surge.

◉N24 Sailfish Tree and Rivermouth

◉	**Depth**	21 m
◉	**Visibility**	fair
◈	**Currents**	mild
◉	**Dive Type**	day boat

Heading from Wimbe Beach across to the opposite side of the bay, then north along the coastline, you eventually reach the delta from the Tari River. A little way past the river mouth, a solitary casuarina tree stands sentinel over a deserted white beach. Known as Sailfish Tree, this marks the entry to another shallow wall. No doubt because it is on the Indian Ocean coast, this stretch of reef is far more impressive than the ones in the bay: the hard corals are in amazing condition, spreading across the seabed and walls to create lovely gardens. The short wall drops from about two metres below the surface and is interspersed with overhangs and shallow caverns. Large fan corals and black coral bushes grow outwards into the currents that run between the wall and some rocky outcrops off to the ocean side. These are also well coated with low-lying hard corals and attract many schools of fish. There are snappers and sweetlips and masses of different coloured anthias. Larger fish are not seen very often, but there are occasional pufferfish and even bigger groupers. Despite fringing the open ocean, visibility is still low, and reduces even more on a second dive at Rivermouth, which is actually an extension of the first site.

While gassing off between these dives, you can usually snorkel in the mangrove forests that sit just inside the river mouth. The water is fairly clear and you will see young cardinals, morays and nudibranchs.

Reef scenes from Rivermouth, Playground and Sailfish Tree

Medjumbe

Running north from Pemba are 32 tiny coral islands. They stretch up as far as the Rovuma River which creates the border with Tanzania. Collectively known as the Quirimbas Archipelago, these islands are sandwiched between the coast and the Mozambique Channel, which is said to drop to over 400 metres deep.

Along with a vast area of mainland forest, the southernmost 11 of these coral islands form the Quirimbas National Park. This entire area is incredibly remote. Flying overhead in a small aircraft reveals that there is virtually no human habitation, yet the marine realm is a well-populated, but very much unexplored, region.

Dives here are conducted around the whims of the daily tides. The broad lagoon that encapsulates tiny Medjumbe is a breathtakingly beautiful sight but it does extend for quite some way, restricting the movement of the boats. At certain times, you literally have to wait for the sea to return so you can travel to the fringing reef. This also means that the sand is moving constantly and visibility can be low. At the same time, this means you are forced to sit and admire the view and the seabirds, and that is no great hardship.

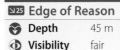
N25 Edge of Reason

🕐 **Depth**	45 m
🌓 **Visibility**	fair
🌀 **Currents**	mild
🌊 **Dive Type**	day boat

Definitely the most spectacular dive near Medjumbe's shores, this sheer wall drops vertically from the lagoon top. Enormous fan and whip corals jut out from a series of soft-coral-clad ledges and caverns. Each has a sandy bottom which harbours

schools of fish: silver sweetlips mix with surgeonfish and often mask a giant grouper. At nearly two metres long this might be a goliath grouper. He bolts out from the back of the cave, taking his 50 or so pilot fish with him. The flat reef top lies at 15 metres and is covered in thick patches of seagrass (much of which is swept over the wall to disturb the visibility). In between are hundreds of triggerfish nests – and just as many triggerfish, who fortunately are not aggressive. During a safety stop, you might spot huge turtle on the sand.

Whip coral goby; a goliath grouper and a coral-clad cavern on Edge of Reason

❝❞ Who knows why the dive was named the Edge of Reason... perhaps it was because the wall is so amazing, and it drops off so steeply, that going over it seems against all reason. (But we go anyway!)
Lindy Chazen,
Divemaster, Mediumbe Private Island.

⬇26 Sambi-Sambi

Depth	30 m
Visibility	fair
Currents	mild
Dive Type	day boat

North of Medjumbe and just beyond the lagoon, this gently sloping wall has a thick covering of hard corals. These are mostly gardens of lettuce leaf coral that are so prolific you can't see the seabed. The first part of the dive takes you east, where the bottom of this reef drops down as far as 80 metres. Looking to greater depths you can see a lot of big fans below the hard corals while back up on the reef top, at less than 10 metres, this changes to huge swathes of staghorn corals. As this area is both protected and undived, all the corals are very healthy although the fish are not so numerous. On a second dive along this reef, you can head west, which is shallower but the corals are equally prolific and pristine. Occasionally, a giant barracuda will be hovering.

⬇27 The Restaurant

Depth	14 m
Visibility	good
Currents	mild
Dive Type	day boat

This flat plateau at the top of, and behind, Sambi-Sambi is covered in a fantasy realm of table corals, hence the name. These are in fantastic condition, to the point that you almost don't see all the small fish lurking around as they are lost in amongst the graphic table shapes.

⬇28 Joe's Ridge

Depth	18 m
Visibility	poor
Currents	mild
Dive Type	day boat

The flat reef at Joe's Ridge lies off the southern side of the island on the edge of the lagoon. The visibility can be low due to tidal changes but the seabed is covered in small, low-lying outcrops of hard and soft corals. These harbour a variety of juvenile fish: tiny angelfish and butterflies, a baby bicolour parrotfish and a brushtail tang juvenile with its huge, startled eyes. There are a few small nudibranchs and some twin-tailed slugs, whip coral gobies, anemones and their clownfish and the rarely seen leopard blenny hiding in the hard corals.

Hard corals at the Restaurant; a juvenile brushtail tang

☺ Big-fish tales

There was a sense of excitement and anticipation as we kitted up on the deck of dive centre. We'd come to Inhambane in southern Mozambique to dive with whalesharks and manta rays and if the divemaster's reports were to be believed, we weren't going to be disappointed.

We were looking forward to our first dive. It was a beach entry through the surf so we pushed the RIB in and the skipper instructed us to jump on. We held on tightly as he skillfully negotiated the seemingly impassable wall of water and then sped on to the dive site. Without wasting any time we descended to the reef and took up position on one of the three cleaner stations. We waited patiently and within a couple of minutes were rewarded with three gigantic manta rays. They gracefully cruised overhead and passed within arm's reach. Taking up residence on a sandy section we watched the mantas doing 'laps' of the cleaner stations for about twenty minutes before heading off to explore the rest of the reef. Healthy corals, schools of snapper and turtles entertained us and peering into crevices unearthed honeycomb morays, paper – or leaf – fish and even rare, colourful harlequin shrimps.

I always seemed to be unlucky where whalesharks are concerned. All too often I would hear a divemaster say 'Strange, there were ten here last week...' I had been assured that this trip would be different, so with this in mind I frantically scanned the water for signs of these elusive creatures. And then it happened – I heard the word I had been waiting for – 'whaleshark!' With almost a sense of disbelief I grabbed my snorkel and slipped into the water. She was only small, but to me she was magnificent. She allowed our small group to snorkel with her for about ten minutes before descending into the depths. It had to be the perfect end to an amazing dive!

Tim Beard, IT consultant, London, UK

Drying out

It would be utter madness to travel to East Africa and not see her greatest resources – the vast wilderness of the Serengeti plains, the fascinating culture of the Masai tribes, the mass migrations of hundreds and thousands of animals.

When planning your trip, choose your dive destination by coordinating it with a safari, no matter how short. Bear in mind that wherever you go, you are likely to need an overnight stop – or at least a very long layover – in either Dar es Salaam or Nairobi. Dar is by far the nicer city, and the airport has much better facilities than those in Nairobi.

Kenya
Nairobi
Sleeping and eating

$$ **Stanley Hotel**, T+254 (0)2 228830, sarovahotels.com. A part of local colonial legend and once the haunt of the likes of Ernest Hemingway. The Thorn Tree Café located here is another Nairobi tradition. Pizza, pasta and coffee from US$20.

Kenya coast
Diving and sleeping

$$$ **Hemingways Resort**, T+254 (0)42 32624, hemingways.co.ke. In Turtle Bay. Diving with AquaVentures, diveinkenya.com.

$$$ **Turtle Bay Beach Club**, T+254 (0)42 32622, turtlebay.co.ke. Lively resort hotel.

All-inclusive rates include room, food and drinks. Turtle Bay Divers are on site.

$$$-$$ **Papillon Lagoon Reef**, T+254 (0)40 320 2627. On Diani Beach, nice rooms with pretty gardens. Barracuda Diving Team on site, baracudadiving.com.

$$$-$$ **Southern Palms Resort**, T+254 (0)40 3203721, southernpalmskenya.com. Swahili-style rooms at Diani. Dive the Crab are on site, divingthecrab.com.

Eating

$$ **Ali Barbour's Cave**, located right on Diani Beach. This rather unique restaurant is inside a series of naturally formed coral caves and although you sit underground, the roof is open to the stars. The menu is a curious mix of African spicing and modern international style. US$40 per head.

Kenya

Malindi An hour north of Mombasa and just beyond Watamu, this is the biggest attraction on the north coast. First made famous because Vasco de Gama stopped here in 1498, this small but historic town now looks rather frayed but gives an insight into life on the coast. A tour costs around US$60.

Mombasa One of the oldest cities in East Africa, the original town dates back some 700 years and was based on Mombasa Island. The city now sprawls both north and south along the coast, connected by causeways and bridges. This has created a curious combination of old and new, with plenty to see, do and buy. The markets and bazaars are fascinating, despite being manic, noisy and bustling. Tours cost around US$60.

Wasini Island In the Kisite-Mpunguti Marine Park and only accessible by boat. Tours run via the town of Shimoni. The island is steeped in history and a day tour (US$95) includes a visit to the village, lunch at the incredible Charlie's Claw restaurant and snorkelling in the marine park, wasini-island.com.

Shimba Hills National Reserve About 50 km south of Mombasa, this small game reserve is easy to reach from the south coast resorts. The coastal rainforest has orchids and on game drives, you can see elephants, giraffes and several monkey species. Unique to the reserve, is the sable antelope. Day tours from US$150, but an overnight trip is better value at US$250.

	Sleeping	$$$ US$150+ double room per night		$$ US$75-150	$ under US$75
	Eating	$$$ US$40+ 2-course meal, excluding drinks	$$ US$20-40		$ under US$20

A week on safari

There are more safari operators across these countries than you can possibly imagine. Every hotel, dive centre, travel agent or taxi driver will have their favourite. Mostly, they are very good and regulated by the relevant governments.

...in Kenya

Start from the coast and finish in Nairobi, or start from Nairobi and finish on the coast. Whichever way you go, the choices are endless. However, the most remote parks with the best animal populations are inland. Head north to **Samburu**, where landscapes are classic Africa: deep-red soil lush with acacia trees. Unusual animals include the long-necked gerunuk, Grevy's zebra and the reticulated giraffe. A change of pace will take you to endless – and pink – **Lake Nakuru**. The population of flamingos is so enormous that from a distance the water looks rose tinted, especially at dusk when the sun sets across millions of pink feathers. Finally, the **Masai Mara National Park** is where you are likely to see all of the big five. You can also stop and visit ancient tribes who still adhere to their traditional way of life. No TVs out in the mud huts although old film canisters are regarded as one of the better earlobe-stretching devices. Meanwhile, the baboons eat wild figs, which ferment in their tummies until, rather inebriated, they fall out of the trees. Quite amusing when it's around your luxury tented campsite! **Tsavo East** is the main park close enough to the coast to allow a day trip, although you won't get very far inside in less than two days. You might see elephants and lions, but buffalo, giraffe and various deer species are more likely. Day trips from US$200. One week budget safari from US$1,250, luxury from US$2,500. Contact Pollmans in Kenya, pollmans.com.

...in Tanzania

Again, there are countless pre-organized options, but a fabulous route is to start from Arusha, not far from Mount Kilimanjaro. Flying over that is quite a sight and if you fancy the climb, there are several different treks – some are regarded as quite gentle at five days up and one day to get back down. Expect to pay around US$2,000 for the pleasure.

Alternatively, enjoy some cool mountain air at a lodge before setting off for the amazing **Ngorongoro Crater**. This ancient gorge is occupied by elephants, giraffe, rhino, zebra, lions and cheetahs. It is a very intense experience as the animals are concentrated in a small space. At sunset you can sip an icy beer on the rim of the crater while admiring the monkeys and giraffe just feet away. Next explore the wide open **Serengeti**. Days are long, hot and grubby but the rewards are high. All the big cats live here – chances are you will see them – and hippos wallow in ponds. The great wildebeest migration is beyond spectacular, as is watching a pride of cheetahs making a kill. Evenings are spent around the campfire after cleaning up in a hot bush shower. Sleep under canvas listening to the sounds of nocturnal animals on the prowl. No need to panic, there are armed guards. Budget safaris cost from US$1,500; luxury from US$3,500. Contact Ranger Safaris, rangersafaris.com.

and one day maybe Mozambique.

With tourism being so new, and after the long civil war, safaris are only just starting to take off in Mozambique. The quantity and variety of big animals is known to be far lower than elsewhere in Africa, but who knows what the future will bring.

Booking a safari As standards vary, check you will get the following:

- ▸ Small groups so that every passenger has a window seat
- ▸ 4WD rather than a minibus; this gives better access in the parks
- ▸ Vehicles should travel independently, not in a convoy
- ▸ Lift-off roofs provide better views and photo opportunities
- ▸ Company policy on taking children – it varies
- ▸ Campsite standard: 'luxury' may mean a private hole-in-the-ground toilet and a bucket hanging from a tree with heated water for a shower; or it could be permanent rooms built with canvas walls and hanging nets.

Pemba Island

Chake Chake Pemba's largest town is also the administrative capital. There are shops, banks, ruins of an 18th-century fort, a small dhow port and a fish market to visit.

Pujini About 10 km south of Chake Chake are the ruins of a 15th-century fortified palace – the seat of Mohammed bin Abdul Rahman whose name was synonymous with cruelty and hard labour. A day tour including both of these costs about US$60.

Ngezi Forest Lying on the northern tip of Pemba is the last remaining tract of indigenous forest and home to the Pemba flying fox, a bat endemic to the island. The nature trail is good for bird life and local flora. Walking tours cost around US$45.

Zanzibar

Stone Town The old city and cultural heart of Zanzibar is now a World Heritage site. Built in the 19th century on a triangular peninsula, the town consists of a maze of winding alleys, bustling bazaars, mosques and grand Arab houses. The architecture shows Arab, Persian, Indian, European and African influences with ornately carved wooden doors and enclosed verandas. One of the two most visited buildings is Beit-El-Ajaib or the House of Wonders. Built by Sultan Seyyid Barghash as a grand palace,

it is now a museum of sorts. The other is the 18th century Arab Fort which has an amphitheatre and artisan stalls. Stone Town was a major centre for the slave trade and the Anglican Cathedral is built on the site of a former slave market. The town was also a base for many explorers. David Livingstone's house on the seafront has become a trendy restaurant with lovely views – perfect for lunch. The island's most famous 'son' is undoubtably singer Freddie Mercury. One of his homes was on Kenyatta Street and is now the Zanzibar Gallery.

Guided tours of Stone Town can be informative, but are expensive. Buy a map at the Zanzibar Gallery for a DIY tour and don't be put off by the notion that you will get lost in the backstreets – they all lead back to the seafront eventually.

Spice tours The history of Zanzibar is one of spices: nutmeg, cinnamon and pepper brought the Sultans of Oman to the island, initiating the slave trade. Plantation tours demonstrate using spices in cooking, cosmetics and for many ailments. And you can shop!

Jozani Forest In the east central region, this is home to red colobus monkeys. These roam freely beside Sykes monkeys, small bucks and bushpigs.

Day tours around Zanzibar are easily available but can cost upwards of US$100 a head.

Tanzania

Dar es Salaam
Sleeping
$$ Protea Hotel – Oyster Bay, T+255 (0) 22 266 6665, proteahotels.com/oysterbay. Great stopover hotel, smart rooms have a mini-kitchen. Pool and restaurant in the complex; airport transfers can be arranged.

Pemba Island
Diving and sleeping
$$$ Fundu Lagoon & Dive710, T+255 (0)77 443 8668. fundulagoon.com. Classy resort with bungalows disguised as tents.
$$$ Manta Reef Lodge, T+255 (0)77 762 8333, themantaresort.com. Renovated and upgraded resort on the northwest tip of Pemba. Oxygene Pemba Divers on site.
Liveaboards
There are few liveaboards that ply East Africa's waters, however, MY Kisiwani, a modern steel-hulled vessel, is based on Pemba island, divingpemba.com.

Zanzibar
Diving
One Ocean, T+255 (0)24 223 8374, zanzibaroneocean.com. Australian-owned dive operation based at Matemwe Beach Village opposite Mnemba Atoll. Well-run outfit with good, traditional wooden boats and a fantastic crew. Also with a centre in Stone Town and in four other resorts dotted around the island.

Rising Sun Dive Centre, T+255 747 415 049, risingsun-zanzibar.com. British-owned operation and the only PADI National Geographic Centre on mainland East Africa. Based in Breezes Beach Club on the east coast. Guaranteed small groups with personal attention from the very friendly divemasters and staff. Courses run daily. Also in Royal Zanzibar Hotel at Ras Nungwi.
Sleeping
$$$ Breezes Beach Club, T+ 255 (0)77 444 0883, breezes-zanzibar.com. Club style resort with beautifully decorated interiors

Carved Arab wooden door in Stone Town; the House of Wonders; Breezes Beach Club in the southeast of the island.

and lovely gardens. The on-site bazaar is altogether too tempting and the spa has Asian therapists. Also the owners of Baraza Resort and The Palms: same beach but extra doses of romance and luxury.

$$ Matemwe Beach Village, T+255 (0)77 417250, matemwebeach.com. A cluster of palm-thatched bungalows set right on the beach beside the local village. Various room categories are great value for money. Nice touches include coffee served at dawn on the beach.

Other options
Azanzi, azanzibeachhotel.com
Mnemba Island Lodge, mnemba-island.com
Royal Zanzibar, royalzanzibar.com

Mozambique

Pemba
Diving and sleeping
$$$ Pemba Beach Hotel and Spa, T+258 (0)272 21770, pembabeachresort.com. This resort style hotel hangs over the edge of Pemba's Wimbe Beach with gorgeous views to sea. Huge, luxurious rooms (and bathrooms) are decorated in Moorish style, facilities are excellent and the on-site dive centre is very efficient.

$$$ Medjumbe Private Island, T+258 (0)217 15200, medjumberesort.com. The location, the service, the colour of the water, the overall ambience... Not the most expensive or sumptuous resort you will ever visit, but one that has acheived an almost unattainable standard: the balance between casual lifestyle and luxurious touches is simply perfect.

Other options
Matemo Resort, matemoresort.com
CI DIvers, cidivers.com

Mozambique flights
For flight schedules and bookings to northern Mozambique contact national carrier, Linhas Aéreas de Moçambique (lam.co.mz). Rani Resorts, owners of Medjumbe Private Island and Pemba Beach Resort, will also be able to assist and advise.

Pemba

Originally named Porto Amelia after a Portuguese queen, some people describe this small city as rundown, but compared to many an African centre, it is quite a tidy place. Colonial architecture rubs shoulders with fishing villages made of wooden huts. The centre has a sense of faded grandeur, while Wimbe beach is becoming popular with tourists. There is a casino, a couple of top-class hotels and some budget ones. In the centre of town there is a souk that stretches for two km. Silver and crafts are available, but avoid anything that might be made of ivory as selling this is illegal.

Medjumbe

A 45-minute flight over the Quirmbas Archipelago delivers you to Medjumbe. Once you are there, that's it – nothing but peace and tranquility. A walk around the island takes half an hour, depending on how long you stop to wade in the rock pools, watch the populations of seabirds or sit beneath the old lighthouse. The only entertainment is at sunset, when the tide retreats and the sand spit changes into a sea of terns. Thousands arrive, turning the white sand even whiter, but strangely dotted with beady black eyes. They resent being disturbed and lift off en masse, squawking their how-dare-yous. There is an uninhabited island just to the west which can also be visited at times, tide dependant.

Ibo Island

Once the capital of Mozambique, Ibo dates back to the times of Vasca de Gama. It was colonized by the Portuguese in early 1600s, it's economy thriving due to the slave trade, pirate commerce and ivory trading. Many of the colonial houses have been abandoned and walking about feels like stepping back 200 years. Day trip tours vist the Catholic Church and the fort of St Jao Baptista where silversmiths melt down old nickel coins and recraft them as bracelets and pendants.

The courtyard of the Pemba Beach Hotel, flying over the Quirimbas islands, Medjumbe's lagoon, seabirds and their rooms with a view

Fish soup: right across the atolls there are countless numbers of bluestripe snappers, *Lutjanus kasmira*.
Kuda Rah Thila, South Ari Atoll

INDI

INDIAN OCEAN

THE MALDIVES

↘1 North and South Malé ▶▶ p74

North Malé Atoll

↘2

↘9

↘4

↘3

● MALÉ

↘1

South Malé Atoll

↘5

↘7

↘8

↘6

↘1 The Victory, Malé
↘2 Finger Point, Eriyadu
↘3 Lankanfinolhu, outside channel
↘4 Occaboli Thila
↘5 Cocoa Thila
↘6 Vili Varu Giri
↘7 Kandooma Corner
↘8 Kuda Giri

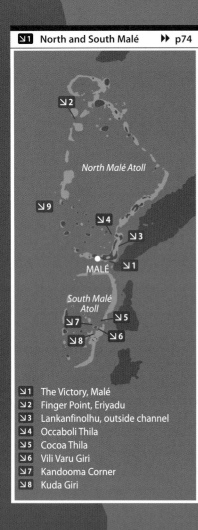

North Malé Atoll

↘1

Ari Atoll

MALÉ ●

South Malé Atoll

↘2

North Nilandhoo Atoll

↘3

↘2 Ari Atoll ▶▶ p78

↘9 Vilamendhoo House Reef
↘10 Maaya Thila
↘11 Bodhufinolhu Thila
↘12 Kalahandi Huraa

↘12

↘9

South Ari Atoll

↘11

↘10

One and Half Degree Channel

Equatorial Channel

75 km

Introduction

SRI LANKA

COLOMBO ●

◥3 North Nilhandhoo Atoll   ▶▶ p80

↘14
↘13
↘15

Felitheyo

North Nilhandhoo Atoll

↘16

All those dreams of playing Robinson Crusoe – being cast away on your own private island and getting back to nature – can all come true in the Maldives. What's more, you can have the fantasy complete with hot and cold running water, someone to wait on you hand and foot and go diving at the same time.

Your first glimpse of the Maldives will be the spectacular aerial view of her diminutive islands as you fly in to the capital, Malé. As you try to work out which one is yours, rest assured that they are all equally beautiful and all have fabulous diving.

This tiny, waterborne country was bypassed for centuries due to the hazardous fringing reefs that are also its saving. Their untarnished natural beauty, both above and below the waterline, is now their prime appeal. There are fish, fish and yet more fish, all attracted to these isolated Indian Ocean atolls, which are actually the tips of an ancient volcanic mountain range. There's other marine life too, but there is nowhere else quite like this for swimming amongst pretty tropical fish.

Drying out time, however, isn't exactly a succession of cultural diversions. In the Maldives you make your own entertainment. For here, watching the stars in the sky can be far more rewarding than watching them on screen.

Maldives rating

Diving
★★★

Dive facilities
★★★★

Accommodation
★★★★

Down time
★★

Value for money
★★★

Essentials

Getting there and around

Getting a flight to the Maldives used to be fairly challenging but the country is now so popular that flying to the capital, Malé, is simplicity itself. There are dozens of charter flights that arrive on a daily basis, mostly from European cities. To access them you need to book a package via a travel agent in your home country. If you are coming from Australia, Asia, North America – or Europe but want to travel in substantially more comfort – there are also scheduled airlines that fly in regularly. These include Emirates (emirates.com), Sri Lankan Airlines (srilankan.lk), Singapore Airlines (singaporeair.com) and Qatar (qatarairways.com).

Once you arrive at the airport, you will be collected by your hotel, dive centre or liveaboard. There is very little in the way of independent travel; it does exist although arriving without a booking is not advised. Transfers from the airport are mostly by seaplane. This is a great experience – flying in a 20-seater seaplane over fantastic seascapes until you reach your own little paradise isle. A few resorts, mainly those in North Malé Atoll, will collect guests by speedboat as the trip is less than an hour. These journeys can be bumpy so be prepared with seasickness tablets if your stomach is sensitive. Once you are on your island, you're not going very far – maybe to the next island on an organized day trip – so getting around is just not an issue.

Local laws and customs

The Maldives is a Muslim nation but you won't come across much in the way of religious customs. Many staff – such as waiters and receptionists – are from India or Sri Lanka. Originally this was an attempt to ensure that the locals were not unduly influenced by western ways. Now, more and more native Maldivians are working within the tourist industry. The resorts are tolerant of other cultures but do ask that you respect the private compounds where staff live, and especially the small mosque that is on every island. Women are asked not to sunbathe topless and it is regrettable that some visitors ignore this request; the Maldivians are such nice people that you do have to wonder why. If you visit a nearby non-tourist island, or go into Malé, dress conservatively.

Safety

You're on holiday somewhere that looks like paradise and it's hard to imagine that anything could go wrong. Personal safety has always been an almost insignificant concern. If there was to be any petty crime or theft it would probably be at the hands of a fellow tourist, certainly not a local; however, don't tempt fate by leaving cash or valuables on show.

Of course, things do go wrong, as the Christmas 2004 tsunami demonstrated. However, this freak disaster indicates that the biggest risk you run on the Maldives will be nature taking revenge. Kick some hard coral and you will get cut. Put your hands down on fire coral and you'll get stung. It's important to read up on the marine life and learn what you can and can't do safely.

Traditional fishing craft

Maldives	
Location	3°15'N, 73°00'E
Capital	Malé
Population	396,334
Land area in km²	300
Coastline in km²	644

Language

When the country was first opened to tourism, as mentioned, many workers were imported from elsewhere and English became the most commonly used language. Now, many of these migrant workers can speak almost any language you care to throw at them. The native language is Dhivehi, which has many influences from right across the region. It is also the root of one of the most used words in this book – atoll. Anyone who has tried to learn a little Arabic may notice some similarities.

hello/goodbye	*salaam alekum*	sorry!	*ma-aafu kurey!*
yes	*aan*	how much is...	*agu kihaavareh ...*
no	*noon*	good	*rangalu*
thank you	*shukriyaa*	great dive!	*barabaru feenume*

And what about impressing the boat boys with 'what is the name of this reef?' which is *mi farah kiyanee kon nameh.*

Health

There are medical facilities in Malé and many resorts have a nurse or doctor on call. They may not be on your island but will be close by. However, there is little in the way of risks here. Food standards are generally high, though you should drink bottled or purified water. Mosquitos are more prolific on lush islands than ones with less natural vegetation. The sun, however, can be fearsome, which you may not realize due to those cooling sea breezes. Use lots of sunscreen and drink plenty of water to avoid dehydration.

Costs

As everything is imported into the Maldives, costs can be high. By 'everything' we mean everything – from staff to drinking water, lettuce to T-shirts. There is virtually no agriculture, no food or drink industry, no manufacturing. Hotel rates run from a reasonable US$80 per night to an astronomical US$1,000. Meals are also expensive but almost all resorts include breakfast and most will offer room rates that include lunch and dinner.

The trend to rebuild the original hotels as upper-class resorts continues. These are beautiful but expensive and not aimed at serious divers anyway. The best way to keep your costs down to a reasonable level is to book an all-inclusive resort or a liveaboard as there will be fewer hidden extras. Otherwise, everything is signed for and charges tallied at the end of a stay. It's easy to run up larger than expected bills so keep an eye on these to ensure you only pay what you have signed for. Tipping is expected. At the end of your holiday leave a 'gift' for your waiter or room boy, who will have taken care of you consistently during your stay as the system allots specific staff members to each room. Around US$10 per week is often suggested. For dive staff see page 12.

Tourist information → The government website can be found at visitmaldives.com. There is additional information at maldivestourism.net.

Fact file

International flights	Singapore Airlines via Singapore, Emirates via Dubai, Sri Lankan via Colombo, Qatar via Doha
Departure tax	Mostly included in ticket or US$12
Entry	Visa for 30 days issued on arrival
Internal flights	Maldives Air Taxis and Sun Express
Ground transport	Water taxis
Money	The US dollar is the accepted currency
Language	All European languages are widely spoken
Electricity	230v, plug type A (see page 16)
Time zone	GMT +5
Religion	Muslim
Phone	Country code +960; IDD code 00; Police 119

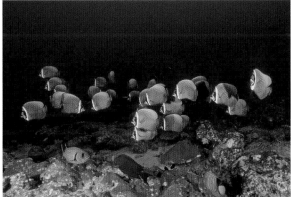

Free swimming leopard shark; schooling white collared butterflyfish

Dive brief

Diving

Fish, fish and yet more fish. There's no doubt about it, this is the place to go for them. Like no other tropical destination, the atolls here host the most amazing quantities of colourful fish due to the isolated nature of these tiny specks of land. The fringing reefs provide the only habitat for many miles in any direction so diving feels like being immersed inside a great big aquarium.

On the other hand, this is not the place for prolific corals. The 1998 El Niño took its toll in these shallow waters but get down a little deeper and you'll hardly know that had happened. Even before that event, coral was never the main attraction so if you don't go expecting to see lush colour-ridden reefs, you won't be disappointed. Despite that, there are patches of soft corals and hard corals live and regenerate in deeper, cooler waters, providing a backdrop to the myriad fish life.

Currents are the other defining feature of Maldivian diving and these vary with the seasons. Before you choose a resort check what direction the prevailing winds will be coming from. Currents run in line with the winds and bring in clearer waters from the open ocean. May to November is the southwest monsoon. Winds transport clearer water from that direction so you will get better visibility if you go to the west of an atoll. December to April is the northeast monsoon, so at that time it's better on the east of an atoll.

Snorkelling

There are those who like to claim that you can see as much while snorkelling as you can diving and this is one place where that might just about be true. The small fringing or house reefs that encircle nearly every island are full of life. During the day, you can spend long hours floating over a shallow reef watching all sorts of pretty creatures like the ubiquitous powderblue surgeonfish. At night you can sit dangling your feet off the jetty and watch baby sharks congregate, attracted by the lights.

Marine life

Fish, fish, fish. Snappers by the million, parrotfish and butterflies by the hundreds. There's never just one of something. While schools of pelagic fish like jacks are less common, some bigger animals are well known. Nothing is ever guaranteed but there are feeding stations for mantas, reefs that whalesharks are known to haunt and a good supply of sharks, especially in areas that get stronger currents.

Maldives
animal
encounters

Seasonal	mantas and whalesharks
Not seasonal	masses of fish

Chomping on the reef in Nilhandhoo

Our first ever dives, way back when, were off tiny Bandos. On Christmas Day, we came face-to-face with a whitetip shark and were utterly, completely hooked. The Maldives have since become pretty busy, which is not to say that the islands have lost the Robinson Crusoe atmosphere that made them famous. However, if you're looking for true isolation, with no other people and no other dive boats in sight, you may find it a bit too crowded.

Making the big decision

The Maldives tend to be where most European divers graduate to after they've done the Red Sea. It's just a little bit further but a lot more exotic. The tiny islands are romantic and standards are generally high. Although the greatest draw is still the marine life, this country has also become highly attractive for those who want to sail, windsurf, be pampered in a spa or bake in the sun.

There are around 100 designated resorts and the castaway style is cultivated and exploited at them all. Choosing the perfect one can be confusing. Most are perfect for couples while others cater for families. Some are managed by a specific nationality and that attracts guests of the same nationality.

Serious divers should opt for an island with a good house reef, where shore and night diving is available. Families may want to look for islands with bigger beaches and more facilities. Location is another consideration – the closer to the airport, the shorter the transfer time but the remote islands will be less busy. Finally, if you can abandon the island castaway dream, try a liveaboard and dive more than one atoll.

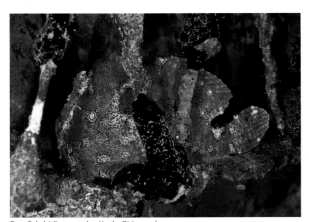

Frogfish hiding on the Kuda Giri wreck

Dive data

Seasons	The southwest monsoon is May to November: go to the west of an atoll
	The northeast monsoon is December to April: go to the east of an atoll
Visibility	Varies according to location and season, from 10-30 metres
Temperatures	Air 25-30°C; water 25-29°C
Wet suit	3 mm full body suit
Training	Courses available on all resort islands, however pre-booking is essential
Nitrox	Becoming more common; check in advance
Deco chambers	Bandos and Malé

Bottom time

Maldives	Stretching across the Indian Ocean for 820 kilometres north to south and 120 east to west, this country consists of 1,190 coral islands making up 26 major atolls. Addu Atoll, the most southerly, is just below the Equator, and boasts the country's highest point at 2.4 metres. The remainder of the country lies to its north.
North Malé Atoll ▸▸ p74	Location of capital city, Malé, this is the most explored atoll, the most dived but possibly still the best, especially for fish numbers.
South Malé Atoll ▸▸ p76	Less populated and visited, South Malé has adventurous channel dives with strong currents and a lone wreck.
Ari Atoll ▸▸ p78	A popular destination with wide open spaces and the biggest variety of dive styles – reefs, wrecks and walls.
North Nilandhoo Atoll ▸▸ p80	Remote and quiet diving in barely investigated waters, North Nilandhoo is a newer destination.

Diversity — reef area 8,920 km²

HARD CORALS	63
FISH SPECIES	1,116
ENDEMIC FISH SPECIES	2
FISH UNDER THREAT	19
PROTECTED REEFS/MARINE PARKS	0

All diversity figures are approximate

North Malé Atoll

More correctly known as Kaafu Atoll, this is home to both the capital, Malé, which you are unlikely to see before getting whisked off to a waiting transfer, and the international airport. Because of that, the resorts on islands nearby were the first to be developed.

Islands vary in size from those that require only a 10-minute walk to circumnavigate, to those that take as much as 40 minutes. In general, North Malé resorts tend to be smaller but more sophisticated than ones further afield because, as time has passed, the original ones have been rebuilt to higher standards. Where once a Maldives holiday was all about the simple life with brackish, cold water showers, now it's jacuzzis and spas, fancy eco-resorts with international style restaurants, gyms and sports facilities. A few are still as rustic as when they were first built, a little on the rundown side but more in tune with the feel of the islands.

All the same, diving in this atoll is some of the best in the country. There is a mix of channel and thila (small submerged reef) diving and this creates very exciting conditions for the prolific marine life. For some divers, strong currents can be off-putting, which in terms of conserving the reefs is not such a bad thing as fewer people are there to damage them. Yet, with so many resorts, many divers regard both the region and the diving as a little overcrowded.

⛴ The Victory, Malé Airport	
🐢 **Depth**	30 m
◐ **Visibility**	fair to good
〰 **Currents**	slight to very strong
🌊 **Dive type**	day boat

The *Victory* sank on Friday, 13th February, 1981, although no one is clear what really happened. The most touted theory is a navigational error as all the crew escaped. The wreck is a 110-metre steel cargo ship that you descend to via a rope attached to the midship mast. Surface currents can be strong so the rope is a necessity but once you reach the deck, you are sheltered. From here you can investigate the holds which are teeming with fish or head around the outside of the hull. There are often some big pelagics like turtles and grouper around the seabed near the anchor. Part of the accommodation area and the bridge is open for investigation but space is tight. Most dive centres limit this site to experienced divers due to the current and depth.

Whitetip reef sharks circling over Finger Point

N2	Finger Point, Eriyadu	
Depth	27 m	
Visibility	good	
Currents	slight to ripping	
Dive type	liveaboard	

A well-known adrenaline-rush dive, entry is over a small thila attached to the main reef by a sandy saddle. The current here can be extremely strong, which attracts big animals. Napoleon wrasse hover over the sand as do whitetip sharks, and then, as you descend to the point of the thila, you can spot eagle rays on a fly past. Whitetips circle just off the reef edge and even grey sharks are standing off in the blue. The thermoclines can be severe too, but it's an exciting dive. Back on the main reef where the coral is mostly rubble (natural effects taking their toll), you are likely to see octopus, a lot of small schooling fish and juvenile turtles.

N3	Lankanfinolhu, outside channel	
Depth	15 m	
Visibility	fair to good	
Currents	slight to strong	
Dive type	liveaboard	

At this well-known manta cleaning station, dives start with a drift along the channel, passing an occasional shark and schooling fish until you reach a depression behind a small outcrop. Occupied by cleaner wrasse, the mantas head in to get spruced up while diver groups sit and wait for them to appear. Sometimes it's juveniles circling closer and closer, swooping between all the divers' bubbles, at other times adult mantas swoop past divers then head out into the blue. The coral here has sadly been turned to rubble by the diver activity and there is little other life on the cleaning station. Some days you only see them further along the channel.

❝ ❞ Descending into Occaboli's canyon feels like being a kid with your nose pressed against the glass wall of an aquarium. There is a peculiar sense of complete disbelief – you are looking at so many fish at once that you just can't absorb how many or what they all are. After being nudged by a two-metre-long Napoleon you just give up and start grinning instead.

N4	Occaboli Thila	
Depth	32 m	
Visibility	fair to good	
Currents	slight to very strong	
Dive type	liveaboard	

While perhaps not the most exhilarating dive in the Maldives, this site sums up the best of being in a real-world aquarium. Just an hour or so north of Malé, the site consists of a circular main reef, a small narrow thila lying off its southeastern corner and a coral rock which creates a canyon between the thila and the main reef. The canyon is a real magnet for fish attracted by the currents that pass through. There are resident Napoleon wrasse, several tuna and many small schools of jacks all whizzing about. At depth there are groups of bluelined snapper and oriental sweetlips. Fish life is prolific with parrotfish, surgeons, banners, butterflies and so many other species you can't absorb it all. An overhang is thick with glassfish and as you approach them they part in silent waves to reveal a giant grey moray behind. Back on the top, the reef slope is covered in small table corals just inches across and lots of little soft corals and colourful tunicates in between. There are more small tropical fish and bottom feeders such as blennies.

Maldives Dive log North Malé Atoll

Octopus parading in the shallows; Humpback snappers cluster in large groups

South Malé Atoll

With the upper rim of South Malé Atoll just about touching the bottom of North Malé, you could almost consider these two regions to be one and the same. The style of the resort islands are much as they are elsewhere in the country – each is ringed by rooms tucked under trees with views out over the reefs or lagoon. However, this atoll is slightly less developed with fewer hotels as it's that bit further from the airport.

The south of Kaafu is separated from the north by the deep Vadhoo channel and, being smaller and due south, is protected by its bigger neighbour from the more severe wind and sea conditions. Diving is mostly on the east side in narrow channels that carve through the rim of the fringing reef. There are only six of these so the tides sweep in and out at a great rate and the currents can really rip! At certain times of year the visibility will be flawless; at others it can drop right down but this attracts the bigger animals to feeding stations.

◪5 Cocoa Thila

◉	**Depth**	26 m
◐	**Visibility**	fair to good
≋	**Currents**	mild to ripping
◓	**Dive type**	liveaboard

This large, flat-topped, oval-shaped reef is surrounded by a sloping wall that runs most of the way around its sides. At one end, the slope becomes quite steep and is interspersed with small overhangs covered in pastel-hued soft corals – pink, lemon and mauve. On the reef top, if the current is running, you encounter huge schools of collared butterflyfish hovering beside equally large groups of oriental sweetlips. The site is also known for green turtles and there are several in residence. You need to approach them very carefully as they take off if spooked. The adults can grow to be enormous, at least two metres from head to tail. They are sometimes seen sleeping under the ledges or moving about the plateau feeding, but mostly you see them as they take off to the surface for a gulp of air.

◪6 Vili Varu Giri

◉	**Depth**	18 m
◐	**Visibility**	fair to good
≋	**Currents**	mild
◓	**Dive type**	liveaboard

This small, flat thila makes a perfect night dive. The very top level is exposed at low tide so there are a lot of boulders and rubble where, under cover of darkness, all the nocturnal animals emerge to hunt. As you descend onto the plateau, you can spot decorator crabs that are incredibly well camouflaged, some spider crabs, lots of sleepy fish nestling into the cracks and crevices and scorpionfish in the rubble area. A sandy slope then drops to a low wall on one side which is encrusted with dendrophyllia corals and small tunicates. Amongst these are more nocturnal crabs and shrimp, ornate ghost pipefish hiding in black coral branches and a couple of shallow caverns where green turtles rest.

◪7 Kandooma Corner

◉	**Depth**	23 m
◐	**Visibility**	good
≋	**Currents**	strong
◓	**Dive type**	liveaboard

This long, thin reef extends out to a point or corner where there are often fierce currents that attract big pelagic action. More often than not, though, it won't be possible to dive here as the currents are simply too strong. Fortunately, the other, calmer side can be equally as interesting. From the flat top there is a small ridge and overhang that slopes down to 30 metres or so. There are lots of tubastrea corals and quite a bit of dendronephthya soft coral surrounded by masses of fish. In the overhangs you can often find small green turtles munching on some lunch, or a resting whitetip shark. On the top of the reef there are huge schools of parrotfish, black surgeonfish and rainbow runners. These appear in massive waves to feed on algae-covered rocks.

Hiding in the corals at Vili Varu Giri, an ornate ghost pipefish

8 Kuda Giri

	Depth	27 m
	Visibility	fair to good
	Currents	mild
	Dive type	liveaboard

What makes this such a special dive is that it's really two dives rolled into one. Just a short distance from Dhigufinolhu, there is both the intact wreck of a cargo boat and a small pinnacle to explore, although the real reef does tend to take second place to the artificial one to its side.

No one seems to know the cargo boat's real name although it is said that it sank somewhere else and was moved to the giri (meaning submerged reef) to create a dive feature. And it certainly has done that, attracting a lot of marine life. The hull lies pointing towards the reef with her bow at 18 metres and the stern dropping past 30. The hull is about 30 metres long with one cargo hold at the back, which you can enter though it is a bit too dark and confined to penetrate very far. The outside is in perfect condition and you can see how well the small cup corals, sponges and tunicates and algaes are colonizing the sides as you drop to the propeller. This sits at 27 metres and is covered in more crusting corals. Ascend back up to the midships section past some black coral bushes to find the rear deck has some raised scaffolding. This open structure attracts plenty of small fish while an old cage has a resident grey frogfish inside it.

After diving the wreck it's time to head over to the pinnacle to gas off. There are some small caverns and overhangs that are full of fish, and up at the 10 metre mark, a bed of staghorn corals is home to even more: there are leaffish, filefish and even the Maldivian clownfish. Another great feature of this site is that strong currents are rare, although the visibility can drop at times.

Ari Atoll

The largest atoll in the country, and some way south and west of the Malé atolls, Ari – or Alifu – is still comparatively close to the airport with seaplane transfers generally taking less than an hour. This atoll has resorts right around its rim and there are also a few on islands in the central lagoon which have access to dive sites in all directions.

This is a huge atoll with, potentially, the most varied diving in the country. There are many thilas, which are less prone to strong currents than channel and outer rim dives, and this is a big bonus for less experienced divers. There are also lots of caverns and overhangs to explore, plus there's one more thing that gives Ari an edge at certain times of year – the southeastern corner is known to be a whaleshark haunt and you might be lucky enough to see several in a day. Visibility can be low, however, as they come here to feed when the plankton blooms.

Powder blue surgeonfish; male redfin basslet; the cave on Vilamendhoo house reef, exit 10

⌖9 Vilamendhoo House Reef

🕐	**Depth**	28 m
◐	**Visibility**	good
≋	**Currents**	usually mild
◓	**Dive type**	shore dive

This is one of the most diver-friendly islands in the country and shore dives are marked by exit numbers from the beach. Exit 10 is on the northern side of the island. The wall here is almost completely vertical, dropping to 28 metres, then sloping to the seabed. It isn't all that pretty, with lots of scrappy coral and rocks interspersed with dark green tubastrea, but quite dramatic all the same. Fish life is good and there are some unusual nudibranchs and tiny morays with yellow and black spots. There is a small cave at about 15 metres deep that is bursting with glassy sweepers. At its entry there are pretty pipefish, flatworms, lots of different types of shrimp and a large grey moray just inside.

⌖10 Maaya Thila

🕐	**Depth**	20 m
◐	**Visibility**	low to fair
≋	**Currents**	medium to strong
◓	**Dive type**	day boat

One of Ari's better-known dive sites, Maaya Thila is also a protected zone. The thila is a typical submerged oval that you can easily swim around in a single dive. There are some outcrops off one end that display feeding corals. It's worth swimming across to them, especially if there is current, as grey sharks often patrol the sandy channel. Likewise, back on the main reef, there is the most activity when you hit oncoming currents so dives here are always best when these are strongest. You can see all sorts of impressive marine life: there are resident batfish, oriental sweetlips, clown and titan triggers, octopus, morays and the ever-present powderblue surgeons.

⌖11 Bodhufinolhu Thila

🕐	**Depth**	32 m
◐	**Visibility**	poor to good
≋	**Currents**	medium
◓	**Dive type**	day boat

As well as having good dive sites running along its edge, the southwestern rim of Ari is a known whaleshark highway. The divemasters watch for tell-tale shadows enroute to a dive and often spy one or two in the depths before coming across one shallow enough to snorkel with. Then it's a mad leap into the water before the magnificent beast drops down and heads away. On a good day, this pattern will be repeated several times. Whalesharks can be extremely nosy and will come right up to the boat providing no one is in the water splashing about. They even lift their heads out to see what's there. At this dive site, the visibility is low – the whalesharks come to feed on the plankton – but on the small thila there are passing squads of mobula rays, whitetips circling and a small school of barracuda above.

⌖12 Kalahandi Huraa

🕐	**Depth**	32 m
◐	**Visibility**	fair to good
≋	**Currents**	medium to strong
◓	**Dive type**	day boat

This steep, sloping wall is covered in crusting corals. The current can be quite strong but the wall is interspersed with a series of swim-throughs where jacks and sweetlips shelter. There are overhangs with fans and soft corals. Back up on the wall you encounter small whitetips or Napoleon wrasse. Part of the way along the wall is a coral outcrop connected to the main part of the reef by a saddle where you might find a lurking leopard shark. These usually docile creatures seem unperturbed by divers and swoop around nosily before settling on the sand. Up on the top of the reef there are wrasse, more whitetips and plenty of schooling fish.

◉ Eye-to-eye contact

We had only been up from our dive a few minutes when another whaleshark appeared. Another – the fifth of the day – but this one was the biggest and the closest. We could tell this because she parked her entire seven metres down the length of the dhoni, raised her head and peered at us. I wasn't even close to ready so Beth jumped in with the camera. The crew made me wait while they swung the boat around, then yelled for me to jump. When the bubbles cleared, I discovered I was just inches away from the whaleshark's face. She made eye contact with me for several very long seconds then, gliding away, gave me a gentle whack with her tail as if to say goodbye. The next day I found a nice little bruise on my arm as a reminder! As if I needed one.

Shaun Tierney, photographer, London

North Nilandhoo Atoll

Due south of Ari, North and South Faafu – Nilandhoo – Atolls were only opened for development in 1999 and so far there are just three resorts. Comparatively isolated, there is a stronger presence of Maldivian people here as the islands are bigger and require more staff who come from other parts to work in the resorts.

The diving is a little different to North and South Malé, more like the slightly flatter topography in South Ari. Inside the atoll, thilas are protected from stronger tidal currents, making them easier sites. There are still plenty of channel dives and steep walls on the outer rim. And as there are so few resorts, dive sites are never crowded. Boats may leave the dive centre at the same time but they scatter to different points. Strangely, the marine life seems more wary of divers here. There are plenty of pelagics but they soon scatter.

↘13 Little South Channel

🧭 **Depth**	36 m	
◐ **Visibility**	poor to good	
〰 **Currents**	mild to medium	
🌓 **Dive type**	day boat	

Dropping in over the channel, divers are briefed that they will see some bommies below. These supposedly attract pelagic species but if the visibility is low you will miss them, despite going deep. All the same, several large tuna might cruise by but heading back to the reef wall is more promising for the dive. On the wall there are a few small caves and ridges that are full of dense soft corals in pink and lemon hues. One little ridge is used by groups of lobster to keep out of the way. There are small turtles in the shallows and if you wait long enough you will see them head to the surface, take a gulp of air then come back to the reef for a good chew on some sponges.

↘14 Lighthouse Channel

🧭 **Depth**	33 m	
◐ **Visibility**	good	
〰 **Currents**	generally strong	
🌓 **Dive type**	day boat	

This dive also involves dropping into an open channel to look for big animals. There are usually large schools of passing rainbow runners, and very occasionally, a manta ray will swing up from great depths, peer about, then swim away again. A little further along, where the currents hit the side of the reef, a group of young whitetips patrol the ridge just over the drop-off. Ascending back up to the reef, there is a broad slope, from 30 metres to 10, where patches of hard coral are surrounded by anthias, sweetlips and butterflies. Amongst the corals are green leaffish and different coloured nudibranch egg rings, including ones being laid by the funeral jorunna nudi.

🌀 Secret manta spot

We had received a hot tip. Lots of mantas had been seen in the area and we knew the place was a hotspot for mantas surface feeding. There had to be something to attract the animals beyond a food source. It was likely there was an undiscovered 'cleaning station'. We cruised to the area where the reef met the channel and marked the point with the GPS. It takes many years of experience to read the water and reef beneath the boat with any accuracy and the patience and skill of our skipper was called upon to hit the right spot.

We gathered the divers and briefed them for an exploration dive – we just asked them to stick with us and hopefully we would see some mantas. We felt a little nervous as they suited up. We didn't know what to expect and could just find a lot of sand. We jumped in exactly on the GPS point, down a shallow slope of hard coral reef towards a sandy area. We saw lots of lovely hard corals but no sign of a manta. We decided to swim slowly into the current and take a look inside the channel. There was a wide expanse of snowy white coral sand beyond the reef heaped into drifts. Suddenly we saw a large shape out across the sand. We slowly made our way towards it and beckoned the divers to follow us.

As we got closer we made out a group of three mantas slowly circling on the far side of the channel. We stayed very low and continued to swim across the channel until we were kneeling watching the mantas circling above our heads and being tended by cleaner fish. The longer we stayed the more mantas appeared and we all became mesmerized by the spectacle.

Over the past three years we have dived this site many times and it continues to amaze. We have regularly seen over 40 mantas visiting the cleaning station and it remains our special site as very few other dive guides have learnt of our secret spot.

Anne-Marie Kitchen-Wheeler and Matt Kitchen, cruise directors for Maldives Scuba Tours, have been diving in the Maldives since the early 1990s.

↘15 Seven Stingrays

🧭	**Depth**	28 m
◑	**Visibility**	good
🌊	**Currents**	generally strong
⬤	**Dive type**	day boat

This site is highly indicative of the atoll's diving. The long, flat reef has seven gentle mounds rising from its contours; these are all quite small except the last which is far wider and only in about eight metres of water so it's a good last stop. Entry to the site starts from the north and drops you right into the current so you drift out into the blue to search out large animals. These are mostly tuna and there seems to be little other activity, although that all depends on the day. Back over the reef, you can count the 'stingray' mounds passing below as the current grows stronger. By the time you have reached the sixth, it can be pretty stiff and you are unlikely to stay still. There are substantial schools of yellow snapper and rainbow runners and on the seventh mound, there are broad swathes of carpet anemones with clownfish, porcelain crabs and white-eyed morays hiding beneath.

↘16 M'n'M

🧭	**Depth**	19 m
◑	**Visibility**	good
🌊	**Currents**	mild
⬤	**Dive type**	day boat

This almost circular thila is inside the reef lagoon so is quite an easy dive. It also has a distinctive structure: on the north side a perfectly straight wall drops from just below the surface to 35 metres. There are quite a few little caverns and a couple of very nice caves to swim through. These have a healthy covering of small white fan corals which are extremely delicate. There is a lot of colour here too, with the wall covered in multi-hued soft corals, sponges and tunicates. Nudibranchs crawl amongst them and mantis shrimp can be spotted on the cavern floors. The very unusual comet fish can be found here. This fish's skin is black with tiny white spots: it mimics the white spotted moray, especially if threatened. They are resident on the wall near the entry and exit point. The south of the thila has more gentle terrain and, being less dramatic, is dived less often.

The wall at M'n'M; lobster and oriental sweetlips on Seven Stingrays; Sabretooth blenny smiling from his tunicates

Drying out

There are obviously many more resorts in the Maldives than are listed here and they are all of a good standard. Many do not have websites but can be contacted via an agent or the dive centre which is based there. There is also a trend for them to periodically close and reopen a short while later as a more sophisticated version. Budget hotels are harder to come by but mid-range and all-inclusive options can be good value.

North and South Malé Atolls
Diving and sleeping
$$$ **Bandos Island Resort**, T+960 (0)664 0088, bandos.com. Half an hour by boat from the airport, it has one of the two decompression chambers in the country, plus shops and wet and dry sports facilities. Tiny deserted Kuda Bandos is a few minutes away. Dive Bandos are on site.
$$$ **Kurumba**, T+960 (0)332 3080, kurumba.com. 10 mins from the airport and done up to ultra-trendy spa specifications. Proximity to the capital's shipping lanes makes this resort feel a little busy but it's a brilliant stopover pre- or post- liveaboards.

$$$ **Rihiveli**, T+960 (0)644 1994, rihiveli-maldives.com. Seaplane transfer in 45 mins to the far end of South Malé. In a lagoon with two uninhabited islands just a short walk – yes, walk – away. Refurbished island with Euro-divers, euro-divers.com, on site.
$$ **Eriyadu**, T+960 (0)664 4487. On the northwest of North Malé, an hour by speedboat. An escapist's island with no unnecessary frills, just simple bungalows hiding under the palms. Diving run by Euro-divers, euro-divers.com.
$$ **Helengeli**, T+960 (0)664 4615, helengeli.net. On the northeast corner of North Malé, also an hour by speedboat. Charming, budget orientated and with Ocean Pro Dive team on site.

Ari Atoll
Diving and sleeping
$$$ **Lily Beach**, T+960 (0)668 0013, lilybeachmaldives.com. About 45 mins by seaplane from Malé. This resort was built over the site of a small garden island. It is quite spacious and the large bungalows have their bathroom in the garden.
$$$-$$ **Vilamendhoo**, T+960 (0)668 0637, About 45 mins by plane from Malé, this is one of the country's older resorts. Strong

focus on diver service and a great house reef. The gardens are well established and feel very tropical. Diving run by Euro-divers, euro-divers.com.

North Nilandhoo Atoll
Diving and sleeping
$$$ **Filitheyo**, T+960 (0)674 0025. An hour and 15 mins by seaplane. The lone resort in the north of the atoll sits on a comparatively large, green island. On one side is a perfect white sand beach. Rooms are billed as Balinese style, meaning lots of timber, and mostly sit in pairs. Sold as a 'romantic' destination (water bungalows sit over the reef edge), in reality this is a family resort as the beach and pool attract a lot of people with children. Diving run by Werner Lau Centres, nitrox available.

❂ Temperatures rising

As time goes by and island development continues, the Maldivian government opens ever more atolls for tourism. There are close to 100 resorts across 11 atolls: Baa and Raa in the far north, once regarded as the frontier, now have six resorts between them. In the south, Meemu Atoll has opened its first resort. It has even been suggested that a second international airport will be built near Gan, the 1940s British naval station that became a resort in 1996. This atoll, Addu, is 450 km from Malé and a real outpost.

Despite this, the islands do manage to retain that castaway feel but 'undeveloped' is no longer a word most would use. The resorts shut down and rebuild on a regular basis creating an ever more sophisticated set of destinations. When the devastating tsunami of Boxing Day 2004 hit the region, many islands were flooded. Fortunately, these low-lying atolls escaped the more aggressive tidal effects as the water simply rose over them and then receded. The resorts used this as another reason to renovate and increase costs. Likewise, liveaboards that were once purely the domain of the adventurous are becoming classier and more luxurious.

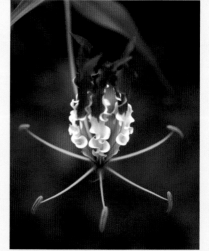

Sleeping	$$$ US$150+ double room per night	$$ US$75-150	$ under US$75
Eating	$$$ US$40+ 2-course meal, excluding drinks	$$ US$20-40	$ under US$20

Other atolls

The resorts above have been experienced – and enjoyed – by the authors. But that's not to say that there aren't many more excellent ones right across the country. Most have an on-site dive centre, some are independent and others part of larger groups. If you are undecided, look to dive centres run by well-regarded operations.

Pro Divers, prodivers.com, can be found at Kuredu, Komandoo and Vakarufalhi.

Diverland, diverland.com, have bases at Embudu, Summer Island and Gan.

TGI, tgidiving.com, have bases at Halaveli, Alimatha and Dhiggiri.

Liveaboards

If you are having trouble choosing a resort, hop on what is endearingly called a 'safari boat' in the Maldives. From the airport, a 10-min transfer will drop you onto a comfy floating hotel. Depending on the prevailing weather, you then sail around two or even three atolls. Evenings are spent moored near uninhabited islands, while days are filled by hopping onto the dive dhoni which shadows your floating home, taking you to find the best dives.

Sea Queen and Sea Spirit, T+44 (0)1449 780220, scubascuba.com. Owned and run by British firm Maldives Scuba Tours, these two liveaboards are based on traditional Maldivian craft and although small are very comfortable. A dhoni runs in tandem with each main boat so all diving and equipment is kept separately.

Ocean Dancer, T+1 (1)305 669 9391, PeterHughes.com. Part of the Peter Hughes fleet with high standards of luxury and service. Seven nights from US$2195.

Dream Catcher II, T+ (960) 334 1860, sunprincess.com.mv. Stunning new luxury vessel run by a team with many years of Maldivian hotel experience.

The Maldives

When asked what there is to do when you're not under the water, the answer is pretty much to get in the water. Apart from diving, you can swim, snorkel, sail or windsurf. Some resorts run night fishing trips and some run trips to other islands. Away from the water, entertainment is centred inside the resorts. Newer resorts have spas and gyms. Many will organize guest versus staff volleyball or soccer matches. Sometimes a band visits for a weekly disco but beyond that, you can read a book under a palm tree, watch the sun set or try to name star constellations.

Malé If you are staying near the capital, you could hop over for a visit. It takes about 20 minutes to walk from end to end so in a couple of hours you could see the new Presidential Palace, the two mosques, wander along the seafront and go to the market or a souvenir shop.

Local islands If you are near a designated locals' island you can often go across for an hour or two, talk to the kids, buy a soft drink and a T-shirt and head back.

Spas If you are looking for some post-dive body pampering, choose a resort with a spa. These are increasingly more sophisticated with both Indian and Balinese massage programmes, yoga, reflexology and all sorts of therapies.

Clockwise from top: Vilamendhoo beach; island and dive dhoni; heron at sunset; taxi, Maldivian style; atolls from the air

Maldives Drying out

Thailand

Gentle giant: five full metres
of awe-inspiring juvenile
whaleshark, *Rhinocodon typus.*
Western Rocky, Mergui Archipelago

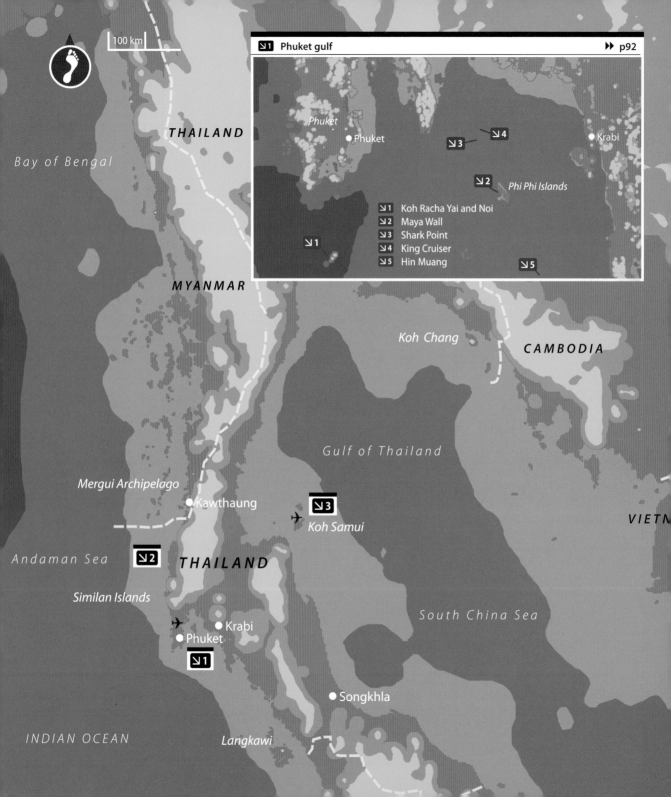

100 km

THAILAND

Bay of Bengal

MYANMAR

⬂1 Phuket gulf   ►► p92

Phuket

● Phuket

⬂3 ⬂4

● Krabi

⬂2

Phi Phi Islands

⬂1 Koh Racha Yai and Noi
⬂2 Maya Wall
⬂3 Shark Point
⬂4 King Cruiser
⬂5 Hin Muang

⬂1

⬂5

Koh Chang

CAMBODIA

Gulf of Thailand

Mergui Archipelago

● Kawthaung

⬂3

⬂2

Koh Samui

VIETN

Andaman Sea

THAILAND

South China Sea

Similan Islands

● Krabi

● Phuket

⬂1

● Songkhla

INDIAN OCEAN

Langkawi

2 Similans to Myanmar ▶▶ p94

- ↘6 East of Eden
- ↘7 Elephant Rock
- ↘8 Breakfast Bend
- ↘9 Christmas Point
- ↘10 Boon Song Wreck
- ↘11 The Pinnacle, Koh Bon
- ↘12 Koh Tachai
- ↘13 Richelieu Rock
- ↘14 Western Rocky
- ↘15 Burma Banks
- ↘16 South Twin
- ↘17 High Rock

↘17
↘16
↘15 ↘14
Mergui
Archipelago   Kawthaung
↘13
↘12
↘11
↘8
↘9 ↘7
Similan   ↘6
Islands
↘10 ● Khao Lak
Phuket

3 Gulf of Thailand ▶▶ p99

↘19
↘20   Koh Tao
↘18
- ↘18 Hin Bai
- ↘19 Chumphon Pinnacle
- ↘21 White Rock   Koh Phangan

Sitting right on the western edges of Southeast Asia, Thailand could be regarded as the region's dive outsider. Geographically beyond the borders of the Coral Triangle, Thailand still reflects much of the marine beauty of her neighbours, but her principal dive sites are rather more influenced by the effects of the Indian Ocean rather than the Pacific.

From the smaller, peaceful reefs south of Phuket to the high drama of the Mergui Archipelago to the north, the variety of diving can be impressive. Even the murky waters around the islands in the Gulf of Thailand are lush enough to keep most divers smiling.

Thailand may not be as diverse as other parts of Asia – biodiversity rankings are lower by quite a way – but with more than its fair share of pelagic animals, you can forgive it almost anything. Especially as this is one of the most likely places you will get to dive with that revered gentle giant, the whaleshark.

When it's finally time to let the nitrogen leach out, days on land can be a treat. Thai culture is rich – think orange-clad monks and golden Buddhas – the nightlife is heady and the cuisine outstanding. And the often contradictory elements of tradition and cutting-edge modernity are somehow held together by the charming people.

Introduction

Thailand

Thailand rating

Diving
★★★★

Dive facilities
★★★★

Accommodation
★★★★

Down time
★★★

Value for money
★★★★

Essentials

Getting there and around

Thailand is one of Southeast Asia's easiest countries to travel in. There are international airports right around the country, a decent bus system, trains linking Bangkok with the south and ferries to all the islands.

As the best diving is based in the south of the country, international flights via Singapore are often the most practical option. The city is great for stopovers (see page 141) and as airports go, Singapore's Changi is one of the best. Indoor gardens, free internet, on-site hotels and pool all mean it's worth routing this way, rather than via Bangkok. Singapore Airlines' flight network (singaporeair.com) is excellent, no matter where you start from. At Changi swap to their regional airline, Silk Air (silkair.com), which has twice daily flights to Phuket. If you're heading to Koh Samui use Bangkok Airways' daily connection (bangkokair.com). Of course, if you've never been to Bangkok, you may think it's worth having a stop there in which case Thai Airways (thaiair.com) have plenty of good connections to all the dive regions.

Transfers from your arrival airport are no problem – just ask your hotel or dive centre to pick you, and all that heavy luggage, up. Depending on the package you have booked, this may cost a nominal sum, or be free. For internal travel and land tours, rely on your dive centre or hotel for advice and assistance. It is perfectly OK to wander about on your own. Although traditions are still evident, westernised standards prevail. Thai nature means you will always find someone willing to help. Nearly everyone speaks English or another European language.

Local laws and customs

Thai etiquette is based around courtesy and calmness. Keep a cool head at all times and you won't go wrong. On the subject of heads, never touch a Thai there, not even an affectionate pat for a child. Never show the soles of your feet or use a foot to point. Feet are the lowest part of the body so it's considered an insult. The Thai Royal Family are much revered, so criticism is never allowed, not even in jest. Buddhist monks should warrant equal courtesy and women should never touch one. If you visit a temple or are away from the beach, sensible, modest clothing is preferable. On the beach, well anything goes!

Safety

Thailand is a relatively stable country and although personal safety hasn't been much of an issue, there is some occasional unrest. However, common sense should keep you safe. There is a continued threat of terrorist attacks in the provinces in the far southeast of the country, closer to the Malay border.

Thailand	
Location	15°00'N, 100°30'E
Capital	Bangkok
Population	65,905,410
Land area in km²	511,770
Coastline in km	3,219

Similans scenery

This is not a dive region so it isn't really an issue unless you intend to head to the islands in the Malay Gulf. If you do, consider flying.

Women should be aware that they may get hassled a little so teaming up with a dive buddy could be a good idea. Petty crime can be more of a problem, especially in tourist areas. In places where nightclubs are upscale and up tempo, drink spiking does occur. There are also tales of travellers on buses or trains being handed a drink by a friendly local then waking up hours later having been relieved of their wallets. Dive centres tend to be in well populated, traveller-friendly places but camera carriers should be aware that Pelican cases scream an invitation to a petty thief, as do laptop bags and mobile phones. Don't leave dive equipment unattended, especially not swanky dive bags with big logos plastered all over them. Note that penalties for possession of drugs are severe and can include the death penalty.

Language

Thai is a tonal language – two words may look and be spelt the same way but pronounced differently and mean different things. That makes it hard for your average westerner to learn and to make matters worse, it has a different alphabet. But like most countries, the Thais are honoured, and amused, if you try a few words. Here are a few to help you charm your divemaster or waiter:

hello	*sa-wùt dee krúp (kâ)*	how much is...	*tâo-rài...*
yes/no	*chái/mâi chái*	where's the...	*yòo têe-nai...*
thank you	*kòrp-kOO/mâi ao*	great dive!	
no thank you	*kòrp-kOOn*	*Dam naam dee mak mak*	
excuse me	*kor-tôht krúp (kâ)*	(Use krúp for males and kâ for females.)	

Health

In tourism-focused areas, staying healthy is not an issue. Standards are high, hotels will have doctors on standby and decent medical facilities are available should you need help. Basics, like aspirin and insect repellent are easy to get. Beware of too much sun, mosquitos at dusk and drink bottled water. There is very little risk of malaria in the southern coastal regions and mosquitos don't make it out to sea. Be smart when it comes to extra-curricular activities – Thailand has an epidemic of HIV infection and AIDS and HIV is common amongst prostitutes of both sexes.

Costs

Thailand is good value for money for divers. Although everyone's version of value varies, you can easily get a decent three-course meal and a local beer or two, while sitting under a coconut palm watching the sunset. And all for less than US$20 dollars. A beer is less good value though, with the excellent local brew, Singha, around US$2 a bottle. Room rates can be whatever you need them

Tourist information → The government website can be found at tourismthailand.org.travel. This site has links to various regional sites and is in a variety of languages.

Fact file

International flights	AirAsia, Bangkok Airways, Singapore Airlines/Silk Air, Thai Airways
Departure tax	Included in your ticket
Entry	EU, US and Commonwealth – valid passport required for stays of up to 30 days
Internal flights	Bangkok Airways, Thai Airways
Ground transport	Good countrywide bus connections, trains and ferries to all islands
Money	US$1 = 35 Thai baht (THB)
Language	Thai but English is widely spoken
Electricity	220v, plug types A/C (see page 16)
Time zone	GMT +7
Religion	Principally Buddhist
Phone	Country code +66; IDD 001; Tourist Police 1699

to be – US$40 will buy a comfortable but simple room, while a more upmarket hotel can cost far more and rates are higher in Bangkok, where it's worth paying for comfort. Tipping isn't the norm, although in touristy areas it's becoming more common and good service should be rewarded. On restaurant bills, consider 10%. For dive crews see page 12.

Tiger-tail seahorses are seen in Burmese waters

Dive brief

Diving

Thailand's diving is defined – or perhaps confused – by its position between two seas. The western coastline faces the Indian Ocean and is heavily affected by its deep water currents and contrasting monsoons. May to October sees driving, onshore winds pushing in from the southwest. By November, calmer conditions return to the Andaman Sea as the monsoon swaps over to the northeast. Over in the Gulf of Thailand, wind patterns have the opposite seasonal effect.

There are reef structures all the way along both coastlines but on the west these are far more extensive, particularly around the offshore islands. All the way from south of Phuket and right up into Myanmar, there is fantastic diving. Sea fans and colourful soft corals are plentiful. There are enormous granite boulders, spectacular swim-throughs and swarms of colourful fish. Pinnacles rise from the deep and submerged reefs offer protection in isolated regions. In contrast, the Gulf and her islands are subject to their position in a very shallow sea. At less than 60 metres deep, and with twice daily tides, they are susceptible to heavy sedimentation and river run off. These harsh conditions have restricted reef diversity and coral numbers. All the same, there is good diving to be had around a few of the southern islands but the further north you go, heading towards Bangkok, the more likely it is that visibility will disappoint.

Snorkelling

Thailand is a mixed bag: currents can be unpredictable and often strong, and wind conditions can change rapidly, making for rough surface conditions. Many of the better dive sites visited by liveaboards are exposed and submerged pinnacles may be off-putting for all but the strongest swimmers. However, there is decent snorkelling in most shallow coastal areas.

Marine life

Despite being outside the Coral Triangle, the reefs off the western side of Thailand are lush with hard and soft corals that attract and support a huge variety of species. These are typical of the Indian Ocean and include everything from mantas and whalesharks right down to the tiniest crustaceans. Life in the Gulf is somewhat more limited as the shallow waters are separated from the main oceanic currents. All the same, there is plenty to see.

Thailand
animal
encounters

Phuket gulf	ornate ghost pipefish
Similans	Similans angelfish
Richelieu Rock	whalesharks
Mergui	silvertip and nurse sharks

White collar butterfly fish

When we're asked why we keep returning to Thailand – or why we recommend it – we can only quote some of the special moments... floating over the crystal clear, turquoise waters of the Similans. Dawn on the Burma Banks watching whales breach. The time the light went out at Richelieu Rock as a whaleshark swam over us and when we met another in the Mergui Archipelago a day later. Discovering a perfect pink ghost pipefish on a perfect pink coral. Exploring the inky depths of a wreck at night. And just simply knowing that below lies a marine adventure that's hard to rival. We've never been disappointed diving off Thailand's west coast.

Making the big decision

Once you have decided to dive Thailand, choosing a specific destination may seem daunting. However, Thailand is highly seasonal, so first of all decide when you can go. If it's between November and May, then you're heading to the west of the country. If you are limited to May through October, the Gulf of Thailand will make for a better holiday, although not necessarily the best diving. If you're a qualified diver, then there is no better way to explore the wonders of the Andaman Sea than being on a liveaboard.

A much wider selection of Thai destinations are reviewed in Diving Southeast Asia, see page 6 for details.

Bluespotted sting ray on the ocean floor

Dive data

Seasons	November to May on the west coast, May to October on the east coast
Visibility	5 metres inshore to 'infinity' in the Andaman Sea
Temperatures	Air 30-34°C; water 27-30°C
Wet suit	3 mm full body suit
Training	Courses available in Phuket, Krabi or the Gulf
Nitrox	Available on land. May be limited on liveaboards
Deco chambers	Pattaya, Bangkok, Phuket and Koh Samui

Bottom time

Andaman Sea	Lying off Thailand's western coastline is a wealthy marine ecosystem with rich and colourful reefs and two unusual wreck dives.
Phuket gulf ▸▸ p92	Three well developed holiday centres – Phuket, Krabi and the Phi Phi Islands – form an imaginary enclosure for some delightful day-trip diving.
Similans ▸▸ p94	The ultimate Thai marine park with picture-postcard perfect islands and equally impressive reefs. Head out on a liveaboard to explore both sides of these incredible reef systems.
Koh Bon, Koh Tachai, Richelieu Rock ▸▸ p96	Two open water pinnacles that attract the big stuff are a prelude to legendary Richelieu Rock: the do-not-miss dive of the country and quite possibly of your life.
Mergui Archipelago ▸▸ p98	The waters of the Andaman Sea just across the Myanmar border are relatively unexplored but often equal those in neighbouring Thailand.
Gulf of Thailand	The reefs that surround the delightful Gulf Islands are subject to variable conditions but are still pleasant dives.
Koh Samui and Koh Tao ▸▸ p99	Pinnacle dives are occasionally sensational while gentle, local reefs are good training grounds.

Diversity reef area 4,000 km²

HARD CORALS	
	428
FISH SPECIES	
	1,428
ENDEMIC FISH SPECIES	
	20
FISH UNDER THREAT	
	57
PROTECTED REEFS/MARINE PARKS	
	16

All diversity figures are approximate; combined reef area Thailand and Myanmar

The Andaman Sea

Phuket gulf

The area that is ringed by Phuket island, the Phi Phi Islands and the nearby town of Krabi is the starting point for diving in Thailand. These places embrace some of the country's most idyllic scenery and have masses of facilities both for divers and non-divers.

The island of **Phuket** has it all, from loud and raucous but very pretty Patong Beach to calm and quiet Chalong Bay. Ao Chalong is also the departure point for day boat dive trips, liveaboards to the treasured Similan Islands Marine Park and cruises further north to the Burma Banks.

Thousands of divers flock to Phuket yet dive sites close to the island tend to have reduced visibility, sometimes as low as 10 metres, but sail offshore for an hour or so and the difference can be surprising.

If you are looking for something a bit less developed, head to **Krabi**: less than two hours' drive away, it's comparatively peaceful and laid-back. Originally a haunt of long-term travellers, the beaches and offshore islands near this compact and bustling town are idyllic and, despite their increasing popularity, have managed to

achieve a comfortable balance. The final option for island lovers are the famous **Phi Phi Islands**. These are the ones that attract serious crowds as they really are intensely beautiful, with steep limestone cliffs dropping to gorgeous sweeps of sand.

All dive sites in the Phuket Gulf are reachable from any of these access points so you can stay at any one and still dive the whole area.

↘1	Koh Racha Yai and Noi	
Depth	24 m	
Visibility	fair to good	
Currents	slight to medium	
Dive type	day boat	

These sister islands (large rock and small rock) have some of the best year-round diving near Phuket. At the top of Racha Yai two delightful bays feel just like swimming pools. They gradually drop to the sandy seabed and the currents are mostly gentle. The nutrient-rich coastal waters attract large schools of tropical fish. Perfect for novices! The reefs at Racha Noi on the other hand are a bit deeper and the currents stronger than at her sister island to the north. There are huge underwater boulders and a good chance to see manta rays, reef sharks and bluespotted rays.

On the wreck of the *King Cruiser*

⊠2 Maya Wall, Phi Phi Lei

🕐	**Depth**	20 m
◑	**Visibility**	fair to good
〰	**Currents**	mild to strong
🌊	**Dive type**	day boat

Just beyond Maya Beach, this dive is a continuation of Phi Phi's dramatic topside scenery. The wall of the island and a row of enormous granite boulders that sit a few metres away form a long enclosed channel. Swimming through you encounter several large turtles and a lot of fish. At the end of the channel the boulders become more sporadic, creating lots of nooks and crannies to investigate. The hard corals are interspersed with brightly-hued fans, and there are a huge number of impressive 'comb' corals that grow vertical branches. A shallow cave has nudibranchs, clown triggerfish and the Similans angelfish.

⊠3 Shark Point (Hin Musang)

🕐	**Depth**	16 m
◑	**Visibility**	fair
〰	**Currents**	slight to strong
🌊	**Dive type**	day boat

The story goes that a dive company owner called this reef Shark Point to get people to go there. It really should be called Soft Coral City or something similar. The dive starts near an exposed pinnacle that has surf and surge pushing across it. Below is an extensive series of pinnacles, bommies and outcrops, all plastered with enough soft corals to wow even the most hardened diver. The visibility can be as low as five to seven metres, which divemasters describe as a good day. Regardless, the reefs are very beautiful with lots of barrel sponges ringed by ever more soft corals and fans. There are some good macro critters on the sand: stonefish, nudibranchs, dragonets and stingrays. Bommies are colonized by whole gardens of anemones with apricot-coloured skunk clownfish while a nearby hard coral table has a dozen white-eyed morays running about its surface at speed.

⊠4 King Cruiser

🕐	**Depth**	31 m
◑	**Visibility**	fair
〰	**Currents**	slight to medium
🌊	**Dive type**	day boat

The *King Cruiser* passenger ferry was en route to Phi Phi when it found itself several kilometres off course. It ran into a pinnacle and sank slowly. There were 500 people on board but fortunately no loss of life. In just a decade the hull has become a rich artificial reef sitting upright on the seabed at 32 metres: it is 85 metres long and 25 metres wide. There are the most amazing numbers of fish swirling between the two rudders with small sardine-sized silver baitfish preyed on by gangs of aggressive lionfish. Swimming between the two hulls, you see the giant barracudas that lurk here, no doubt equally well stuffed with the smaller fish. Ascending upwards, the hull is well covered in newly developing corals, sponges, oysters and barnacles. This wreck can't be penetrated, as the cabin sections are starting to collapse, but you can peer inwards though the old window holes and see the passageways that would have led to the cabins.

⊠5 Hin Muang (Purple Rock)

🕐	**Depth**	25 m
◑	**Visibility**	good to excellent
〰	**Currents**	mild
🌊	**Dive type**	day boat

If you ask a divemaster what you'll see, the likely response will be anemones and clownfish. And what an understatement that would be. This completely submerged reef is aptly named. Purple-hued anemones form enormous carpets; then there's the purple and pink soft corals that drip down the gully and, if you look closely, you'll see that the whole reef has purple-toned fish: scorpionfish, lionfish and even octopus display indigo hues hoping to stay hidden. There are some bigger animals hanging around too, but it's hard not to focus on all the tiny critters hidden in the folds, branches and crevices. The macro life is wonderful. Tiny caves are full of purple cleaner shrimp and, occasionally, you'll find rarer creatures hiding along with them. Ornate ghost pipefish – in shades of purple – are often seen by those who take the time to look. The furthest south of these sites, Hin Muang is in open water so the visibility tends to be much better.

Soft corals at Shark Point and comb corals around the Phi Phi islands

The Similans

For many people a dive trip to Thailand means just one thing – the Koh Similans National Marine Park. This chain of nine tiny islands, 55 nautical miles northwest of Phuket, is ringed by perfect beaches and amazing coral reefs. Visibility rarely drops below 20 metres and can reach mythical proportions.

What makes the Similans so attractive are their two completely different sides. To the east the islands have pure white sand and hard coral gardens that slope gently down to over 30 metres. The diving is easy and the pace is calm. The west is much more dramatic, with currents that swirl around huge granite boulders creating spectacular swim-throughs. It's a bit like diving between skyscrapers that have been reclaimed by the sea. It is possible to see and dive the Similans in a long day trip from Phuket, however, the islands are so beautiful, do yourself a favour and book a liveaboard. It's unlikely you'll want a lot of down time but when you're not diving, you can admire the pristine views or walk on an idyllic, deserted beach.

↘6 East of Eden

Depth	21 m
Visibility	good to excellent
Currents	slight
Dive type	liveaboard

Off Similan No 7, this sloping wall drops to a secondary reef completely encrusted with big fans and rainbows of huge soft corals. Masses of glassy sweepers flit and dance in the light like sparkling stars. Tuna and schooling trevally swim above while the upper reef hides plenty of delicate small creatures like ornate ghost pipefish.

You can even catch sight of the indigenous Similans sweetlips here. At night, the site reignites with nocturnal activity. Nestling in almost every crevice are cleaner shrimp or tiny pink crabs. Hermit crabs scramble everywhere, arrow crabs poke their noses up from a fan. Stay completely still, but divert your beams a little away from the wall and you'll be rewarded with tiny, shy cuttlefish peeking out from matching crinoids. Heading back uphill to the sandy sea floor, decorator crabs are on the prowl, along with cowries and cone shells. A stealthy octopus will wait for the right moment to nip out for a quick meal.

↘7 Elephant Rock

Depth	28 m
Visibility	good to excellent
Currents	can be strong
Dive type	liveaboard

This is one of the Similans' most famous sites purely because of the unusually shaped granite boulders that reach up from invisible depths and emerge on the western side of the island. On land they are said to mimic the shape of an elephant's head. Beneath the water they tumble over each other to form a complex of arches and tunnels and some of the most dramatic swim-throughs in the entire chain. Small fans nestle into crevices for protection from the surge while critters crawl on the sheer rocky surfaces. Small tubastrea trees add a hint of green while hawkfish perch on their branches. There are sea cucumbers that host fantastic imperial shrimp; mantis shrimp skitter about in the rubble with blennies while gobies bob up from the rocks. Back up around the boulders there are groups of trevally and schools of small yellow grunts under a ledge.

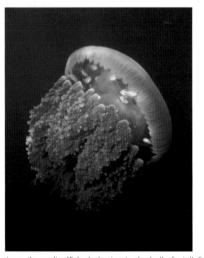
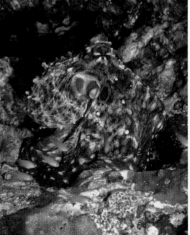

Juvenile cardinalfish sheltering in the bell of a jellyfish; common octopus; diving East of Eden

⎘8 Breakfast Bend

Depth	31 m
Visibility	good to excellent
Currents	slight to medium
Dive type	liveaboard

At the very top of the Similans chain is Koh Banggu (No 9), and on her eastern side is this charming and easy dive. They say it got its name as diving here makes a great start to the day with sunrays penetrating down onto the gentle sloping reef. There is a lot of rubble but it's interspersed with hard coral patches and there are small soft corals in the shallows. The marine life is good with many nudibranchs, including chromodoris and phyllidia types, crawling over the uneven seabed. (Phyllidias are those ones with warty looking spots on their bodies.) Another far less peaceful creature is the titan triggerfish. Many live on this reef, but they are aggressive only when nesting and the rest of the time you can catch them being cleaned by shrimp. There are also morays, lobster, sweetlips, groupers and plenty of other small fish flitting about.

⎘9 Christmas Point

Depth	20 m
Visibility	excellent
Currents	mild to strong
Dive type	liveaboard

Wonder how this one got its name? The site marks the top end of the Similans chain and the visibility here can be very, very good, no doubt as it is swept by clear open ocean currents. These can be strong at times and surface conditions a little rough, but below there is a good reef with the classic Similans scenery of square cut boulders interspersed with bright-hued fans. On one side of the dive, there are some large stony arches to swim through and these are mobbed by schools of fish. Trevally are quite common. Down on the rubble-strewn seabed are blue and black ribbon eels, lots of spotted jawfish and lovely, pure white egg cowries displaying their jet-black mantles. Occasionally you may find a leopard shark resting here. This is also a good site to spot the indigenous Similans sweetlips, clown triggerfish, puffers and angelfish.

⎘10 Boon Song Wreck

Depth	18 m
Visibility	poor to good
Currents	slight to mild
Dive type	liveaboard

Also known as the Bansak wreck as it sits just a little way from Bansak beach on the coast, this site is usually visited last and on the way back to port. Like most wrecks, the *Boon Song* is far more than it appears at first glance. The hull of a tin dredging boat, she is now a solid square of metal resting on the seabed. She sank in 1984 so the structure is very well preserved. You can even see some of the mechanical parts such as gear wheels and metal scoops. Visibility can be quite poor, due to the silty surrounds, but it really doesn't matter. Her real value is as a haven for a wealth of tiny critters. Circumnavigating the hull is like a nudibranch treasure hunt with many more shapes, sizes and colours than you are likely to see elsewhere. While focusing on these diminutive creatures, you also start to notice a whole lot more – estuarine stonefish, tiny flounders on the sand and unusual miniature spindle cowries that grip on to baby whip coral branches. There are honeycomb morays and blotched morays in crevices, lots of lionfish and tiny peacock flounders. Of course the wreck is also known for its resident leopard sharks that nestle on the sand and a school of porcupine puffers that hover constantly over the top deck.

Ornate ghost pipefish; the blue-ringed angel is called a Similans angel here; imperial shrimp on a sea cucumber

Travelling north from the Similans, just before you hit Burmese waters are a chain of islands formed by a series of enormous underwater pinnacles. The jungle-covered granite outcrops of Koh Bon and Koh Tachai are part of the Similans National Park, while Koh Surin National Park is home to Richelieu Rock.

All these are enveloped by excellent reefs and prolific marine life: the islands of the Koh Surin National Park are exposed to deep ocean currents so there are frequent pelagic sightings. All sorts of sharks, manta rays and schooling barracuda are regular visitors. At the end of this string, and just 20 kilometres from Surin, is the dive site that has it all – Richelieu Rock. In fact, if the gods are smiling on you and your dive buddies, this could be the one do-not-miss dive of your life. But, as ever in diving, nothing is guaranteed.

⟩11 **The Pinnacle, Koh Bon**	
🌀 **Depth**	35 m
◐ **Visibility**	poor to stunning
🌊 **Currents**	generally strong
🌓 **Dive type**	liveaboard

⟩12 **Koh Tachai**	
🌀 **Depth**	35 m
◐ **Visibility**	good to excellent
🌊 **Currents**	generally strong
🌓 **Dive type**	liveaboard

The water around Koh Bon can be gloomy from suspended plankton. The sharp-sided pinnacle rises up from who knows where to about 20 metres. All the rocky surfaces are smothered by yellow soft corals, with clusters of golden-toned fans surrounded by yellow snappers. The effect of all the sunny hues in the deep, dark water is rather surreal. Leopard sharks often rest on a ledge while a little way off in the blue are mingled schools of batfish and jacks. There could be as many as 200, perhaps more. The water can be as thick with fish as it is with plankton. The soup attracts a mass of animals to feed: it is a marvellous sight. Unfortunately, hovering at such depth for too long isn't all that wise and a safety stop on a nearby shallow reef is required. Although it will be hard to drag yourself away, you may be rewarded with a glimpse of a manta. They often make appearances, swimming swiftly through the small channel between the pinnacle and the nearby reef, no doubt attracted by the seasonal smorgasbord.

Southeast of the island lies a submerged reef made up of hard corals and scattered boulders. As the currents are nearly always swift here, a mooring rope leads down to a point where it's possible to shelter from the currents. There are soft corals coating the bommies and the many crinoids add a splash of brighter colour. At the bottom of the reef a resident school of batfish hovers around a cleaning station, a sea snake passes by and a gang of puffers stand off to the side. An unusual carpet anemone protects porcelain crabs and eggshell shrimp (these have white spots down the insides of their transparent bodies). Around the boulders are masses of swooping jacks; both trevally and mackerel nip in and out to feed on glassy sweepers. To complete the complement of pelagic fish, a massive shoal of chevron barracuda swirls constantly above the dramatic pinnacle.

Chevron barracuda at Koh Tachai (above); leopard shark on Koh Bon

Richelieu Rock

🌀	**Depth**	32 m
🔆	**Visibility**	medium to stunning
🌊	**Currents**	none to strong
🌊	**Dive type**	liveaboard

The idea of describing the splendour that is Richelieu Rock in a paragraph or two is more than a challenge – it's nigh on impossible. This isolated, submerged hill is without doubt the dive site that has it all, from the tiniest of critters to the ultimate in grace, size and beauty: the whaleshark.

Entering over the top of the rock, it's worth heading straight down to the base where there are masses of healthy, brightly-coloured soft corals and several enormous groupers. Back on the slopes there is a wealth of smaller creatures to admire: lion and trumpetfish, seasnakes, cowries, angels and butterflies, seahorses, white-eyed morays, clownfish and mantis shrimp. Then there's the bigger guys: turtles, reef sharks, barracuda, potato cod and even occasional mantas. Every surface seems to house yet another fascinating resident.

But at all times, keep an ear out for the sounds of manic tank banging. This is the signal that a whaleshark has been seen and you should make a mad dash towards the sound. When the conditions are right, you may be really lucky and see several in a day. Both adults and juveniles are attracted to this isolated reef, which is one of the few places in the world where you can still dive with them. Pay them the respect they deserve.

❝ ❞ **On a single dive we saw minute harlequin shrimp pairs and four enormous whalesharks, two curious turtles and several elegant seahorses. Not to mention masses of morays, giant groupers, nudibranchs, ghost pipefish, schooling snappers... the list could go on and on. Suffice it to say, you could spend days here and still not see everything the Rock has to offer.**

A first for everything

There were so many firsts: our first time in Thailand, first time on a liveaboard and the first time I'd achieved a lifelong ambition. To set the scene, I'm half way through a glorious morning dive with my head down a crevice trying to position my camera for a shot of two harlequin shrimp when I felt this hand grab my ankle. As I turn around, all my buddies are screaming, pointing and most of all grinning and I soon realise why... a whaleshark is gliding over our heads. I knew they were sometimes seen here, but never in my wildest dreams did I think it would happen for me. Back on the dive deck it's group hugs all round but what we didn't realize was that the Rock hadn't finished with us yet. After a surface interval that seemed like an eternity we're back in the water, sort of looking at the reef but with one eye firmly out in the blue. We didn't have to wait long and this time a four-metre baby appeared along with its big seven-metre sister, gliding past us as if they didn't have a care in the world. That day was definitely a 'Dom Perignon' moment for me.

Andrew Perkins, manager, retail superstore, Telford, UK

Mergui Archipelago

These days most liveaboard operators extend their itineraries to include some time amongst the spectacular reefs in the south of Myanmar – and for good reason. The diving here is superlative and relatively untouched.

Just a short sail north of Richelieu Rock you cross the border to Kawthaung. A visa is not required but some convoluted formalities take place on the boat, before it resumes its trip to Mergui Archipelago, passing some incredible scenery on the way. The reefs are not significantly different to those that run north from Thailand but they are mostly pristine.

↘14 Western Rocky

Depth	25 m
Visibility	excellent
Currents	slight
Dive type	liveaboard

How do you improve on diving Richelieu Rock? Simple, sail up to Burma's Western Rocky. This area was closed for quite some time to allow it to regenerate. Now it is a site that rivals her Thai neighbour. An huge submerged pinnacle is ringed by sheer walls that plummet vertically from the surface. The sharp sides are covered in glistening cup corals and bright crinoids. There is a splendid cathedral-like arch at the end of the south wall. Finning through it you are surrounded by masses of stripy snappers. Further east there are a series of smaller pinnacles. Reaching them requires passing over fantastic fan corals that are smothered in glassy sweepers. Banded sea snakes investigate tiny caves and porcelain crabs and eggshell shrimp shelter in flat carpet anemones. Schools of squid take refuge in the lee of a wall and nurse sharks hide in the caverns. You might even be fortunate enough to encounter a young whaleshark.

Tiger cowrie with mantle extended

↘15 South Twin

Depth	30 m
Visibility	fair to excellent
Currents	none to slight
Dive type	liveaboard

South Twin has gentle conditions and an enormous variety of marine life. The reefs feel similar to parts of the Similans with granite boulders that tumble down onto a sloping reef. Gullies are full of fans and soft corals. There are blue ribbon eels, honeycomb and yellowmargin morays. Shells are prolific with spider conchs and cowries under tiny overhangs. The tiger cowrie is easy enough to spot, but not the *Mauritia maculifera* cowrie, which has no common name but lives here. Up in the shallows, young whitetip sharks lurk beneath hard corals, while flitting about above are typical fish species like anthias, damsels and rainbow runners.

↘16 Burma Banks

Depth	25 m
Visibility	excellent
Currents	slight
Dive type	liveaboard

It's a great pity that when a site gets well known as the place to see sharks, it also gets a bit too well known to fishermen. A few years ago the Burma Banks were absolutely bereft – not a shark to be seen. However, more recently they have returned and the area is once again a great shark spotting destination. The Banks consist of several different sea mounds but Silvertip Bank is the most visited. Rising from 500 metres to about 15, the top plateau is carpeted with small fans and some pretty, soft corals. Peer down into the depths and you're likely to glimpse the whitetips that pass by. Back up on the flat section, other species make irregular appearances – reef sharks, nurses and even large silvertips. They swoop around divers and seem quite curious but slide away just as easily. The rest of the site has more to see but that gets lost in the excitement when the crew sets up a bait bucket. This attracts a few wary silvertips and Max, a resident nurse shark. There are several dogtooth tuna and octopus while much smaller fish include rockmover wrasse and sand gobies.

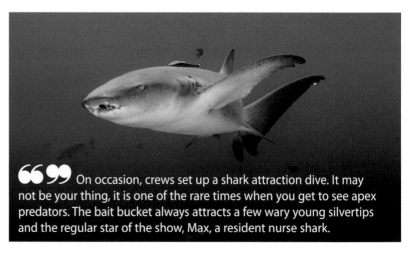

66 99 On occasion, crews set up a shark attraction dive. It may not be your thing, it is one of the rare times when you get to see apex predators. The bait bucket always attracts a few wary young silvertips and the regular star of the show, Max, a resident nurse shark.

Gulf of Thailand

Beautiful white-sand beaches, lush green hills and turquoise-blue waters. You could hardly go wrong visiting any of the scenic islands that pepper the Gulf of Thailand. There'll be many who feel the region deserves more attention than is given here and credit where it's due, there are plenty of reasons to visit this side of the country, the main one being that when the weather is off on the west, it's just delightful here.

However, as the east coast is not open to the rigours and influences of the Indian Ocean it has less in the way of prolific reefs. Koh Samui is the island that attracts most tourists. Koh Tao, however, is better located for dive sites and has the best shore diving. Sheltered bays make it ideal for novices or those who like peaceful dive days in between visits to the more up tempo ones.

18 Hin Bai (Sail Rock)

Depth	30 m
Visibility	good to excellent
Currents	mild to strong
Dive type	day boat

Jutting out of the water 18 kilometres off Samui's north shore, this isolated rock rises from 30 metres to just above the surface. It is covered in beautiful green and yellow corals and frequented by large marine animals like reef sharks and rays. Its unique feature, though, is the spectacular journey upwards through an underwater chimney that is flooded with beams of sunlight. It feels like ascending inside a cathedral spire. The entry point is at 19 metres and the exit at five, where you emerge to find carpets of anemones and their many resident clownfish. The outer walls are carved with lots of small holes with, it seems, a white-eyed moray in each. Visibility here is some of the best in the Gulf as the pinnacle is an exposed site and the currents keep plankton and sediment on the move.

The chimney at Sail Rock; Trevor the terrible passing by

19 Chumphon Pinnacle

Depth	36 m
Visibility	fair to great
Currents	none to strong
Dive type	day boat

The best dive in this area is undoubtedly Chumphon Pinnacle, where tales of big marine mammals have hit legendary status. A massive granite pinnacle soars from 40 metres to 16 metres below the surface and is surrounded by a group of smaller ones. Diving here is a bit like wandering through an underwater mountain range. There are large plateaux covered in healthy hard corals, sponges and seawhips which lead back up the pinnacles to reveal a huge variety of life. Giant groupers and batfish are always hovering around while white-eyed morays reside amongst the colourful coral gardens. Not only are huge schools of jacks spotted regularly, but occasionally there are also whalesharks and sailfish. Even whales have been seen.

20 White Rock

Depth	23 m
Visibility	fair to good
Currents	mild to medium
Dive type	day boat

Ko Nang Yuan is said to be the only place in the world where three islands are joined together by sandbars. The islands are ringed by a variety of shallow dive sites and there are some beautiful arches to swim through. The most exciting dive is probably White Rock, which is actually two submerged granite boulders sitting 12 metres apart. The site is a great place for finding reef creatures like stingrays and butterflyfish. Being quite shallow, it also makes a good night dive. However, its main claim to fame is local personality Trevor, the terrible triggerfish. This giant trigger is a chap with an attitude problem and, despite being a permanent resident on a fairly busy dive, has been known to nip at unwary divers' fins.

Drying out

Right across Thailand you will be spoilt for choice with masses of liveaboard and land-based options. And there are plenty of things to do when you are gassing off or if you are travelling with a non-diver.

The Phuket gulf

Phuket

Dive centres

Calypso Divers, T+66 (0)76 330869, calypsophuket.com. Everything from local day trips, 5-night Similans liveaboards and an overnight trip to the Phi Phi Islands with a hotel included – a great use of time. Day trips from US$100, Phi Phi special, US$300.

Sea Fun Divers, T+66 (0)76 330124, seafundivers.com. Local day-trip specialists with a smart and spacious boat. Full range of courses available. Day trips from US$120.

Sleeping

$$-$ Ao Chalong Villa and Spa, T+63 (0)2 854 8888, aochalongvillaandspa.com. This small resort is tucked away in a lane a short distance from Chalong Jetty. Variety of great value, comfy rooms, some front the bay and the rest are in delightful gardens. The onsite restaurant is superb.

$ Kata Minta, T+66 (0)76 333283, kataminta.com. Boutique-style hotel just off Kata Beach. Good facilities, nice rooms.

Eating

Restaurants include stalls in night markets (Patong's is amazing!) to 5-star cuisine in top hotels. At Chalong, there is a row of famous seafood restaurants, which serve well-priced, delicious fish under the trees.

Phi Phi

Sleeping

$$-$ Bay View Resort, T+66 (0)75 601127, phiphibayview.com. Large resort complex on Phi Phi Don. Bungalows sit on a tree-lined, terraced hill. No on-site dive centre but there are several close by.

Ao Nang, Krabi

Dive centres

Aqua Vision, Ao Nang, T+66 (0)75 637415, aqua-vision.net. One of Ao Nang's newer and larger dive centres, works with many hotels including Wanna's.

Sleeping

$$-$ Wanna's Place/Andaman Sunset, T+66 (0)75 637484, wannasplace.com. On the front at Ao Nang in a convenient spot, although it is quite busy nearby.

Eating

Like on Phuket, the range and variety of restaurants is wide. A special mention has to go to Wanna's Place as the Thai beef salads are simply amazing.

Other options

There is no reason to be limited to staying on Phuket island. Khao Lak, a short drive north has closer access (hence shorter day trips) to the Similans or Koh Lanta, south of Krabi, is much a quieter island, nearer to Hin Muang but still within sight of Phi Phi.

Sea Bees Diving, sea-bees.com. Extensive business with a base in Ao Chalong on Phuket and also on Khao Lak beach.

Lanta Divers, T+66 (0)75 684208, lantadiver.com. Based on Koh Lanta, with full packages and diving around the south.

The Similans to Myanmar

Diving the Andaman Sea beyond Phuket is best done by liveaboard. There are many operators from budget to luxury but, of late, there have been big changes to the local scene. Remember that boats costing more are usually of a higher quality. Many routes include the waters just over the Myanmar border; your operator will handle all the necessary formalities. Check out:

MV Black Manta, whitemanta.com
MV Mermaid I, mermaid-liveaboards.com
MV Philkade, philkade.com
MV Queen Scuba, coralgranddivers.com
SY Siren, worldwidediveandsail.com

Gulf of Thailand

Koh Samui

Diving

Samui International Diving School, T+66 (0)77 422386, planet-scuba.net. Several offices on Koh Samui and also on Koh Tao as Planet Scuba. Full range of dive services.

Sleeping

$$$ Poppies Samui Resort, T+ 66 (0)77 422419, poppies-samui.com. Part of the delightful group born in Bali, cottages are set in lush gardens. The on-site restaurant has great Thai food and a lovely ambience.

Koh Tao

Diving and Sleeping

$$$-$$ Koh Tao Coral Grand Resort, T+66 (0)77 456431, kohtaocoral.com. This large resort has nice bungalows of differing standards plus restaurants and bars. Coral Grand Divers, coralgranddivers.com are on site with courses from novice all the way up to IDC plus local and day-trip diving.

Myanmar: a message from the publishers
The diving in Burmese waters is superb but should divers visit a country with one of the worst human rights records in the world? Footprint would advise all potential visitors to make themselves aware of the current political situation in order to make a fully informed decision.

 Sleeping $$$ US$150+ double room per night $$ US$75-150 $ under US$75

Eating $$$ US$40+ 2-course meal, excluding drinks $$ US$20-40 $ under US$20

Phuket gulf

There is a lot to do on **Phuket** if you can force yourself away from the marine realm. Entry fees are modest – a couple of dollars will get you into most sights. **Wat Chalong Temple** is one of 29 Buddhist monasteries on the island but by far the most important. The buildings are very ornate. **Thalang National Museum** contains ancient artefacts and exhibits on the famous Battle of Thalang. The **Phuket Aquarium** on Cape Panwa is surprisingly good. There is a turtle hatchery, jellyfish exhibits, a walk-through tunnel and nature trails. And, of course, there is always **Phuket Town**, a retail therapy haven. If you're in Phuket in April, you'll catch **Songkran**, the Thai New Year water festival. Masses of Thais fill plastic bins with water and ice, drive the streets then ditch them over the unwary. And they do love dousing tourists! The tradition behind this lively event lies in the cleaning of hands and washing away of bad thoughts or actions. Great fun and completely harmless so join in the spirit of the day.

For a longer day out, **Khao Sok National Park**, north of Phuket, is a protected lowland rainforest with animal conservation projects, canoeing and elephant treks. All-inclusive trips cost US$75. **Koh Tapu**, also known as James Bond Island, is incredibly pretty but touristy. A day trip, passing Nail Island and a sea gypsy village can be as much as US$100.

If you don't stay on the **Phi Phi Islands** you can always retread Leonardo di Caprio's steps for a day and visit Maya Beach, where *The Beach* was filmed. Return ferry trips up to US$30, day tours substantially more.

Krabi Town has good shops and from here you can easily reach the **Tiger Cave Temple** with its nature trail and many shrines set in caves. It's all of 1,237 steps to the mountain-top statue of the Buddha.

Gulf of Thailand

The most populous of the Gulf islands, Koh Samui has some interesting cultural sites. Again, mostly are free or just a few dollars. **Wat Phra Yai** is known as Big Buddha Temple. It boasts a 12-m high statue and has superb views over the island. More of an oddity is **Wat Khunaram**, which contains a perfectly mummified monk. If you fancy some **Thai kickboxing** head for the Chaweng stadium, from US$12. **Nathon**, Samui's main town, is full to bursting with shops and markets, or to see a working Thai town, catch a ferry to **Surat Thani** on the mainland. It's especially worthwhile in mid October to see the **Chak Phra Festival**, literally 'the procession of hauling the Buddha image' and marks the Buddha's return to Earth.

The attractions around **Koh Tao** tend to be nature orientated – hiking, kayaking, waterfalls, idyllic beaches and so on. Around-the-island cruises stop at scenic hotspots to swim and snorkel.

Bangkok

Completely manic, outrageously noisy and entertaining beyond belief, 24 hours in the capital guarantees a high-voltage stopover. A single day's itinerary will give a taste of the city's best features. Start by taking a three-wheeled tuk-tuk ride to the **Grand Palace**, a superlative example of traditional architecture. Inside the complex is **Wat Phra Kaew**, the Temple of the Emerald Buddha, Thailand's most sacred. Next, walk the short distance to the **Chao Praya River**. Pass by the unusual **Royal Barges Museum** then on to Tha Chang Pier. Hop on the Chao Phraya Express river boat to lovely **Wat Arun**, the Temple of the Dawn, which is opposite. Re-embark for a short cruise upriver and back, for a local's view of Thai river life. Hop off at Thra Phra Arthit jetty and walk to *the* place for cheap designer goods, **Khao San Road**. This travellers' hang-out is full of shops and good restaurants. Finally, for a touch of class, take a taxi to the museum at **Jim Thompson's House**. Credited for creating the silk industry, his home is now full of interesting exhibits.

If you have a second day, within easy reach of Bangkok is the ancient Siamese capital of **Ayutthaya**, a World Heritage site with amazing ruins of temples and palaces. Damnoen Saduak is famous for the **floating markets** where canals are packed with boats piled high with fruit and vegetables and there is the **River Kwai** if you are interested in war history. Tours that cover the above cost upwards of US$60.

Sleeping

$$$ **The Peninsula Bangkok**, T+66 (0)2 861 2888, bangkok.peninsula.com.
$$ **Holiday Inn**, T+66 (0)2 2384300, ichotelsgroup.com.

Eating

With everything from fast food to top-notch cuisine, be bold and walk into any restaurant where you see locals eating something good.

Transport

Tuk-tuks offer big-thrill rides through the city, but always negotiate the price. Taxis are less fun but metered and air-con.

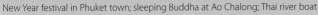

New Year festival in Phuket town; sleeping Buddha at Ao Chalong; Thai river boat

Malaysia

Form a circle: chevron barracuda,
Sphyraena genie, **manoeuvre into a**
spiral as a way to confuse predators.
Barracuda Point, Sipadan

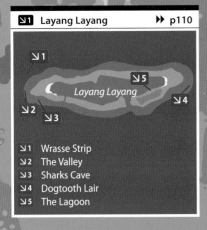

⭢1 Layang Layang ⏵⏵ p110

- ⭢1 Wrasse Strip
- ⭢2 The Valley
- ⭢3 Sharks Cave
- ⭢4 Dogtooth Lair
- ⭢5 The Lagoon

Layang Layang

⭢2 Lankayan ⏵⏵ p112

- ⭢6 House Reef & Jetty Wreck
- ⭢7 Froggie Fort
- ⭢8 Jawfish Lair

Lankayan

⭢3 Sipadan, Kapalai & Mabul ⏵⏵ p113

Mabul

Kapalai

- ⭢9 Sipadan Drop-off
- ⭢10 Barracuda Point
- ⭢11 Kapalai Jetty & House Reef
- ⭢12 Mid Reef
- ⭢13 Recep 1
- ⭢14 Paradise 1 & 2
- ⭢15 The Oil Rig

Sipadan

South China Sea

MALAYSIA

✈ ● KUALA LUMPUR

Tioman
⭢4

Sumatra
INDONESIA

✈
SINGAPORE ●

BRUN

● Miri

MALAYS

Sarawak

● Pontianak

INDONES
Kalimantan

⭢4 Tioman ⏵⏵ p117

Tioman

- ⭢16 Tiger Reef
- ⭢17 Pulau Labas
- ⭢18 Jack Rock

⭢18 — *Jack Rock*

Mersing ●

Java Sea

Bangarmasin ●

130 km

PHILIPPINES

Sulu Sea

↘2

● Kota Kinabalu

Sabah

Semporna ●

↘3

Celebes Sea

✈

likpapan ●

INDONESIA

Sulawesi

Introduction

Malaysia's dive profile is something of a double-edged sword. Divided by the South China Sea, one part of the country creates the western edge of the Coral Triangle so is a rich and lush destination with extremely high biodiversity rankings, while the other part is, like neighbouring Thailand, something of an outsider.

Both regions sit in Southeast Asian waters, but it is the island of Borneo that is the most revered, its ocean-rimmed position ensuring it is a magical, mystical dive realm. Descend into the waters around the northern state of Sabah to find a theatrical mix of pelagic predators living in tandem with rare and unusual creatures that are rarely bigger than your hand.

Across the sea, the small islands and reefs off the mainland are totally different but charming destinations in their own right, and can be well worth exploring in the right season.

Drying out days become another voyage of discovery as Malaysia once again demonstrates its split personality. This is the most multicultural of any Asian country, with Malay, Chinese and Indian influences combining to create a unique experience.

Malaysia rating

Diving
★★★★★

Dive facilities
★★★

Accommodation
★★★

Down time
★★★

Value for money
★★★★

Essentials

Getting there and around

Finding your way to Malaysia is far from difficult, although reaching the island of Borneo, where the best diving is found, involves a little extra effort. First of all, target getting to Kuala Lumpur. Malaysia Airlines (malaysiaairlines.com) have many flights from across the world to the capital. From there you will need to transfer to Kota Kinabalu on Borneo and onwards again to reach your final dive destination. There are many other carriers flying to KL – Singapore Airlines, Qantas, Qatar and Delta and even low-cost carrier Air Asia (airasia.com) now has international flights.

Internal flights are frequent with good connections and although you may do a few hops, you can usually get to where you need to go fairly quickly. Malaysian and AirAsia both serve Kota Kinabalu and Tawau. Once you are on Borneo, your dive centre will advise on transfers. For Layang Layang, the resort charters a small aircraft every couple of days. For Lankayan, you will be collected from Sandakan airport for a scenic speedboat transfer. The resorts that are clustered in the Sipadan area collect their clients from Tawau airport and transfer by road to Semporna then by boat to the

relevant hotel. As all these resorts are on offshore islands, heading out to explore the countryside would involve a transfer back to the coast, in which case, it would make more sense to arrange a tour. See page 119 for ideas.

Finally, should you decide to stay on Peninsular Malaysia, to head to Tioman or Redang perhaps, it's likely that you will need to transfer from KL's international airport to Subang Airport on the other side of the city. The mainland has some lovely diving but transfers are not easy. Take advice from your resort on the best way to get there.

Local laws and customs

Malaysia is Asia's melting pot. About half the country consists of indigenous Malay people, a third are Chinese and are10% Indian. The rest a curious melange of backgrounds. As such, cultural norms are an interesting and occasionally odd mix. On the mainland, some areas are strongly Muslim, so be sure to dress conservatively. Women should take note of what locals are wearing. The Borneo states are far more Chinese influenced, though, with quite a large population of Filipinos working in dive related areas. These people are so friendly that the usual levels of courtesy and politeness will go a long way.

Safety

Generally, crimes against tourists are rare in Malaysia. Like anywhere, be sensible in big cities, leaving valuables like cash and passports in your hotel safe. Don't leave flashy dive or camera bags unattended and no one should accept drinks from strangers. Of course, once you reach your dive resort, these concerns become almost irrelevant as there's nowhere to go.

It's been a few years since terrorism hit Malaysia. After the Sipadan kidnappings back in 2000, the government stationed Armed Forces on all offshore islands. These places are now about as safe as you can get and the soldiers who watch over you are all utterly charming. However, many governmental advisories still

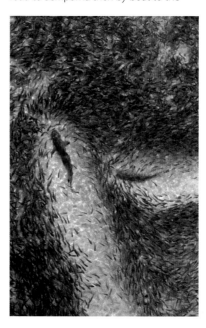

Malaysia	
Location	2°30'N, 112°30'E
Capital	Kuala Lumpur
Population	25,715,819
Land area in km²	328,550
Coastline in km	7,282

recommend caution. Before planning a trip, take advice from those on the ground (your travel agent, dive centre or hotel) and bear in mind that government websites naturally err on the side of caution. Also be aware that Malaysia probably has the strictest Asian laws on possession of drugs, which carries a mandatory death sentence.

Language

The national language of Malaysia is Bahasa, which is used by the 50% of the country's inhabitants. However, with large groups of other language speakers, English is used widely. Despite the similarity in name, Bahasa Indonesia and Bahasa Malaysia are not exactly the same.

good morning (till 1200)	selamat pagi
good afternoon (1200-1400)	selamat tengah hari
good afternoon (1400-1900)	selamat petang
good evening	selamat malam
welcome	selamat datang
goodbye (if you are leaving)	selamat jalan
and if you are staying	selamat tinggal

yes	ya	sorry!	ma'af
no	tidak	how much is...	berapa harga ini...
please	sila	good	bagus
thank you	terima kasih	great dive!	menyelam yang bagus!
you're welcome	sama-sama	one beer/water	satu bir/air

Health

Apart from the usual hot sun and stinging bug warnings, Malaysia has few health issues for visitors, though note that you need to be careful with drinking water. All the offshore islands are reliant on watermakers (often reverse osmosis) or importing water by tanker and you will probably be supplied with drinking water in your room. Should anything out of the ordinary occur, it is good to know that both doctors and chemists are well trained, many in the UK, as there are close links between UK and Malay universities.

Costs

When it comes to costs, standards and value, there is little to worry about with Malaysia. All the island resorts tend to be charming but simple, with just enough creature comforts to keep most happy. The only downside is that there is little choice. The only island with more than one accommodation option is Mabul. Meals and diving are generally included in accommodation rates so your only extras will be souvenirs and drinks, which are not too heavily marked up – a beer is about US$1.50. Should you choose to stop over in Kuala Lumpur or Kota Kinabalu, there are

 Tourist information → The official government website can be found at tourism.gov.my. This site has links to various regional sites. For Sabah go to sabahtourism.com.

Fact file

International flights	AirAsia, Delta, Malaysian Airlines, Qatar, Qantas, Singapore Airlines, Silk Air
Departure tax	Included in your flight price
Entry	Visa not required for EU, USA and Commonwealth citizens
Internal flights	AirAsia, Malaysian Airlines
Ground transport	Buses, ferries and taxis
Money	US$1 = 3.5 ringgit (MYR)
Language	Bahasa Malaysia, English is widely spoken
Electricity	240v, plug type B (see page 16)
Time zone	GMT +8
Religion	Muslim, Buddhist, Hindu, Christian
Phone	Country code +60; IDD code 00; Police 999

plenty of hotels in all categories. Tipping is not expected – bigger hotels and restaurants include a service charge on their bills. On the islands, most resorts have a staff fund box in reception or will leave an envelope with your final bill. What you leave is entirely up to you and should reflect the level of service you were given.

Curious cuttlefish; Kapalai resort

Malaysia Essentials

Dive brief

Diving

Malaysia is a geographically widespread country. She has 11 'mainland' states which sit between Thailand and Singapore plus another two states, and a federal territory, on the island of Borneo.

When it comes to diving, Borneo is the place to head. Her two states, Sabah and Sarawak, and the Territory of Labuan, are washed by the South China, Sulu and Celebes Seas. Being surrounded by open ocean currents makes for an incredibly diverse set of marine environments. Sabah – which translates as the 'Land below the Wind' – is ringed by marine reserves, idyllic islands and 75% of the country's reefs. The diving here is superlative and your only problem will be choosing between resorts.

Sarawak, surprisingly, has little or no organized diving and although Labuan has some interesting wrecks, the unreliable conditions mean the territory is mostly bypassed.

Peninsular Malaysia, which sits between the South China Sea and the Straits of Malacca, has plenty of diving but suffers in comparison to spectacular Sabah. The west coast is not regarded as much of a dive destination to those in the know. A history of heavy shipping, trade and industry has taken its toll on the marine environment. However, over on the east coast, a string of picturesque islands are favoured by Asian divers who live close by. The diving here can be surprisingly good, but difficult transport connections mean it is regarded somewhat as a 'stopover' or weekend destination for training.

Snorkelling

Location, location, location – it's all down to where you are. The diverse environments around Borneo mean that some places you can and some places you can't. If you are travelling with a non-diver who loves to snorkel, Kapalai's beautiful lagoon is probably the best option. Elsewhere will be limited by weather and sea conditions. Likewise, on the peninsula, conditions vary with the seasons.

Marine life

Borneo sits firmly inside the Coral Triangle, so the reefs there play host to an incredible variety of marine creatures. Whether you see big stuff or not is all down to seasons: if you hope to encounter hammerheads at Layang Layang for example, make sure you ask about the right time to visit. There will always be a fabulous small critter about.

Tiger Reef at Tioman island

Malaysia
animal
encounters

Layang Layang	hammerheads
Sipadan	turtles
Kapalai	mandarinfish
Mabul	frogfish

Malaysia is an interesting country no matter what part you are in but for the very best of the diving, there is only one option and that's Borneo. The mainland has some real surprises, but every single resort off the state of Sabah can promise big stuff, little stuff, more little stuff, lovely locations and the people are friendly. But perhaps the one thing that links them all is that the resorts still have that feel that you know you are somewhere a long way from home.

Making the big decision

If you are travelling a long way to dive Malaysia it's a good idea to see more than one area. The islands off the peninsula's east coast are lovely but experienced divers may find them lacking. Sabah, however, has several first-class options. Each island resort has its unique features so choosing where to go should be based on what you want to see. Do you want to swim with pelagics or spend your time with your nose down a hole hunting for weird and wonderful species? Do you want a variety of diving or to be able to chill out on a beach? Travelling between the resorts isn't difficult so it's possible to do a multi-centre trip. The only other thing to consider is the time of year. A couple of these resorts are seasonal so choose your time carefully.

A much wider selection of Malaysian destinations are reviewed in Diving Southeast Asia, see page 6 for details.

Picasso triggerfish in Layang Layang lagoon

Dive data

Seasons	May to September, mostly good countrywide, October to April, restricted in some areas
Visibility	5 metres inshore to 40 metres in open water
Temperatures	Air 22-32°C; water 26-31°C
Wet suit	3 mm full body suit
Training	Courses are not common – ask in advance
Nitrox	At some resorts on Mabul
Deco chambers	Kuantan, Labuan, Singapore

Bottom time

Sabah		This northern Borneo state is the centre of the Malay dive industry for good reason.
Layang Layang	▸ p110	Nicknamed the Jewel of the Borneo Banks, this isolated atoll has Malaysia's most impressive open water diving with hordes of pelagics.
Lankayan	▸ p112	The only resort in the Sulu Sea, this lush green island is a nature lover's retreat. In the water it's heads down for a marine treasure hunt.
Sipadan	▸ p113	A legend amongst legends, the perimeter walls of tiny island drop to unimaginable depths in the Sulawesi Sea. You can no longer stay on the island but visit from nearby Mabul and Kapalai.
Kapalai	▸ p115	Edging the shallow Litigan Reefs, the jetty dives rank right up near the very top of the 'best muck diving in the world' list.
Mabul	▸ p116	Just moments by boat from Kapalai, Mabul's diving is another marine treasure hunt with a few surprises to keep you on your toes.
Peninsular Malaysia		Small marine parks circle charming islands while offshore pinnacles add drama.
Tioman	▸ p117	Well suited to the beginners who flock here to train, there is some lively and more challenging diving way offshore.

Diversity   reef area 3,600 km²

HARD CORALS	
	568
FISH SPECIES	
	1,242
ENDEMIC FISH SPECIES	
	4
FISH UNDER THREAT	
	54
PROTECTED REEFS/MARINE PARKS	
	44

All diversity figures are approximate

Dive log

Sabah

Layang Layang

Fly an hour north-west from Kota Kinabalu into the South China Sea and you will find yourself hovering over a series of land masses known as the Spratly Islands. Sitting at the southern end is Layang Layang, just one of many islands whose ownership has long been fought over.

For decades, China, the Philippines, Vietnam and Taiwan have laid claim to the isolated and mostly uninhabited islands nearest their territorial waters. As Layang Layang sits closest to Borneo, a Malaysian Navy outpost was built there to ensure Malay interest over the Spratlys was not lost in the mêlée. And as it was surrounded by incredible coral reefs, creating a dive resort as well seemed an obvious choice.

Layang Layang, or Swallow's Reef, is a submerged oval with just one tiny, barren island. This was expanded to create an airstrip which hangs above the outer edge of the reef. Beside that runs a strip of land bordering a delightful, turquoise lagoon. Steep walls, constructed of pristine hard

corals, drop away from the outer edge of the lagoon and offer a haven to masses of pelagic life. While the corals and reef life alone are worth a visit, most come for the curious hammerhead phenomena. Every Easter, large schools swarm into Layang then head off again a few weeks later. At other times, turtles, reef sharks and schooling pelagic fish are common.

Conditions are variable as the atoll is so exposed: winds can whip the sea into a frenzy and the dive boats struggle to exit the channel to the outer reef. Currents can be strong and surface conditions rough. Late in the year, when the winds really pick up, the resort closes for a few months. However, in season, when conditions are good, they are very, very good – and visibility can seem limitless.

◪1	Wrasse Strip	
🕙	**Depth**	35 m
◑	**Visibility**	fair to stunning
🌊	**Currents**	medium to strong
🌊	**Dive type**	day boat

On the northern side of the atoll but at its westernmost end, Layang's dive sites tend to be sloping reefs rather than a rapid drop down to a sharp wall. This makes for excellent multi-level diving. Most of the time there is a current on Wrasse Strip, but it's a manageable one, although on a 'good' day, the current will even carry you along to the Valley so you get to do two sites at once. However, this dive is best when the current is less strong and you have time to admire the shallower parts of the reef. The gentle slope is covered in a variety of hard corals and crusting sponges. It's fairly pretty terrain, inhabited by soldier and triggerfish and all sorts of wrasse. Many cluster under table corals where you can also spot reef fish such as boxfish, angels and butterflies. Just past 20 metres the slope drops into a sloping wall where there is a bed of waving gorgonians, whip corals and some lush soft coral growth.

Jacks, aka big-eye trevally

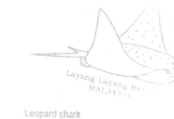

Leopard shark

Layang Layang Reef
MALAYSIA

www.whitemanta.com

⊠2 The Valley

Depth	35 m
Visibility	stunning
Currents	medium to strong
Dive type	day boat

At first glance, this site looks like nothing much, just a flat slope with small crusting corals, sponges and some fish. But descend to 30 metres and the action starts: lots of small whitetip sharks and handfuls of large grey reefs appear out in the blue; there are dogtooth tuna and several giant trevally. These swoop to and fro in currents that push against the western tip of the lagoon. A cluster of blackfin barracuda joins the throng then, as you start to ascend, another huge ball of barracuda appears overhead. Up in shallower waters there is a 'valley' scooped out of the reef where you can find large turtles resting, many juvenile whitetips under some bommies and a gigantic ball of schooling jacks. Napoleon wrasse, batfish and more turtles arrive and you can also see parrotfish and razorfish.

⊠3 Sharks Cave

Depth	31 m
Visibility	stunning
Currents	medium to strong
Dive type	day boat

Dropping down this nearly vertical wall, you will encounter two different sandy shelves. Depending on the currents you will probably drop to the deeper shelf first. It sits at 35 metres where an overhang creates a small cave. The divemasters are at pains to point out that there are no sharks in it despite the name. The cave rim has nice soft corals though and there are often large grouper tucked into a recess. Heading back up the wall, you pass a lot of small fish living on the corals, while off the wall the schooling fish are prolific, with large groups of butterflyfish. When you hit 25 metres you should find the second cave, which is a little larger than the first and is more likely to have sharks in it.

⊠4 Dogtooth Lair

Depth	25 m
Visibility	fair to good
Currents	mild to strong
Dive type	day boat

Lying behind the resort, this site gets mixed currents. From the surface you can admire a racing pod of dolphins playing in the waves while below, your profile becomes a zigzag pattern along the wall and slope. The dive site is named after the pack of enormous tuna that often lurks here but it is equally likely to have schools of jacks and turtles – although every dive on Layang has turtles. You would have to be asleep to miss them. Rumour has it that this is also another prime site for the schools of hammerheads that appear in huge gangs around Easter when the resort is at its busiest. At other times whitetips park at the cleaner stations for a spruce up as do honeycomb groupers. In the flat reef areas, there are nudibranchs and robust ghost pipefish and banded coral shrimp.

⊠5 The Lagoon

Depth	10 m
Visibility	poor
Currents	none to slight
Dive type	day boat

If you are interested in fish nurseries, then it's worth diving right in front of the resort. You can start from the boat jetty or walk a little way past the swimming pool and slowly fin back. The visibility is never that outstanding but there are loads of critters. On the sandy seabed are masses of little dragonets, upside-down jellyfish, gobies with their commensal shrimp partners, twintail and headshield slugs and pipefish. Holes in the sand reveal the spearing mantis shrimp surrounded by sail fin gobies. Small corals are ringed by tiny white triggerfish, baby lionfish, juvenile butterflies, damsels and sweetlips and you will see the outrageously coloured Picasso triggerfish. Look out for the unusual anemone with pink tips that protects tiny tomato clownfish.

Malaysia Dive log Sabah: Layang Layang

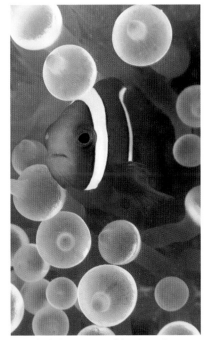

Juvenile Clarke's anemonefish – this is the orange variation; whitetip at rest

Lankayan

Just an hour or so by boat into the Sulu Sea, Lankayan is surrounded by a set of flat plateaux that gradually shelve and drop-off into a healthy reef system. There are no great walls here but gentle slopes covered, primarily, in hard corals.

In 2000, the island was declared a Marine Conservation Area after a survey confirmed both high biodiversity and nesting sites for green and hawksbill turtles.

Conditions are easy, strong currents only occurring every now and then, and the water's surface is smooth. However, visibility is often quite poor due to shallow reef structures, proximity to the mainland and high levels of plankton. Diving is all about looking for the animals that thrive in these nutrient-rich conditions, although there are also several wrecks to explore. Whitetip and nurse sharks are seen, and a very special treat is walking with blacktip sharks: the shallows are a nursery for them. You can stand in ankle-deep water and have 50-centimetre long babies swim around your toes! The resort announces the passing migration of whalesharks every year but you can never guarantee them being there for any long-term planning.

↘6 House Reef & Jetty Wreck

Depth	16 m	
Visibility	fair	
Currents	slight to medium	
Dive type	shore	

This site is the one that gets done more often than any other, partly because it can be done whenever you want, day or night, and partly because there are several sections to the dive. Entry is right under the pier where a rope on the seabed leads to the wreck of a small fishing boat. You could spend quite some time around the pylons and struts that form the jetty itself. Each surface is coated by small corals, sponges and algaes forming miniature reefs. Following the rope, there is lots of activity on the way to the wreck: clusters of catfish, trunkfish and cardinalfish shelter inside a group of tyres, their treads coated in hingebeak and cleaner shrimps. When you reach the wreck there are puffers and lionfish while decorator crabs and spider crabs shroud the slowly rotting timbers. A school of jacks hovers over the mast. On the way back, another rope leads divers past two timber pyramids. These artificial reefs attract nudibranchs and batfish. On the sand are cowries and bluespotted rays.

↘7 Froggie Fort

Depth	22 m	
Visibility	poor to good	
Currents	mild to strong	
Dive type	day boat	

A sloping oval-shaped reef, this dive is something of a surprise. Around its base, emerging from the sand, are rows of short, pastel-toned gorgonians. And beneath these is where you often find the star of the dive – a rare *Rhinopias frondosa* or weedy scorpionfish. This outrageously patterned and highly decorated fish is only about the size of a hand and is also flat like its relative, the leaf scorpionfish, but is distinguished by beautiful markings and fronds on its skin. Up at the top of the mound, where the hard corals are in particularly good condition, is a broad bed of staghorn coral. Several white leaffish reside among the branches, adults sitting beside their young.

↘8 Jawfish Lair

Depth	22 m	
Visibility	poor to fair	
Currents	mild	
Dive type	day boat	

True to its name, this site is renowned for its resident giant jawfish. The divemasters delight in showing off their pets and tempt them out of their burrows with scraps of fish. The jawfish will come right out and, despite having a huge head, are actually much smaller than that smiling, tennis ball-sized face would have you think. These chaps grow to 25 centimetres or so long, unlike a standard jawfish which rarely tops 10 centimetres. The remainder of the dive involves investigating the extensive variety of corals looking for pipefish, frogfish and orang-utan crabs, all of which are regularly found here. You may even spot a baby nurse shark taking refuge under a table coral.

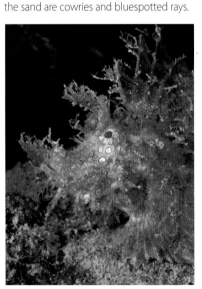

One of Lankayan's wrecks; a *rhinopias frondosa* or weedy scorpionfish

Sipadan, Kapalai and Mabul

A legend for divers the world over, Sipadan is one of those dive destinations that everyone knows about and everyone wants to see. This deep green, circular island, rimmed by bleached white sand and encapsulated by a perfect blue sea, is now shut but, fortunately, only in terms of accommodation. Meanwhile, neighbouring islands, Kapalai and Mabul have become the rising stars in this region.

In 2004, a move was made to turn Sipadan into a World Heritage Site. Concerns voiced by environmentalists over continually increasing diver numbers and the already fragile ecosystem led to a court case in Kuala Lumpur. All resort operators were asked to leave and a programme to rehabilitate the island commenced.

Divers now stay at the nearby resorts on Mabul and Kapalai which schedule dives to Sipadan. Numbers are restricted and it should be noted that while some people report easy access, there are just as many stories of permits being refused. Time will tell how much this helps with the regeneration of the reef system and whether World Heritage status will be granted. Sadly though, the arguments surrounding these plans continue with ever more concerns regarding diver numbers, incidences of illegal fishing and the lack of on-the-ground protection.

Regardless of all this, if you are looking for big stuff, then Sipadan is a must. Turtles are everywhere, so prolific and inquisitive that they will follow you around. Sharks are easy to spot and there are phenomenal numbers of barracudas. Currents are variable and most dives are done as drifts. Although they are not always that strong, the currents can quickly turn fierce, resulting in a complete about-face halfway through a dive. Across on Kapalai and Mabul, conditions are a little easier and although there are currents, most dives are shallow and easy going. The real contrast – and what makes this region so exciting – is that both of these islands are ringed by horizontal, sandy shelving reefs that attract the most phenomenal number of small and unusual creatures.

Longnose hawkfish in hiding and a resident turtle at Sipadan

9 Sipadan Drop-Off

Depth	35 m
Visibility	fair to good
Currents	slight to strong
Dive type	shore

What made Sipadan so popular was the jetty drop-off. You could simply wander off the beach and onto the amazing wall. It was known as the best house reef in the world for many a year. Within a 10-metre or so fin you can slip over the lip of the reef and find schools of batfish or jacks right there to greet you. You descend past small crevices and overhangs all painted with brightly coloured coral and every tropical fish imaginable. It is likely that you will see at least a shark or two, and a dozen or so turtles. At night, the shallows are alive with crabs and shrimp, the sandy beach area has shells and gobies and beneath the jetty are many urchins, starfish and schools of catfish. To the east of the jetty, at around 18 metres, is the entrance to Turtle Cave, a series of interconnecting caverns. It is fairly dangerous inside, full of the remains of drowned turtles: it is thought they go in at night and get lost as there is no light to guide them back out. Beware – the same could happen to divers who enter without both a torch and a divemaster.

10 Barracuda Point

🜨 **Depth**	28 m	
◐ **Visibility**	good to stunning	
≋ **Currents**	mild to ripping	
⬯ **Dive type**	day boat	

Perhaps Sipadan's most famous dive, this submerged point sits to the east of the boat jetty. The wall is sheer and the crusting corals and sponges make it incredibly colourful. As you descend to 30 metres there is a full quota of schooling small fish – butterflies, tangs and surgeons – but most outstanding is the enormous number and sizes of black coral bushes. Every one seems to have a longnose hawkfish in it, or be swarmed by lionfish, and interspersed with gigantic fans in many colours.

Turtles swim along with divers to keep them company; sometimes one will have a batfish hovering beneath his belly. At the top of the reef the corals are less impressive but gangs of whitetip sharks rest peacefully on the sand. Grey reef sharks approach from behind, heading for the school of jacks that are just around the bend. Large turtles visit cleaning stations while Napoleon wrasse and giant tuna pass by in the blue. Although the dive starts along the wall and drifts towards

them, the infamous barracuda school is usually spotted from the surface. There are hundreds in the ball, maybe thousands, sitting right on the top of the reef. They move slowly in perfect synchronicity, sliding apart for a few moments only to reconfigure swiftly into a perfect spiral – simply breathtaking.

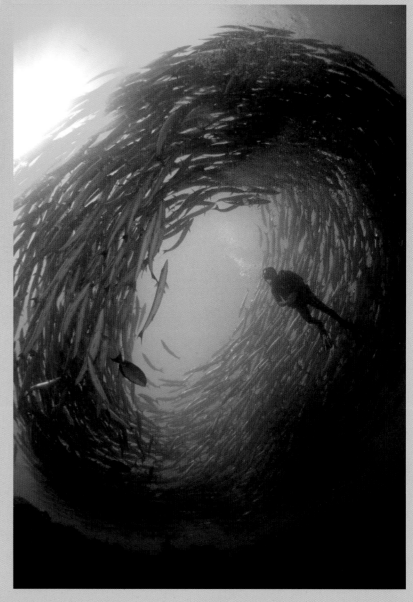

❝❞ To find a world of beauty, separated from the ordinary, that is the siren song of diving. Occasionally, the experience far exceeds the dream. This was one of those moments. Floating in the middle of the universe, never wanting to leave.

Bruce Brownstein, Venice, California

⑪ Kapalai Jetty & House Reef

🧭 **Depth**	25 m	
💧 **Visibility**	fair to good	
🌊 **Currents**	slight	
🌀 **Dive type**	shore	

Kapalai's dive jetty extends out at a right angle over a small drop-off. The area under and around it is perhaps the most popular dive here – yet dive in the single tense is misleading. You can stay under the jetty in the lagoon, drop down and turn left, or right, or head straight out and down to the wreck. A popular option is to head down to the wreck then back to the wall. This old wooden fishing boat has little on it in terms of its original purpose, but many interesting creatures hide on the rotting hull, including frogfish decorated with splotches and hairy bits. Beneath, there are lots of morays neatly lined up in a row and the seabed nearby reveals gobies and the spearing mantis shrimp.

Swimming back up towards the jetty, the corals are a mixture of hard and soft, none particularly big or prolific but it's still a substantial and healthy system. Sponges, tunicates and hydroids provide plenty of hiding spaces for critters, including ornate ghost pipefish hovering inside whip corals and banded pipefish in a cavern.

Across the upper section of reef you can see squat lobsters in crinoids, lots of decorator crabs, slipper lobsters and plenty of shrimp. The more exotic creatures seen regularly are flamboyant cuttlefish and the incredible blue-ringed octopus. These are spotted at dusk and often near Mandarin Valley: a patch of the reef that is just a metre or so square but where a colony of miniscule, glamorous mandarinfish can be seen every night. Go at dusk and sit still until they emerge from the rubble, perform their courting rituals, then spawn.

Directly under the jetty (perfect for a night dive) are crocodilefish and peacock flounders, while the brightly coloured fans growing on the pylons are full of pink and white striped squat lobsters. There are more tiny crabs on the sponges, sleeping parrotfish in their mucous bubbles, a few juvenile batfish and even baby nurse sharks on a fly by!

⑫ Mid Reef, Kapalai

🧭 **Depth**	21 m	
💧 **Visibility**	fair to good	
🌊 **Currents**	slight to medium	
🌀 **Dive type**	day boat	

A divemasters' favourite, this is just one of Kapalai's high-voltage critter hunts. The seabed is rife with crawling critters and you are likely to spot the solar powered nudibranch. Whip corals are rich with tiny animals like the highly camouflaged *Xenocarcinus conicus* crab and lots of tiny 'bumble bee' shrimp, all jostling for prime position on the narrow surface. There are many small gobies and jawfish on the seafloor, plus this site has some bigger animals including a gang of turtles. Some healthy fan corals house spider crabs, longnose and pixie hawkfish. One patch of finger sponges has the tiniest of pink frogfish. (A year after doing this dive, we returned and he was still in exactly the same place. The divemasters monitored him for the whole year and watched him grow into an adult.)

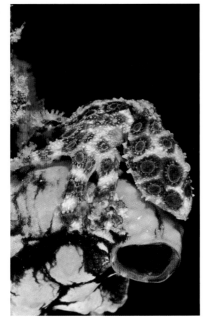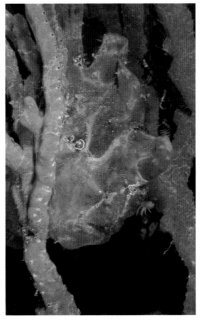

Kapalai critters: an angry blue-ringed octopus; pink frogfish in matching sponges; ornate ghost pipefish mother and baby

⬂13 Recep 1, Kapalai

⬙	**Depth**	26 m
◐	**Visibility**	poor to good
〰	**Currents**	slight to strong
🌊	**Dive type**	day boat

This is a classic Kapalai critter dive. From the moment you hit the undulating seabed until you are nearly out of air, you will see curious critter after curious critter: drop down over the small wall into a gully with a sandy bottom. Spot a blue ribbon eel then a white leaffish. The gully leads to a flat hard plateau where there are robust ghost pipefish, ornate ghost pipefish and many whip corals. On them are tiny stripy shrimp, then clear-bodied shrimp on the next whip with minute cowries sitting by them. There are masses of nudibranchs, leaffish, ribbon eels, very tame mantis shrimp and an octopus. At the top of the little wall are orang-utan crabs and turtles. The current across the plateau here can be really strong so when that happens it's best to stay up at the top levels and look for baby cuttlefish hiding in soft coral.

⬂14 Paradise 1 & 2, Mabul

⬙	**Depth**	21 m
◐	**Visibility**	fair to good
〰	**Currents**	none to strong
🌊	**Dive type**	day boat

Paradise 1 is another cracking dive where you hop from one weird animal to the next with hardly a moment to admire each: flying gurnards, fingered dragonets, dwarf lionfish, snake eels, inimicus (or devilfish), filefish and longsnout pipefish. There are even weirder fish such as hairy decorated filefish, a wacky long-legged crab and juvenile stonefish just millimetres long. Mantis shrimp peek out of their burrows and flounder try to disguise themselves. Small octopus hide beneath coconut shells and even smaller blue-ringed octopus sneak into old beer bottles. Palm fronds get caught on buoy lines and are used by squid to lay their eggs. A little further to the west is Paradise 2, which has fewer 'muck' critters but more free swimmers like batfish and young wrasse and many clownfish in their host anemones.

⬂15 The Oil Rig, Mabul

⬙	**Depth**	18 m
◐	**Visibility**	poor to good
〰	**Currents**	slight to medium
🌊	**Dive type**	day boat

The massive, ugly oil derrick parked just off Mabul's shores is an exercise in nature's power over man. Humanity does its best to mess up the landscape but nature has its own cunning ways of turning that around. The pylons supporting the rig are eerie, reminiscent of a wreck dive, and swarmed by jacks and snappers. Below, the seabed is studded with detritus, yet the creatures have started their own recycling programmes: ropes have been colonized by iridescent sponges that shelter tiny gobies; building materials have stonefish squatters; and a giant moray called Elvis lives under an old cage. There are flying gurnards and crocodilefish carpeting the sand, ornate ghost pipefish in fans and lime green frogfish hang out in old car tyres. A pile of metal sheets and pipes has yet more frogfish in varying colours, morays and scorpionfish are everywhere; and there are mantis shrimp and jawfish, cardinals and nesting sergeant majors. The list could go on. This is a superlative dive.

The flamboyant cuttlefish being flamboyant; seahorse on Paradise 1

Peninsular Malaysia

Malaysia's mainland is a hot destination for Asian residents. Both qualified and trainee divers head to the islands off the east coast to relax, do a little diving or continue with courses they have started at home. The conditions here are perfect for that, with sheltered bays, gentle currents and warm waters making an ideal long weekend.

Tioman

Although Tioman's coastal bays are renowned for their calm and easy diving, exciting and challenging dives can be found just a little way offshore. Visibility is never crystal clear but the underwater landscape is reminiscent of parts of the Similan Islands with huge boulders tumbling together. These create interesting swim-throughs coated in soft corals and attracting a wealth of marine creatures. This is seasonal diving though, with weather conditions limiting a visit to the months between May and October.

⤵16 Tiger Reef	
🕐 **Depth**	22 m
◐ **Visibility**	fair
🌊 **Currents**	none to strong
⬤ **Dive type**	liveaboard

Off the north of Tioman, Tiger Reef consists of a series of pinnacle-shaped boulders. Entry is over one with the mooring buoy at about five metres. You then drop to 12, swim through a crevice and make your way around all the pinnacles to see what is about. And there is a lot of life: snappers, needlenose barracuda, Similans sweetlips and bluespotted rays. At the base of the dive in a sandy bowl, you might encounter a family of bumphead parrotfish. All the stunning nudibranchs pale in comparison.

⤵17 Pulau Labas	
🕐 **Depth**	13 m
◐ **Visibility**	good
🌊 **Currents**	slight
⬤ **Dive type**	liveaboard

Because there are two distinct sides to this moon-shaped reef, it is often used for night dives. On the inner side are crevices and tunnels between the rocks; the outer side gets strong currents. At night, you spend time investigating around the sheltered rocks and under the hard corals. There are sleeping bumphead parrots as well as smaller parrots in their bubbles. Tiny crabs cling to fans while hermit crabs skitter across the coral rubble trying to avoid all the urchins on the surface.

⤵18 Jack Rock	
🕐 **Depth**	20 m
◐ **Visibility**	poor to fair
🌊 **Currents**	none to ripping
⬤ **Dive type**	liveaboard

This lonely pinnacle is in the middle of nowhere, halfway back to Singapore. It drops from two metres above the surface to 22 metres at the flat seafloor. The visibility is renowned for being awful, and currents strong, so when you drop in on one side, and find the visibility is up to 10 metres, you are relieved. The first part of the dive is on the clear side of the rock and takes you down to the base which is covered in hard, soft and whip corals. A couple of crevices are known baby shark haunts – you can just see their tails. There are unusual nudibranchs and large starry puffers. A bit of the dive is then spent around on the murky side and then, as you come back up to about five metres on the clear side, you come into the current and one of the most amazing moments in diving – there are swarms of small silvery fish, but the excitement isn't due to their presence but because of the speed they are moving, both around the pinnacle and the divers. It's impossible to describe.

Drying out

For trips to Borneo, chances are you will need a night in Kota Kinabalu. There are many hotels in all price ranges, and even dive operations if you fancy that. However, once you head for the islands, there is usually just the one choice of operation as most (Mabul excepted) are a single, dedicated dive resort.

Sabah
Kota Kinabalu
$$$ Sutera Harbour Resort, T+60 (0)88 318888, suteraharbour.com. A convenient and pleasant complex with several hotels, a spa, golf course, sports facilities, many restaurants and free airport transfers. The resort also owns the North Borneo Railway and can arrange a variety of day trips.

Diving
City-based diving is rarely a first choice but if you have a couple of days to spare, you could visit the nearby marine park. Check Borneo Dream, borneodream.com and Down Below, downbelow.co.uk.

Layang Layang
$$ Layang Layang Island Resort, T+60 (0)3 2162 2877, layanglayang.com. On an isolated island in the Spratly Group, this resort's rooms are built in 'longhouses' and feel rather like a comfy, old-fashioned American motel. All rooms have balconies and good views towards the sea. Weekly packs for roughly US$1,400 include all meals and diving.

Lankayan
$$ Lankayan Island Resort, T+60 (0)89 765200, lankayan-island.com. Again just one resort on this tropical island. Simple, comfortable rooms are dotted amongst the trees and face the sea. Laid-back atmosphere. Weekly packs from US$1,200 include all meals, transfers and diving.

Sandakan
$ Sepilok Nature Resort, T+60 (0)89 765200, sepilok.com. Delightful wooden chalets overlook a tropical garden-rimmed lake. This very peaceful resort is near to the departure point for Lankayan, has a collection of 150 different Asian orchid species and is just a few minutes' walk from the orang-utan sanctuary entrance.

Kapalai
$$ Sipadan Kapalai Resort, T+60 (0)89 765200, sipadan-kapalai.com. This water village resort is simply delightful – the bungalows are spacious and bug free, no air-con, just sea-breeze cooled. The resort has been expanded and upgraded since Sipadan closed but is said to have retained its atmosphere. The divemasters are master critter spotters. Weekly packs cost around US$1,200 and include all meals, transfers and unlimited diving. Sipadan trips are subject to permits.

Mabul
$$$-$$ Sipadan-Mabul Resort & Mabul Water Bungalows, T+60 (0)88 230006, sipadan-mabul.com.my. Long-established operator with two resorts, the original with basic accommodation and a second,

better, set of water bungalows. Weekly packages, from around US$1,200-1,800 including all meals, transfers and diving. Sipadan trips are subject to permits.

Liveaboards
MV Celebes Explorer, T+60 (0)88 224918, borneo.org. The only liveaboard in this region. Cruises depart from Semporna jetty for 3-day, 4-day or weekly itineraries.

Peninsular Malaysia
Tioman
$$-$ Minang Cove Resort, T+60 (0)7 799 7372, minangcove.com.my. On the south of Tioman and set in a lovely cove. The reef just offshore is said to be great for snorkelling. Run by a British-Malay couple.

Liveaboards
White Manta Diving T +65 9677 8894 whitemanta.com. This highly professional Singaporean company has 2 vessels, *White* and *Black Manta*. From November to May, they sail and dive Thai waters, but from June to October they cover north and east of Singapore. Trips vary from 2-4 days to Tioman, Pulau Aur and Kuantan in Malaysia plus some wrecks and islands in nearby Indonesian waters. *Black Manta* is very comfortable and the food is fabulous.

MV Black Manta at Jack Rock; Layang Layang Resort; Lankayan Island

 Sleeping $$$ US$150+ double room per night $$ US$75-150 $ under US$75

Eating $$$ US$40+ 2-course meal, excluding drinks $$ US$20-40 $ under US$20

Kota Kinabalu

Take a day to see this pleasant, small city and her surrounds. The **KK Heritage Walk** is a guided two-hour walk around the city's landmarks and costs about RM100 per person. Those with the inclination to climb mountains will be sorely tempted to take a slightly longer break and scale **Mount Kinabalu**. Trips take two days so if time is short, visit Malaysia's first World Heritage Site, **Kinabalu Park**, and see just a little of the incredible range of plant, animal, insect and bird life. **Poring Hot Springs** are nearby and day trips that cover both will be around US$60. A slightly more relaxed day can be had by taking the North Borneo Railway journey to the agricultural region of Papar. The restored 100-year-old train chugs past mangrove swamps, villages and markets. Return trip about US$70.

Sandakan

Sepilok Orang-utan Sanctuary Founded in 1964 to rehabilitate orphan orang-utans, the sanctuary consists of 43 sq km of protected land at the edge of Kabili Sepilok Forest Reserve. Up to 80 orang-utans live in the reserve, the aim being to help them readjust to life in the wild. Public access is strictly managed. At feeding times, the animals come down to platforms so are easy to see and older, permanent residents will approach visitors. There is a boardwalk trail through the forest where you can see snakes and local plants.

Turtle Island Marine Park Not far from Lankayan is this set of three islands where turtles come to nest. Now a marine park, there are no established diving facilities here and accommodation is very limited, but it's a good day out for non-divers.

Sabah's rainforests

This one Malaysian state is regarded as having some of the world's most important flora and fauna species. Over half of the state has been set aside to create rainforest reserves and wildlife parks to ensure the protection of the interior and the many unique plants and animals, although you may find this hard to believe as you pass coastal palm oil plantation after palm oil plantation. To see the real Sabah, you will need to head far inland: there are over 200 mammals living in these forests but you will be lucky to see them as they retreat at the faintest hint of disturbance. Join and escorted walking tour to a reserve and you can stay overnight. The best time to visit is during the fruiting and flowering season from March until October. Options include the **Danum Valley Conservation Area,** which is home to Asian elephants, and the rarely seen endangered Sumatran rhinoceros, sun bears and clouded leopards. The **Tabin Wildlife Reserve** has the Borneo Pygmy Elephant, Sumateran Rhinoceros and Tembadau (a species of Asian wild cattle), while wildlife in the **Kinabatangan Wildlife Sanctuary** include proboscis and leaf monkeys and crab-eating macaques.

Tioman

Most people come to Tioman to relax, swim and dive. There isn't much else to do and chances are you won't move far from where you are staying. The main day out is to walk across the island from Tekek to Juara on the east coast. It's a long haul uphill and takes about four hours through the jungle. Take plenty of water and catch a ferry back.

Peninsular Malaysia

Malaysia is built on its cross-cultural differences and nowhere is this reflected more than in the capital, **Kuala Lumpur**. If you're up for a few days of city lifestyle, KL is as lively as any, and for many, too lively. Admire architecture that ranges from aging colonial mansions to the state-of-the-art Petronas Twin Towers.

The historic city and port of **Melaka** could be worth a diversion as it's only 2½ hours away. A prosperous trading post in the 16th century, the Portuguese, Dutch and British all colonized here. For cool air, the **Cameron Highlands** are 1,500 m above sea level and famous for their pleasant weather and tea plantations and cool temperatures. The peninsula's **East Coast** is punctuated with several small cities and large towns. There is little to hold diver tourists here for more than a day although places like Mersing will give you a feel for a rustic Malay sea port and Kota Bharu is an introduction to more traditional Malay culture.

Jessica at Sepilok Orang-utan Sanctuary; golden buddha; shopping on the East Coast

Indonesia

Photography daydream: more bigeye trevally, *caranx sexfasciatus,* than you could ever have the right lens for. *Nusa Laut, the Spice Islands*

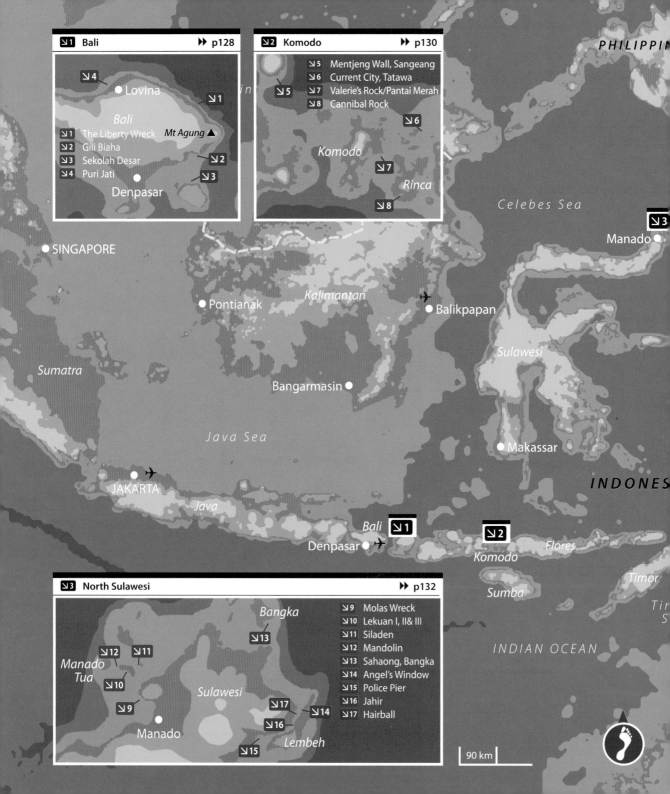

↘1 Bali ▶▶ p128

↘4 Lovina

Bali ↘1

↘1	The Liberty Wreck
↘2	Gili Biaha
↘3	Sekolah Desar
↘4	Puri Jati

Mt Agung ▲

↘2

↘3

Denpasar

↘2 Komodo ▶▶ p130

↘5	Mentjeng Wall, Sangeang
↘6	Current City, Tatawa
↘7	Valerie's Rock/Pantai Merah
↘8	Cannibal Rock

↘5

↘6

Komodo

↘7

Rinca

↘8

PHILIPPIN

Celebes Sea

↘3 Manado ●

● SINGAPORE

● Pontianak

Kalimantan

✈ Balikpapan

Sulawesi

Sumatra

Bangarmasin ●

Java Sea

● Makassar

✈ JAKARTA

Java

Bali ↘1

↘2

Flores

I N D O N E S

Denpasar ● ✈

Komodo

Timor

Sumba

*Tir
S*

INDIAN OCEAN

↘3 North Sulawesi ▶▶ p132

Bangka

↘13

↘9	Molas Wreck
↘10	Lekuan I, II& III
↘11	Siladen
↘12	Mandolin
↘13	Sahaong, Bangka
↘14	Angel's Window
↘15	Police Pier
↘16	Jahir
↘17	Hairball

↘12 ↘11

*Manado
Tua*

↘10

Sulawesi

↘17 ↘14

↘9

↘16

Manado

↘15

Lembeh

| 90 km |

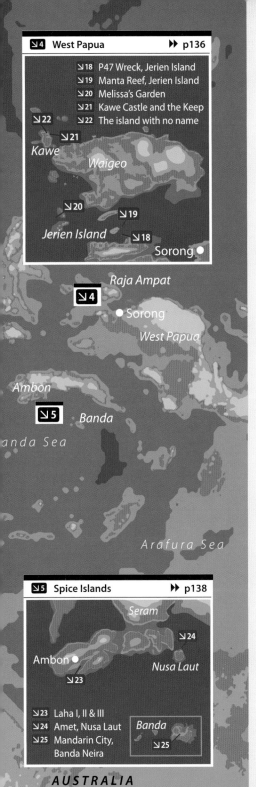

Introduction

Indonesia is the largest archipelago on the planet and by far the biggest of the Southeast Asian countries. Her extensive arc of islands forms the southern edge of the Coral Triangle, reaches up past Malaysian Borneo and abuts the Melanesian nations to the east.

Not only is this a physically immense country, Indonesia is also where the world's marine biodiversity rankings are at their highest, and these factors combined mean that there are more opportunities to explore the underwater realm than anywhere else in the region, if not the world.

Every inch of water has the potential for mesmerizing diving: some is up-tempo and adventurous, some just as calm as you could wish for. Many marine animals that are rare elsewhere are common here. No matter what it is you look for, chances are you will find it.

Despite the massive changes the country has seen in recent years, Indonesia has completely retained her sense of tradition. On land there are almost as many religions, cultures, arts and cuisines as there are islands. Diversity is not confined to Indonesia's world beneath the seas. From peace-loving Bali to the outer reaches of Raja Ampat, this water-bound land is one of the world's most fascinating places to experience.

Indonesia rating

Diving
★★★★★

Dive facilities
★★★★★

Accommodation
★★★★★

Down time
★★★

Value for money
★★★★★

Essentials

Getting there and around

Travelling to Indonesia is simplicity itself with international flights arriving from almost everywhere. Airlines include Eva, Qantas, Qatar, Thai and United amongst many others. Garuda, the national carrier, only has a nominal long-haul network but Singapore Airlines (singaporeair.com) and regional subsidiary Silk Air (silkair.com) have flights to diver-orientated destinations including Bali, Lombok and Manado. The city is also an ideal stopover (see page 141). There are several low-cost regional options like AirAsia (airasia.com) or Jetstar (jetstar.com) that connect Bali and Jakarta to Australia and other Asian countries.

As this is such a widespread country, there are endless internal travel options including masses of local airlines: Garuda, Merpati and Lion Air (garuda-indonesia.com, merpati.co.id, lionair.co.id) are the most reliable but as online booking is not easy, ask your dive operator to handle this for you. Don't be too concerned if they book you on an unheard of airline: new ones appear almost by the minute. What won't work by the minute though are schedules, which are permanently on 'Indonesian' time. Internal flights run like buses, hopping from one island to another, and delays can have a knock-on effect.

Airport to hotel transfers are almost always included but taxis are reasonably priced and usually metered. If you fancy a day or two to explore land-based sights, ask your hotel or dive centre to arrange a driver and car to escort you around. Alternatively, simply wander up the road until someone asks, "Transport, mister?" This is one of Indonesia's most universal sayings. You'll hear it along every street, on the beach or in a restaurant. It's the way a lot of people earn a living and, as long as you set a price first, you're unlikely to have any problems.

Local laws and customs

Religions in Indonesia are highly varied so it's difficult to define a behavioural pattern for tourists except to say that anywhere divers are likely to go will be 'tourist tolerant'. Take local advice if you are unsure. Much of the country is Muslim but there are substantial Buddhist, Christian, Hindu and Animist communities. The Indonesian version of Islam is strongly influenced by these other religions, which in turn influence each other. However, the religion most people encounter is Balinese Agama Hinduism which is not the same as Indian Hinduism. Its calming presence is strongly felt in day-to-day life.

Safety

Indonesia has experienced more than its fair share of trouble and strife over recent years. Terrorist actions, natural disasters and racial tensions in out-of-the-way regions have all hit the headlines, creating a mood of concern. It's worth taking advice from those on the ground (your dive centre or resort) who will have the most up-to-date information and views. Also check your government's travel advisory website for the official view. That said, crimes against tourists are rare, except in highly populated towns which may have been affected by an economic nosedive. Sadly, it is budget travellers who bear the brunt of this as they tend to use public transport and stay in cheaper, less secure hotels. Divers travelling to a suitable resort and using

Indonesia	
Location	5°00'S, 120°00'E
Capital	Jakarta
Population	240,271,522
Land area in km²	1,826,440
Coastline in km	54,716

private transport are unlikely to encounter trouble. If you are out at night take only what you need and keep valuables concealed. Lone women should be aware of the mixed message they are sending to a society that regards sexual openness as taboo, yet is inundated with Western culture that promotes sex as a selling tool.

Language

There are many indigenous languages right across Indonesia but government education policies have ensured that the national language, Bahasa Indonesia, is spoken everywhere: people just love tourists who greet them in Bahasa. It's easy enough to learn and pronunciation is straightforward. The only confusing issue is getting to grips with variations within a simple saying – the way you say hello varies by the clock!

good...		yes	*ya*
morning (until 1100)	*selamat pagi*	no	*tidak*
day (until 1500)	*selamat siang*	please	*tolong*
afternoon (until dusk)	*selamat sore*	thank you	*terima kasih*
evening	*selamat malam*	sorry	*ma'af*
bye... if leaving	*selamat tinggal*	how much is...	*berapa harganya...*
...if you are staying	*selamat jalan*	good	*bagus*
welcome	*selamat datang*	great dive!	*menyelam yang bagus!*
you're welcome	*kembali*	one beer/water	*satu bir/air*

Health

Malaria and other mosquito-borne diseases occur in some areas. It depends on who you talk to as to how much of a risk this is. For some time Bali was declared malaria free but occasional cases are now being reported. Get up-to-date advice and always use a repellent. Many hotels have purified tap water or supply bottled. There are plenty of medical facilities but these vary depending on the relative wealth of a particular locality. Medical consultations are costly for locals and many simply can't afford it. For a visitor, a trip to the doctor is just a few dollars but rest assured that for minor illnesses doctors are well-trained and know their stuff.

Costs

Of Southeast Asia's destinations Indonesia consistently provides the best value for money. You can spend a fortune on an all-singing all-dancing hotel room with a private pool and maid, but it will still be only half of what it would cost elsewhere. The variety of accommodation is incredible, from ultra-modern to quietly traditional; a small, simple bungalow will be as little as US$30; spend over US$100 and you can have luxury; over $200 and you will feel like you have a palace. Where you are limited to a lone resort, these will be of a good standard and reflected in the price.

Tourist information → The government website can be found at my-indonesia.info; other websites include indonesia-tourism.com; Bali: balitourismboard.org; Komodo: komodonationalpark.org; West Papua: diverajaampat.org Sulawesi: divenorthsulawesi.com, north-sulawesi.org.

Fact file

International flights	Air Asia, Eva, Jetstar, Malaysian, Qantas, Qatar, Singapore Airlines/Silk Air, Thai, United
Departure tax	International 150,000 IDR; Domestic 20,000 IDR
Entry	Visas required for most nationalities, US$25 on entry
Internal flights	Garuda, Lion Air, Merpati
Ground transport	Plenty but use private rather than public
Money	US$1 = 11,000 rupiah (IDR)
Language	Bahasa Indonesia, English is widely spoken
Electricity	220v/110v, plug types A/C (see page 16)
Time zone	GMT + 8 (Bali/Manado) GMT + 9 (West Papua)
Religion	Muslim, Hindu, Christian, Animist
Phone	Country code +62; IDD code 001; Police 110

Food is much the same: a delightful meal in a small, local restaurant may be less than US$10 a head or visit an ultra-trendy affair a mile along the bay and pay much more. Drinking is cheap too; a large bottle of the local brew, Bintang, will be US$2, but more in resorts which add their own mark-up. Tipping is the done thing and, in general, about 10% on meals and similar services would be reasonable. Bear in mind that salaries are very low by Western standards so you can afford to be generous. For dive crews, see page 12.

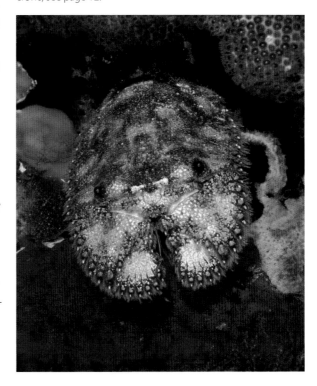

Indonesia Essentials

Dive brief

Diving

Indonesia is the largest of Southeast Asia's countries with an estimated 18,000 islands that stretch east to west for over 5000 kilometres. Compare that to continental America at only 4400 kilometres wide and realize just how big this archipelago is. As her myriad land masses sit surrounded by six different seas and two oceans and include around 18% of the world's coral reefs, you can take it for granted that the diving is impressive. What's more, Indonesia's southern islands mark the edge of the Pacific Ring of Fire and the country falls completely within the Coral Triangle, the most diverse marine region on the planet. There are also many localized features which go even further to ensuring that no matter which part of Indonesia you visit, there will be a fantastic ecosytem to explore.

The incredible number of diveable regions is only outdone by the number of dive sites at each. However, what makes this such a special destination is the recognition that this is also an important business. A couple of decades ago there were few formal dive facilities but that is no longer the case. Areas that are easy to get to have many professional dive operators catering for all budgets and tastes, while for those with an adventurous spirit there are distant areas that can be reached only by liveaboard.

Conditions and dive styles vary region by region and sea by sea according to which monsoon season is prevailing. Surprisingly, this is good news, as you are not restricted to visiting in specific months like in some countries. Simply choose a destination according to when you can go.

Snorkelling

With so many coral reefs the options for snorkelling are endless. On Bali, reefs reach right into shallow bays; at Bunaken Island off Manado, you can hover over the top of her steep walls. More distant, adventurous regions have fewer options as currents can be strong, but that should not put non-divers off. Good liveaboards always ensure the dive tender stays nearby if someone is in the water. And what could be more alluring than snorkelling over a reef in Raja Ampat so remote that the closest island doesn't even have a name?

Marine life

It is important to recognize that Indonesia is regarded as the world's most biodiverse marine environment. Research studies have found more species in Indonesian waters than anywhere else, even in other Asian countries, although new research is pushing the Philippines closer to taking that accolade. A recent survey recorded the Raja Ampat islands as having 950 fish species, 450 corals and 600 molluscs. Four

Indonesia animal encounters

Bali	mola-mola
Komodo	toxic fire urchins
Manado	pygmy seahorses
Lembeh	mimic octopus
West Papua	wobbegong sharks

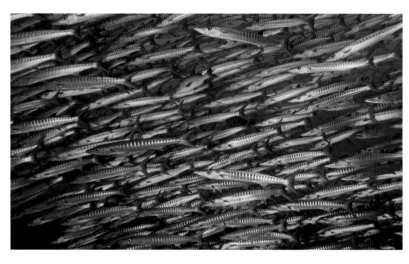

> If there was only one country in the world we could dive, Indonesia would be it. We have seen it develop and change; we have been there both in peaceful and troubled times and we still love it the most. The marine realm is superb and there is something about the people and their incredible integrity that keeps it at the centre of our affections. On the dive side, every season there is something fresh – a new area opens up as an old one goes out of favour, only to bounce back a few years later.

new fish species and seven new corals were discovered and the area is being proposed as another World Heritage Site. Likewise the Bunaken National Park, Banda and Derawan Islands are all on the tentative list for World Heritage status while the superlative Komodo National Park already is. All this makes it impossible to list exactly what you will see here, but you will see plenty.

Making the big decision

It isn't easy to recommend one area of Indonesia over another as they all have something to offer. One way to choose would be to decide what else you want to do. Bali is by far the most developed island, with everything you would expect from a major resort destination including incredible land attractions. In comparison, a liveaboard trip to Banda or Raja Ampat won't suit if you like to have all the mod cons (no mobile phones or TV way out there), while Manado would sit somewhere in the middle of all that. Or choose by dive style: big open waters with pelagics in West Papua or the ultimate in muck diving in the Lembeh Straits. Whichever way you look at it, there is always somewhere exciting to go.

A much wider selection of Indonesian destinations are reviewed in Diving Southeast Asia, see page 6 for details.

Dive data

Seasons	May to September, SE monsoon (dryer); November to March, NW monsoon (wetter)
Visibility	5 metres inshore to infinity in open water
Temperatures	Air 19-36°C; water 23-32°C
Wet suit	3 mm full body suit, add 2 mm extra for Komodo
Training	Look for PADI 5-star (or equivalent) agencies
Nitrox	Generally available on land. Limited on liveaboards
Deco chambers	Bali, Manado, Jakarta, Singapore

Bottom time

Diversity   reef area 51,020 km²

HARD CORALS	602
FISH SPECIES	3,374
ENDEMIC FISH SPECIES	113
FISH UNDER THREAT	113
PROTECTED REEFS/MARINE PARKS	40

All diversity figures are approximate

Dive log

Bali

This tiny volcanic island is one of the world's most stunning. Even the Balinese call their home the 'Island of the Gods'. The combination of a balmy climate, unique culture, delightful people and great diving all adds up to one supremely good dive destination.

Strangely, Bali is often overlooked by divers who use it as a staging post to head to more distant marine parks, yet her fringing reefs are too good to miss. The southern tip of the island, where the main resort areas are, has only a minimal reef system as the coastline is hit by surf from the Indian Ocean. But head east or north and it's all very different.

At the island's easternmost point lies mighty, active Mount Agung. This towering volcano faces the Lombok Channel and the combination of a rich volcanic soil and some rushing offshore currents ensures there are healthy and impressive reefs with diverse diving. There is the famous wreck at Tulamben, gentle reefs, muck dives and you can even head across to do the drift dives around Nusa Penida island.

Travelling to the northern coast, many small and extremely shallow bays attract fascinating and unusual creatures while the offshore islands of the Menjangen Marine Park are superlative with deep walls and clear water.

↘1	The Liberty Wreck	
🌀	Depth	30 m
◑	Visibility	fair to stunning
🌊	Currents	none to medium
🌗	Dive type	shore

Part of diver folklore, the Liberty lies just 30 metres from shore. A Second World War US supply ship, she was torpedoed in 1941 by a Japanese submarine and lay beached for 20 years before Mount Agung erupted and pushed her down the sloping seabed. Now, she is one of the best artificial reefs you will ever see. Visibility varies depending on the season and run-off from the nearby river mouth but, even when it's low, the dive is magnificent. As you fin towards the hull you pass the resident oriental sweetlips, then the wreck materializes from the blue. There are jacks swirling above, a Napoleon wrasse in amongst them and, occasionally, mola-mola are seen. The superstructure is thick with corals, sponges, fans and crinoids. Peer inside to see guns, toilets, boilers and the anchor chain. Right at the bottom are some gorgonians that are known to have pygmy seahorses on them. There are also leaffish, dragonets and more nudibranchs than you thought possible in one dive.

◤2 Gili Biaha

🌀	**Depth**	26 m
◑	**Visibility**	good
〜	**Currents**	slight to strong
⬡	**Dive type**	day boat

Sailing to this small island outcrop takes about 30 minutes from Padangbai. As the crescent of land emerges from very deep water, the sea temperature here can be much lower than other dives nearby and is likely to take your breath away as you drop in. There can also be strong currents and surge but the dive is well worth it. At one end you drop onto one of Bali's most impressive walls, encrusted in an incredible amount of soft and hard coral and, because of the current, there are swarms of fish. The current is likely to push you inwards to the wall, where a small cave seen on the surface opens up to a much bigger cavern below the water. There are often baby and adult whitetip sharks swinging in and out of it. Further along the wall another small cave is a riot of life: two blue ribbon eels, three different coloured leaffish, a mantis shrimp and mating nudibranchs near to a freshly laid, lacy egg ring and all this in a very small space.

◤3 Sekolah Desar, Nusa Penida

🌀	**Depth**	34 m
◑	**Visibility**	fair to good
〜	**Currents**	none to ripping
⬡	**Dive type**	day boat

Further offshore is Nusa Penida which sits firmly in the often strong currents of the Lombok Channel. This dive starts at the Sekolah Desar (primary school) and is a popular section of the reef. The scenery is a gently undulating slope that leads down to a short wall where there are some very large barrel sponges and a few nice fans. In some sections, hard corals form a flat carpet across the topography while in others there are broad patches of sand punctuated by outcrops with gorgeous soft corals. There is some damage – from the currents more than anything else – although there has been some destructive fishing in the past. All the same, large tuna, jacks, mackerel and turtles are seen here quite often. However, the highlights of the dive are just as likely to be small: there are orang-utan crabs and porcelain crabs, lots of clownfish on anemones and lively mantis shrimp, providing the currents allow you time to look.

◤4 Puri Jati, Siririt Bay

🌀	**Depth**	25 m
◑	**Visibility**	fair to good
〜	**Currents**	slight
⬡	**Dive type**	shore

This is the latest 'in-thing' on the north coast, an absolutely marvellous critter-hunt dive. The seabed geography is very flat, staying at under 10 metres until a very long way offshore. A sudden drop then falls quite steeply to depth but the principal interest is in the shallows. Patches of seagrass are interspersed with large leaved halimeda algae. The critters found amongst these are outstanding: coconut octopus, the mimic octopus, seahorses, juveniles of frogfish, lionfish, and filefish. There's slipper lobsters, cockatoo waspfish, imperial shrimp on sea cucumbers, squid eggs, cowrie shells – even cowries with imperial shrimp sitting on them. Nudibranchs crawl up blades of seagrass and as you stare you realize there are tozeuma shrimp, harlequin crabs, sand divers, dart gobies, shrimp gobies, snake eels, garden eels, tiny white faced stone fish, crab on a fire urchin and most exciting, if it's possible to define that here, a frogfish that was five millimetres long.

On Sekolah Desar; a tiny lionfish and a seahorse at Puri Jati

Komodo

A long chain of islands stretches east from Bali, ending eventually at Timor. The most famous of these is tiny Komodo, home of the world's largest – and most offensive – lizard and now a World Heritage Site and National Marine Park.

Other islands are sometimes forgotten in the rush to reach Komodo, yet this island chain encompasses some of the planet's most interesting geological features.

A century ago, British naturalist Alfred Russel Wallace recognised that an invisible line divided the region. This later became scientifically acknowledged as the 'Wallace Line'. It separates Bali from Lombok: to its west, islands are tropical Asian; to the east they resemble arid Australia. The chain also separates the Indian Ocean from the Java Sea, so currents are unpredictable. At times they can toss you about like a washing machine and, what's more, the cold water upwellings can be breathtaking.

It's not like that all year but the harder conditions often correlate with the best animal spotting seasons. It must be noted though, that this is some of the most challenging diving in Indonesia. However, the reefs are spectacular with large and small animals on every dive.

◤5 Mentjeng Wall, Sangeang

🕐	**Depth**	45 m
🌓	**Visibility**	fair to good
🌀	**Currents**	none
🌊	**Dive type**	liveaboard

Just outside the Komodo Marine Park, Sangeang's southern point disguises a fantastic dive. The upper levels of the bay are covered in hard and soft corals but the real excitement lies on the wall where you see such curiosities as colonial anemones. It bottoms out at 20 metres into a black sand seabed and at the base are masses of unusual critters like crinoids with ornate ghost pipefish and sea whips with gobies or tiny commensal shrimp. There are saron shrimp, frogfish and for the eagle-eyed, tiny boxer crabs hide under small rocks. Yet the biggest attraction are nudibranchs. Nicknamed 'butterflies of the sea', at the last count nearly 40 different species had been logged on a single dive.

◤6 Current City, Tatawa

🕐	**Depth**	16 m
🌓	**Visibility**	fair to good
🌀	**Currents**	none
🌊	**Dive type**	liveaboard

There are times when there aren't currents at Current City – it just depends on when you do the dive and how many times. However, whether the water is ripping or almost still, this is a great site. At slack times, you can see the walls are thick with sponges, soft corals and fans. Masses of brightly coloured crinoids hang on to them for dear life (they know what will come later) and curious morays poke their noses out from the wall. You might even spot a crocodilefish sitting on a ledge. An hour later, a second dive, and it's all changed. As you drift at speed along the wall, you see the barrel sponges are now quivering in the current. An eagle ray passes by so quickly you almost miss it, as does a small turtle, but schools of trevally and rainbow runners manage to keep pace.

◤7 Valerie's Rock/Pantai Merah

🕐	**Depth**	45 m
🌓	**Visibility**	fair to good
🌀	**Currents**	none
🌊	**Dive type**	liveaboard

This pinnacle, rumoured to be named after Valerie Taylor, is not far from the entrance to the Komodo National Park. A shallow bay encloses a sloping reef and a tower of rock rising from 30 metres to reach the surface. The site seems like perfection until you hit the water and find Komodo at its most temperamental. Temperatures can drop from a comfy 28°C to a brain-numbing 20°C in seconds. The currents can rip and if you're not careful you will be over the site and out the other side in moments. At other times, however, it can be the most impeccable dive in the world: calm, warm water and all sorts of weird and wonderful creatures such as leaffish, scorpionfish and sea hares. Bits of detritus turn out to be the solar-powered nudibranch, you can spot toxic fire urchins or a dozen mobula rays as they sail over your head – provided you're looking up at the time, of course.

Frogfish with his lure extended; the wall at Current City

8 Cannibal Rock

Depth	33 m
Visibility	fair to good
Currents	slight to strong
Dive type	liveaboard

Horseshoe Bay is within the Komodo Marine Park, at its most southerly point. Nestled between Rinca Island and Nusa Kode, the bay is now world famous for its incredible diversity. You name any small critter and it's bound to have been seen here. There are several dive sites but Cannibal Rock is the most famous for its all-round variety. The site is a sloping, submerged sea mound that can just about be seen from the surface. Rolling in over the rock feels a bit like rolling into a rainbow: the entire mound is luminescent, smothered in bright soft corals, olive green tubastrea corals, many-

coloured crinoids and iridescent sea apples. These animals are a member of the sea cucumber family, their round shape having a vague resemblance to red apples – until they poke their yellow and white tipped tentacles out to feed. They are extremely rare elsewhere. Then there's the macro life. Amongst the corals you can find frogfish, mushroom coral pipefish, seasnakes, tiny shrimps in bubble coral and orang-utan crabs. A lot of the more bizarre life is at great depth so it's easy to go into deco if you're not careful. Tiny pygmy seahorses are seen on pink gorgonians at 32 metres and toxic sea urchins cluster on the slopes beyond 30 metres. Night dives are a treat, where every tiny crustacean seems to come out and hitch a ride on another animal – squat lobsters sit on urchins and zebra

crabs on fire urchins. There is some pelagic life here too but visibility is variable so you may only see passing tuna. Minke whales are said to pass through the bay: you might only see a fin or fluke, but you'll certainly hear them calling.

Indonesia Dive log Komodo: Cannibal Rock

66 99 Whole gangs of fire urchins wandered over the slope, spines waving a warning. Carefully hovering, noses down, we spotted almost all of their commensal hitchhikers, Colman's shrimp, zebra crabs, tiny cardinals, then – at last – the miniature squat lobster.

North Sulawesi

Bizarrely shaped Sulawesi sits in the centre of the Indonesian archipelago but it's the tip of the far northern arm reaching towards the Philippines that has captured the hearts and minds of both scientists and divers. Way up on this narrow stretch of land are two destinations with the most incredible diving. Their styles are diametrically opposed yet complement each other perfectly.

This entire island is ringed with coral reef systems so it may seem odd that most dive centres are based around the northern city of Manado. However, there are good reasons why Manado Bay, the offshore islands and the coast that leads around to the Lembeh Straits have become diving hotspots. For a long time scientists believed that this small area contained the greatest marine biodiversity in the world and was at the heart of the Coral Triangle. Although research wasn't conclusive, exceptionally high levels of certain species had been noted. The underlying causes are, as always, location and sea currents. This top end of Sulawesi is swept by strong northeasterly currents that originate in the Pacific Ocean. In addition, many smaller counter currents bring in rich nutrients that feed and sustain the coral reefs, which in turn sustain all the fish and marine life.

Manado

Perhaps the most famous and certainly the most favoured destination for many divers is the Bunaken Marine Park, sitting just off Manado. Established in 1991, there are five islands inside the park zone. Coral gardens and steep walls are the main features, with good year-round visibility and comfortably warm waters. These conditions extend to the islands near Bangka just outside the park to the north.

▨9 Molas Wreck

🕐 **Depth**	39 m
◐ **Visibility**	fair to good
🌊 **Currents**	ripping
⬛ **Dive type**	day boat

Named the *Molas* Wreck after the nearest village, this ship is thought to be a Dutch cargo vessel that sunk in 1942. Regarded as an advanced dive due to the depth, what can actually make this a hard dive at times are the often extreme currents. You can go down the mooring line in perfectly still water only to find a complete change within minutes. It's worth it though as this is now a lovely artificial reef. The bow is at 24 metres, but it's best to head straight down to the propellers at 42 metres. These are heavily encrusted in coral and small sponges. The sides of the hull display good soft coral growth, as does what remains of the cabin. This is full of young fan corals so it's difficult to swim through, although it is

occupied by lots of young batfish. Many more are being cleaned at the bow where they can shelter from currents.

▨10 Lekuan I, II& III

🕐 **Depth**	25 m
◐ **Visibility**	fair to good
🌊 **Currents**	mild to strong
⬛ **Dive type**	day boat

The Lekuan dives sites sit along the inner curve of Bunaken's south coast and at the heart of the marine park. Lekuan means 'curves' or 'bends' and refers to the winding nature of the wall. No matter where you start the dive, the topography is similar all along the wall, consisting of a vertical drop coated in plenty of bright fans, sponges and soft corals. As you drop towards the bottom, there are small caverns where turtles take a break. They often have huge remoras sitting on their shells. Others swim up and down the wall, rising to the surface for a breath then coming back down. These guys are in great condition, with pristine, healthy shells. Eagle rays pass by and there are huge schools of midnight snappers. Napoleon wrasse are always about, along with blacktip and whitetip sharks, tuna and pufferfish. When it comes to smaller fish, it's the usual suspects like anthias, damselfish and butterflies.

◉ S11 Siladen

◉ **Depth**	17 m
◉ **Visibility**	fair to stunning
◉ **Currents**	none to mild
◉ **Dive type**	day boat

The reef at Siladen is a consistently excellent and beautiful dive. The sloping wall is thick with hard and soft corals and decorated by enormous clouds of ever-present pyramid butterflyfish. The currents are rarely strong so there is plenty of time to pause and look for smaller creatures. Inside the blue vase sponges are tiny white crabs that are almost impossible to spot, so stick with your divemaster who will point these out. Scorpionfish hide in sponges too, their skin textures mimicking the surfaces around them. There are a variety of nudibranchs crawling over the wall and munching on the tunicates. Out in the blue you might spot a passing eagle ray or a small turtle. In the shallows huge swathes of leather corals compete with brain and staghorns, untold numbers of anemones and clownfish and many anthias and chromis.

◉ S12 Mandolin

◉ **Depth**	33 m
◉ **Visibility**	good to excellent
◉ **Currents**	slight to strong
◉ **Dive type**	day boat

Situated in the passage between Bunaken and Manado Tua, this is one of the area's more impressive dives. A sharp drop-off leads to a wall completely covered in soft corals and tunicates. It is a riot of colour that almost makes you forget you are under water. In the depths, there are big gorgonian fans and barrel sponges. Narrow shelves display long whip corals growing out in parallel rows to the light. (Rumour has it that someone once thought these looked like mandolin strings.) Turtles and Napoleon wrasse swim past in the blue while on the wall you find masses of interesting smaller animals such as balls of catfish. There are white leaffish at the top of the reef and if you spend some time hunting around the bommies, there are orang-utan crabs, robust ghost pipefish and squat lobsters in a crinoid.

◉ S13 Sahaong, Bangka

◉ **Depth**	33 m
◉ **Visibility**	good to excellent
◉ **Currents**	mild to strong
◉ **Dive type**	day boat

Marked by an underwater pinnacle that dramatically breaks the surface, the surge and currents here can be challenging but the landscape beneath the water makes it unmissable. Dropping down to the wall, you pass a phenomenal number of fish. The current is doing a bit of a dance and attracts a school of midnight snappers in from the blue until a whitetip shark buzzes them and they take off. After time on the pinnacle, it's up to a plateau covered in huge step-like boulders with everything carpeted in the most stunning soft corals. The whole thing is a riot of colour, glowing in tones of red, orange and yellow. A little further around the bend, you encounter a whip coral, thick with waving razorfish, then a tiny fan, which has an even tinier pygmy seahorse on it. The smaller creatures add a bit of scale to all the big things around.

Indonesia Dive log North Sulawesi: Manado

◉ This is what diving is all about

It was our first trip to Indonesia and the diving surpassed anything we had ever seen... We spent four days diving the reefs of Bangka and a week around Bunaken. At Bangka the dives were vibrant with vivid soft corals reaching up to the surface. The reef was packed with activity: Moorish idols, emperor angels, butterflies, crocodilefish, scorpions, razorfish and particularly attractive anemonefish guarding their homes. At Batamundi the sheer numbers of fish amidst the beautiful corals were too much for my maximum log book ratings and the comment in it, which reads 'this is what diving is all about', sums it up best.

Our first dive at Bunaken had a lot to live up to, but it was more than ready. The trip across to the marine park was just stunning, with Manado Tua growing as we approached. Dive 1 was to be at Lekuan 1. We descended onto a huge reef wall full of corals and only moments later resting on a crevice was the biggest turtle we have ever seen. We passed by slowly thinking how lucky we were, only to see another and then another. A slight current pushed us through 1000's of pyramid butterflyfish while above, a Napoleon wrasse passed by and towards the bright blue a school of fusiliers darted around shimmering in the sun. Amazing.

This holiday in Indonesia went by far too fast. It was so good that we went back the following year and we just can't wait to visit again. Just beautiful.

Mike and Samantha Muir, Warwickshire, England

Bignose unicornfish (left); frogfish nestled in a Bangka sponge

Lembeh Straits

While many places like to claim they are best of this or that, world famous, world class, there is no doubt that this small stretch of water is actually the best at what it is: a muck diving paradise. The Lembeh Straits deliver what they promise. This is the destination for seeing the weird, unusual and normally unseen marine critters.

The narrow and dark Lembeh Straits have become a 'must' for marine biology enthusiasts. With Sulawesi to the west and Lembeh Island on the east, the narrow channel between is riddled with dive sites fed by rich, volcanic nutrients. This is by no means pretty diving; visibility is always low, but it is one of the few places where you can be guaranteed sightings of some of the world's most unusual animals. You really can say 'seahorse' to a divemaster and they will ask "What type?" Although muck diving made the area's reputation there is also some nice wall diving and a couple of Second World War wrecks.

⌖14 Angel's Window

🕙 **Depth**	24 m
◑ **Visibility**	fair to good
🌊 **Currents**	slight to strong
🚤 **Dive type**	day boat

This is such a pretty dive, with so much variety you can understand why it is one of the most popular. Based around a pinnacle with two peaks, and linked by a sandslope, the visibility can be as much as 15 metres, not bad for the Straits. At times the currents can become strong, especially across the sandy area, but there are plenty of places to get away from it. The plan is always the same: descend over the wall then down to the cave – the Angel's Window – and through to the base of the pinnacle. There are fans on either side of the exit and these have the barbiganti pygmy seahorse on one and the miniature Denise pygmy on the other. Ascending past these, you can spend some time on the slope. There are small patches of coral and some rocks so look around these for leaffish, orang-utan crabs, imperial shrimp, whip corals and their resident gobies. There are even squid eggs on the sand. Around the bend of the reef there is a small wall which leads to a rocky area covered in a purple hue – this is made by sergeant major eggs and there are untold sergeant majors trying to defend them against the onslaught of butterflyfish. (Curiously, this has happened on every dive we have done here across a period of 12 years.) Huge scorpionfish also perch on these boulders.

⌖15 Police Pier

🕙 **Depth**	21 m
◑ **Visibility**	fair
🌊 **Currents**	slight
🚤 **Dive type**	day boat

As its name implies this site lies below the pier used by the police. A gentle slope is covered with alternating patches of algae, sponges and piles of rubble. It is a great dive site for finding thorny seahorses which use finger sponges as their home patch. Likewise, masses of frogfish utilize the small rounded sponges. It's hard to remember how many small froggies you have seen, as there are so many different shapes and sizes. At night, there is a variety of shells, snake eels in the sand, decorator crabs, squat lobsters, dragonets, tiny bobtail squid or banded seasnake. Banggai cardinalfish are common too, despite being indigenous to the Banggai islands some way south. The story goes that a fisherman had a cargo hold full of them bound (illegally) for the aquarium trade. The police got wind of this and pulled the captain over to the pier. He moored up and promptly dropped his cargo into the sea, and of course the Banggais colonized right where they were dropped.

Lembeh Straits soft corals; the Banggai cardinal

⬐16 Jahir

🕙	**Depth**	16 m
◐	**Visibility**	fair
🌊	**Currents**	none to medium
🛥	**Dive type**	day boat

Jahir is one of the divemasters' favourites, a fabulous hop from one 'pet critter' to the next; so much so that a dive log looks like a fish ID list: cockatoo waspfish, juvenile cuttlefish, dwarf and juvenile scorpionfish, tiny stonefish, thorny seahorses, mating crabs, hairy crabs, decorator crabs, flying gurnards, flounder, frogfish in many hues and varieties, *Inimicus* (or devilfish), robust ghost pipefish and the Pegasus seamoth. At night the site is even better as nocturnal creatures emerge – free-swimming snake eels, moon snails and tiny shells trucking across the sand, and masses of crabs. This is also a known nursery site for flamboyant cuttlefish with newly laid eggs often found inside coconut shells. Jahir is also a good spot for the mimic octopus.

⬐17 Hairball

🕙	**Depth**	25 m
◐	**Visibility**	poor to fair
🌊	**Currents**	none
🛥	**Dive type**	day boat

Hairball is all about the ways animals try to remain hidden. The seabed is level with black sand in every direction. There is a lot of fine silt (watch your fins!) and almost no landmarks but it is the place to go to find hairy critters. Some grow skin filaments so they can hide in small patches of algae; others use the muck or each other as camouflage: fire urchins reveal zebra crabs while other crabs carry urchins on their backs. A tiny octopus will be spotted with just his eyes poking out of a tin, a snake eel has a shrimp living on his nose, a coconut crab will be wrapped in three clam shells. And then there are the hairy creatures: frogfish that are fishing constantly and the Ambon scorpionfish who is even harder to spot than hairy ghost pipefish.

Critters from Lembeh, clockwise: the inimicus or devilfish; hairy frogfish; pygmy seahorse; flamboyant cuttlefish feeding; mating mandarinfish; mimic octopus; rhinopias; ornate ghost pipefish

One of the newer Indonesian regions to come under diving scrutiny is the western end of New Guinea. Officially known as West Papua but often called Irian Jaya, these waters are as remote as anywhere can be, yet are surprisingly easy to reach.

The eastern tip of West Papua is the Bird's Head Peninsula and lying offshore are a group of islands known as Raja Ampat, or the Four Kings. This lovely archipelago consists of over 1,500 small islands, cays and shoals. When the reefs around them were surveyed a few years back by a group of Australian scientists, their research registered the world's highest counts of corals, molluscs and crustaceans.

Not long after their reports hit the press a whole new dive industry developed. However, the momentum didn't stop with that one survey. Raja Ampat's reefs have been monitored frequently since and the numbers appear to rise with every new report. One of the most recent noted some 1,200 species of fish plus dozens of unrecorded species, including the headline hitting 'walking' sharks. Almost 600 species, around 75% of the world's known total of reef-building corals have been identified in this small area.

With the Halmahera Sea and Pacific Ocean lapping the northern edges and the Ceram Sea to the south, this is an incredibly diverse area and while many others regions promote high diversity, there is no doubt that West Papua has something of an edge. Conditions are variable, like anywhere in Indonesia, but never difficult enough to be off-putting even for novice divers.

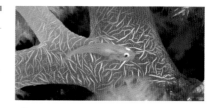

⑱ P47 Wreck, Jerien Island

🧭	**Depth**	35 m
👁	**Visibility**	good to stunning
🌊	**Currents**	mild
⚓	**Dive type**	liveaboard

On 2 October, 1944 two American fighter squadrons, the 310 and 311, took off from their base at Noemfoor Island near the city of Biak. Their mission was to attack a Japanese fleet thought to be near Ambon Bay but, on arrival, they discovered that the reports had been misleading. After strafing a few enemy craft they decided to return to the closest base: 310 Squadron landed at Middleburg but 311 was caught in bad weather; they flew until they ran out of fuel and were forced to ditch near Jerien Island. All seven crew were rescued. There are now two plane wrecks sitting on the base of the reef; one belonged to flight leader, Steven O'Benner (P47D-21), the second was element leader Kenneth J Crepeau's (P47D-16) although no one is sure which is which. One plane is deeper and not easily accessible, while the other is upside down at 30 metres. It is virtually intact and covered in light coral growth.

⑲ Manta Reef, Jerien Island

🧭	**Depth**	8 m
👁	**Visibility**	good to stunning
🌊	**Currents**	medium to strong
⚓	**Dive type**	liveaboard

As the boat approaches this reef the crew watch for wing flaps and the race is on to see if there are mantas. As you drop into the water the smaller ones are flying right beneath the dive tender. The current rips across the plateau, pulling divers away from the entry point but in the same direction as the mantas. There is little coral so the strategy is to find some dead rock and use a reef hook to stay still. Waiting for just a few minutes is usually enough for them to return. Larger ones sit still, feeding in the current (no hooks required by them). You can creep closer but need to be cautious as these animals are still wary of visitors.

SJ20 Melissa's Garden

Depth	25 m	
Visibility	fair	
Currents	can be strong	
Dive type	day boat/liveaboard	

Melissa's is a flat, oval-shaped reef topped by three small rock islands. The entire area is coated in hard coral outcrops with small soft corals, masses of crinoids and fish – although fish in the singular is something of an understatement when it comes to describing the substantial numbers here. Sandy-bottomed edges are smothered in garden eels and rocky areas are home to octopus. Peek under a hard coral head to find a juvenile batfish still displaying his orange rims. Further along are snapper and sweetlips, whitetip sharks, a turtle and one huge barracuda being tailed by a school of small ones. There are plenty of smaller animals too, including imperial shrimp, mushroom coral pipefish and a juvenile rock mover wrasse. This is also a good site for spotting wobbegong sharks. Tuna swim by out in the blue and banded seasnakes appear around every outcrop.

SJ21 Kawe Castle and the Keep

Depth	31 m	
Visibility	fair to good	
Currents	none	
Dive type	liveaboard	

Kawe Island sits right on the Equator and much is made of the fact that you can moor in the southern hemisphere and dive in the north. The area is noted for its dramatic underwater pinnacles. Approaching this circular, straight-sided seamount you are met by forbidding walls that rise like castle walls topped with battlements. A gouge cutting through the outcrop is filled with midnight snappers. At its mouth, a bright pink fan houses a whole family of pygmy seahorses. Descending to the base, a complete circuit reveals a small cave. This dungeon has a tiny exit higher up the wall. Batfish patrol outside like sentries while masses of small fish cower in black coral bushes. The sheer walls are tempered by corals and crinoids, marbled dragonets, nudis and flatworms. Another sharp knife cut in the wall is packed full of soldierfish and a lone barramundi cod.

SJ22 The island with no name

Depth	32 m	
Visibility	good	
Currents	mild	
Dive type	liveaboard	

A few feet from the Equator, this beautiful island has, rather surprisingly, no name. The dive site starts on a steep wall and at its base there is a deep cave to explore. At the rear are flame fire shells that reveal an electric current running through their tentacles. Back out on the wall a tiny fan houses the Denise pygmy seahorse. The wall itself is smooth-sided with sponges, crusting algae and tiny corals. It flattens to a ridge beneath the limestone cliff where the rocky topography is barren. Amongst the boulders are some unusual creatures like Paguritta hermit crabs and blue-ringed octopus. This dive can be done at night, when the wall comes alive with nocturnal crustaceans and nudibranchs. Psychedelic bobtail squid nestle on the wall beside decorator crabs. It's easy to enter the cave accidentally so be careful! Back on the top, cuttlefish feed in the shallow waters.

Indonesia Dive log West Papua

A wobbegong shark on Melissa's; batfish on sentry duty; Raja Ampat soft corals

Spice Islands

Several hundred years ago Ambon and Banda were the most important islands on the planet, the lone source of a commodity that, per ounce, was worth more than gold: nutmeg.

The fabled Spice Islands were so vital to16th and 17th century trade they sparked many battles between Europe's great seafaring powers. Now though, they are visited for their mountainous rainforest interiors and incredibly diverse coastal waters. Ambon is an oddly-shaped land mass almost divided into two halves; the water in between is known as Amboyna Bay and it was this harbour that first attracted divers. However, these days more dive operators are exploring further afield and the tiny Banda islands, dominated by the towering presence of active Gunung Api, are opening to dive tourism.

The marine ecosystem in this developing region is close to pristine with mostly easy conditions. In season, the seas tend to be calm and currents are fairly mild when they do occur. Really strong currents are rare but those dives are often delayed until things settle down.

ⓝ23 Laha I, II & III, Ambon

🕐	**Depth**	up to 42 m
◐	**Visibility**	stunning
🌊	**Currents**	none to strong
🌊	**Dive type**	liveaboard

Also known as the Twighlight Zone, these are the dive sites that first made Ambon hit the diver radar as the critter life rivals the more famous Lembeh Straits. A sloping seabed drops away from the shoreline to reveal a series of small bommies that house frogfish and leaffish. The slope leads past eels, shrimp, crabs, even a saron shrimp and thorny seahorses while nearby there are a whole load of mandarinfish skittering about even in the daylight. By sunset, they are mating. If you drop to the 40 metre mark, you will find rhinopias but there are also fire urchins with their hitchhiking zebra crabs and Coleman shrimp. Coming back up the slope you can encounter seahorses,

puffers, tiny trunkfish, dwarf cuttlefish and a miniature yellow mantis shrimp. Other easy spots are pipehorses, the inimicus, stonefish, dwarf lionfish, ornate ghost pipefish and lots of different morays.

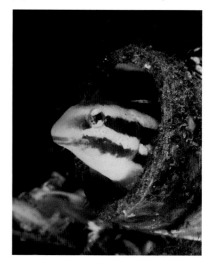

ⓝ24 Amet, Nusa Laut

🕐	**Depth**	25 m
◐	**Visibility**	excellent
🌊	**Currents**	slight
🌊	**Dive type**	liveaboard

Due east of Ambon is the small island of Nusa Laut. Local villagers actively protect their reefs from outside fishermen and it shows – Amet's are pristine. An underwater promontory drops down to a sandy slope coated with whip corals. This is edged on either side by a flat sand bar. A gang of bumphead parrotfish hang near the edge of the sand bar and just beyond are two gigantic schools of jacks. The number of fish is phenomenal. They seem unafraid of divers, continuing to move together and apart, swimming in perfect synchronicity. The shallows reveal bluespotted rays, beds of garden eels, dancing razorfish and mantis shrimp. The reef slopes are coated in good hard corals which harbour creatures such as tomato clownfish and shrimp in an anemone, and if you pause above these, you may see a spotted eagle ray pass by.

ⓝ25 Mandarin City, Banda Neira

🕐	**Depth**	18 m
◐	**Visibility**	poor to fair
🌊	**Currents**	none to slight
🌊	**Dive type**	liveaboard

The most famous dive in the Banda islands is right under the jetty in Banda Harbour. This amazing muck dive can be brilliant in daylight but dusk is the time to see the mandarinfish. Described as 'mandarins on steroids', these little beauties are larger than any you will see in other places, even neighbouring Ambon. Entry is over a dark sand bottom with low visibility: currents running between Gunung Api and Banda Neira are not strong but fast enough to stir up the silty seabed. At depth you can search for, and will find, Colman's shrimp and squat lobsters on fire urchins. Back up the slope a little, and hiding in anything they can find are banded pipefish, coral banded shrimp, the jewelled blenny, snowflake morays, razorfish, octopus and juvenile butterflies. There is much more – this site is prolific.

Corals at Nusa Laut; above, fang blenny in a bottle

Drying out

Bali

Right across the island there is an array of dive operators, hotels and resorts. Many target a specific nationality – check this to ensure you get a suitable operator. Some hotels have on-site dive operations but that doesn't obligate you to use them.

South coast
Dive Centres

AquaMarine Diving – Bali, T+62 (0)361 730107, aquamarinediving.com. Bali's only British-owned and managed dive shop is in Seminyak. First-class service, full client insurance and great dive guides. They will organize accommodation, tailor-made land excursions and round-island dive tours.

Blue Season Bali, T+62 (0)361 282574, baliocean.com. Spacious boat and a good location in Sanur for easy access to Nusa Penida. Customized safaris around the island. Also located at Zen Resort in North Bali, zenresortbali.com.

Sleeping

$$$ The Elysian, Seminyak, T+62 (0)361 730999, theelysian.com. At the far end of the Kuta-Seminyak beach strip in a quiet location. Fantastic boutique-style villas, each with a private pool. Just back from the beach near many higher-end facilities.

$$ Tamukami, Sanur, T+62 (0)361 282510, tamukamibali.com. Charming, small hotel in Sanur with large rooms in tropical gardens that surround a free-form pool. On-site is **Alise's Restaurant** with delicious, well-priced local and international food.

Other options

Patra Bali Resort, Kuta, patra-jasa.com
Poppies Cottages, Kuta, poppiesbali.com

Eating

From über-trendy to cheap and cheerful, you could never want for a restaurant in the south of Bali. Fabulously trendy **Ku De Ta** in Seminyak has incredible fusion food and breathtaking sunsets. Just along the beach is **Tekor** with genuine Balinese food. Or you could head down to Jimbaran Beach for exquisite, unbelievably cheap seafood at the open-air **Jimbaran Seafood Café**.

East Coast
Sleeping

$$ The Watergarden, Candidasa, T+62 (0)363 41540, watergardenhotel.com. Peaceful and charming hotel; each room has a deck that sits over a magnificent koi carp pond and is surrounded by private 'jungle' gardens. Great restaurant as well.

$$ Mimpi Resorts, in both Tulamben and Menjangen, T+62 (0)363 21642, mimpi.com. The original divers' resort in Tulamben and just south of the *Liberty* wreck. Their resort at Menjangen is opposite the National Park.

Other options

Alila Manggis, Candidasa, alilahotels.com
Anda Amed, Amed, andaamedresort.com

North coast
Sleeping

$$$–$ Taman Sari Bali, Pemuteran Bay, T+62 (0)362 94755, balitamansari.com. Garden hotel with both budget cottages and high-end villas. The restaurant is very good. Bali Diving Academy are on site.

Bali

Although much developed in the south, Bali has a beautiful landscape, distinctive culture and is world-famous for its crafts, art, dance and music. The town of **Ubud** is the cultural heartland, full of art galleries, music and retail therapy to die for. Make sure you catch a traditional dance which represents the everlasting struggle between good and evil. Inland, the **Kintamani** region of volcanoes and crater lakes is surrounded by deep green rice paddies, while at **Lake Bratan** is mystical Pura Ulun Danau, one of Bali's most beautiful temples. **Tanah Lot**, the island's most important temple, is built on a rocky outcrop overlooking the sea. It is just half an hour from Kuta and is worth seeing – although busy – at sunset. For a little history, visit the **Bali Aga** village at Tenganen. The Aga, the island's inhabitants before the arrival of Hindu Javanese, retain ancient customs by allowing only minimal contact with outsiders. The **Bali Barat National Park** covers woodlands and coastal areas and houses some of Bali's resident wildlife including rare birds, monkeys and iguanas.

The Balinese are Agama Hindus, an ancient religion influenced by many things including Indian Hinduism. For travellers, religion seems ever present, interwoven with daily life through offering rituals. Festivals are just as prevalent: it is said there is a **Balinese festival** every day of the year – somewhere – as they are the essence of Balinese life. If you hear of one, go: etiquette requires you to stand politely back, but tourists are not resented.

Sleeping **$$$** US$150+ double room per night   **$$** US$75-150   **$** under US$75
Eating **$$$** US$40+ 2-course meal, excluding drinks   **$$** US$20-40   **$** under US$20

Komodo

If you are travelling to Komodo or any of the Nusa Tengarra islands, the best option is to go by liveaboard as dive facilities, apart from on Lombok, are limited.

Liveaboards

Archipelago Adventurer II, T+62 (0)361 282369, archipelago-fleet.com. Top-class vessel with British-American management. Trendy, extra-spacious cabins, with large picture windows, smart ensuites and desks for the all photography and computer kit. Highly knowledgeable guides and a variety of regional routes. Great meals too.

Dive Damai, T+62 (0)361 281311, dive-damai.com. New vessel custom-built by a well respected team that have worked in Indonesia for many years. Large boat but with only four luxury cabins.

Kararu, T+62 (0)361 282931, kararu.com. Company has a long-standing pedigree in the region, with a great crew, food and management. Their new boat, a phinisi schooner is, by all accounts, spacious, very comfortable and with good facilities.

Other options

As Indonesia's most sailed route, there are many operators from budget to luxury. Remember that vessels that cost more will be of a higher quality – ask enough questions to ensure your choice has the right facilities (see page 8). Check out:

Baruna Adventurer, komodo-divencruise.com

Bidadari, kmbidadari-cruises.com

Komodo Dancer, peterhughes.com

Mona Lisa, monalisacruises.com

Seven Seas, thesevenseas.net

North Sulawesi

This region has many accommodation options from budget to top class. Most resorts are self-contained, meaning they have a dive operator, restaurant, pool and other facilities inside the complex. This tends to be a land-based region.

Manado

Dive resorts

$$ Cocotinos Resort, T+62 (0)812 430 8800, cocotinos.com. Located in a picturesque bay, this resort has beautifully decorated rooms and very personal service from the staff and the crew in the dive centre: hand over your kit, everything is done for you. Opposite the marine park, it's only a short ride to the dive sites. Great value packages.

$$ Seaside Resort Santika & Dive Centre Thalassa, T+62 (0)431 850230, thalassa.net. Located opposite Bunaken, this 4-star hotel has modern rooms with views over Manado Tua. On site is 5-star PADI **Dive Centre Thalassa**, a professional Dutch-run operation with fantastic facilities and friendly guides. This is a great place to do a course.

Other options

Kima Bajo, kimabajo.com

Murex Dive Resorts, murexdive.com

TwoFishDivers, TwoFishDivers.com

Lembeh Straits

Dive Resorts

$$$-$$ Kungkungan Bay Resort, T+62

(0)438 30300, kungkungan.com. The American-owned resort that 'discovered' diving in the Lembeh Straits. Now larger and busier but still charming and with great shore diving. Rooms are spacious.

$$ Lembeh Resort, T+62 (0)438 550 0139, lembehresort.com. Sitting on the slopes of Lembeh Island, this is a relaxed, friendly resort. Bungalows are built onto the hillside to capture the cool breezes and have fantastic views of the strait. Diving is run by **Murex** with very knowledgeable guides.

Other options

Black Sand Dive Retreat, blacksanddive.com

Kasawari Lembeh, kasawari-lembeh.com

West Papua and the Spice Islands

Facilities are limited in these far flung corners, but the good news is that what is there – be it hotels, dive centres or liveaboards – is of a very good calibre.

Liveaboards

Archipelago Adventurer II, archipelago-fleet.com, **Kararu**, kararu.com and **Dive Damai**, Dive-damai.com all sail this area according to season. Reviews above.

Diving and sleeping

Kri Eco Resort and Sorido Bay Resort, iriandiving.com. On Kri Island near Sorong.

Misool Eco Resort, misoolecoresort.com. On Misool island in south Raja Ampat.

Maluku Divers, divingmaluku.com. The only land-based dive resort in Ambon.

CocoTinos Resort, Manado; Archipelago Adventurer in Banda; the Komodo Dragon

 Sleeping $$$ US$150+ double room per night $$ US$75-150 $ under US$75

Eating $$$ US$40+ 2-course meal, excluding drinks $$ US$20-40 $ under US$20

Indonesia Drying out

Komodo

Everyone goes to the National Park to see the Komodo dragons. These enormous, ugly beasties are not to be trifled with – a park ranger will escort you to the feeding station. The world's largest monitor lizard grows to over three metres and weighs up to 165 kg. With huge jaws, squat muscular legs and sharp claws they prey on live deer, goats and wild pigs. Youngsters spend their time in trees but adults cannot climb so hunt from the long grass. Solo treks are not encouraged.

North Sulawesi

Not as culturally rich as Bali, there is still plenty to explore in this area. The Minahasa Highlands are covered with spice trees and rice fields, local villages specialize in pottery or traditional house building. **Airmadidi** is a fascinating site where an ancient cemetery is full of Waruga, tombs dating back to the ninth century. Carved stone chambers are hollowed out and corpses placed inside in a sitting position. The triangular lids display motifs indicating the sex and status of the

occupants. **Lake Tondano** lies 2,000 ft above sea level in the Lambean Mountains. The area is lush with paddy fields. **Lake Linow** is a beautiful but strange lake, which changes colour from red to green and sometimes blue. There are hot springs and many birds in the park surrounding this peaceful stop. **Bukit Kasih** or the 'Hill of Love' was built around a steaming, sulphorous series of hot springs, and billed as a spiritual epicenter for followers of different faiths to commune and worship in open air. However, the most visited area in the region is the **Tangkoko Rainforest**, right on the Lembeh Straits. This spectacular area is home to rare species of monkeys, birds, butterflies and the tarsius – the smallest primate in the world.

Spice Islands

With such a rich and incredible history, there is much to see in the Spice Islands. **Ambon** city has lively market areas near the harbour; there are cemeteries dedicated to those who fought in the Second World War and memorials like the one dedicated to freedom

fighter **Martha Christina Tiahahu** which looms over the town. **Victoria Fort** was built by the Portuguese in 1575, the huge walls facing the bay are still preserved while parts of the interior now lay in ruins. The **Siwalima Museum** is a charming but old-fashioned museum which aims to preserve all aspects of local heritage. Banda's **Nutmeg Plantations** are still its main source of wealth because nutmeg trees grow here naturally. Tours with a master horticulturist are quite something, as he picks the nuts off the trees and peels them apart, explaining the riches inside. **Banda Neira Town** is an absolute must-see. In front of the Maulana Hotel there is a collection of swivel guns and memorabilia. The town streets are lined with wooden Dutch colonial houses and some are being renovated – the small town **museum** is in one. The now deserted **governor's palace** can be seen but the most overwhelming sight is **Fort Belgica**, which hovers ominously over the town. This pentagonal structure has far-reaching views.

Manado Tua; Banda Neira town; just picked nutmegs

Singapore

Southeast Asia's Lion City is an amazing place for a stopover, to acclimatize to the heat and lifestyle of this tropical continent. Changi Airport is without doubt one of the best and most efficient in the world, and the city itself is a fabulous amalgamation of cultures and colours. Start with a trip to **Chinatown** to investigate this historic area with its temples, gardens and great street market. Stop for lunch before walking up to **Clarke Quay** on the Singapore River. Old 'bumboats' ply the river so hop on for a short cruise, ending at the mouth of the river where you can view the **Merlion** statue, Singapore's mascot.

Next, cross over to the **Singapore Flyer** for a bird's-eye view from the 42-storey-high ferris wheel. Then head to **Orchard Road** for some retail therapy, but beware – it's a long road. Finally, end the day at the city's most famous landmark, **Raffles Hotel**. Step into the bar and billiard room for a Singapore Sling and,

if late, stay for dinner too. The evening buffet is incredible. If you have a second day there's also **Sentosa Island**, a 'theme' park of sorts but with an aquarium that's worth seeing: you can even dive in the shark tank! Plus there's a great zoo and night safari, a bird park and the botanical gardens, Little India, museums and so much more.

Sleeping
$$$ **Novotel**, novotel.com
$$ **Albert Court**, albertcourt.com.sg
$$ **Gallery Hotel**, galleryhotel.com.sg
Transport
Clean, quick and cheap, transport includes buses, the MRT (metro) and metred taxis. Pick up a map as you arrive at Changi.

Philippines

Just passing through: the hawksbill
turtle, *Eretmochelys imbricata,*
displaying the claws on his fore-fins.
Apo Point, Mindoro

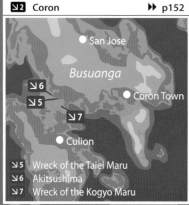

3 Tubbataha ▶▶ p154

Tubbataha Reef North Atoll

↘8 Shark Airport
↘9 Eiger Wall
↘10 Black Rock, South Atoll
↘8
↘9
↘10

Tubbataha Reef South Atoll

4 Panglao ▶▶ p155

Tagbilaran ●

↘14
Panglao
↘12
Balicasag
↘11
↘13

↘11 Alona Beach Sanctuary
↘12 Arco Point
↘13 Blackforest
↘14 Pungtud

5 Dumaguete ▶▶ p156

Negros
↘15
Dauin ●
↘16
↘17

↘15 El Dorado Reef
↘16 Dauin
↘17 Masa Plod Sanctuary
↘18 Coconut Point
↘18

Apo Island

PACIFIC OCEAN

The islands of the Philippines are surrounded by the second largest expanse of water inside the Coral Triangle, forming its northern apex. The rich marine biodiversity here has only recently been acknowledged. The country may be just a short hop away from more popular routes for well-heeled divers but it should come as no surprise that the numbers of coral and fish species rank as high as anywhere else, even competing with neighbouring Indonesia.

The variety of diving can be outstanding. Sandwiched between the Pacific and the South China Seas, the reefs are tantalizing: thick with tropical fish and colourful gardens of coral. In some areas there is a wealth of unusual small marine animals, while in others there are swarms of pelagics or the chance to explore a fleet of Second World War wrecks.

Considered something of an enigma, above the waves outlying island destinations retain a charming sense of the past. Idyllic sea views are interrupted only by rows of brightly painted *bancas* – traditional timber and bamboo outriggers – lined up awaiting the next day's quota of divers. It would be hard to beat the romance of sitting at night under a coconut palm on a snow-white Filipino beach, cool sand between your toes and wondering what the next day will bring.

Introduction

Philippines

Philippines rating

Diving
★★★★★

Dive facilities
★★★

Accommodation
★★★

Down time
★★★

Value for money
★★★★

Getting there and around

Philippine Airlines once had an extensive network that went right around the world. Now though, their long haul flights are principally from America or Australia. Other flights are likely to be a code share with another airline. Most frequent is probably Singapore Airlines but there are also flights with Asiana (flyasiana.com), Northwest, Qatar and many others. All these deposit travellers in Manila on a regular basis. Silk Air (silkair.com) and Qatar have flights to Cebu City located in the central Visayas.

For those already in Asia, low cost carrier Jetstar (jetstar.com) flies to Manila; Tiger Airways (tigerairways.com) and Air Asia (airasia.com) fly to Clark Airport three hours' drive north of Manila. Philippine Airlines (philippineairlines.com) and Cebu Pacific (cebupacific.com) both have good regional and internal networks although there are several other airlines also. Between them they can get you almost anywhere but internal trips between the islands can often be easily achieved by ferry or fast catamarans (oceanjet.net). Note that their schedules change frequently.

One of the peculiarities of Filipino dive trips is that hotels and operators rarely include transfers from the airport. This is because they usually involve a small hop on a ferry to another island. However, you will be given full instructions and advice.

Local taxis are cheap and the drivers helpful, ensuring you reach the first available ferry as sometimes an extra one will have been added or, in low season, stopped. In the cities there are ultra-colourful, but crowded, jeepney buses – you will probably find taxis a better option.

Local laws and customs

This is a deeply religious land though it's easy to forget that as you stand beneath a city skyline obliterated by posters depicting American movies, pop stars and mobile phone companies. Move your eyes just a little to see that the rest of the horizon is lined with churches. The Philippines were a Spanish colony for 350 years and 85% of the country is Catholic. The country was sold to America in 1898 for US$20 million, remaining a US possession for 50 years. The American influence seems dominant on the surface but deep down the Filipino nature is devout. Outside Manila or Cebu, life is more relaxed with fewer Western influences. Remember to be respectful but otherwise there are no specific dress codes or courtesies to be observed.

Safety

When it comes to safety, geography is all important. All government advisories warn against travel to Mindanao and the Sulu Archipelago (Basilan, Tawi-Tawi and Jolo). These very southern islands are the base

Philippines	
Location	13°00'N, 122°00'E
Capital	Manila
Population	96,976,603
Land area in km²	298,170
Coastline in km	36,289

for the extremist Muslim Abu Sayyaf group, so should be avoided. The good news is that the dive regions included here are over an hour's flight from Mindanao and have been mostly unaffected by political problems.

There have been isolated terrorist actions throughout the country, including in Manila, so before wandering off from your hotel get some local advice. Having said that, the risk is probably no worse than in any major city: don't carry valuables around especially after dark, don't leave a bag unattended and don't move away from well lit and well populated areas. Once you are on the islands, it is extremely unlikely that you will find anything to trouble you; even petty crime is minimal as it really doesn't sit well with the people's religious nature. What also doesn't sit well is any form of drug use and the penalties are severe.

Language

Despite the centuries of Spanish domination, English is actually the language of the Philippines and is spoken by pretty much the entire nation. The national language, Filipino, is a derivative of Tagalog, the most widely spoken indigenous language. If you ask any divemaster what they speak, they look at you quizzically then usually come up with Tagalog. Here are a few words:

hello	kumusta	thank you	salamat po
goodbye	paalam	sorry!	paumanhin po!
welcome	mabuhay	how much is...	magkano...
yes	o-o	good	mabait
no	hindi	great dive!	tamang sisid!
I don't know	di ko alam	one beer/water	
please	paki		isa pa pong beer/tubig

Health

Healthcare facilities depend on where you are. Manila has plenty and the islands have fewer and of varying standards. However, health risks are generally low. AIDs is spreading, as is the sex trade, so be wary. There are insect borne diseases but these tend to be in remote, hilly regions rather than on the coast. Malaria is almost unheard of in the Visayas but is a problem in Palawan. Water can be an issue. Some hotels will have purified tap water but check before drinking on the islands. Some still have only brackish water so you will know straight away not to drink that.

Costs

Travelling in the Philippines is very good value. Accommodation options vary both by cost and quality. There are few resorts that rank over four star – most tend to be in the two to three star range, yet in some places it's easy to find small, pleasant cottages

Fact file

International flights	Cebu Pacific, Philippine Airlines, Qatar, Qantas, Singapore Airlines, Silk Air, United Airlines
Departure tax	US$18
Entry	EU, USA and Commonwealth – valid passport for stays up to 21 days
Internal flights	Asian Spirit, Cebu Pacific, South East Asian Air,
Ground transport	Jeepney buses, ferries and taxis
Money	US$1 = 47 pesos (PHP)
Language	English and Tagalog plus regional dialects
Electricity	220v, plus types A/C (see page 16)
Time zone	GMT +8
Religion	Roman Catholic
Phone	Country code +63; IDD code 00; Police 166

with rates so low it's hard to believe it. Naturally, these are simple and facilities can be basic. In more popular areas, standards are higher with a greater variety of hotel styles and price brackets. Most dive-specific resorts will be mid-range. Whatever you book, remember that their quality is reflected in the room rates so compare carefully.

The cost of food and drink can also be aligned to location. For example, at a simple beach bar, a local beer may be just under US$1 compared with an average of US$2, while in smarter resorts the cost will creep up to as much as US$4.

When it comes to tipping, most dive resorts and smaller hotels will simply leave a tips box on the reception desk. It's completely up to you if you leave something but rounding up the bill seems to be the done thing. High-end establishments may add a service charge of 10% and some show a government tax of 12%. In better restaurants tipping is the norm, at around 5-10%; in small ones, round up the bill. For drivers, guides and divemasters, see page 12.

Tourist information → The WOWPhilippines official websites can be found at wowphilippines.co.uk and .com.us, .com.sg, com.hk, .com.ca and philippinetourism.com.au.

Dive brief

Diving

Can you imagine a country with 7107 (or so) individual islands all ringed with coral reefs? That must be something like 70,000 dive sites to choose from. What a concept.

The Philippines are located within the Pacific's Ring of Fire and, just as significantly, make up a segment of the Coral Triangle. This imaginary boundary is bordered by nearby Indonesia, the Solomon Islands, Malaysian Borneo and the Philippines. Within this small space there are more marine species than anywhere else on the planet – more varieties of coral, more fish and more critters.

The Filipino islands have their fair share of this wealth and, in fact, new research indicates that the levels of diversity may be far higher than was previously thought. There are luxurious coral reefs, awesome walls, mysterious wrecks, critters by the bucket load and countless marine reserves. This is also a dive destination that once suffered from a reputation for serious fish bombing and environmental damage to the reefs. However, you will be surprised at the number of small exclusion bays that are patrolled by local villagers. The people have learnt the value of creating protected nursery grounds, if only to be able to fish beyond the no-go zones. There are also two UNESCO Biosphere Reserves and two World Heritage Sites.

Conditions are fairly easy going. The islands are naturally tidal and currents can be strong but dive centres sensibly divert to protected sites when necessary. Visibility is usually good; murkier in the shallows and crystal clear in oceanic open waters.

Snorkelling

For the non-diver who likes to join in the fun, the Philippines is a feast. Small reefs run right up to the beach, shallow drop-offs are protected and currents are fairly predictable. The water is warm and usually clear enough for surface huggers to still get a good peak below the water line.

Marine life

With so much diversity, you can safely assume that you will see a high variety of tropical species, both pelagic animals and reef-based fish and critters. However, a few dive regions in the Philippines are particularly seasonal with diving restricted to a few short months each year. Go out of season and you are likely to lose your diving. If you want to see something specific, check before you book.

Philippines
animal
encounters

Tubbataha	turtles and sharks
Puerto Galera	fish
The Visayas	critters

The first time we visited the Philippines, we would sit content at the end of each day and wonder why we had never considered this destination before. The diving was so good, we went back within a year just to see if it really was as good as we first thought. It wasn't – it was better. Another trip later, even better, yet we still know we need to go again.

Making the big decision

No matter where you go, the Philippines is a friendly, welcoming country with plenty to offer the travelling diver – not least a well established dive industry across a wide range of destinations. There are only a few liveaboards so to get a broader view of the country it's best to choose two slightly different destinations and build a two-centre holiday: a week of wrecks and one of macro say, or a liveaboard to an isolated atoll followed by a week at a more lively island resort. There are a variety of dive types in each area so if you simply want to kick back and relax in just one place, that will work too.

A much wider selection of Philippine destinations are reviewed in Diving Southeast Asia, see page 6 for details.

Dive data

Seasons	June to October, rainy; November to February, cool and dry; March to May, hot and dry; typhoon risk in May
Visibility	10–40 metres
Temperatures	Air 23°–32°C; water 25°–30°C
Wet suit	3 mm shorty or full body suit
Training	Courses available in most resorts, standards vary
Nitrox	Not easily available
Deco chambers	Manila, Batangas and Cebu

Bottom time

Mindoro	This northern island is just over two hours from Manila and is much loved by locals.
Puerto Galera ▸▸ p150	Bright, lively, well developed and well explored, this resort region has something for everyone from critters to wrecks.
Palawan	The western edge of the country is the access point for her two most unique dive regions.
Coron ▸▸ p152	One of the dive world's most interesting wreck destinations with many Second World War era ships sitting on the seabed.
Tubbataha ▸▸ p154	This isolated World Heritage Site in the middle of the Sulu Sea is the best in the Philippines for (almost) guaranteed big animals.
Visayas	More delicious white-sand-edged, coral-ringed islands than you can possibly imagine.
Panglao ▸▸ p155	A huge variety of dive sites – reefs, walls, steep drops, shallow bays and caverns surround the island of Panglao and white-sand Alona Beach.
Dumaguete ▸▸ p156	Doing its best to rival some of the world's best-known critter havens but with open ocean Apo Island close enough to vary the pace.

Diversity   reef area 25,060 km²

HARD CORALS	577
FISH SPECIES	2,986
ENDEMIC FISH SPECIES	120
FISH UNDER THREAT	76
PROTECTED REEFS/MARINE PARKS	52

All diversity figures are approximate

Mindoro

Puerto Galera

One of the Philippines' larger islands, Mindoro is divided from Luzon – location of capital Manila – by the Verde Island Passage. Some say this narrow body of water is the most biodiverse on the planet. You could be forgiven for blindly agreeing as you cross it accompanied by a pod of pilot whales and frolicking dolphins.

First colonised by Spanish explorers who realized that the deep natural harbour gave easy passage through the extensive coral reefs, northern Mindoro is now one of the most lively dive-tourism areas in the country.

These waters were first declared a marine reserve way back in the mid-1930s; in 1973, they became a UNESCO Man and Biosphere Reserve. A recent study by the International Union for Conservation of Nature indicates that this area may even be far richer than anyone imagined, with pointers to it having the highest marine biodiversity in Asia. However, the same study also states that the waters are under threat as the Verde Island Passage is one of the busiest shipping lanes in the country. Extremes of weather also conspire to cause damage to some of the shallow reefs, although from a diver's point of view this may not seem particularly obvious. Drop onto any dive site around the Puerto Galera promontory and it's soon clear that diversity here is high regardless.

↘1 Giant Clams	
🌀 **Depth**	17 m
🕐 **Visibility**	poor to fair
🌊 **Currents**	none to strong
🌙 **Dive type**	day boat

Inside Puerto Galera Bay and exactly at the point where the currents converge means conditions at this site are highly variable. The visibility can drop way down as the movement stirs up silty sections of the seabed. Despite that you are bound to see the dive's most famous residents, seahorses.

You enter in the shallows beside a cluster of giant clams that vary from the size of a football to way over a metre. From here, it's down to a sand patch where algas, seagrasses, soft corals and small sponges support a wealth of macro animals. There are minute frogfish, crinoids stuffed full of commensal residents (squat lobsters, tiny fish and shrimp), the Pegasus seamoth, razorfish, morays and a few nudibranchs. And of course, there are the seahorses, who wander from sponge to stick to soft coral. Apart from the life on the seabed, there are also a few pretty coral outcrops.

Whitetip shark hiding in Shark Cave

◈2 Alma Jane Wreck

◈	**Depth**	31 m
◐	**Visibility**	fair to good
◈	**Currents**	slight
◐	**Dive type**	day boat

On the edge of Sabang Bay, three minutes from shore, this old cargo boat was sunk to make an artificial reef. The *MV Alma Jane Express* was scuttled in March 2003 and settled upright at 30 metres. She was a 60-ton, 35-metre-long steel-hulled cargo ship built in 1966. Little remains to indicate her past working life but the boat has become a special dive as it attracts a huge number of pelagic fish. Dropping to the rudder you meet the first school of curious batfish then, as you ascend, another, larger group hover around the metal framework at deck level. There are schools of fusiliers, snappers, golden rabbitfish, lionfish and a solitary flutemouth that follows divers around.

Suddenly Goto, our divemaster, went ballistic, performing a wild victory dance underwater. We watched amused until he slowed enough to show us what he had found.

◈3 Shark Cave

◈	**Depth**	28 m
◐	**Visibility**	poor to fair
◈	**Currents**	none
◐	**Dive type**	day boat

One of Puerto Galera's deepest dives, this is located well away from the coast. There is no sloping reef so it's not possible to do a multilevel dive. Instead you drop into the blue then down to what seems like a

◈4 Boulders

◈	**Depth**	26 m
◐	**Visibility**	fair to good
◈	**Currents**	slight
◐	**Dive type**	day boat

Sitting on beneath an almost vertical, sharp cliff face you are faced with a series of large boulders that break the surface. Rolling back into the water between them, you find some of the most interesting terrain around this coast. The boulders seem to have tumbled down from the cliff, falling close together and forming swim-throughs that create a winding path down to the level base of the site. Despite wanting to stop to explore the caves and tunnels for

flat plateau but is actually a series of long terraces. Beneath these are some very deep cave-like fissures that are known to have sharks inside. Small whitetips pace to and fro under the protective ledges before disappearing into the dark recesses. Out on the plateau the level surfaces are surprisingly pretty as they are carpeted in masses of tiny pink soft corals. A few large fans punctuate the level areas while on the seabed you can spot seagrass ghost pipefish and balls of catfish.

all the marine life that lives inside them, the divemaster signals to head down to the base that flattens suddenly. A rubbly area is coated in sponges, hydroids and algas. It's the spot to go searching for the resident thorny seahorses – and it's no problem to find them. They are always there, along with peacock razorfish, the usual range of clownfish in anemones, nudibranchs, adult blue-ribbon eels and young cuttlefish. More of a surprise as you move back up to the boulders is when the divemaster you are with goes crazy. You know he has found something but he's too excited to tell you he's just found a stunning, and rather unimpressed, blue-ringed octopus. This sort of thing doesn't happen all that often, but when it does...

At the bottom of the Alma Jane; blue-ringed octopus on Boulders

Palawan

The island province of Palawan is just about as far west as you can go and still remain inside Philippine waters. It is an area famed for its outstanding natural landscapes as much as its incredible underwater realm.

The area is also one of the most frequently targeted by divers as it is home to both the unique Tubbataha National Marine Park and the historical Second World War wrecks in Coron Bay.

Coron

Island upon island mark the 1,400 or so square kilometres of the Calamian Island group. To the east is the Sulu Sea, to the west the South China Sea, so you could expect this location to be subject to strong currents as sea moves around the islands. Instead, the channels and bays are mirror calm and currents below the surface are minimal. These are the conditions that attracted the Japanese in the Second World War. They moored a fleet of support ships there but these were later bombed by US forces. The remains are seen as second only to those in Truk Lagoon.

To date around a dozen wrecks have been located and their historical value is boundless. For divers, they are particularly attractive as they are so much easier to dive than Truk: this lagoon is shallow and calm. To an extent, that is also to its detriment as the visibility is never very clear. However, Coron isn't just wrecks: small reefs here are in good condition too.

⊙ **Depth**	28 m	
◑ **Visibility**	fair	
⬳ **Currents**	none	
⬮ **Dive type**	liveaboard	

The *Taiei Maru* was an oil tanker which, at 180 metres long, is one of the larger wrecks in Coron. She sits upright on the seabed with a slight list to the port side. The buoy is hooked on at 10 metres and the deck is at 15-ish so there is plenty of time to look around. After descending, it's a good idea to head straight down to the rudder. Swarming around this are masses of pelagic fish: schools of batfish, yellow snappers and some sweetlips. The seafloor reveals animals, including some unusual nudibranchs. The divemasters then take an unusual turn and swim through the narrow propeller shaft behind the rudder, emerging 30 metres later in the engine room. This is a very tight passage so once you are inside you must go forward. Most people will find it easier and just as much fun to head back up to near the deck, from where you can penetrate some of the well lit holds and the engine room.

⊙ **Depth**	38 m	
◑ **Visibility**	fair to good	
⬳ **Currents**	none	
⬮ **Dive type**	liveaboard	

The only warship sunk inside Coron Bay, the *Akitsushima* was a seaplane tender 118 metres long and 16 metres wide. The hull is now lying on its side. At the stern there was a crane, which was used to lower the planes down into the water. However, when the ship was hit the stern broke away and the crane is now found a short distance away on the seabed. The visibility can be murky and seems to get worse the further down you go. There is a lot of gold and silver black coral, especially on the two masts jutting horizontally out over the seabed. Beneath these you can find a school of young, teenager stage, batfish. Swimming inside the wreck you can explore the holds, which originally covered three levels, but time will be against you. On the deck are two circular gun placements. These can be seen at the bow and midships, sitting between the two masts.

Philippines Dive log Palawan: Coron

The deck of the *Taiei Maru* and inside its engine room; at the base of the *Akitsushima*

7 Wreck of the Kogyo Maru

Depth	37 m
Visibility	fair
Currents	none
Dive type	liveaboard

This Japanese freighter is 158 metres long and was carrying construction materials supposedly for building an airfield. She is now lying on her side with some of those still inside the holds. After dropping down the mooring line, which is tied to the central bridge, it's best to fin downwards past the mast before entering the nearest open hold. Inside are rolls of fencing or some other diamond-shaped, webbed material. (They are heavily coated in silt so it's hard to see precisely what the material is.) The next hold along has some bags of cement and an almost intact bulldozer inside. It's a little easier to pick out shapes here. Next, you can swim through parts of the engine room before heading back up to the mast area where the black corals are very lush and there are lots of fish. The top level is actually the side of the hull (now facing up) and is covered in a huge amount of lettuce leaf and leather corals.

66 99 The water in Coron Bay may be murky but it is the constant flow of plankton and nutrients that has turned each of these wrecks into sumptuous artificial reefs.

Tubbataha

It's a long sail out to Tubbataha but when you do arrive it's to steep-sided walls that rim oval reefs with visibility to die for. In the open water, reef sharks, barracuda and tuna all cruise by at a lazy pace. Rays flit by and turtles ponder over reef tops.

This huge open space in the middle of the Sulu Sea is home to the Philippines' most impressive World Heritage Site, a marine park consisting of three reefs: Jessie Beazley, North Reef (or atoll) and South Reef.

Due to their exposed positions, the Tubbataha reefs can only be dived in the late spring. At other times, potentially rough seas make the crossing nigh on impossible. Currents are variable and most dives are drifts. Tenders follow diver bubbles in case of a change of direction but arrive early on a spring morning and you are likely to be greeted with a glassy surface and nothing but sunshine. While this is not the prettiest of reef systems – reef tops have been damaged by past illegal fishing and coral growth is inhibited by natural weather conditions – this is definitely the place for big guys.

8 Shark Airport

Depth	35 m	
Visibility	stunning	
Currents	can be strong	
Dive type	liveaboard	

One of the north atoll's gentler dives, a long slope drops away from the reef rim before turning into a wall. Dotted with caves and crevices, this drop into no man's land has visibility so amazing you can see all the way down. The wall is decorated with sea fans and some soft corals while pelagic fish pass by. Jacks, rainbow runners and the ever-present whitetips hover on the tails of snappers. Heading back up, the slope pans out into a long strip of sand – the 'airport' – surrounded by coral heads. This ledge is almost always covered in whitetip sharks which rest here in neat squadrons. This is a great site for a night dive too, with many hermit crabs.

9 Eiger Wall

Depth	38 m	
Visibility	stunning	
Currents	mild to strong	
Dive type	liveaboard	

Sitting between the north and south atolls, this site is subject to some fairly strong currents. Entry is over a flat reef top, then a very steep vertical wall drops sharply to over 50 metres. Swimming downwards you pass humungous gorgonians and as you reach the 30 metre mark you can see a lot of soft corals below. A cavern at 38 metres reveals its upper surface is just dripping in small white soft corals, like an upside-down snowstorm. Ascending back up the wall you pass a few more sharks, including sonme blacktips this time, before arriving on the top plateau to be greeted by a school of jacks silhouetted against the sun.

10 Black Rock, South Atoll

Depth	38 m	
Visibility	stunning	
Currents	slight to strong	
Dive type	liveaboard	

The geography of the south atoll is a little gentler than the sharp walls of the north and this sloping reef is a good example of the dives here. It eventually drops well beyond where you should be – you have to watch your depth when the visibility is so clear. The wall has a substantial number of gorgonians and impressive barrel sponges swarmed by schools of reef fish. Rainbow runners are interspersed with an occasional tuna or barracuda while on the wall there are squirrel and soldierfish, lionfish and morays. Eagle rays have been seen here but most exciting, on the right day, are the mantas. They are not a regular attraction but when they do arrive there are often several of them. It is most likely that you will get to snorkel with them rather than dive as they hang around for hours at a time, lazily flapping about.

Whitetip resting at Shark Airport; on Eiger Wall; manta at Black Rock

The Visayas

Panglao, Bohol

Just a quick hop from Cebu to Bohol and you'll find a destination loved by anyone who has ever been out this way. Bohol is renowned for its natural attractions, interesting history and offshore islands ringed by coral reefs. Panglao island is the most popular. It's connected to Bohol by a causeway but is really best described as an island.

Alona Beach was the first to be developed and is now a lively place with many beach-front hotels. It has become more sophisticated but still manages to retain that 'no news-no shoes' feel. There are great dive facilities and masses of stunning sites all within minutes of shore. Or head a little further offshore to reach the satellite islands of Cabilao and Balicasag with their deep walls smothered in corals.

≥11 Alona Beach Sanctuary

Depth	12 m
Visibility	good to great
Currents	slight to medium
Dive type	day boat

Pristine Alona Beach is very shallow, so much so that at low tide boats struggle to cross it. To protect the reef from damage a section is buoyed off and the area below is now a sanctuary. At high tide the reef is at 10 metres and at its edge, the drop-off descends to about 20 metres. The wall is cut with vertical crevices and there is a broad array of corals and fans, tunicates and small sponges. It's colourful with plenty of fish to admire both day and night. In fact, the reef top is one of the best night dives in the area and slow inspection of the many small outcrops will reveal a myriad of weird critters. There are parrot and cardinalfish, flatworms, shells, nudibranchs, frogfish, tiny cuttlefish, more tiny cuttlefish nabbing cardinalfish and lionfish preying on whatever they can.

≥12 Arco Point

Depth	28 m
Visibility	good to great
Currents	slight to medium
Dive type	day boat

Heading east from Alona beach is this small, submerged point. In the top of the reef, sitting right in the beautiful white sand, is a blue hole about two metres wide. This descends through the reef and emerges on the wall at about 20 metres. The tunnel is lined with soft corals and whips, lots of small morays and fish. After exiting the cave you swim to the base of a completely vertical wall where there is one of the largest purple fan corals you will ever see. A patch of tubastrea coral is a known haunt for giant frogfish. The wall winds in and out, lined with plenty of corals, then it's back up to the sandy flat reef for a safety stop. You can go critter hunting over the sand where there are motionless pipefish, ribbon eels, pufferfish and many sand dwellers: look for the *inimicus* or devilfish.

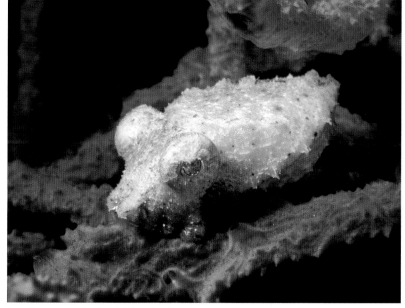

Juvenile stumpy-spined cuttlefish in the Alona Sanctuary; the cave at Arco Point

Philippines Dive log The Visayas: Panglao, Bohol

◼️N13 Black Forest

🕐	**Depth**	33 m
🌓	**Visibility**	good to stunning
〰️	**Currents**	slight to strong
🌊	**Dive type**	day boat

The island's principal dive, Black Forest, is a swathe of incredibly prolific black corals that shimmer in tones of gold and silver whenever the current is running enough for them to extend their tentacles to feed. Black corals are in the scientific order *Antipathiaria* and tend to be found in deep waters. However, the ones here grow right up to 30 metres. It is thought that they have adapted to the shallower depth as they are living in the shadow of the island. Cool water upwellings supply deep-water nutrients so the corals are fooled into thinking they are deeper than they are. There are many animals hiding around the branches – giant frogfish and flutemouths are regular finds. Meanwhile, out in the blue are balls of jacks, batfish and moorish idols. A school of barracuda passes by; then, as you ascend, you find ledges and patches of sloping sand where you will spot many nudibranchs, pipefish and some tiny scorpionfish.

◼️N14 Pungtud

🕐	**Depth**	24 m
🌓	**Visibility**	good
〰️	**Currents**	slight to medium
🌊	**Dive type**	day boat

Bordering the submerged wall on the western tip of Panglao, this dive can be swept by currents. As you descend over the first section of wall, it blazes with brightly coloured feeding soft corals. There are snapper and mackerel off in the blue and large puffers sit closer in. As you round the bend, the current drops away and you have more time to investigate the wall's residents. You can find interesting small creatures like orang-utan crabs and bright nudibranchs. Up on the reef flat are ever more curious critters: snake eels, twintailed slugs and spinning balls of catfish. Banded seasnakes are surprisingly common; you can see several swimming up and down the wall to feed. Ornate ghost pipefish are another special find but you will have to poke your nose into all the crinoids to see them.

Dumaguete, Negros

Running parallel with long, thin Cebu, Negros island is a draw for divers who travel to her southern tip and the city of Dumaguete. To her south, the coastline is riddled with dark sand bays and some fantastic muck diving. From here you can also reach Apo Island, the country's most successful marine sanctuary.

The coastal reefs were once regarded as overfished but local fishing communities learned about the value of the dive dollar and the area is now riddled with projects for sustainable fishing. This is probably one of the best macro locations you will ever find. Think of a critter, mention it to the divemaster and off you go to see it. And just in case you might (unbelievably) get bored with all that, a short sail away is Apo Island, home to turtles, schooling pelagics and pristine hard corals.

◼️N15 El Dorado Reef

🕐	**Depth**	16 m
🌓	**Visibility**	fair to good
〰️	**Currents**	slight to strong
🌊	**Dive type**	shore

Right in front of El Dorado resort is this amazing beach dive. Wander out from the restaurant then fin down over the dark-sand slope, descending to about 20 metres then around a circular bed of staghorn corals, past some coral bommies and back up to the seagrass bed near the start. There is some rubbish about: a few tyres and logs that encourage animals to hide. It's a bit like a treasure hunt. At night, in a single dive you can see five or six different types of frogfish, crinoid shrimp, and a few leaffish. Shining your torch around, you may suddenly spotlight a barracuda, which is a bit of a shock in the dark! Then there are plenty of shells, flatworms, crabs, shrimps and blue-spotted rays moving around the sandy areas.

Black corals at Balicasag; small, brightly-coloured fish flitting along an Alona wall

⬂16 Dauin

🧭	**Depth**	30 m
◐	**Visibility**	fair to good
〰	**Currents**	slight
⬓	**Dive type**	day boat

For those interested in small cryptic marine dwellers, this is simply heaven. For those who would give their right arm (or more likely their camera) for a glimpse of a ghost pipefish, cuttlefish or even a mimic octopus, this one bay ranks right up there with the best. As you head south across the crest of the slope, there are logs surrounded by balling catfish, old tyres with dwarf lionfish and flying gurnards. A little further along snake eel noses poke from the sand then it's down to a hollow where a crinoid houses tiny ornate ghosties. At the base of the slope, a rubbish pile is the homepatch of several seahorses. The spot is also good for morays, flamboyant cuttlefish and stonefish encounters. A little north of here are the wrecks of some old cars which are smothered in life – lionfish, scorpions and batfish. There is even a rare, juvenile zebra batfish on occasion. Or you could turn south and uphill to spin along the edge of the coral sanctuary with its baby sharks and butterflyfish then back along the crest

until – if you are really lucky – you spot the mimic octopus. Finally, there is a patch of seagrass in shallow water that makes a perfect, extended safety stop. In fact, you can spend a very long time here hunting for critters in amongst the green blades. There are more frogfish and seahorses, juvenile razorfish, fingered dragonets, devilfish and a spectacular find for patient spotters is the Pegasus seamoth.

⬂17 Masa Plod Sanctuary

🧭	**Depth**	22 m
◐	**Visibility**	fair to good
〰	**Currents**	none
⬓	**Dive type**	day boat

One of the first sanctuaries in the area, this one is roped off so that no fishing can take place. Consequently fish life is prolific. The reef falls gently down to about 25 metres and is covered in patches of hard coral. It's one of those reefs where the lower you go the more you will see, as so many creatures take refuge under the corals. There are big groupers and juvenile whitetips, plenty of triggerfish and some sweetlips. On the sand are mantis shrimp while under are pipefish and young batfish hiding. You may even spot some passing tuna.

⬂18 Coconut Point, Apo Island

🧭	**Depth**	28 m
◐	**Visibility**	stunning
〰	**Currents**	slight to ripping
⬓	**Dive type**	day boat

Coconut Point is the big-thrill experience. It catches some very strong currents, especially as you head out to the point, and as ever it's the currents that attract the fish. The dive commences over a flat reef with a good cover of hard corals. It then slopes out to a tongue with steep walls where jacks, snapper and rainbow runners patrol. There is a sandy cut that provides shelter for when the current is really ripping and from here you can watch turtles, groupers, Napoleon wrasse and whitetip sharks. Schools of big eye trevallies compete with Spanish mackerel, barracuda and midnight snappers. Clouds of anthias and fusiliers are always seen here and damsels dance around the hard coral. The sloping section of this site is a very good place to look for turtles – one friendly resident is very old and his shell is encrusted with barnacles – and sea snakes on the prowl.

Juvenile zebra batfish, frogfish and seahorses are found at Dauin

Drying out

Across such a large country, there is bound to be a huge selection of resorts that have excellent dive facilities. Once you have picked a region, remember to balance standards with budgets. You do get what you pay for and this is especially true with liveaboards.

Manila
$$ Heritage Hotel Manila, T+63 (0)2 854 8888, millenniumhotels.com. Only 8 mins from the airport, this comfortable, first-class hotel is perfect for quick stopovers. Transfers are included.

Mindoro
Puerto Galera
Dive Resorts
$$ Atlantis Dive Resorts, T+63 (0)43 287 3066, atlantishotel.com. A resort that truly focuses on its diver guests. In the middle of Sabang Beach bay, the hotel is built on terraces in a fun style with white-washed, curved walls. Rooms vary in size and shape but are all well decorated and with internet access. Classy in-house restaurant; well thought-out dive facilities and a camera and computer room. Dive courses available. Packages with all meals and unlimited diving are fantastic value.

Other options
Buri Resort and Spa, buri-resort.com
Marco Vincent, marcovincent.com
Oceana, oceanadive.com

Palawan
Coron
Liveaboards
Expedition Fleet, T+63 (0)2 890 6778 expeditionfleet.com. The only consistent dive liveaboard operator in the Philippines with a variety of boats. Vessels are large and stable, cabins are very simple but comfortable. Itineraries change by season and include direct routes or transition trips that include more than one destination.
Hans Christian Andersen, T+45 (0)86 182 488, hcaexplorer.com. This 20-cabin large, Danish-owned and operated vessel runs 7-day cruises from Puerto Galera to Coron. There are only minimal diving facilities on board so it is best suited to occasional divers or divers with families.

Other options
Sangat Island Reserve, sangat.com.ph
Dive Link, Uson, divelink.com.ph
Discovery Divers, Decanituan, ddivers.com

Tubbataha
Liveaboards
Expedition Fleet, T+63 (0)2 890 6778 expeditionfleet.com. Review as above.

Other options
Oceana Maria, adventurebound.com.ph
Philippines Siren, worldwidediveandsail.com

Visayas
Bohol
Dive Resorts
$$ The Ananyana, Panglao. T+63 (0)38 502 8101, ananyana.com. Top-class dive resort with beautiful rooms overlooking Doljo Beach. Not the cheapest option, but sometimes you just have to indulge. On-site dive centre, spa and restaurant.

Other options
Alona Palm Beach Resort, alonapalmbeach.com. Affiliated to atlantisdivecenter.de
Sun Apartelle & Sun Divers, sun-divers.net
La Estrella, laestrella.ph. On Cabilao.

Dumaguete, Negros Oriental
Dive Resorts
$$ Atlantis Dive Resorts, T+63 (0)35 425 2327, atlantishotel.com. Sister resort to Atlantis in Puerto Galera with similar standards of service and facilities. Located on Lipayo Beach bay, 20 mins south of Dumaguete. Rooms are nicely decorated. Dive courses available. Packages with meals and unlimited diving are fantastic value.

Other options
Bahura Resort and Spa, bahura.com
El Dorado Beach Resort, eldoradobeachresort.com

Atlantis Resort, Puerto Galera; sailing into Coron

	Sleeping	**$$$** US$150+ double room per night	**$$** US$75-150	**$** under US$75
	Eating	**$$$** US$40+ 2-course meal, excluding drinks	**$$** US$20-40	**$** under US$20

Puerto Galera

Puerto Galera town, **Poblacion**, was once a fishing village. It has banks, restaurants, shops and a public market. Beside the Catholic Church is the Excavation Museum which has ancient Chinese artefacts and pottery found in the area. If you fancy a change from seawater to fresh, there are waterfalls at **Tamaraw**, near the village of Villaflor (14 kilometres from Puerto Galera). They have a natural swimming pool at their base. **Mangyan Village** is home to Mindoro's once coastal nomads. These tribes have tried to avoid any outside influences in order to protect their own culture. Nearby, on **Small Tabinay River** are gold-digging sites.

Coron

Arrive in Coron Bay by boat and you will never forget the breathtaking vistas of towering, sharp volcanic walls dotted with small green trees clinging on for dear life. Inside the channel, the walls give way to soft and gentle hills then it all drops into the deep blue sea. **Busuanga** is the largest island in the group and attracts those who like to get out into the great outdoors. There are river mountain and jungle walks, hot springs and horse-riding. It is also the location of **Coron Town**, which is quite small and easy to explore on foot. You could stick to the town market, souvenir or pottery shops or trek the 720 steps up Mount Tapyas for a 360º scenic view. **Calauit Island**, off the northwest tip of Busuanga is an animal sanctuary with both endemic and African animals: zebra, giraffes and gazelles live alongside local Calamian deer and Palawan peacocks. **Culion Island** is the most renowned in this region, famous for once being a leper colony. Established in 1906, the community grew when families followed their afflicted relatives there. It was said to be the safest place in the country during the Second World War as the Japanese would not set foot on the island for fear of getting ill.

Bohol

Spend a lazy day touring **Tagbilaran**, the island capital and location of an old Spanish settlement. There are a few 17th- and 18th-century churches and some attractive tree-lined plazas, colonial homes and a small museum. **Loboc River** cruises travel along the jungle-rimmed river in a pumpboat, passing local villages. The most famous Bohol attraction is the **Chocolate Hills**, a weird landscape of 1,200 grassy mounds that look like someone tipped up bags of sugar in rows. In the summer, the domes turn brown as the covering, grassy vegetation dries out, transforming the area into rows of 'chocolate' mounds. The province is also home to the world's smallest primate, the tarsier. This truly diminutive creature is endangered. You can see them at the **Tarsier Research and Development Centre** at Corella. There is a netted enclosure, where the tarsiers are fed, bred and monitored. Alternatively, take the tarsier trail through the forest and watch out for one.

Negros

The busy coastal city of **Dumaguete** is home to Silliman University. The shops and markets are fun to visit and there is some colonial architecture including an 18th-century bell tower. The botanical gardens, zoo and aviary are worth a visit. **Casaroro Waterfall** is an hour by car in the Valencia Mountains. The small nature reserve nestles in the river valley. Hiking for an hour takes you to the waterfall which drops into a stunning natural swimming pool. Another day out is to **Twin Lakes**. Located in the mountainous area above San Jose, and inland from Dumaguete, Balinsasayao and Danao Twin Lakes are a haven of pristine flora and fauna. Kayakers can rent a small *banca* and cross to the deserted side of the lake under a dark forest canopy.

Diving bangka at Alona Beach; fish market; the diminutive Tarsier; local jeepney bus

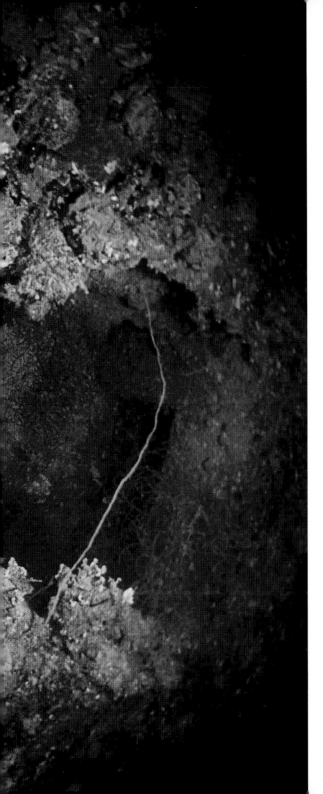

Micronesia

Rest in peace: this 114-metre freighter fell victim to Operation Hailstone, but was reborn as a coral reef.
Kansho Maru, Truk Lagoon

Guam

NORTHERN MARIANAS

FEDERATED STATES O

Yap ✈ ● Kolonia

CAROLINE ISLANDS

↘ 2

Palau ✈

↘ 1

● Koror

*Philippine
Sea*

↘ 1 **Palau** ▶▶ p168

↘ 1 Ulong Corner and Channel
↘ 2 Jellyfish Lake
↘ 3 Blue Corner
↘ 4 Peliliu Wall
↘ 5 The Iro Maru
↘ 6 Chandelier Cave

Babelthaup

↘ 6

↘ 1

↘ 3   ● Koror

↘ 5

Rock Islands

↘ 2

↘ 4

Peliliu

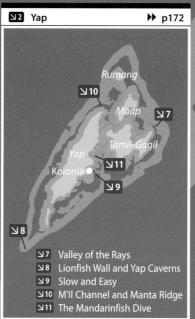

↘ 2 **Yap** ▶▶ p172

Rumang

↘ 10

Maap   ↘ 7

Tamil-Gagil

Yap
Kolonia ●   ↘ 11

↘ 9

↘ 8

↘ 7 Valley of the Rays
↘ 8 Lionfish Wall and Yap Caverns
↘ 9 Slow and Easy
↘ 10 M'll Channel and Manta Ridge
↘ 11 The Mandarinfish Dive

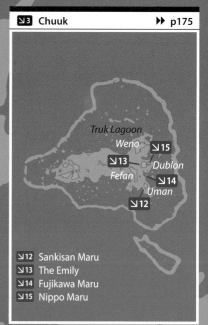

↘ 3 **Chuuk** ▶▶ p175

Truk Lagoon

Weno   ↘ 15

↘ 13   *Dublon*

Fefan   ↘ 14

Uman

↘ 12

↘ 12 Sankisan Maru
↘ 13 The Emily
↘ 14 Fujikawa Maru
↘ 15 Nippo Maru

Jayapura ●

Bismark Se

INDONESIA

*PAPUA
NEW
GUINEA*   ● Wewak

CRONESIA

Weno

Chuuk Islands

⊿3

PACIFIC OCEAN

Solomon Sea

100 km

Introduction

Flying in to Micronesia is quite an experience. The aerial views are of awe-inspiring beauty: handfuls of green islands sprinkled over deep blue seas. There is no development here, no high rise, no motorways. Just never-ending seas that promise – and deliver – some remarkable diving experiences.

The island groups of Palau, Yap and Chuuk are like a set of triplets: all charming but, for divers, each with its own distinct personality. Palau is precocious, leaping to the fore to show off her many marine talents; she has a bit of everything and something for every diver. Yap is shy, modest about her attractions, yet quietly proud of her year-round populations of manta rays. Nearby lurks Chuuk, moody and mysterious but admired for her Second World War wrecks. Although each has their own specific features they are all set against the prolific backdrop of a marine realm born of the deep ocean trenches of the Western Pacific.

Micronesia sits quietly apart from the 'real' world. These islands have developed at differing paces: one rushing headlong towards a western future; one shying away from outside influences; and one that's not sure which way to jump. The challenge is in being open-minded – you think you know what to expect, then you realize you didn't have a clue.

Micronesia rating

Diving
★★★★

Dive facilities
★★★★

Accommodation
★★★★

Down time
★★

Value for money
★★★

Essentials

Getting there and around

There's hard to get to, there's expensive to get to, and then there's Micronesia. But before you give up, do bear in mind that there are potentially huge rewards for those who make the effort to go.

The only airline that runs any sort of consistent service to the Federated States of Micronesia (FSM) and the Republic of Palau is Continental Micronesia, part of Continental Airlines (continental.com). This subsidiary has almost no competition so can charge what it likes – and does. Flights depart from Manila, Tokyo, Los Angeles, Honolulu and Cairns to Guam, which is a US Territory, so you will need to go through American immigration before departing on another flight to your final destination. The best option is from Manila as there are twice weekly, non-stop flights to Palau. One of these flies onwards to Yap. On other days, or to get to Chuuk (Truk), you have to transit in Guam. Many airlines have flights to the hub cities listed: look for those with links to Continental to make a through booking. It also appears that US agents have access to cheaper fares than those elsewhere.

Transfers on the islands will be handled by your dive operation or hotel. Taxis are the best way to go sightseeing on Palau, while on Yap, most of the sights are within walking distance but you can also take a taxi. On Chuuk, you are unlikely to go very far – see safety below.

Local laws and customs

The Pacific islands that are loosely grouped together as Micronesia were inhabited by seafarers from the countries we now know as Indonesia and the Philippines. Their ancient cultures were quite sophisticated with highly structured social groups but as each island developed in isolation from each other so their cultures differ. For more on this, see pages 178-179. Bear in mind that on all islands, you should dress neatly (women should cover their legs beyond the knees) and be respectful of the elderly. One thing that is consistent across all the islands is heavy penalties for possession of a firearm and drug offences. Homosexuality is technically illegal and laws are occasionally enforced.

Safety

It may be hard to believe that a tiny Pacific paradise can be a troubled one but then nowhere is immune these days. **Palau** is considered safe but a curfew is in force from 0230-0500 in an attempt to control local drinking. There are high incidences of road accidents so use taxis rather than hiring a car. **Yap** is more laid-back with few alcohol-related issues, probably because most people spend their days chewing betelnut. Peeled and chewed with lime (the stuff they put in mortar) and a green leaf, this has a mild narcotic effect and disintegrates teeth. How does this rank as a danger? Well, you have to be wary of the

Palau
Location
7°30'N, 134°30'E

Capital	Melekeok
Population	20,796
Land area in km²	458
Coastline in km	1,519

Micronesia
Location
6°55'N, 158°15'E

Capital	Palikir
Population	107,434
Land area in km²	702
Coastline in km	6,112

Diver and soft corals in Micronesia

constant jets of bright red saliva produced by users. **Chuuk** is troubled by a lack of employment. Young men move to Weno, the main island, hoping to make their fortune but there simply is no work. This leads to the usual social problems and specifically to alcohol abuse. The island is supposedly dry but there is little evidence that it is. You should stick to your hotel and take advice before heading out on your own. There are tales of people being attacked, even in a hire car, so talk to reception who can link you up with a local guide.

Language

The lingua franca is English. Those wishing to try local languages may well find themselves up against it. In Palau many dive crews are Filipino, in Yap they all seem to come from Chuuk, while in Chuuk they might be from an outlying island and look at you blankly when you attempt a few words. All the same, it can never hurt to try:

	Palauan	Yapese	Chuukese
hello	alii	mogethin	ras annim
goodbye	mechik'ung	kefel	kenne nom
yes	choch'oi	arrogon	uu (wu)
no	diak	danga	apw
please	adang	wenig	kose mochen
thank you	ulang	kammegar	kinisou
sorry!	komeng!	sirow!	tirow!
no problem	diak a mondai	dari fan	lese wor (or)

Health

There are no specific inoculations or warnings for either Palau or FSM. There is malaria but reported incidences are rare. Take the usual precautions to protect against insect bites. Drinking water is either bottled or filtered and food standards are generally high. All three islands covered in this chapter have recompression chambers and there are good medical facilities.

Costs

These islands could be described as expensive but costs aren't so high as to be prohibitive. Most things are a little bit more than in the US. There is little in the way of agriculture so much has to be imported: a beer will be US$3-4, a glass of wine US$4-5. Meals are international style and around US$12 for a main course. Hotels are limited everywhere except in Palau which has the most options in all price ranges. Yap has just a handful and the lower end places are not really worth investigating. Chuuk has only two land options and these are similarly priced. There are marine park fees in Palau (US$35) and Chuuk (US$30). Tipping is expected.

 Tourist information → Government websites can be found at visit-palau.com, visityap.com and visit-micronesia.com which includes pages on Chuuk (Truk).

Fact file

International flights	Major carriers to hub cities as listed
Departure tax	Manila: US$20; Palau: US$20; Chuuk: US$15
Entry	Visas not required but check US regulations for transiting through Guam
Internal flights	Continental Airlines
Ground transport	Taxis or use private options
Money	US dollar
Language	English is widely spoken
Electricity	110v, plug type A (see page 16)
Time zone	Palau and Yap: GMT +9. Chuuk: GMT +10
Religion	Various Christian denominations with many fringe and evangelical forms
Phone	Palau country code +680; FSM country code +691; IDD code 011; Police 911

The Rock Islands in Palau

Dive brief

Diving

Micronesia is a very loose, geographic description and, depending what atlas you look in, her resident nations can vary. The only reason some are even grouped together is that after the Second World War, the UN and US formed federations of certain Pacific island groups. Some of these lasted and some didn't. Each island has its own distinct history influenced by wars, colonialism, missionary infiltration and geopolitical interests right up until today.

The three most visited destinations – for divers – are the Republic of Palau and, in the Federated States of Micronesia, Yap and Truk Lagoon – more properly known as Chuuk. As you fly in to **Palau** you get your first view of just how breathtaking her landscape is. (Sell your grandmother for a window seat or you'll find yourself sitting on a stranger's lap.) Once you hit the water you won't be disappointed as the diving can be equally breathtaking. **Yap** is less than an hour's flight north and is famous for just one thing: her large resident manta populations, although there is so much more here. **Chuuk**, with her renowned lagoon, is a few hours away. If you are into wrecks and war history, this is an unrivalled diving destination.

Conditions vary considerably from one island group to the next and are influenced by local geography. The only similarities are water temperature and tropical marine life. Biodiversity is highest in Palau and decreases the further east you head.

Snorkelling

This is another of those location, location, location moments. The majority of wrecks in Chuuk are beyond 20 metres deep so snorkelling will be limited, but there are some wonderful aeroplane wrecks in shallow waters near Eten Island.

Over in Yap, the mangrove-rimmed channels can be murky with some strong currents during tidal changes. Some of the outer walls come up to 10 metres but again, currents can be strong so you will need to be advised by your dive team.

In Palau, there are lots of beautiful white sand beaches with offshore reefs where a snorkel can be rewarding but these sites are not likely to be where the dives are. Parts of the Rock Islands are closed to protect nesting species such as turtles but of course, Palau does have one of the planet's ultimate snorkelling destinations: the Jellyfish Lake.

Micronesia
animal
encounters

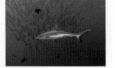

Palau	sharks
Yap	mantas

Palau's cavernous reef openings; artefacts on the deck of the Kiyosomi Maru

> We were lucky enough to be able to take an extended trip out to these islands and it still wasn't long enough. A week in Palau gave us a week's great diving but not enough time to enjoy her cosmopolitan island lifestyle. Five dive days in Yap gave us manta after manta encounter but barely time to see her charming southern reefs, and six dive days on Chuuk – on land – was enough. But, oh to have been floating over that amazing lagoon on a boat. The question is, would we go back? Yes, to Palau and Yap in a heartbeat; but to Chuuk, only if we could get on a liveaboard.

Marine life

Divers come to these islands for the large, famous animals, the sharks in Palau and the mantas in Yap. However, diversity is high and the macro life in these seas is just as good, as long as you take time to look for it.

Making the big decision

This is probably the longest, least convenient dive trip you will ever do so there is no question that you should do all three islands at once. However, that will mean taking the best part of three weeks, or four if you really want to do it properly. Transport issues mean you may lose up to two days getting there and another two each time you transit between islands. If you have less time then Palau and Yap work well together providing you can commence your trip from Manila. It would be hard to see Palau in less than a week. Yap needs five days; any less in low season and you would risk missing the mantas. Chuuk? Well, a week if you are on a liveaboard, four or five dive days from land, though you may still not see as much as you should.

The tiniest of hermit crabs in Yap, *Paguritta species*

Dive data

Seasons	Year-round diving but with the most rain between July and October
Visibility	10 metres inshore to 40 metres further offshore
Temperatures	Air 26-32°C; water 28-30°C
Wet suit	3 mm shorty or full body suit
Training	Courses in Palau or Yap
Nitrox	Check with your resort or liveaboard
Deco chambers	Palau, Yap, Chuuk and Guam

Bottom time

Micronesia	These islands may well be linked by airline routes and political alliances but there the similarities end. In all other ways, especially diving, they couldn't be more different, each having a unique feature or two.
Palau ▶▶ p168	An incredibly impressive variety of dive types with masses of pelagic fish over the reefs, Second World War wrecks and submerged limestone caves, but by far the most popular attraction has to be the sharks.
Yap ▶▶ p172	Mantas, mantas and more mantas – and they are as guaranteed as any event in the marine world can be. However, there is much more to discover than these incredibly graceful beasts, like the large populations of diminutive mandarinfish in shallow waters.
Chuuk ▶▶ p175	The legendary war graveyard where a whole fleet of Japanese planes, cargo carriers and warships sits on the bottom of a mirror calm lagoon. There is little else though, as most of the outer reefs have been battered both by man and nature.

Diversity

combined reef area 5,500 km²
Micronesia | Palau

HARD CORALS	
	68	61

FISH SPECIES	
	1,197	1,420

ENDEMIC FISH SPECIES	
	6	1

FISH UNDER THREAT	
	14	18

PROTECTED REEFS/MARINE PARKS	
	2	2

All diversity figures are approximate

Micronesia Dive brief

Palau

The legend goes that these islands were formed after the birth of a boy named Chuab. He grew into a giant, consumed all the village's food and even some of the other children. The villagers were so worried they decided the only solution was to kill him. They built a bonfire and tricked him into standing in the middle of it by saying it was for a special feast. The fire engulfed him and he fell into the sea. The parts of his body that protruded from the sea became the many islands of Palau.

Geographically, these islands are either limestone or volcanic in origin (not human, obviously) and nearly all are ringed by reefs. These drop to extreme walls perforated by caves and tunnels that have been flooded by the sea. The largest island is Babeldaob but most diving centres around the islands to her south. Koror, the capital, and Malakal, the harbour, are linked by road bridges

and the lagoon nearby has enough wrecks to give Chuuk a run for its money. There are plenty of macro-specific sites and some rather unusual shallow cave dives. Further south are the picturesque limestone Rock Islands which have dramatic undercuts and look almost like they are hovering above the sea. This is also where you will find the stunning Jellyfish Lake, one of several marine lakes and an unmissable experience. At the bottom of the chain is Pelilu Island which was the scene of a horrendous land battle in the Second World War.

Palau sits between the North Pacific and the Philippine Sea so her marine life is influenced by both. Conditions tend to be fairly easy; when there are strong currents, they are at sites that attract pelagics. The diving here is year round, although there are a few seasonal features: shark mating is February to April, moorish idol migration is March, groupers spawn from May to June, and manta rays, though seen all year, mate from December to April.

⛩ Ulong Corner and Channel	
❂ **Depth**	33 m
◐ **Visibility**	good
⬳ **Currents**	medium to ripping
◓ **Dive type**	liveaboard

Ulong Island is where the US version of TV's *Survivor* was filmed. The island is a pretty stop but more significantly leads to an exposed dive area. Ulong Corner and Channel are swept by currents which attract sharks – and divers. Entry is over a small wall which leads to a natural amphitheatre where divers hook on and wait for the show to commence. There are small whitetip sharks waiting in the wings but they keep away while several larger and more inquisitive greys approach those sitting in the front rows. The greys swoop in so close you feel the need to pull back. After a while at this spot, it's time to move the show down the channel and, unhooking from your rock, you are

swept away, accompanied by schools of snappers and trevally. The current is quite frisky and it's off for a rollercoaster ride through steep walls and schooling big-eyes. Part way along you reach an extensive patch of lettuce leaf corals. The delicate folds are a deep brown with many rabbitfish tucked in between them. A few sharks and a turtle keep you company towards the end of the ride but they disappear as soon as the current spits you out over a patch of bright white sand.

Ulong Corner, a grey reef up close and personal

↘2 Jellyfish Lake

⌖	**Depth**	33 m
◐	**Visibility**	good
≋	**Currents**	none
⬯	**Dive type**	snorkelling

The marine lake on Mecherchar Island is just one of many found in Palau. Their depths are seawater and fed by hidden channels that lead from the sea, while the top layer of water is fresh, diluted by rain. The animals that live inside these lakes have grown and adapted to exploit this unusual environment. Reaching this particular lake requires a trek through the jungle, up a steep and very slippery track. It's quite hard going but it only takes 10 minutes before you descend again to a pontoon overlooked by emerald hills and surrounded by mangroves.

The water in the lake is murky around the edges which are well shaded, with just an occasional polka-dot cardinal hovering around, but as you swim across the lake you see one, then another, until suddenly there are hundreds of mastigias jellies in pale apricot plus an occasional moon jelly. The mastigias species lost their capacity to sting as their only predator is a small anemone that lives under the mangroves. They spend their days circumnavigating the lake, following the movement of the sun's rays. Under the mangroves are cardinals, tube worms, anemones and tiny puntang gobies.

As you snorkel, be aware of what you are doing with your fins – a hefty kick will destroy any jelly you make contact with.

Mastigias jellyfish en masse

66 99 The sensation of swimming with these velvet skinned, pulsating animals is both bizarre and beautiful, a very calming experience.

3 Blue Corner

🧭	**Depth**	32 m
🕐	**Visibility**	fair to stunning
〰️	**Currents**	can be ripping
🌊	**Dive type**	liveaboard

Palau's most famous dive is justifiably so – a spectacle of epic proportions. Entry is over the edge of a wall that curves outwards to a promontory. Divers often drop straight into a massive school of chevron barracuda, or sometimes it's an equally large one of jacks. Next, it's a swim along the perfectly vertical wall to a deep crevice lined with fan corals. The wall is quite pretty but mostly ignored as just beyond this point is where divers ascend to the plateau above and hook on to a rock, to wait for the show. Looking down into the crevice there are a few grey reefs in the deep and then, on the other side of the plateau, a second jumbo school of jacks appears. As the current lifts to rip-your-mask-off levels, the real action starts. Lots more sharks – greys, blacktips and whitetips – appear and swoop across the vista. They are surrounded by schooling fish such as fusiliers and redmouth triggers. Napoleon wrasse swim in and out and you notice a few turtles sitting on the plateau behind, calmly chomping on sponges.

The sharks circle closer and closer while masses of jacks hang close to their tails. The greys and whitetips continue patrolling below the front of the wall surrounded by blue trevally and yet another school of barracuda.

Eventually, you have to lift off. The current will take you either along the reef rim, over beds of lettuce leaf coral with the whitetips still cruising below, or back over the plateau to spot morays and turtles.

❝❞ A school of chevron barracuda thickens the water to the point of obliterating the sun. Suddenly they disperse, the first grey reef shark has appeared from nowhere...

⊠4 Peliliu Wall

🌀 **Depth**	28 m	
🌓 **Visibility**	excellent	
🌊 **Currents**	medium to ripping	
🌀 **Dive type**	liveaboard	

Both sides of the southern tip of Peliliu are swept by currents where the Pacific and the Philippine Sea meet. This dive starts by swimming into a circular hole in the reef about three metres across with small soft corals lining its walls. Dropping another few metres, you exit through another hole in the wall and directly below, reaching to about 35-40 metres, is the most colourful and spectacular garden of soft corals. There are so many different bright hues, it's almost gaudy. There are black coral bushes and rows of fans that have grown in horizontal tiers to catch the sunlight from above. The rainbow effect is multiplied by large pufferfish, queen triggerfish, banded angels and anthias. Pyramid butterflies and redmouth triggers hover in the blue with a couple of passing sharks, Napoleon wrasse and mackerel.

⊠5 The Iro Maru

🌀 **Depth**	33 m	
🌓 **Visibility**	good	
🌊 **Currents**	medium to ripping	
🌀 **Dive type**	liveaboard	

The *Iro* was a Japanese fleet oiler built between 1919 and 1921. Used specifically to haul stores, munitions and 8,000 tons of oil to war fleet units, her movements during the war are reasonably well documented. On 31 March 1944, she was attacked by Yorktown VB-5 bombers and hit twice: once on the port side forward of midships, the other on the aft starboard quarter. The view of this wreck as you descend falls somewhere between awe-inspiring and intimidating. This is one very big ship at 145 metres. Dropping past the bowmast, the first thing you see is a large bandstand gun platform. On top of this 'spoked wheel' is a 5.5-inch bow gun that measures nearly nine metres long, with the barrel about five metres. Travelling along the deck you come to a small cabin where two very curious batfish lurk. A little further is an open hold which contains oil drums and machinery. The whole wreck is covered in masses of corals and the hard corals are in pristine condition – surprising on such a well-dived wreck. There are also hundreds of living shells – clams, mussels, barnacles, oysters and razor clams – and many dead ones littering the decks. Alternating masts and kingposts rise from the deck to about eight metres and the forward one is a great place to offgas as you can hunt for small fish and nudibranchs at the same time.

⊠6 Chandelier Cave

🌀 **Depth**	10 m	
🌓 **Visibility**	excellent at the top	
🌊 **Currents**	none	
🌀 **Dive type**	liveaboard	

In a lovely cove just across from the port at Malakal is this hidden cave system. Entry is just before a buoyed-off area which stops boats mooring too close. The cave mouth is perhaps five metres wide but as soon as you go inside it opens to a gaping space. The stalactites at the beginning are quite rounded, perhaps reshaped by the movement of seawater. There are four chambers inside the cave. You can ascend inside each to the space where the air gap allows fresh water to percolate through from the land above, creating spectacular sculptures. The formations are breathtaking, glittering with absorbed minerals and appearing as pleats of fabric or pencil-thin icicles. It's incredibly pretty but can get crowded with divers. Ensure you stay well above the bottom to avoid stirring up the silt and take a good torch (or two).

Vibrant colours on Peliliu Wall; investigating Chandelier cave; descending over the *Iro*

Yap

From the air Yap appears as a single triangular island. However, on closer inspection, her gently rolling landscape is divided by three channels into four tightly-knit land masses: Yap, Tomil-Gagil, Maap and Rumung. There are also 134 outlying islands and atolls.

The marine world here is something of a surprise. The channels that separate the islands are rather shallow, lined by dense mangrove swamps and edged by seagrass. The water is nothing if not murky but head seawards, over the surrounding lagoon, and it's all change. Where the surf breaks against the submerged reef the visibility clears to reveal a lively series of coral-clad hills and valleys. Fifteen miles to the east is the Yap Trench, one of the deep water trenches that form part of the Pacific Ring of Fire. The water plummets to a depth of over 8,000 metres which explains its deep shade of blue. Of course, you won't get down that far but you will see plenty of the pelagic species that are attracted to this region: Yap's manta populations are world famous. Sharks congregate here as well. The area is also becoming known for its macro life. There is a good selection of the small and often wacky reef-building animals to look for if you can just drag yourself away from the mantas. The reefs in the south are impressive and, despite some typhoon damage a couple of years ago, there is plenty of coral.

Conditions vary from the east, or windward, side to the west of the island, so there is always somewhere to go, even when the weather is less than perfect.

⏷7 **Valley of the Rays**	
🌀 **Depth**	16 m
◑ **Visibility**	medium to great
🌊 **Currents**	mild to strong
🌀 **Dive type**	day boat

Yap's resident mantas love the plankton-rich waters that flow out from her shallow channels. At this site on the east coast the channel descends to a deep valley with a sandy bottom. There are three cleaning stations that are known to attract the mantas – Merry-go-round, Carwash and Manta Rock. The dive involves swimming from one to another until you find them. At first this may seem hopeless, until you suddenly notice the grey wing flap of an approaching manta. Effortlessly, it glides towards your group. Soon after, a gang of four or five settles right over the nearest cleaning station. The mantas are so close you could touch them; in fact, you know that as you sit on the sand in absolute awe they are watching you too, no doubt with barely disguised amusement.

More mantas arrive in small groups, take turns at the cleaning station, then move off again. At the same time, those waiting their turn pull into the channel behind so you need to have eyes in the back of your head. The currents can be strong (a reef hook is a must) but this does not deter these magnificent animals from scooping the plankton and bits of floating weed into their mouths.

❝❞ **We've only been in Yap a few hours, in the water a few minutes, and it's hard to believe this is happening.**

⬊8 Lionfish Wall and Yap Caverns

🕐	**Depth**	26 m
◑	**Visibility**	good to great
🌊	**Currents**	mild to strong
🌀	**Dive type**	day boat

There are dives all the way to the south of the island where the reef veers away from land. The water can be a bit rough as the surf pushes in from different directions. As you round the southern tip of the reef, the walls become much steeper than those on the east and much prettier. The vertical surface of Lionfish Wall drops to about 45 metres and is covered in pastel tree-fern corals. There are moray noses sticking out and even a lionfish or two. More prominent though are the incredible number of big-eyes, coral trout and groupers. Looking into small cracks and crevices you can spot leaffish, carpet anemones with 'popcorn shrimp' crawling on them and nudibranchs. The terrain becomes rockier as you move along the wall to the Yap Caverns. These cuts and tunnels in the reef wall are just big enough to swim in and out of. You are likely to meet a young whitetip en route and one cavern harbours a substantial school of copper sweepers. Above the caverns for a safety stop are carpets of cup corals, dragonets and lots of anthias.

⬊9 Slow and Easy

🕐	**Depth**	19 m
◑	**Visibility**	poor to good
🌊	**Currents**	mild
🌀	**Dive type**	day boat

Heading away from town through the main channel there are several dives just before the break in the reef. On the left, against a mini-wall, is this critter hunter's favourite. Although the site can get quite murky, depending on the tides, there are lots of interesting creatures to see. The edge of the reef slopes down from about three metres to 18 metres where the sandy seabed is peppered with coral bommies. Amongst the varying bits of terrain are lionfish, anemones with their commensal clowns, crabs and nudibranchs. Huge pufferfish sit stationary on the sand with shrimp and goby partnerships beside them. There are clusters of pipefish, lone crocodilefish and pairs of lizardfish. Hiding under a rock is the juvenile six-lined soapfish. Nearby, the legs of a lonely stand of staghorn are hidden by yellow cardinalfish while blue anthias dance above.

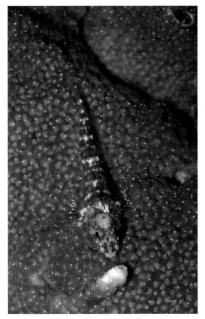

⬊10 M'Il Channel and Manta Ridge

🕐	**Depth**	27 m
◑	**Visibility**	medium to great
🌊	**Currents**	mild
🌀	**Dive type**	day boat

The ride from Kolonia north through the channel that divides Yap from Tomil-Gagil and Maap is a mysterious tour through mangroves and past silent villages with their traditional buildings and meeting houses. At the mouth of the channel the boat moors over one of Yap's most famous sites. In the middle of M'Il Channel is a manta station. Divers wait on the rubbly bottom but if the rays haven't arrived within about 10 minutes the divemasters head off down to Manta Ridge. Along the channel are outcrops of coral, anemones and clownfish but you'll be keeping your eyes on the blue to catch a glimpse of what's out there. It could be a manta speeding past, a flock of eagle rays or a small shark. At the ridge there is another cleaning station and here the mantas arrive silently to sit over everyone's heads, waiting to be cleaned by the small fish that are on duty for the day. This is the area where, between December and April, the mantas come to mate, doing belly rolls and acrobatics to impress each other.

Micronesia Dive log Yap

Lionfish on his namesake wall; Triplefin blenny at Slow and Easy; Manta fly-by in M'Il Channel

⛟11 The Mandarinfish Dive

⚙	**Depth**	9 m
◑	**Visibility**	poor
🌀	**Currents**	none
⬤	**Dive type**	day boat

A few minutes from Manta Ray Bay but inside the channel are a cluster of small, uninhabited islands. The divemasters know several residential areas for mandarinfish: in less than 10 metres of murky water are some stands of coral surrounded by rubble. Descending seconds before dark, you spot the male mandarins skittering about but they are still wary in the fading sunlight. As it gets darker they become more active, chasing the ladies around the reef until eventually, they begin mating. Rising up into the water column they are disturbed, inevitably just before spawning, by the equally numerous but very aggressive – and hungry – pyjama cardinals.

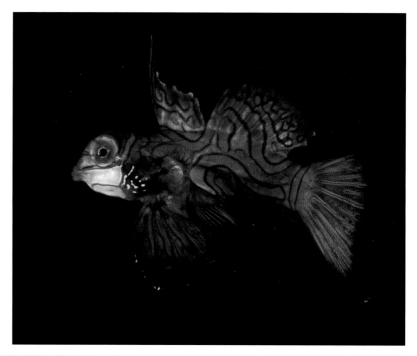

✹ Lost in the Blue

Palau, to me, 20 years ago was a delightfully 'local' Pacific paradise. It offered little for flower-shirted tourists seeking 5-star Western luxury and everything for the traveller savouring unspoiled culture and nature combined. Little had changed in 2005 although some 5-star resorts are now dotted around. The pace is still as slow and the people just as relaxed and friendly.

Snorkelling was the limit of my passion all those years ago and my vivid memories are of the fish nurseries – aggregations of millions of multi-species' juveniles sheltering in the protected shallow water between the Rock Islands for which Palau is famed. This recent trip finally revealed where all those fish end up as adults – this time I was a diver. Several previous remote diving expeditions in this prolific Pacific region hadn't prepared me for the sensual feast that is on offer at the southern end of Babeldaop: a famous dive called Blue Corner.

Blue Corner is the fish dive to end all fish dives. Secured by a reef hook in a strong current at the reef edge, hovering slightly buoyant above hundreds of metres of blue, I lost myself in the fish festival frolicking around me. Huge schools of snapper and jacks heaved through the blue, patrolled by whitetips and grey reef sharks, dwarfed by the odd lone Napoleon wrasse and the occasional tuna. The finale was a squadron of chevron barracuda, gliding slowly in over the reef top from behind then moving into formation in the blue, turning in unison into the current once settled into position. What an incredible sight all this action was; one we went back to for a second and third time.

Yap is a logical add-on to a Palau adventure and is a tiny, delightful backwater with a rich cultural feel – its large stone money discs lying around the villages and along the village paths are a highlight. Underwater, Yap presents a myriad of great sights, and none more spectacular than their resident manta rays. Just like the barracuda 'squadrons' on Blue Corner in Palau, manta rays in Yap appear at the reef channel sites at feeding times like a squadron of bombers. They appear through the blue and approach the shallows in formation – we saw up to seven at once – then settle together over the cleaning station, gently finning their wing-tips to stay stationary. We laid underneath them, in awe, closer and for longer than we could have hoped; in the end it was our air supply that ended the dive, not the departure of the mantas.

Sue Laing, managing director, the risk store, Sydney, Australia

Chuuk

It's 0530 on 17 February 1944. Japanese radar detect the approach of an aircraft squadron. The attack begins within the hour. An estimated 100 American planes (out of a total of 450) blitz what was thought to be an impenetrable fortress. After that first wave, Operation Hailstone continues for two days and annihilates the entire Japanese fleet stationed in Truk Lagoon.

Standing on a flawless beach, beneath a rustling palm looking at a perfectly calm sea, it's hard to imagine the devastation of those two days. The islands of modern Chuuk seem so far removed you could almost convince yourself it had never happened until you get below the water. The Japanese Imperial Fleet had long recognized the value of Chuuk's completely enclosed lagoon. They felt that having a few entry and exit channels would make the lagoon easy to defend against a naval attack – but it also made it a trap.

There are 40 or so shipwrecks lying on the lagoon floor and each and every one is a sumptuous artificial reef, an incredible tour through a moment in history. Each is a testimonial to her purpose: you will find the remains of tanks and jeeps, anti-aircraft guns and torpedo tubes and far more ammunition than you care to think about. There are broken aircraft and abandoned submarines but you won't find any human remains: as many as could be recovered were returned to their homeland, an action regarded as vital to Japan's religious beliefs.

You also won't see as many artefacts as you may have thought. Sadly, many small items have been systematically plundered – by tourists desperate for a souvenir, by locals trying to profit from selling artefacts and by local fishermen who have salvaged explosives for their own use.

The dives here tend to be deep – not so deep as to be dangerous but most are well beyond 20 metres. Some wrecks sit at 50 metres plus, well beyond Nitrox limits. Air divers should approach these carefully and plan thoroughly, taking safety stops at several levels. Operators hang emergency tanks at five metres. Water temperatures are consistent with an average of 28°C. Currents are rare, with just occasional surface movement, and visibility can be said to be good year-round although less clear in the rainy season when there are also plankton and jellyfish blooms. There are also dives on the outer reefs, but a combination of natural and man-made damage means that these reefs are not really worth diverting from the wrecks.

ⓝ12 Sankisan Maru

🌀 **Depth**		48 m
◑ **Visibility**		fair to brilliant
🌀 **Currents**		no
🌀 **Dive type**		day boat

Regarded as Chuuk's prettiest wreck, the *Sankisan's* history is unknown. She may have been Japanese, launched in 1942, or American, launched as the *Red Hook* and later captured by the Japanese. Whatever the truth, the ship was around 4,700 tons, 112-115 metres long and nearly 16 metres wide. Sitting off Uman Island, her demise was caused by strafing from American aircraft but there are no accurate records confirming this. As a dive, the *Sankisan's* reputation is for coral gardens – a strange introduction to the wrecks in the lagoon. As you descend over the hull, the view is one of rainbow-hued reefs rather than disintegrating metal. Divers visit the first hold, which is carpeted in bullets and shells, then back up to deck level, past the remains of vehicles, then down to the next hold. This has a truck and a flat-bed lorry, plus boxes full of medicine bottles, their contents an ominous, chalky white. The divemasters then swim through a warren of corridors to a third hold, with spare parts for engines. On the deck the midships section is quite broken up but covered in corals. Metal joists and beams drip with colour and you see fish you normally see on a reef – longnose hawkfish, moorish idols and mimic filefish. You can plan to dive the ruined stern (48 metres) to see the remains of the propeller and rudder or spend time investigating the incredible growth on the foremast.

Inside and outside the *Sankisan Maru*

N13 The Emily

Depth	17 m
Visibility	fair to good
Currents	no
Dive type	liveaboard

Japanese flying boats were manufactured by the Kawanishi Company. Prior to the war they had been associated with Short Brothers of Belfast, makers of Sunderland and Sandringham flying boats. However, the Japanese Navy wanted faster, stronger boats so after making several modifications Kawanishi developed the H8K, later known as *Emily*. Regarded as the finest flying boat of the war, she was nicknamed the *Flying Porcupine* due to her heavy armaments used for bombing and reconnaissance. The *Emily* lies just to the south of Dublon Island at 17 metres. Like many other wrecks, her history is a little blurred and no doubt embellished over the decades. One tale is that she was shot down while returning some Japanese dignitaries to base after a

trip to Palau. This theory is questionable as there are no signs of bullet damage. Another theory is that she may have been low on fuel and resorted to flying on her inner engines, landed heavily and then flipped over. The propeller blades of her outer engines are not bent while the inner props are bent forward, indicating that she was moving backwards as she went under. You can muse on all this as you fin around her and under her wings. The cockpit is crushed but segments of the fuselage are intact. Poke your nose inside to see glassy sweepers sheltering or small colonies of coral and sponges starting to form. Like all the wrecks, artefacts have been moved around: parts of the cockpit dashboard and telecommunications equipment sit in the sand. Not far away is the wreck of a Zero fighter that is almost completely intact. She sits just off Eten Island in about 10 metres. Although you can't do them both on one dive, you can snorkel over the Zero while gassing off.

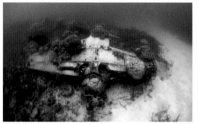

N14 Fujikawa Maru

Depth	34 m
Visibility	fair to excellent
Currents	no
Dive type	liveaboard

The most popular wreck in the lagoon must be the *Fujikawa*, a passenger ship built for the New York run. Requisitioned in 1940 by the Imperial Navy, she was used as an armed transport ship for the delivery of aircraft and spares, amongst other things. She was damaged at anchor in Kwajalein and towed to Chuuk for repairs, arriving on 31 January 1943. The *Fujikawa* is now an excellent wreck dive but showing obvious signs of wear. This is probably since she is upright and one of the shallower dives with plenty of interest on the deck at just 17 metres. Descent is straight down to the very impressive, coral-encrusted bow gun which rests at about 12 metres, bathing in

the sun's rays. Her coating of crusting hard and soft corals is incredibly lush, although you can hardly see them for the amount of fish that swarm around. Just below the gun mount on the deck are two memorial plaques: one for the ship itself and another for well-respected local diver and explorer, Kimiuo Aisek. The two front holds are full of aircraft paraphernalia – propellors, wings, engines and the fuselages of four aircraft

said to be Zero fighters. Heading out of the second hold you can swim through the engine room, a fascinating maze of walkways and engines lit by sunshine filtering from above. One cabin still has a bathroom area and you can see wash basins and urinals. All the holds heading to the stern can be investigated but the most curious is the last, full of sake bottles, china and mess kits.

The Emily and a Zero fighter on the sea bed (above); encrusted bow gun on the Fujikawa

Depth	38 m
Visibility	fair to excellent
Currents	no
Dive type	liveaboard

The *Nippo* was built in 1936 in Kobe as a cargo-passenger vessel then requisitioned in 1941 and refitted to carry water tanks, ordnance and munitions. She arrived in Chuuk in a convoy transporting troops a week before being hit three times in the midships area by 500-lb bombs. The *Nippo* was discovered in 1969 by the Cousteau expedition near Eten Island although her location was 'lost' until the late 1980s when the ship's bell was discovered, engraved with both English and Japanese characters. At 107 metres long the remains of the *Nippo* could easily take three dives to fully investigate and, as she is sitting at over 50 metres, dives should be carefully planned. The stern is most impressive. As the light fades, and the hull takes on that ghostly quality, a series of three howitzers emerge. To their side are a series of gun mounts and a barrel gun platform. Inside the deepest hold is more artillery, while the next one heading upwards has medical supplies, bowls, wheels and tyres. Another has water tanks, shells and beer bottles. To the port side of the deck is a preserved armoured tank, although its turret gun is missing. A final entry is made into the shallowest hold – and perhaps the most harrowing – where you are reminded what went on here. Surrounded by a swathe of bullets are several gas masks.

Medicines and the bridge on the *Nippo Maru*

Drying out

Micronesia's land attractions may take a back seat when compared to other countries but there is just enough to do to give a flavour of life on these Pacific islands. Generally, accommodation options are limited (Palau has the biggest variety) so always choose in conjunction with your dive centre.

Manila

As the best flight for Palau and Yap leaves Manila early in the morning, chances are you will end up spending the night there. Book into a hotel close to the airport overnight (such as the Heritage) and catch up on some sleep before flying out again. Refer to the Philippines chapter, page 158 for details.

Palau

Dive centres

Fish 'n' Fins, T+680 (1)488 2637, fishnfins.com. One of Palau's most diverse and professional operations with full daily dive programmes, dive courses, photo facilities, a shop and a restaurant. They will collect divers from any hotel and assist with all bookings across the island.
Sam's Tours, T+680 (1)488 1062, samstours.com. PADI 5-star centre that also runs land-based tours.

Liveaboards

Big Blue Explorer/Eco Explorer, T+63 (0)890 6778, explorerfleet.com. Large vessels with plenty of deck space and camera rooms but cabins are small and simple. Good for divers on a budget. Great dive set-up with spacious, shaded dive tenders.
Ocean Hunter 1 & III, T+680 (1)488 2637, oceanhunter.com. Two luxury vessels of varying sizes. All cabins are en suite and very smart. On-board facilities depend on choice of boat but are all of a high quality. Part of Fish 'n Fins.

Sleeping

$$ The Carolines Resort, T+680 (1)488 3754, carolinesresort.com. Small boutique hotel with traditional Palauan bungalows.
$ West Plaza Malakal, T+680 (1)488 5291, wphpalau.com. One of a series of good quality, locally owned hotels. Huge rooms just a hop from the harbour so a good choice for pre- or post- liveaboard trips.

Palau

Palau's history reaches back centuries to a once highly family-orientated, matrilineal society: during the Stone Age women were in charge of finances and the men had to ask permission to spend! More recently, periods of European colonialism led to Japanese occupation during the Second World War followed by American rule. Independence was finally granted in 1994. The result here, unlike Yap and Chuuk, is a cosmopolitan atmosphere created by the melting pot of cultures. The biggest influence is probably Chinese but with residents coming from Japan, the Philippines, America and Europe.

On Koror, the main island, there are tours to traditional villages that still retain their ancient meeting houses. There is

Eating

$$ Ba-ra-cu-da Restaurant, part of the Fish 'n' Fins clan. Catch a taxi to M dock for their superb Mediterranean-inspired food.
$$ Palm Bay Bistro and Brewing Company, opposite the West Plaza Malakal. Eat on the deck for views over the bay. Home of locally brewed Red Rooster beer.

also a National Museum (US$5) and the Etpison Museum, which has some art and ancient artefacts. The International Coral Reef Centre (aka aquarium) is at M dock and entry costs US$7. On Pelilu, there are several Second World War sites and memorials. You are unlikely to see much else in the way of crafts or traditions, except perhaps some old money beads in a souvenir shop. One thing you are likely to see though, is the use of turtle shell and corals for making knick-knacks. Don't buy these as the trade should be discouraged and import of turtle shell to many other countries is illegal.

Other activities are water-based – walks to a waterfall, kayaking, snorkelling around the Rock Islands and so on.

Terry's dive brief for the *Iro*; boarding time for a Palau liveaboard; deserted beaches and islands

	Sleeping	$$$ US$150+ double room per night	$$ US$75-150	$ under US$75
	Eating	$$$ US$40+ 2-course meal, excluding drinks	$$ US$20-40	$ under US$20

Yap

Dive centres

$$$ Manta Ray Bay Hotel and Yap Divers, T+691 (1)350 2300, mantaray.com. What can you say – the original, the best, setting the standards. Lovely rooms, morning coffee delivery, good restaurant, great dive set-up, camera facilities and a unique PADI Speciality Manta Ray Awareness course.

Sleeping

$$ O'Keefe's Waterfront Inn, T+691 (1)350 6500, okeefesyap.com. Delicious New England style inn right beside Yap Divers. Friendly owner, small but perfectly formed rooms and a great bar.

Eating

$$$ Traders Ridge Resort, uphill behind the Oasis. Impressive 'fusion' style meals.

$$ The Mnuw, a schooner-cum-restaurant moored at Manta Ray Bay. Serves a mix of American and oriental food.

$ The Oasis, a small café opposite Manta Ray Bay. Good local style meals.

Chuuk

Dive centres

$$ Blue Lagoon Resort and Dive centre, T+691 (1)330 2727, bluelagoonresort.com. The better located of the two resorts with beautiful grounds, good restaurant and lovely rooms. Perfect for a few nights pre-liveaboards but let down by a neglected dive operation in need of upgrading.

$$ Truk Stop Hotel and Dive Centre, T+691 (1)330 4232, trukstop.com. This modern hotel suffers from being right in the centre of town. The dive operation is said to have good facilities and professional guides. Rumour has it that it is possible to stay at Blue Lagoon and dive with Truk Stop.

Liveaboards

Odyssey Adventures, T+1 (1)904 346 3766, trukodyssey.com. American-run liveaboard leaves from the Blue Lagoon's dock. It can take up to two years to get a booking.

Other options

The **SS Thorfinn**, thorfinn.net sails around Truk Lagoon. This vessel appears to be more budget orientated.

Yap's stone money and the high street in Kolona; recovered war artefacts; the edge of Truk Lagoon

Yap

The ancient Yapese empire was a powerful one but almost unknown until European explorers came looking for riches like spices and *beche de mer*. Many foreign countries influenced life here until the Japanese took hold during the two World Wars. Control then passed to the US. Despite this, Yap is the most traditional of the islands. The village remains the social hub and each chief holds sway over his clan. The sexes live fairly separate lives and there is a resolve to keep traditions alive.

People are friendly but come across as shy. If you are out walking, say hello to anyone you pass, and ask to walk across land. Always ask to photograph someone and don't step across sitting people. Also, carry something: empty hands are said to show signs of a troublemaker!

Take a morning to see compact Kolonia, the capital. From Manta Ray Bay, walk around the coast towards the hospital, stopping at the Yap Art Gallery to admire the work of local artists. Then go back towards town and up the stone path by the defunct Ocean View Hotel – a stone money disc marks the route, which is lined with plants and flowers. At the top you come to a paved road where you can turn left and go past St Mary's church, head right all the way up Medeqdeq Hill or go straight across and down a slippery stone path to Chamoor Bay. In the bay is the Ethnic Art Institute where you find women weaving cloth or men carving. Another walk leads from here to the village of Balabat, known as the stone money bank as the road is lined with a large collection of *rai*, the huge stone discs that were used to display the wealth of a village.

Chuuk

Unlike Yap, contemporary history seems to have eroded much of Chuuk's past. Foreign contact arrived in a similar way and had much the same effect, until it culminated in the total occupation of these islands by the Japanese Imperial Navy during the Second World War.

Chuuk is now Micronesia's most populous state with the highest quota of government senators, yet it appears to be struggling to cope with the modern world. Island life was once based on a clan system but this is no longer apparent. The elderly are still greatly respected and women bow to men but both unemployment and alcoholism are rife.

There are few facilities for general tourism. The airport is comparatively sophisticated so your first view of the town as you drive through may come as a shock. You could take a day trip to explore the recent history: these cover Nefo Cave, the Japanese War Memorial, Gun and Lighthouse, from where views over the lagoon are revealing. There are few chances to see other islands except Eten, its shape changed by the Japanese who excavated the hill for an airfield: now it resembles an aircraft carrier. The Officer's quarters are still standing despite US bombing.

Crafts are rare, but you will see lovesticks: a slender, dagger-shaped, wooden rod that was traditionally carved on Fefak. Male islanders carve their personal notches on the lovestick for a would-be sweetheart. At night, the chap would kneel beside the thatch wall opposite where his intended lay sleeping, poke the stick through the wall and entangle her long hair, hopefully awakening her but not her family.

Micronesia Drying out

Australia

Undescribed but awe-inspiring: the dwarf minke whale is a subspecies of *Balaenoptera acutorostrata*.
Ribbon Reef No.3, Great Barrier Reef

INDONESIA

Banda Sea

PAPUA
NEW
GUINEA

JAKARTA   *Java*

Bali

↘4

↘3   *Christmas Island*

Cocos Keeling

Timor Sea

● Darwin

↘2

↘
Cairns

Rowley Shoals

● Broome
✈

● Exmouth

AUSTRALIA

▲
Uluru

INDIAN OCEAN

✈

● Perth

↘1   **Great Barrier Reef**   ▶▶ p188

↘1	Double Bommie
↘2	Tongue Reef
↘3	Mackay Bommies
↘4	Flare Point Reef
↘5	Steve's Bommie
↘6	Pixie Pinnacle
↘7	The Cod Hole
↘8	North Horn
↘9	The Entrance
↘10	Half Way Wall
↘11	Round the Bend

↘8
↘9
↘10
↘11

↘7

↘6

↘5
↘4

↘3

Daintree National Park

↘2
↘1

Port ●
Douglas

Cairns ●

↘2   **Rowley Shoals**   ▶▶ p194

Mermaid Reef
↘14

Clerke Reef
↘13
↘12

Imperieuse Reef

↘12	The Channel, Clerke Reef
↘13	Blue Lagoon, Clerke Reef
↘14	Cod Hole, Mermaid Reef

↘3   **Cocos Keeling**   ▶▶ p195

Horsborough Island
↘15
↘16

Direction Island
↘17

South Keeling Atoll

↘15	Clare's Corner
↘16	Cologne Gardens
↘17	Cat's Cables

Coral Sea

ort Moresby

350 km

● Brisbane

PACIFIC OCEAN

● Sydney

4 Christmas Island ▶▶ p197

21

20

18 Settlement ●

19

18 Perpendicular Wall
19 Thundercliff
20 Flying Fish Cove/Kelana's Mooring
21 Coconut Point

Introduction

Geographically isolated from the rest of the planet, the Australian continent is a place of timeless beauty: from sun-warmed landscapes to dense tropical rainforests; chilly southern beaches to roasting barren deserts. The mind-boggling list of natural attractions is, for many, the biggest drawcard of them all.

'Big' is an adjective often used in conjunction with Australia. Its sheer size can be overwhelming and visitors rarely realize just how enormous the place is. For divers, there's also the biggest reef system on the planet – the Great Barrier Reef. Stretching over vast tracts of sea, it encompasses several distinct geographical and climatic zones. You can even snorkel with one of the ocean's biggest animals, the dwarf minke whale.

The Reef isn't the only diving in Australia's tropical waters, however: those continually searching for the next frontier will find unspoiled, undiscovered islands and atolls off the west coast.

On land, there are more sights than you could ever hope to see. Major cities share a love of art and culture, sport and the great outdoors; you can sail past the Sydney Opera House and climb the Harbour Bridge; fly over Uluru; tour wineries; camp beside kangaroos or trek in the Kimberley. Just don't hope to do it all in one trip.

Australia rating

Diving
★★★★

Dive facilities
★★★★

Accommodation
★★★★

Down time
★★★★

Value for money
★★★

Essentials

Getting there and around

Most major airlines fly to Australia so there are no problems getting there. However, flying halfway round the globe in one go is guaranteed to get you nicely jet-lagged so do consider taking a stop en route. For divers, reaching the Great Barrier Reef (GBR) means getting to Cairns but there are far fewer direct flights than there once were. Brisbane, a two-hour flight away, is the closest option, though you are likely to get a better price flying via Sydney. The latter is also a great city for a stopover (see page 200). To fly direct to Cairns from Bali, New Zealand, Singapore or Japan, try Qantas subsidiary Jetstar (jetstar.com) or from New Zealand and the US there are flights on Virgin Blue (virginblue.com.au).

For Western Australia, head to Perth. Nearly as many major airlines land there as on the east coast. Or if you are routing via Asia there is a weekly flight to Christmas Island. The tourist board has up-to-date details (christmas.net.au).

Once you reach Australia, transport needs a little more thought. Because this is one enormous island, moving between any two points will take time. If you intend to see more than one state, flying is the only way to go. The main internal carriers are Virgin Blue (virginblue.com.au) and Qantas (qantas.com.au). Flights to Western Australia's offshore islands are charters and best booked through your dive operator who will have up-to-date schedules. Australia has good bus and train networks, but as the trip from Sydney to Cairns takes up to 48 hours, that's not a sensible choice. Car rental is relatively cheap but again the distances involved make this less

attractive. The best option is to fly over the long hauls and drive through the scenic areas. Airport transfers are rarely included although minibus shuttles and taxis are reasonably priced. Dive operators will advise how to make the best connection. Most people hire a car for at least part of their time. Aussies are mostly gregarious so you will always be offered help and advice.

Language

English, though certainly not the Queen's variety, is the national tongue. The local dialect has been nicknamed 'Strine' in honour of the Aussie capacity to shorten every word and lengthen every vowel. Don't expect a local to pronounce a three syllable word when they can shorten it to two. Hence chardonnay becomes 'chardy' and relatives becomes 'rellos'. Then there's a whole plethora of non-words that have almost become a parody of themselves. Here are a few common ones:

hello	*g'day*
goodbye	*hooroo*
you're welcome	*no worries*
thank you	*good on ya, mate*
go away	*rack off*
gosh	*strewth (god's truth)*
good	*bonza, ripper*
beer	*amber nectar*

… and some really curious ones:

true	*fair dinkum*
condom	*franger*
crazy	*kangaroo loose in the top paddock*

And if you see 'flake' in a fish and chip shop, it's shark meat.

Local laws and customs

Australia and etiquette? Aussies would be the first to laugh at that idea. Things are informal there. People generally live an outdoor life with an easy-going attitude. The national motto has got to be 'no worries, mate'. There are few pretensions, though places such as Sydney and Port Douglas have trendy establishments where smarter clothes for evenings out are a good idea. Beyond that it would be hard to insult an Aussie – unless you pinch their drink!

Australia	
Location	27°00'S, 133°00'E
Capital	Canberra
Population	21,262,641
Land area in km^2	7,617,930
Coastline in km	25,760

Whip corals on Christmas Island

Safety

Australia is a fairly isolated place. Its sheer size coupled with the small population means that even the biggest cities can feel like small towns to travellers from London, New York, Paris or Tokyo. The upside is that the crime rate is relatively low.

Personal safety, even in the state capitals, is no serious cause for concern. Although there are incidents, they're not common. However, when something awful does happen, it will get more press than you'd expect to hear about back home. Be careful if you're out for a late night walk, especially lone female travellers. And if you visit one of the rowdier nightlife areas, such as Sydney's Kings Cross, keep your wits about you.

Dive regions are immensely traveller friendly but anywhere can attract a small-time thief. Dive and camera bags are best safely stowed in the boot of a car.

Health

When it comes to medicine and health care, Australia is a world leader. Should you be unfortunate enough to get ill, you will be extremely well looked after. The chances of being unwell, however, are low. There are mosquitoes, but non-malarial, and other tropical diseases such as dengue are rare. The sun is very strong so a high factor sunscreen is a must. The Aussie saying is 'slip, slap, slop': slip on a shirt, slop on sunscreen, slap on a hat. It's good advice.

Costs

Compared to other Western countries Australia is reasonably priced, but less so in tourist regions. Petrol is cheap compared to the UK (currently around AU$1.45/litre) making car hire affordable. There are restaurants to suit every budget; the major cities boast world-class eateries and little Port Douglas is home to three of the country's top seven restaurants. Very much based on the concept of fusion food, a three course meal there can cost well over AU$50 per head without wine, but it will be some of the most interesting food you will ever eat. At the other end of the scale, you can eat quite cheaply in a tavern or pub where basic steak and chips will be around AU$20. Similarly with alcohol, a bottle of wine in a store can be just a few dollars while the same bottle in a restaurant will require a credit card.

Australia is very much a destination where you get what you pay for. Hotels work along much the same lines; cheap will mean basic or a little run down but usually clean; higher rates bring corresponding standards. Tipping is not the norm: Aussies rarely do as the minimum wage is comparatively high and strictly adhered to. You should only feel obliged to tip if someone has given excellent service and then it's mostly 10% or less.

Fact file

International flights	American, BA, Cathay, Emirates, Malaysian, Qantas, Singapore, Tiger Airways etc to Brisbane, Perth or Sydney; Jetstar or Virgin Blue to Cairns; National Jet to Christmas Island and Cocos (Keeling).
Departure tax	Usually included in ticket or AU$40
Entry	Everyone except New Zealanders needs a visa. Most airlines issue an electronic travel authority with their ticket for which there may be a small fee
Internal flights	Qantas, Virgin Blue, National Jet Systems
Ground transport	Countrywide buses, trains and car hire
Money	US$1 = 1.38 Australian dollars (AUD)
Language	English
Electricity	240v, plug type E (page 16)
Time zone	GMT +8 Perth, GMT +10 Sydney
Religion	Christian
Phone	Country code +61; IDD code 0011; Police 999

Napoleon wrasse on the Great Barrier Reef

 Tourist information → Local government websites are at Queensland: tq.com.au, Western Australia: westernaustralia.com, Christmas Is: christmas.net.au, Cocos Keeling: cocos-tourism.cc.

Dive brief

Diving

What makes Australia fascinating for divers is that it has over 25,000 km of coastline and spans several distinctive climate zones. The very tip of northern Queensland is just 10 degrees short of the Equator while the island of Tasmania in the far south has weather that's not unlike northern England.

This vast expanse is also bordered by two of the world's largest oceans and many different seas, which all add up to the most varied diving on the planet with cold water wrecks, bathtub temperature reefs and isolated atolls in the middle of nowhere.

Although you could pick up a tank and dive almost anywhere, there are two main areas. The destination that lures most, divers and non-divers alike, is the Great Barrier Reef in Queensland. A few years back it was even voted second in a major survey of 'top things to do before you die'.

Directly across the continent, Western Australia is also on the hot list, not because it, too, has a single major dive attraction but, in contrast, because it has several small, isolated destinations that are perfect for adventurers or those who might feel they've done everything else.

Snorkelling

Snorkellers are well catered for wherever you are but not necessarily in the same places as divers. On the GBR, much of the better diving is located a long way from shore, while easy snorkelling tends to be nearer the coast. Special day trips are run to the closer reefs which will ensure fun for both parties, but these tend to be on large cruise-style boats to designated zones that have a plethora of commercial services attached. Ask a dive centre for advice on smaller, more personal trips.

The facilities are much the same on the west coast, with the exception of organized whaleshark snorkelling tours at Ningaloo. Christmas Island's shoreline is also great for snorkelling but get advice on daily currents and tides.

Marine life

Commonly seen marine creatures range from the very biggest – such as the blue whales that slide down the eastern seaboard and the populations of reef sharks on isolated atolls – to the very smallest seahorses, which you can spot during a shore dive in the middle of Sydney.

Australia
animal
encounters

Great Barrier Reef	minke whales
Rowley Shoals	tiger sharks
Cocos (Keeling)	bottlenose dolphins
Christmas Island	dragon morays

Soft corals in the depths at Osprey Reef; a turtle in the Christmas Island shallows

"" Australia is my birthplace, and if only I had a dollar for every time I'm asked why I left. Well, apart from marrying a Brit, the answers would fill a whole book! What I would say though is that Oz is, without doubt, one of the world's most beautiful countries; an incredible natural phenomenon. Unique wildlife, remarkable landscapes, colours so rich and seas so varied you can't possibly believe they are real. Even if it's a once-in-a-lifetime experience, it's one you definitely must have.

Making the big decision

As this is the single longest haul you are ever likely to make there is absolutely no point in travelling so far to do just one thing. On the other hand Australia is so vast it's also impossible to do it all. Choose the one dive destination you fancy most and build a trip around that. It won't be difficult as Aussie tourism is set up to work in short, sharp bursts. In a three week trip you can dive, visit a rainforest or desert, see a major city and still return home without feeling you already need another holiday.

The harlequin tuskfish living up to its name

Dive data

Tropical regions only

Seasons	Summer (December to February) can get uncomfortably hot and humid, while winter (June to August) has pleasant air temperatures but comparatively cool water
Visibility	5 metres inshore to 40 metres+ in open water
Temperatures	Air 30-34°C; water 25-30°C
Wet suit	3 mm full body suit, 5 mm for GBR in winter
Training	Courses available everywhere: look for PADI, NAUI or SSI training agencies
Nitrox	Available in Queensland. Most liveaboards also carry, but quantities may be limited so pre-booking is advised
Deco chambers	Brisbane, Freemantle, Sydney, Townsville

Bottom time

Queensland	Edging the western side of the Pacific Ocean, the planet's longest coral reef shadows the coast of the tropical state of Queensland for 2300 km before petering out just above the Tropic of Capricorn.
Great Barrier Reef ▶▶ p188	Colour and variety traverse the planet's largest and most famous coral reef system.
Coral Sea ▶▶ p192	Pristine hard corals and amazing visibility over deep, open-water atolls.
Western Australia	Sitting alongside the Indian Ocean, the biggest of Australia's five states is an empty but immensely impressive wilderness. This is reflected in her isolated marine attractions.
Rowley Shoals ▶▶ p194	A remote dive adventure, accessible for only three months a year.
Cocos (Keeling) Islands ▶▶ p195	Australia relocated to an almost unknown isolated Indian Ocean atoll.
Christmas Island ▶▶ p197	Known as 'Australia's Galápagos' for its amazing environment and exceptional numbers of indigenous wildlife.

Diversity

reef area 48,960 km²

HARD CORALS	75
FISH SPECIES	4,522
ENDEMIC FISH SPECIES	494
FISH UNDER THREAT	90
PROTECTED REEFS/MARINE PARKS	15

All diversity figures are approximate

Dive log

Great Barrier Reef

Starting in Papua New Guinea, and even visible from the moon, the Great Barrier Reef meanders down the coast of Queensland until it finally disappears just above the Tropic of Capricorn.

This enormous natural phenomenon consists of nearly 3,000 individual reefs, 1,500 species of fish, 400 corals and 4,000 molluscs. It is also a World Heritage Site, but that's not to say it's pristine along its entire length. The GBR is an active, working, continually changing resource where divers co-exist with fishermen, tropical cyclones and exotic marine fauna such as the devastating crown of thorns starfish.

It's easy to get the impression that visiting the GBR is relatively straightforward. However, it's a substantial sail offshore for most of its length, only nearing the coast in the far north near Cape Tribulation. Its geography creates three distinct sectors to the reef. The **Inner Reefs** sit on the lagoon created by the reef edge and the coast. These are within easy striking distance and are good day trips for novice divers and snorkellers. Next come the **Ribbon Reefs**, the barriers that create the outer edge of the reef just before it drops to the deeper continental shelf. Here, the waters are much clearer and the diving more exciting. Finally,

there are the **Outer Reefs**, sitting a good 12 hours' sail offshore in the Coral Sea. Actually outside the Great Barrier Reef, these are located in open ocean, with virtually no land, and are by far the most challenging diving you can do in this area.

It doesn't matter where you are based in this region as diving is a well-developed industry with its heart in the city of Cairns. Once a slightly seedy, down-at-heel outpost that only attracted vacationing miners and crews from the outback, Cairns cleaned up its act and is now a major heavyweight on the Australian tourist scene. The city has lost ground over the last decade or so to the more sophisticated coastal resorts further north but it still remains the best-serviced hub for divers. The airport is just minutes outside town and there are masses of dive shops, training facilities and organized tours.

Ultra-trendy Port Douglas, an hour's drive north, realised the value of turning its small river basin into a thriving marina. It's a more user-friendly town with a bit of a Mediterranean feel and still enough operators to ensure that anyone who wants to dive or snorkel can do so.

You can dive from many other towns along the Queensland coast but bear in mind that the further south you go, the longer the sailing time from shore to the beginning of the reef.

Arriving at Osprey Reef in the Coral Sea

Inner Reefs

Within a couple of hours' sail from shore, these sites are usually under 20 metres deep and season dependent. Visibility is OK in the summer but in winter the water becomes murky. However, the sea remains calm while more distant reefs are exposed to incoming winds. Small coral outcrops are awash with tropical fish and some interesting critters lurk on the sand. These dives are often used for snorkelling and training novice divers. The restrictions this imposes (time and depth) may be frustrating for more experienced divers but they are good for a day trip or just to get back in the swing of things.

◥1 Double Bommie, Thetford Reef

Depth	12 m
Visibility	poor to good
Currents	mild
Dive type	day boat

Head due east from Cairns for an hour or so to find Thetford Reef, which consists of a complex of coral outcrops. There are several different dive sites dotted around it. Double Bommie is a nice, easy dive. The coral species are not all that colourful or prolific but the reef's character is built on lots of small cut-throughs and tunnels. The outer edge attracts a bit more fish life; moorish idols and sea perch are quite common. Thetford also makes a great night dive as all the tunnel walls are covered in shrimp and small crabs.

◥2 Tongue Reef

Depth	15 m
Visibility	poor to good
Currents	slight to medium
Dive type	day boat

This oval-shaped reef is a short sail from Port Douglas and is a favourite for trainees and novices. Although the dive isn't challenging there are a lot of bigger animals including a resident turtle and Napoleon – or Maori – wrasse. The reef scenery is principally made up of staghorn corals, which guard lots of smaller reef fish like butterflies and wrasse, sweetlips and coral trout. At certain times you can spot barramundi cod and even their spectacular juveniles, which flutter about like hyperactive butterflies.

◥3 Mackay Bommies

Depth	18 m
Visibility	poor to good
Currents	slight to medium
Dive type	day boat

An hour or so from Cape Tribulation these pretty, patch bommies sit on the inner lagoon and are calm and sheltered. Entry is over a sandy expanse of seabed, which means that visibility can be quite low. Small coral outcrops are interspersed with clams in many different hues. The reef is in good condition with some nice soft corals adding colour. Macro life is impressive: there are crab-eyed gobies, pregnant shrimp in mushroom corals and clownfish and anemone partnerships. Occasional jacks dart by plus this is a good reef to spot the indigenous harlequin tuskfish.

◆ Conservation

Australia is very protective of its natural resources and rightly so. Much of what you will see is unique both in geological formation and position. You will be constantly reminded of this, especially in national parks where much is being done to eradicate non-native species. What is bizarre though is how much of what you see appears contradictory – and you wonder how policy-makers make their decisions. This is the home to the world's largest coral reef system yet the authorities not only allow people to walk on it, they actually encourage it which appears to be counter-productive. There are designated usage zones right down the length of the GBR – some are for recreation and sports, some for research, but most are for fishing. And there is no way for these zones to be effectively policed. All that, along with the natural effects of tides and weather, means that you will not see the best of the GBR unless you take an extended trek away from the coast.

Chromodoris nudibranchs and cuttlefish are both typical of the inner reefs

Ribbon Reefs

Running like a ribbon these reefs mark the continental shelf before it drops into the deep-water Queensland Trench. There are dramatic pinnacles and sloping reef walls that were formed by centuries of wave and tidal action. Visibility improves but currents can be stiffer, attracting larger pelagic species. Dive the famous Cod Hole and, in winter, snorkel with pods of migrating dwarf minke whales.

◢4 Flare Point Reef	
Depth	18 m
Visibility	good
Currents	medium to strong
Dive type	liveaboard

A gentle fringing reef with lots of small outcrops over a sandy bottom where you can find odd creatures like mantis shrimp and the world's largest nudibranch, the *Notodoris minor*. There is a variety of unusual small fish that nest amongst the bommies. Female cuttlefish are frequently spotted here as well, laying their eggs in staghorn coral outcrops whilst being guarded by their male. Other males hover cautiously nearby and large schools of snappers hang out with rabbit fish.

◢5 Steve's Bommie	
Depth	40 m
Visibility	good
Currents	can be strong
Dive type	liveaboard

Another typical pinnacle dive but with a flat, sloping base. The coral at the bottom on the lee side is damaged but fin around into the current and the pace picks up. Schooling jacks hover in small groups and surgeonfish display courtship protocol by performing a male/female colour change dance. Tuna pass by out in the blue surrounded by rainbow runners. The wall has a good cover of tubastrea trees and if you are lucky you can spot the tasselled wobbegong – a very pretty, native shark.

◢6 Pixie Pinnacle	
Depth	28 m
Visibility	good
Currents	mild to strong
Dive type	liveaboard

This small pinnacle rises from the seabed to just below the surface. A slope near the base has nice soft corals and fans. Red and purple anthias dart around a small cave, tiny pipefish keeping them company. Around the pinnacle there is good macro life including the flame fire shell, which has an electric current lighting up its bright red tentacles. It nestles in crevices while nearby white leaffish hide amongst plate corals. Out in the blue are chevron barracuda, trevally and midnight snappers.

Minke madness

Every winter, between June and August, a very special event takes place along the Ribbon Reefs...

Pods of dwarf minke whales appear and, curiously, come to play with dive boats. This strange behaviour was first noted when scientists realised that these minkes were different from both Antarctic minkes and 'true' minkes, which are only seen in the northern hemisphere. The GBR visitors are 2 metres shorter than their Antarctic cousins and have different skin colours and patterns. At up to 8 metres long and weighing around 5 or 6 tonnes, these creatures will be one of the biggest things you'll ever get close to in the water. When a pod arrives, they often circle the dive boat, gradually coming closer and closer. It is possible to snorkel with them, though the rules for this are very strict. Drag lines are attached to the boat for snorkellers to grab while 'under pain of death' should they let go. This is to prevent the whales being frightened off. Scientists have been studying the dwarf minke behaviour and are aiming to understand their migration, lifestyle patterns and – most interestingly for divers – why they hang around boats.

7 The Cod Hole

Depth	25 m	
Visibility	good	
Currents	none to strong	
Dive type	liveaboard	

In the early 1970s, famous Australian biologists and adventurers, Ron and Valerie Taylor, discovered a patch of reef consisting of three parallel coral ridges and gullies with a depression, or hole, to one end. This reef topography created a protected haven for several species of large marine animal, in particular giant potato cod and whitetip sharks. The word got out and not long afterwards, dive operators started feeding the fish to ensure their continual presence for divers. Ecologically this practice is now regarded as unsound and is discouraged. However, the cod have remained and as you enter the water, they come to greet the visiting divers just as they always did.

The giant potato cod is a very curious chap and will hover close by as long as someone is in the water. Likewise, small Napoleon wrasse and large schools of red snapper will do the same. Leaving the hole to explore the ridges and gullies, you'll see that the hard corals along this reef are beautiful and in extremely good condition. In fact, the entire site is very pretty. As you work your way up and down the reef you are likely to meet other cod being cleaned in a crevice or a small turtle resting on a bommie. Whitetip reef sharks often sit on the sandy seabed but take off as soon as divers approach, no doubt feeling that the narrow spaces are just not big enough for everyone. There is also an enormous clam – well over a metre long – nestling in the top of one of the ridges.

For many, the main attraction on the Great Barrier Reef has to be that most famous of dive sites, the Cod Hole. In all truth, we weren't looking forward to revisiting it. We had dived there ten years previously and it had been trashed. Too many divers, too many feeding sessions. Now, ecotourism has kicked in and operators are much more responsible. Although some still feed the cod (mentioning no names), the practice is fading away. The hard corals have regenerated well yet all the animals remain.

Coral Sea

In 1803, this group of isolated atolls were discovered a couple of hundred kilometres from the GBR. The only inhabitants both then and now were a large population of seabirds. There are no land masses, just exposed reef tops. Below the waterline these are in pristine condition as they are only ever visited by liveaboard dive boats and getting there requires an overnight sail. There are several reef systems but the one that attracts the most dive visitors is Osprey. This 21 km-long oval drops to over 700 metres below sea level. It has a shallow inner lagoon, which is ringed by sharp fringing reefs.

▨8 North Horn

🕐	**Depth**	40 m
◑	**Visibility**	good to excellent
🌊	**Currents**	slight to strong
🌀	**Dive type**	liveaboard

North Horn is on the northwestern tip of Osprey and is subject to enough current to always attract schooling sharks. From the second you drop in, the clear visibility ensures a good view of the resident grey whaler sharks. Large barracuda often hang off the wall, which drops to a ridge of huge soft coral trees and fan corals. A horn-shaped coral head juts upwards from about 20 metres and the resident whitetip sharks circle it constantly. There are smaller animals too, like coral trout, gobies and a variety of hawkfish. Doing a safety stop back on the shot line is ever entertaining as the whalers perform belly rolls just below. This dive is quite a rush.

▨9 The Entrance

🕐	**Depth**	25 m
◑	**Visibility**	good to excellent
🌊	**Currents**	slight to strong
🌀	**Dive type**	liveaboard

A group of hard coral bommies surround a narrow channel that leads to the inner lagoon. The sandy seabed harbours many critters like imperial shrimp on cucumbers and masses of commensal shrimp and goby pairs. The dive plan takes you around the bommies where there are colourful schooling fish, clownfish living in carpet anemones, hawkfish and blennies. Between two of the pinnacles, and just under the mooring line, there is a very small double-ended cave. You can swim through carefully and, midway, see an anchor embedded in the coral. No one knows where it came from but it's thought to be late 19th or early 20th century.

▨10 Half Way Wall

🕐	**Depth**	25 m
◑	**Visibility**	good to excellent
🌊	**Currents**	slight to strong
🌀	**Dive type**	liveaboard

This steep wall has sharp cut backs along its face. The mooring line drops to a round hump that masks an overhang full of whip corals that grow, unusually, both up and down. At the base of the wall, a sandy area is home to plenty of damselfish and blue flagtails. There is a patch of lacy fire coral that protects well camouflaged stonefish and puffers. There are some lesser known fish like bluestreaked gobies and midas blennies along with longsnout butterflies, whip coral gobies and ever more whitetips.

▨11 Round the Bend

🕐	**Depth**	33 m
◑	**Visibility**	good
🌊	**Currents**	slight to strong
🌀	**Dive type**	liveaboard

This long wall is covered with large crusting plate corals, mostly montipora species, and interspersed with a variety of interesting algae species: sea grapes, turtle weed, coralline algae and sailor's eyeballs. The top three metres is very pretty with lots of pale lemon, blue and pink corals and sponges while at depth there are huge dendronephthya trees. Small gobies and blennies pepper the wall and critters includes shrimp in mushroom coral.

Whitetip reef shark with remora in tow, North Horn; a bob tail or bottle tail squid on the GBR

Western Australia

The biggest of Australia's five states and almost half her landmass, Western Australia is an empty yet immensely impressive wilderness. With so much coastline you'd be forgiven for thinking WA would be a magnet for dive centres but strangely it's not. There's some cool water diving near Perth, but the only tropical diving on the mainland centres around Ningaloo Reef. And the reason why? Well, distances are enormous, the local populations are small and all diving tends to be seasonal.

That's not to say that you can't dive near Ningaloo all year round. You can, and some diving is said to be first rate, but the main attraction is the whalesharks. Every year between March and May these gentle giants pass along the reef then disappear again. Special day trips are set up: spotter planes fly over the reef and radio directions to the boats below. If a whaleshark is seen all the boats head for it. You can't dive here though, it's snorkelling only and even that is limited by time and numbers.

There are a handful of dive centres in Exmouth, a small town built to service the local military base, and in tiny Coral Bay, 150 km to the south. Both have reasonable facilities but, given the seasonal limitations, it's hard to recommend travelling to just this one area from overseas. Some people go, see loads of whalesharks, love the experience and have a great time. But as many are frustrated so it's best to combine the area with another one close by.

There is fabulous diving to be had if you travel from Western Australia's coast, out into the Indian Ocean. Three offshore destinations are a huge surprise: idyllic and isolated, yet incredibly impressive, are the Rowley Shoals, Cocos (Keeling) Islands and Christmas Island. Each has its own distinct geography and personality. **Rowley** consists of three pear-shaped atolls surrounding shallow lagoons. The walls have near-vertical sides rising from very deep water and are smothered in vast swathes of hard coral. **Cocos (Keeling)** spans two small oceanic atolls that are 24 km apart. The southern atoll has some 52 km of fringing reef surrounding a horseshoe-shaped lagoon which attracts a mass of pelagic species.

Perhaps the most impressive of these offshore destinations though, is rainforest-covered **Christmas Island**, with almost as many endemic land and bird species as in the Galápagos Islands. Christmas is also the location of the famed annual red crab migration. The diving is an incredible mix of steep walls, pristine corals, schools of fish and pelagics. There is even some easily accessible cave diving.

Fish tales

It's a long, red, dusty drive from anywhere but you know you're in Exmouth when you hear the corellas. These raucous birds greet you and then hang around. When we phoned Coral Bay to reserve diving for the next week, the dive shop somehow knew we were in Exmouth. When I asked how he figured it out he said "easy, I can hear the cockies." That's WA for you.

Exmouth has one of the best dives in Australia – Navy Pier. I've done the dive six times and would happily go again (and again). It's easy, shallow and warm, though the giant stride entry can be a bit daunting. Sharks cruise the middle, anglerfish hang on the pylons, nudibranchs are all over, and there is a huge resident turtle. There are flatworms, octopus, wobbegongs and what the locals call a 'toadfish'. Big stuff, little stuff, weird stuff. And then there are the fish! Schools of barracuda, trevally, and striped perch (everything is a perch or a cod to Aussies). My log book is a long list of sightings from my first couple of dives; the last two times I've only recorded depth and time followed by a big blank space. Some dives resist being logged...

Whalesharks are a big draw here, though I must admit, I took a pass. The astronomical price goes up each day as the season progresses and it all seems a bit put on, more geared to non-divers and tourists completing their must-do lists. For my money, I'd rather dive the rest of Ningaloo Reef. It is remote, undiscovered, and pristine. Or go back to Navy Pier!

Joann Gren, emergency medicine specialist, Falcon, Western Australia

Spinner dolphins and soft coral tentacles, both enjoying life in the ocean currents

Rowley Shoals

On the northwestern coast of Western Australia is the town of Broome; a strange and very multicultural little place. Its past is based around the pearl industry of the early 1900s. Chinese and Indonesian populations were here long before white Australians moved in. The pearl industry has since declined somewhat and Broome now has the eerie atmosphere of a post-boom wild west frontier town. You can almost see the tumbleweed rolling down the streets after lunch on a Saturday.

Broome is the closest access point to the Rowley Shoals. This small group of atolls is 260km offshore and reaching it involves a rough 12-hour crossing, which can only be made from September to November as conditions are too difficult at other times. However, once there, you will find some outstanding diving. Clerke and Mermaid Reefs have an unusually large tidal range of over three metres. Consequently there is some powerful but exciting current diving. The water here is always clear, at least in dive season, so there's no risk of missing whatever pelagic life passes by.

12 The Channel, Clerke Reef

Depth	20 m
Visibility	good to excellent
Currents	mild to ripping
Dive type	liveaboard

Between the outer edge of this circular reef and the inner lagoon is a sharp-sided, long and narrow channel that was created by natural erosion. It transports water in and out of the lagoon during the extreme tidal changes and makes for a thrilling drift dive. No matter whether you do it on the incoming or outgoing current, this takes a little nerve, too, as the flow of water propels you much faster through the tight, confined space than you could ever do on your own. It is an outstanding roller coaster ride between the walls, around bommies and outcrops, past reef fish and corals until the current deposits you at the end of the ride into complete calm in the sea. On the outer wall, away from the rush, large schools of jacks hang about in clusters as do bronze whalers and, quite frequently, tiger sharks. The Channel also makes an excellent high speed snorkel especially when the current is heading out to sea.

13 Blue Lagoon, Clerke Reef

Depth	30 m
Visibility	fair to good
Currents	mild
Dive type	liveaboard

This fantastic turquoise blue lagoon is surrounded by sandy patches and small coral bommies. There are lots of pretty soft corals and masses of hard corals, all interspersed with channels and swim throughs. Sailfin snapper, surgeonfish and trevally hover over the wall. Descending beyond the edge of the lagoon, a large sandy amphitheatre is occupied by a gang of inquisitive whitetips sharks. These school around the divers until they get bored. Back on the reef wall, Napoleon wrasse swim by with friendly pufferfish and batfish.

14 Cod Hole, Mermaid Reef

Depth	18 m
Visibility	good to excellent
Currents	mild
Dive type	liveaboard

Not unlike its more famous Queensland counterpart, this Cod Hole is a maze of small bommies, crevices and cut throughs in the reef. There are a lot of very pretty soft corals, some small fans and masses of immaculate hard corals. Three resident potato cod are always around at the start of the dive to greet visiting divers. One is around 1.5 metres long and very curious and is accompanied by another about a metre long. A third, which has a distinctive paler skin, seems to be a loner although all three will come very close, even nudging divers for attention. The rest of the dive consists of a lot schooling fish, including trevally, jacks and red snappers. This is yet another site for spotting bigger predators, like the tiger sharks, which seem indicative of this region.

Soft corals at Blue Lagoon and one of the residents of Mermaid Reef's Cod Hole.

Cocos (Keeling) Islands

The 27 small coral islands and two atolls that make up Cocos are closer to Java than to Australia. A couple of decades ago the local Malay population was given a choice: throw its fortunes in with Australia or turn to Asia for political and economic support. They voted for Australia, which had important military placements there during both world wars, and more recently an animal quarantine station.

A while back it was rumoured this would reopen but that never happened and the island is as sleepy as ever. The international airport has just two flights a week and with only 630 residents, this may be one of the quietest places you will ever visit – until you get under the water. Diving takes place mostly around South Keeling, a horseshoe-shaped atoll dotted with a ring of islands around a central lagoon. Many pelagic species are attracted to hunt around the steep outer walls. There are reef sharks on every dive, something you see in very few places these days. Life is less prolific inside the shallow lagoon but there is the compensation of a few small wrecks.

⎘16 Cologne Gardens

🧭 **Depth**	35 m	
◐ **Visibility**	fair to great	
🌊 **Currents**	mild to strong	
🌀 **Dive type**	day boat	

The outer reef edge off Horsborough Island is completely smothered in hard corals, all in excellent condition. The variety and colours of the leather coral is particularly impressive. Dropping down to 38 metres there are some peach-coloured gorgonians patrolled by young whitetip sharks. Highly inquisitive, they follow divers along for some of the dive. At the top of the wall, where it returns to a gentle slope, there are several different types of trevally swimming in mixed schools, several types of clownfish in anemones and masses of pyramid butterflyfish. The channel beside Horsborough Island is also a regular haunt of a pod of bottlenose dolphins. These absolutely delightful animals are attracted by the sound of the motor as the boat approaches. They wait impatiently for new playmates to drop into the water with mask and snorkel then instigate a frantic game of chase. No prizes for guessing who gets tired first!

⎘17 Cat's Cables, Direction Island

🧭 **Depth**	22 m	
◐ **Visibility**	fair to good	
🌊 **Currents**	mild to strong	
🌀 **Dive type**	day boat	

Inside the lagoon, the sandy seabed is affectionately known as 'diving the desert' as at first glance, it seems quite barren. Far from being a wasteland, however, the flat sand is peppered with smooth rocky ridges and small patches of hard coral where you find giant green morays, tiny pipefish and well-camouflaged flounder. Giant triggerfish mate in this area and whitetips, blacktips and grey reef sharks are all present. The occasional manta makes a fly-by. There is also a small wreck, the remains of a fibreglass refugee boat; the engines and some of the skeletal structure is still intact but the hull is slowly disintegrating. A couple of Second World War telecommunications cables stretch across the seabed. A decaying mechanical cylinder houses lionfish and coral banded shrimp. If you're really lucky you may see Cat, the resident dugong. You can often hear her calling but she has to be in the mood to make an appearance.

⎘15 Clare's Corner

🧭 **Depth**	25 m	
◐ **Visibility**	good	
🌊 **Currents**	mild	
🌀 **Dive type**	day boat	

The top of this reef wall is carved by ridges and gullies dropping to a flat reef and the most enormous table corals. Napoleon wrasse patrol the area and grey sharks stand off in the blue, groups of barracuda and jacks hover over the deeper water. One gully turns into a dog-leg shape and masses of fish shelter inside from larger predators. There are pyramid butterflyfish, angels, snapper and rabbitfish. Returning to the mooring line you pass a flat table coral which extends to over three metres wide and is completely pristine.

Rainbow runners sweeping past Clare's Corner and an old cannon on the floor of the Cocos lagoon

"Expect the unexpected – every dive here is an adventure of discovery... you might encounter a whaleshark, be mesmerized by a seahorse or even buzzed by a school of inquisitive batfish...

Linda Cash, marketing manager, Christmas Island Tourism

Christmas Island

Even closer to Java than Cocos (Keeling), this Australian territory occasionally hits the headlines for the wrong reason – as the site of a controversial refugee station. Although covered in dense jungle, the island's economic mainstay was, until recently, its enormous phosphate mine. The government has now withdrawn all mining licenses giving the natural realm the precedence it deserves – 63% of the island is protected as national park.

The wildlife is beyond impressive: native birdlife includes several endemic species like Abbot's boobies and the Christmas Island frigate bird. There's also a unique fruit bat that is seen soaring on the thermals in daylight. And then there's the forest, the wetlands, the tortuous coastal geography. However, the island's biggest claim to fame is the red crab migration, which occurs in the latter part of the year. When weather patterns are just right, millions of these brightly coloured crustaceans scuttle out of the rainforest and head for the coast to spawn. A few months later all the new born crabs make their way back onshore and return to the rainforest.

The underwater realm is also special. The island is the tip of an ancient volcanic mountain that rises from the edge of the Java Trench at 3,000 metres. Visibility can be outstanding and the reefs are smothered in the most unbelievable, pristine hard corals. Huge pods of spinner dolphins come to play with the dive boats while pelagic species patrol the outer reef edges including, late in the year, whalesharks. No one quite knows why, but these waters attract them in considerable numbers.

Critter life is less evident but recently the island's first seahorse was discovered. There are some outstanding animals such as the rare dragon moray eel and several coastal cave systems that can be safely explored. Snorkelling is fairly easy: the reef shoulder is at 10 metres and as diving is 'live boat' with a skipper always on board, snorkellers can spend time on the reef top with the boat close at hand.

❝❞ **For me, diving the 'Galápagos of Australasia' was all about seeing what dive sites my guests were prepared to sacrifice and how many I could pack into their stay only to find, at the end of their holiday, yet another "positively-not-to-be-missed" list anyway...** *Marcus Cathrein, divemaster*

⬛18 Perpendicular Wall	
🧭 **Depth**	35 m
◐ **Visibility**	excellent
🌀 **Currents**	none to strong
⬤ **Dive type**	day boat

Before arriving at this spectacular dive site you may be lucky enough to encounter some bronze whaler sharks. These are attracted by the boat's engine noise: you can even snorkel with them as they are inquisitive yet have never been known to be aggressive in this situation. A pod of spinner dolphins visit this reef too, so it's another chance to snorkel. The spinners frequently come right up to your mask to say hello. When you do reach the dive site, you'll find an overhang full of parallel fans growing to catch the sunlight like solar panels. You then fin around the bend in the wall where the view is breathtaking. Masses of gigantic gorgonians hang off the wall and there are some even bigger ones in a cave. Out in the blue there are grey reef sharks, a school of jacks and a school of midnight snapper. Back up in the shallows are clusters of hard coral bommies, many hosting brightly coloured christmas tree worms.

Moray and Debelius shrimp at Kelana's Mooring; gangs of batfish on the approach; white leaf scorpionfish in Flying Fish Cove at night

◼19 Thundercliff

🜨	**Depth**	8 m
◑	**Visibility**	fair to stunning
≋	**Currents**	none to mild
◒	**Dive type**	day boat

A dive, a swim and a walk; this is probably one of the most unusual experiences you will ever have. Entering over a shallow section of reef you swim down into a sandy channel, under an overhang and into a wide-mouthed cave. A short fin takes you past a rock that juts almost to the surface and has hundreds of silvery fish swarming it. Continuing on through a narrow tunnel, you reach a dark cavern where you can surface inside to admire the stalagmites before descending into a second tight passage that leads to a much bigger cave. Surfacing again, you find it is decorated by impressive limestone structures. Next, you swim up to a rocky beach and exit onto the rocks, before dekitting for a walk through the cave system to a small pool of brackish water. Inside the pool is a rare red shrimp (as yet unnamed) that is attracted to torch beams, plus a surprise that no one knows about until they've been.

◼20 Flying Fish Cove/Kelana's Mooring

🜨	**Depth**	35 m
◑	**Visibility**	excellent
≋	**Currents**	none
◒	**Dive type**	day boat/shore

This small, pretty bay is the island's only year-round mooring point but is awash with marine life. There are at least two dives. You can start by being dropped at Kelana's Mooring then swim back to shore, or start from shore to dive between the main jetty and the ruins of the collapsed original one. There's even the wreck of a Second World War era supply ship. The mooring is the favoured site for finding the spectacular dragon moray. At 25 metres a substantial stand of corals is filled with morays (at least five different types are tucked inside along with Debelius shrimp). It takes some hunting but a shy dragon is always there. Further up in the shallows, there is less coral but plenty of marine life: octopus, mating pufferfish, huge hawkfish and lots of nudibranchs. At night, and closer to shore or around the old wreck, it's easy to spot critters such as pink leaffish, lionfish, crustaceans and sleeping parrotfish.

◼21 Coconut Point

🜨	**Depth**	38 m
◑	**Visibility**	excellent
≋	**Currents**	none to mild
◒	**Dive type**	day boat

Another site that offers three dives in one, Coconut Point starts at a small sand gully under the cliff. It is surrounded by a flat reef that is completely covered in small hard corals interspersed with critters like rare gold spot scorpions. Swimming over this area, you reach a sheer wall that drops past 60 metres and you can see all the way to the bottom. Indian Ocean triggers and pyramid butterflies mob you as you descend. At 40 metres there are masses of huge gorgonians plus grey reef sharks, dogtooth tuna and trevally patrol the depths. Returning to the gully, a channel leads into a huge cavern with openings to the cliff face on two sides. The light inside has an eerie glow. At the back of the cave you can crab crawl through the surge over beautifully rounded rocks until the light fades. If you turn on your torch, you spy an incredible number of huge lobsters nestled into virtually every crevice.

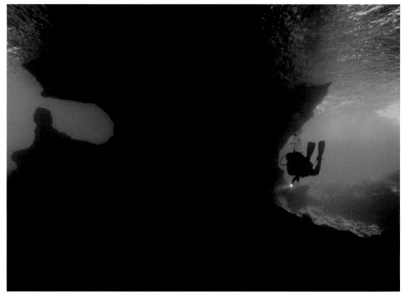

Under the coast and inside the first Thundercliff chamber; the double entrance to Coconut Point.

Drying out

Visiting Australia should be just as much about what to do on land as it is to do with diving – well, almost. Distances between destinations can be immense so limit yourself to one or two states or you'll need a holiday once you get home.

Great Barrier Reef

Cairns

Dive centres

Pro Dive, T+61 (0)7 4031 5255, prodive-cairns.com.au.
Tusa Dive, T+61 (0)7 4031 1028, tusadive.com. Also owns Spirit of Freedom.

Liveaboards

Spirit of Freedom, T+61 (0)7 4040 6450, spiritoffreedom.com.au One of the only luxury liveaboards in these waters with an excellent dive deck, ensuite cabins, outstanding service and food.

Other options

Spoilsort, mikeball.com
Taka, takadive.com.au

Sleeping

$$$ **Rydges Tradewinds**, T+61 (0)7 4053 0300, rydges.com. Reasonably priced, modern hotel.
$$ **Coral Tree Inn**, coraltreeinn.com.au. Good quality 3-star hotel, conveniently located near the centre of town.

Eating

$$$ **Mondo Café Bar & Grill**, T+61 (0)7 4052 6780. Great food with superb views, inside the Hilton Hotel.
$$ **Rattle 'n' Hum**, T+61 (0)7 4031 3011. Casual and fun style with enormous portions of good food.

Port Douglas

Dive centres

Port Douglas Dive, T+61 (0)7 4099 1874, portdouglasdive.com.au
Poseidon Cruises, T+61 (0)7 4099 4772, poseidon-cruises.com.au

Liveaboards

Eye to Eye Marine Encounters, T+61(0)7 4098 5417, marineencounters.com.au. Specialist liveaboard operators who run tailor-made trips on a variety of first-class vessels. The management are well known for mixing scientific research with sport diving and pioneered swim-with-minke-whales programmes. Scheduled cruises cover the minke whale season, tiger shark research at Raine Island and adventure cruises to the far north. It is possible to plan private itineraries for small groups or organise day-diving through this company.

Sleeping

$$$ **Peninsula Boutique**, T+61 (0)7 4099 9100, peninsulahotel.com.au. Stylish apart-hotel with balconies directly opposite the beach, the biggest bathrooms and a very classy in-house restaurant.

$$ **Hibiscus Gardens Spa Resort**, T+61 (0)7 4099 5315, hibiscusportdouglas.com.au.

Eating

Port Douglas is the location of many top restaurants. Eating out is quite an experience, even if you only have a pizza!
$$$ **La Cucina**, T+61 (0)7 4099 6100. Modern Italian creations with a mega-reputation. Bookings required.
$$$ **Salsa Bar & Grill**, T+61 (0)7 4099 4922, salsa-port-douglas.com.au. Famous 'in' place for fusion food. Bookings required.

The Daintree

Dive centres

Odyssey H20, T+61 (0)7 4098 0033, coconutbeach.com.au/odyssey-h2o.

Sleeping

$$$-$$ **Coconut Beach Rainforest Lodge and Ferntree Rainforest Lodge**, T+61 (0)2 8296 8010, coconutbeach.com.au, ferntreelodge.com.au. Good eco-style hotels with large cabins in amazing rainforest settings. Both have classy in-house restaurants.

Eating

$$$ **Dragonfly Gallery Café**, T+61 (0)7 4098 0121. Pretty rainforest setting.

Car hire

All the usual major rental agencies are at Cairns and Perth airports. Small cars start at AU$55 per day, 4WDs from AU$100 per day. Rates tend to be better if you book online and in advance.

The Cairns waterfront; driving in the Daintree; Port Douglas marina

Sleeping	$$$ US$150+ double room per night		$$ US$75-150	$ under US$75
Eating	$$$ US$40+ 2-course meal, excluding drinks		$$ US$20-40	$ under US$20

Western Australia

Perth

Sleeping

$$ **Saville Park Suites**, T+61 (0)8 9267 4888, savillesuites.com. Classy apart-hotel in the business district.

$ **Comfort Inn**, choicehotels.com. The closest accommodation to Perth airport, this budget motel has courtesy transfers and is good for one night stopovers.

Eating

$$$ **Vivace**, T+61 (0)8 9325 1788. Great Italian bistro near Saville Suites.

Broome

Sleeping

$$$ **Cable Beach Club**, T+61 (0)8 9192 0400 cablebeachclub.com. Closest hotel to famous Cable Beach with great views.

$$ **Sea Shells Resort**, T+61 (0)8 9192 6111. Comfy, mid range apart-hotel, a few minutes from exquisite pink Cable Beach.

Liveaboards

Kimberley Escape and Great Escape, T+61 (0)8 9193 5983 greatescape.net.au. Dive trips to the Rowley Shoals in season plus adventure cruises to the Kimberley region (no diving).

Eating

$$ **Sunset Bar and Café,** part of the Cable Beach Club, for al fresco meals.

$$ **The Old Zoo Café**, T+61 (0)8 9193 6200. Beside Sea Shells, modern home-style cooking.

Cocos (Keeling) Islands

Dive Centres

Cocos Dive, T+61 (0)8 9162 6515, cocosdive.com The lone dive centre with very friendly and personal service from the owners. Packs including flights from Perth AU$2600.

Sleeping

$$ **Cocos Castaway**, cocoscastaway.com. Well located and decorated Balinese-style rooms. Right in the centre with sea views.

$$ **Cocos Seaview**, cocosseaview.com. Five minutes walk from the centre, pretty and spacious rooms.

Eating

$$ **Tropika Restaurant**, in the Cocos Beach Motel. Decent cafeteria-style meals, open daily unless the cook gets 'diverted'.

$ **Dory's of Cocos**, cakes, sandwiches and snacks served in the old Admiralty House building. Open for breakfast and lunch, evening meals on request.

Christmas Island

Dive Centres

Christmas Island Divers, T+61 419 759 617, christmasislanddivers.com

Wet'n'Dry Adventures, T+ 61 (0)8 9164 8028, divingchristmas.com Both operators are located right in the centre of town and have great, friendly service. Rates from AU$160 per day.

Sleeping

$$ **Captain's Last Resort, Captain's Cabin and Captain's Retreat**. Stunningly located, comfortable self-catering cottages right on the cliff face. All have marvellous views and good facilities with kitchens.

Contact Christmas Island Visitors Centre for up-to-date flight schedules and rates, accommodation options, car hire and advice on diving, christmas.net.au.

Eating

$$ **Golden Bosun Tavern**, Gaze Rd. T+61 (0)439 969 836. Serves sunset with drinks and pub-style cooking.

$$ **Rumah Tinggi**, Gaze Rd. T+61 (0)8 9164 7667. Modern fusion food on a breezy terrace overlooking the ocean.

A stopover in Sydney

Not exactly on the diver trail, Sydney is the biggest and most cosmopolitan city in the country. Yet it is also a compact city where a short stopover will give you a taste of the Aussie way of life. You can do a walking tour in just a few hours and see the best sights or spend a couple of days seeing a little more.

For a glimpse of the city's most famed attractions, head down to Circular Quay, where the Harbour Bridge sits to the west and the Opera House, east. Walk towards the Bridge to explore The Rocks, the oldest part of Sydney. The area is full of small museums, galleries and shops.

Next wander over to the Opera House to marvel at its bizarre architecture. Behind it lies the peaceful Botanic Gardens.

Back at the Quay take a public ferry across the harbour for the views. The trendy suburb of Manly is 40 minutes away and you could stop there to see its famous beach, shop and have lunch. If you have less time, it's only 15 minutes across to Taronga Park Zoo on Bradley's Head – no need to get off, but it is a good zoo if you have time.

Sydney's nightlife is centred on wild and raucous King's Cross but for a quieter evening try Darling Harbour in the next bay east of the bridge. This is also the location of the Aquarium, more shops, galleries and restaurants and can be reached by ferry, walking or the monorail.

Transport Public ferries are fun and cheap: Circular Quay to Darling Harbour is AU$4.80. The city centre monorail is AU$9 for a day pass. Taxis are metered.

 Sleeping $$$ US$150+ double room per night $$ US$75-150 $ under US$75

 Eating $$$ US$40+ 2-course meal, excluding drinks $$ US$20-40 $ under US$20

North Queensland

Touring in the tropical north is usually a DIY affair. Organized tours are expensive and can be inflexible – hire a 4WD and explore at your own pace.

Cairns The centre of town borders a stylish waterfront. It's a small but lively city, a few square blocks of shops and restaurants, interspersed with travel and tour agents, dive shops and car hire agencies. It's easy to arrange reef trips whether snorkelling, diving or sailing.

Port Douglas Life centres on Macrossan Street, a row of classy restaurants, shops and galleries that link the small town beach and jetty with the beautiful stretch of Four Mile Beach (which does get box jellyfish but areas are netted). The new marina is worth a daydream or two as is the local bird park.

Daintree Rainforest This is a World Heritage Site and regarded as the world's most important lowland rainforest. You can drive through it but will need a 4WD vehicle to negotiate river crossings. Along the winding road are nature trails, aerial walkways and tour facilities. Parts of the forest are designated working regions so you can visit tropical fruit farms and small cottage industries.

Cape Tribulation About two thirds of the way through the Daintree, this Cape was named by Captain Cook as the Endeavour went aground near here. It's the point where the GBR comes closest to the coast. You need to take care though as saltwater crocodiles inhabit nearby creeks.

Western Australia

To travel around the country's largest state, you will either need lots of time and a car or enough money to pay for an air-based tour.

Perth Take a day or two to get over the jet lag. Perth city centre tends to be quiet at night but there's enough to justify a stop. Visit the botanic gardens where the city views are superb. The Swan Bell Tower is home to the original 14th-century bells from Saint Martin-in-the-Fields in London. The Aquarium of Western Australia is just north, while to the south is the oldest city in the country, the port of Fremantle.

Margaret River Tour the newest of Australia's award-winning wine regions. It's at least 4 hours' drive from Perth so explore the small towns and the forests en route. There's also an underwater observatory at Busselton Jetty.

Monkey Mia This small beach resort is 800 km north of Perth and attracts visitors wanting to see the resident pod of bottlenose dolphins. Every day they swim in to knee-deep water to be fed but interaction is highly controlled. A 2-day mini package (flights, hotel and entrance fees) costs about AU$550.

The Kimberley North west of Broome, this national park is spectacular. The landscapes are carved by ancient forces: there are caves, rivers and rock formations to rival Ayers Rock. It's a long drive but you can get to the town of Derby and on to Tunnel Creek relatively easily. Tours cost around AU$300 per day.

Uluru In the middle of Australia – and the middle of nowhere – this gigantic stone monolith, also known as Ayers Rock, is a sacred aboriginal site. Getting there requires a flight from Perth ($2\frac{1}{2}$ hours) or Cairns (3 hours). You can walk to the top and should stay at least one night to see how the rock changes during the day as light moves across it.

Christmas Island

Known as the 'Galápagos of the Indian Ocean' due to its huge number of endemic species, Christmas is the natural world at its most accessible. It takes less than an hour to drive from one end of the island to the other so it's easy to see every unique feature, both above the waterline and below. A 4WD car is an absolute must though!

Walk through virgin rainforest to stand beneath Hugh's Waterfall with some of the 16 indigenous land crabs or watch blowholes on the prehistoric south coast. Explore caves dressed by stalagmites and stalactites; discover beaches occupied by nesting turtles and rare, endemic birds in the treetops. If you can be there during the red crab migration, you'll never see anything like it ever again.

Crocodile warning sign in the Daintree; Koala lunchtime at Taronga Park Zoo; a Christmas Island red crab

Papua New Guinea

Exploring the depths: deep water diving in the crystal clear waters of the Solomon Sea.
Cyclone Reef, Tufi

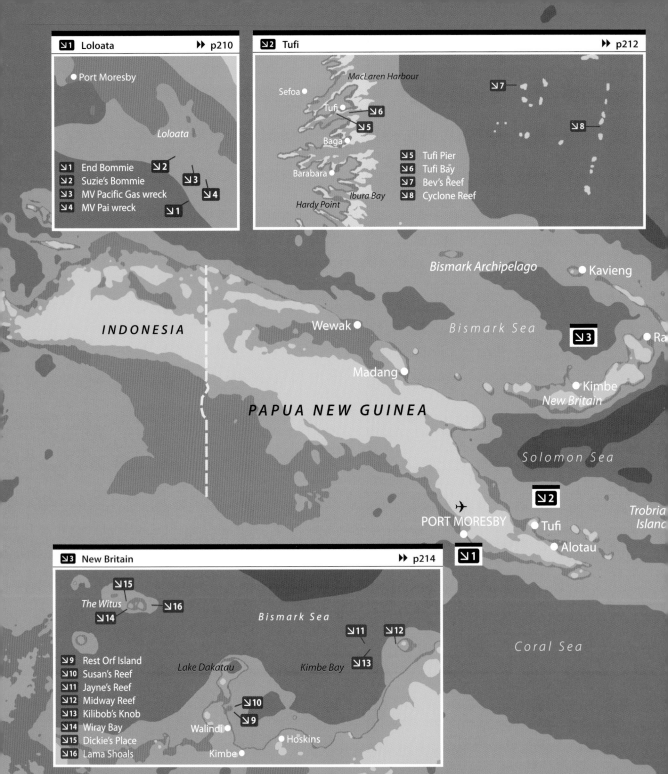

↘1 Loloata
↘ p210

Port Moresby

Loloata

↘1 End Bommie
↘2 Suzie's Bommie
↘3 MV Pacific Gas wreck
↘4 MV Pai wreck

↘2 Tufi
↘ p212

MacLaren Harbour

Sefoa
Tufi ↘6
↘5
Baga

Barabara

Ibura Bay
Hardy Point

↘7

↘8

↘5 Tufi Pier
↘6 Tufi Bay
↘7 Bev's Reef
↘8 Cyclone Reef

Bismark Archipelago

Kavieng

Bismark Sea

INDONESIA

Wewak

↘3

Ra

Madang

Kimbe
New Britain

PAPUA NEW GUINEA

Solomon Sea

↘2

*Trobria
Island*

PORT MORESBY

Tufi

Alotau

↘1

↘3 New Britain
↘ p214

↘15
The Witus
↘14
↘16

Bismark Sea

↘11 ↘12

↘13

Coral Sea

↘9 Rest Orf Island
↘10 Susan's Reef
↘11 Jayne's Reef
↘12 Midway Reef
↘13 Kilibob's Knob
↘14 Wiray Bay
↘15 Dickie's Place
↘16 Lama Shoals

Lake Dakatau

Kimbe Bay

↘10
↘9

Walindi

Kimbe

Hoskins

AUSTRALIA

200 km

PACIFIC OCEAN

Bougainville

SOLOMON ISLANDS

Honiara ●

Introduction

Papua New Guinea is perhaps the last frontier. Not the easiest of places to get to, it is a destination for divers who want undiluted adventure. The landscape is one of high drama both above and below the water line. There are towering mountain ranges where roads simply don't exist; chilly highland forests plummet to lush, tropical coasts, facing idyllic tiny islands while sheer-sided fjords lead to some of the world's least explored and most impressive coral reefs.

Marine biodiversity is just about the highest on the planet with some of the richest and most pristine reefs in the world. These are home to virtually every marine creature you could ever hope to see, from the tiniest seagrass pipefish to pods of spinner dolphins. Wherever you choose to go, this is an outstanding dive experience with consistent year-round conditions.

Back on land, it is said that there are still places where visitors have failed to tread; where indigenous tribes still live traditional lives. Shells and feathers are used as currency, men isolate themselves from women, wear gourds on their penises and spend years in special huts growing ceremonial wigs. You're unlikely to see a lot of this tribal culture as it's all so remote, although small villages close to dive resorts are unfailingly friendly and welcoming.

Papua New Guinea rating

Diving
★★★★★

Dive facilities
★★★

Accommodation
★★★

Down time
★★

Value for money
★★★

Essentials

Getting there and around

Because small nations such as Papua New Guinea have so little in the way of mass tourism – such a bonus these days – getting into the country will cost. There's simply not enough competition to bring flight prices down.

Air Niugini (airniugini.com.pg), the national carrier, has inbound flights from Manila, Singapore, Tokyo, Cairns, Brisbane, Sydney and even the Solomon Islands. The flights that come up from Australia to Port Moresby are often Qantas codeshares (qantas.com.au) so you may end up on one of their planes. From Asia, flight times run at around six hours and are often overnight. The route from Singapore is the most convenient for divers originating in both Europe and America, as it connects with many of Singapore Airlines' schedules (singaporeair.com.sg). The cheapest route is Cairns to Port Moresby at around US$500 plus taxes. Singapore to Moresby return is around US$1,000 plus tax. However, bear in mind that these rates are held by very few international agents and can be hard to find. The good news is that the airline allows divers an extra 10 kg of baggage. Airlines of PNG (apng.com) also have international flights but only from Cairns and Brisbane. Their rates are a little cheaper, starting at AU$350.

There are frequent internal flights connecting the outer islands and sections of the mainland. These are run by Air Niugini or Airlines of PNG. Prices run in the region of US$200 per flight.

Dive resorts arrange airport transfers; just hop off the plane and look for the person who is looking for you. There are so few tourists, it will all be terribly obvious.

Local laws and customs

With its strong colonial influences, daily life in PNG has a tendency to feel quite westernised. Even if you get out into a local village, you won't feel too out of place. Missionary groups have had so much impact that many people regard themselves as Christian although traces of original culture still shine through. Life in the resorts is a casual affair with few pretensions. In Port Moresby the way to dress would be smart casual.

Language

No one really knows how many indigenous tribes live in PNG but there are well over 750 languages, about 20% of the total in the world. Obviously, there is no way you could ever hope to learn even a few words of each even if you were to meet more than one of these groups! Thankfully, there is one that links all the tribes you are likely to encounter – Tok Pisin, an age-old mix of Melanesian and English. Of course, everyone in the diver orientated business will speak English.

hello	halo
see you later	lukim iu behain
yes	ya, yes
no	no/nating
please	plis
thank you	tenkyu
sorry	sori
how much ...?	hamas ...?
good	gut
great!	em nau!
one beer	wan bia
and a computer mouse is lik lik rat!	

Papua New Guinea	
Location	6°00'S, 147°00'E
Capital	Port Moresby
Population	6,057,263
Land area in km²	452,860
Coastline in km	5152

Snorkelling in the shallows of Rest Orf Island

Safety

Unfortunately, Port Moresby has a reputation for not being the safest place in the world. You are warned not to take valuables out with you at any time and to keep out of the city centre at night. This area attracts a lot of poorer, unemployed people. Alcohol problems lead to petty crimes and occasional muggings.

However, as divers you are unlikely to even see the centre of Moresby except on a day trip, which would be escorted by a guide or driver from your hotel. Although the centre has some reasonable shopping facilities, unless you are in dire need of something, there's not really any other reason to go. If you venture into the highlands take an organized tour with a guide who will ensure you stick to tourist-friendly areas. Around the coastal resorts, it's quite different and local villagers are generally welcoming. Divers are often invited to events and festivals.

Health

Standards are high in resorts and hotels, so health concerns only include the usual tropical warnings on water, sun, mosquitoes and so on. There is one thing to note though – the only decompression chamber in the country is in Port Moresby. As much of the diving here is deep, and because the water is warm enough to keep you under for long periods in a day, you do need to be aware of what your dive computer is telling you. Be safe rather than sorry.

Costs

PNG is regarded as one of the world's more expensive diving destinations, and that's mostly because the flight prices are so high. Although Port Moresby is a stone's throw from Australia, this also affects importing goods and then getting those goods to where they are needed. There is little road transport across the mountainous main island so everything has to come by ship, which can be a slow and expensive affair, or by plane. This can be amusing when Chef says, sorry no eggs, the plane is late! Less amusing three days in a row. The knock-on effect is higher rates in the resorts which are mostly run by ex-pat Aussies, so at least they never run out of beer. Tourism numbers are comparatively low, so there are few choices for either general tourism or diving but surprisingly because of all this, what is there is mostly high end. The good news though, is that the resorts and liveaboards do, generally, include all meals and diving in their rates so although the initial cost may seem high, a trip here will be good value. A daily rate for a land resort ranges from US$250-300 per person per day with meals, two boat dives and free shore diving while the liveaboards are around US$350-400 but with up to five dives per day. Some include alcoholic drinks in their rates. Value for money is a better way to judge this unique location, see page 10.

 Tourist information → The government website can be found at pngtourism.org.pg. For listings of all PNG's dive operators go to pngtourism.org.pg/png/cms/diving/diving.htm.

Papua New Guinea Essentials

Fact file

International flights	Singapore Airlines via Singapore; Qantas via Sydney or Brisbane; Air Niugini from above hubs
Departure tax	Included in ticket but there is an additional 30 kina airport tax
Entry	Visa issued on arrival at Jackson Airport (25 kina) or from your closest embassy
Internal flights	Air Niugini, Airlines of PNG
Ground transport	Provided by all dive operations
Money	US$1 = 3 Papua New Guinea kina (PGK)
Language	English and Tok Pisin
Electricity	240v, plug type E (see page 16)
Time zone	GMT +10
Religion	Christianity mixed with indigenous
Phone	Country code +675; IDD code 05; Police 000

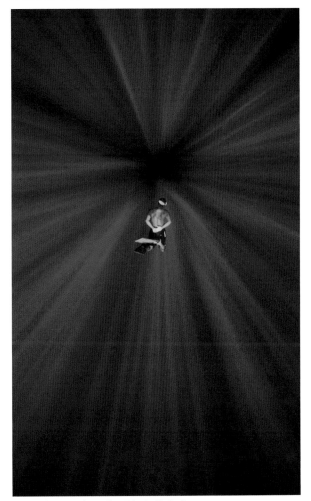

Descending into the endless blue in Kimbe Bay

Dive brief

Diving

The string of islands that make up PNG sit inside what is now being termed the Coral Triangle. This refers to the islands and reefs that stretch from above northern Australia through Indonesia to Borneo and up to the Philippines. Sitting on the edge of the Pacific Ring of Fire, the volcanic band that encompasses the entire ocean, this region is the most biodiverse on the planet. There is, simply put, more of everything – 70% of all the world's coral species are found in the Indo/Pacific region, nearly 900 fish species and 500 corals. These figures sound impressive because they are impressive.

What's more, PNG also boasts every significant marine ecosystem and island type – from atoll reef systems to sea beds, mangrove deltas and deep ocean trenches. There are over 40,000 square km of coral reef found along PNG's coastline, so no matter what your personal marine interest is, you are bound to find it somewhere in the country.

In such a hugely diverse environment what attracts many, especially underwater photographers, is the smaller reef building life, the nursery areas full of weird and wacky creatures. There is also substantial Second World War paraphernalia littered around as many parts of the country were occupied by Japanese forces.

Yet another of the country's major bonuses is that there is no particular dive season. It matters little what time of year you go as conditions are fairly consistent. A final consideration is that diving in PNG is as close to unlimited as you will ever get. Liveaboards schedule five dives a day, most resorts have three boat dives and you are welcome to shore dive whenever you like. Initial costs may seem high but this is a great value-for-money destination.

Snorkelling

Many offshore reefs tend to be very deep affairs with dives starting at around 15 metres and dropping off to unfathomable depths. However, as the visibility is nearly always fabulous, floating over these reefs would be quite a blast. There are exceptions to this; reefs near Port Moresby, for example, have reduced visibility as they are affected by shipping, weather and the tides moving over the shallow seabeds. On the other hand there are masses of coastal reefs that are just a few metres deep.

Marine life

For any diver who is interested in tropical marine life, this area is almost unsurpassed. From the smallest of creatures – minute boxer crabs and ghost pipefish – to uncountable schools of barracuda and jacks, it's all here.

Papua New Guinea animals encounters

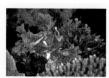

Loloata	lacy scorpionfish
Tufi	harlequin shrimp
New Britain	sharks and jacks

Locals visit Febrina while divers are below

Like many people it took us a long time to commit to going to Papua New Guinea to dive. Until we'd been we just couldn't see the value in upping our travel budget enough to cover the extra costs the journey involved. Then a friend dragged us along and of course, once we had done it, we realized there was no reason to think up excuses again. Now we try to find excuses to go and see another part of the country. This is a superlative destination for serious divers.

Making the big decision

When it comes to a dive holiday in PNG, you really have to get your head around the comparative cost. Yes, it is far more expensive than neighbouring Indonesia and no, it's not so completely, utterly different. But it is different enough that the cost is justified. Once you have made the mental adjustment, selecting a specific area to go to can be the more difficult decision. To travel so far and only do a small part of the country would be a waste.

To get the most out of your time and the flight costs, ensure you do more than one dive region. No one resort or boat is better than the other. All have their own style, whether it's romantic views from colonial bungalows or dive-your-brains-out liveaboards targeted at photographers. The diving is consistently fabulous right across the country.

Breathtakingly beautiful and just 15 mm wide, the boxer crab

Dive data

Seasons	Diving is year round. There are dry and wet seasons, but the changes aren't significant except in the area around Loloata (see p 210)
Visibility	10 metres inshore to 'infinity' in open water
Temperatures	Air: coast 24-35°C; highlands 12-28°C; Water: Loloata 25-30°C, elsewhere 28-30°C
Wet suit	3 mm full body suit
Training	Courses are not generally available, email in advance to make arrangements
Nitrox	Available in some resorts/liveaboards, email in advance
Deco chambers	Port Moresby

Bottom time

Papua New Guinea		**The country's mainland is a melange of geographical features from extreme mountain ranges to flat coastal plateaus that lead to equally diverse marine environments.**
Loloata Island	▸▸ p210	A haven for many unusual marine creatures – and one very rare one – plus some spectacular shipwrecks.
Tufi	▸▸ p212	Where both near and far reefs get into recycling, and they win.
New Britain		**On the edge of the Bismark Sea, this region is defined by the crystal clear water that encompasses the offshore reefs and the pitch black sand close to volcanic islands.**
Kimbe Bay	▸▸ p214	Famous for the many iridescent colours on as many pristine coral reefs.
Father's Reefs	▸▸ p215	Picture-postcard images, both above and below the water line.
The Witus	▸▸ p216	Dramatic diving around the remains of a submerged volcanic crater.

Diversity   reef area 13,840km²

HARD CORALS	73
FISH SPECIES	2,457
ENDEMIC FISH SPECIES	72
FISH UNDER THREAT	47
PROTECTED REEFS/MARINE PARKS	15

All diversity figures are approximate

Dive log

Papua New Guinea

Loloata Island

A few miles south of the nation's capital, Port Moresby, lies this haven of marine splendour. Loloata Island Resort is under half an hour from the airport, just 15 minutes from shore and on the edge of the Papuan Barrier Reef. The resort gets a good through flow of diver and non-diver traffic which adds to its charm. One night you might dine with some fellow divers, the next an Australian politician.

The island itself is a long oval shape with a steep central hill ringed by a flat, craggy strip. There is nothing on the island apart from the resort, which has also become an unofficial wildlife reserve with many rescued native animals. Bungalows line the water's edge and face the day's entertainment – also known as the sunset.

The dive reputation is one of a serious muck diving haven with critters in every shape, size and colour, including almost guaranteed sightings of the splendid lacy scorpionfish. The reefs themselves are impressive, hard coral growth is substantial, soft corals pretty and colourful. The reefs host plenty of schooling fish like jacks, groupers and snapper. Then there's the

wrecks. Local waters are littered with them although they've mostly been scuttled over the years for the benefit of divers.

Unlike the rest of PNG, seasons here are notable. There are two doldrums (April to May and October to December) when the sea is calm and the visibility is better. December to April is wetter and June to October is drier. Diving is still year round.

⬡1	**End Bommie**	
🕐	**Depth**	22 m
◐	**Visibility**	fair to good
🌀	**Currents**	mild
⬳	**Dive type**	day boat

This site is a well-known haunt for the Rhinopias frondosa or lacy scorpionfish. The main reef has a saddle that connects it to a smaller circular outcrop with lots of pristine corals along the outside wall. One section is smothered in tubastrea, purple and white soft corals and vast numbers of anthias all darting in and out. However, it's on the flat reef top where the divemaster will point out the rhinopias – there's no chance of seeing one of these perfectly camouflaged creatures on your own. The resident one is black with yellow and white patterns on his skin, making him very hard to distinguish from the surroundings.

Oriental sweetlips by the hundreds on Suzie's Bommie

❷ Suzie's Bommie

🕐	**Depth**	27 m
◑	**Visibility**	fair to good
〰	**Currents**	can be strong
⬤	**Dive type**	day boat

A cone-shaped pinnacle rises up from about 30 metres to 10 at the top. Around the base are some good fans and plenty of fish but the further up you rise the thicker the fish life becomes. Sweetlips shelter against the tubastrea along with pairs of barramundi cod. Above are masses of anthias and then, as you reach 12 metres, you encounter huge numbers of oriental sweetlips, jacks, snappers, surgeons and batfish. These all school together in a huge ball. A lone Napoleon wrasse hangs around with the other species. Down in the corals, there are leaffish in varying colours – olive, lime and silver – and marbled dragonets. Small longnose hawkfish free swim around whip corals and mantis shrimp run in and out of their burrows.

❸ MV Pacific Gas wreck

🕐	**Depth**	39 m
◑	**Visibility**	fair to good
〰	**Currents**	can be strong
⬤	**Dive type**	day boat

Originally owned by Pacific Gas, this cargo vessel was sunk in 1986 to create a dive site. The currents that wash over her can be quite strong so she has filled up with lots of corals, mostly tubastrea and small soft corals. The propellers are sitting at 45 metres and the main cabin at the stern rises up to over 20 metres. There is less coral cover at depth but plenty of jacks, snappers and a couple of big groupers. Back up at the bow some gear wheels are exposed on the deck and there are two leaffish and a moray sitting below with a cleaner shrimp in his mouth. Travelling up the mast for a safety stop there are masses of anthias, sweepers and crinoids. There's even a resident dendronephthya crab hiding in some soft coral.

❹ MV Pai wreck

🕐	**Depth**	26 m
◑	**Visibility**	fair to good
〰	**Currents**	slight
⬤	**Dive type**	day boat

This wreck of a small prawn trawler is 25 metres long. The mast rises up from the deck at about 20 metres to around 12 and is encrusted by gorgonias, tubastrea and dendronephthya corals in all sorts of colours. They all support a mass of anthias and glassfish. A surprising number of longnose hawkfish sit in amongst it all as well as some pipefish and gobies in crevices. The cabin is intact with fans and corals filling in the old window holes and big silver groupers sheltering inside. One hold is open and can be investigated if you have sufficient bottom time.

The Pacific Gas wreck and the bizarrely decorated *Rhinopias aphanes*, or lacy scorpionfish

Of all PNG's coastal landscapes, Tufi is possibly the most impressive. As you fly in to the landing strip (aka football field and playground) you see a series of deep fjords that cut sharply back into the land. If snow was sitting on the hills, you would think you were in northern Scandinavia. Instead, this highly dramatic landscape is painted in rich green, tropical forests lead down the cliff faces to deep, dark seas.

Sitting right on the top of one fjord is tiny Tufi village and resort. Only accessible by sea and air, it is an hour's scenic flight east of Port Moresby. Diving, and staying here, is quite an experience. Originally built as a Second World War base, the colonial main building is ringed by a cluster of romantic bungalows that face out to sea – the views are to die for. The walk down to the dive jetty involves a daily greeting ceremony with the local villagers. Once you reach it, you get a taste of the critter life that lives there. Baby batfish an inch or so long float less than an inch below the surface while beneath them lurks what may become one of the best muck dives of your life. You name it, you'll probably see it here.

Lying between the coast and the D'Entrecasteaux islands are some fantastic reef systems. The water is gin-clear, corals lush and massive schools of pelagic fish seek shelter around them. A little further away, several war-era wrecks are worth a visit if weather allows. They are deep (over 50 metres) and trips are infrequent. If you miss them, it hardly matters though, as Tufi Bay has its own wrecks, reminders of when US forces were stationed here.

◹5 Tufi Pier

🌀	**Depth**	12 m
◑	**Visibility**	fair to good
🌊	**Currents**	none
🌀	**Dive type**	shore

For serious muck diving aficionados, there is nothing quite like this dive. It is classic muck. Just below the jetty are decades of detritus, from soft drink crates to old beer bottles and tyres. Pieces of plastic net jostle with rotting 40 gallon drums but, no matter what ugly old bit of rubbish you look at, it will be a thriving marine colony. Kitting up on the wooden jetty, you can admire all the juvenile batfish then descend to three metres to find handfuls of ornate ghost pipefish, pairs of robust ghost pipefish and odd hairy ghost pipefish. Inspect a crate to find nudibranchs crawling over it or an old beer bottle for a blenny or two. Seahorses and frogfish live around the pylons and hiding in amongst the algae are scorpions, lionfish and cowries. If you do this dive at dusk you may spot a pair of harlequin shrimp preparing their supper by killing a starfish then eating it limb by limb, or one of the resident mandarinfish that come out to feed under cover of darkness.

◹6 Tufi Bay

🌀	**Depth**	42 m
◑	**Visibility**	fair to good
🌊	**Currents**	none
🌀	**Dive type**	shore

Heading downwards from the jetty past all the magnificent macro life, there is a solitary coral rock where young pinnate batfish live, their orange outline glowing like neon. There are some interesting small animals nestled into the cracks, but past them and down the slope you eventually reach 40 metres. The seabed flattens out into a dark and silty place. Scattered across it is the detritus of the Second World War base. When the American forces shipped out, they dumped many of their unwanted items into the bay. You can see interesting bits of broken metal, engines and chains while pondering their original use. There are the remains of a patrol boat that still has its engine. The inside of the hull is completely covered in cleaner shrimp and small cardinals. Nearby is a nearly intact Land Rover. Its screen is encrusted with muck and small flat corals are forming on the surface. Just a few feet away is a torpedo tube, with the torpedo still in it.

Life in Tufi Bay: dinner time for a pair of harlequin shrimp; a loaded torpedo tube rusting on the sea floor; a harlequin ghost pipefish in the shallows

Bev's Reef

Depth	32 m
Visibility	fair to good
Currents	none
Dive type	day boat

A couple of hours out from Tufi, this is one of the best reefs in the area. Although there is some damage on the top, this is caused by wave and storm action as this site is quite exposed. Circumnavigating the edges you find good soft corals and schools of mating surgeonfish. The walls harbour critters like flabellina – and other – nudis. Eagle-eyed spotters might see a ghost pipefish, crocodilefish or the blacksaddle coral grouper (white with yellow and black markings). As you ascend back to the flat plateau, you are surrounded by a huge number of fish: schools of Spanish mackerel, chevron barracuda, jacks, yellow tailed snappers, damsels and angels.

Cyclone Reef

Depth	50 m
Visibility	good to stunning
Currents	slight
Dive type	day boat

In 1975 a cyclone swept across this reef, rearranging the submerged terrain and even creating a small island that is now used by birds. There are two dives here: one is a pinnacle connected to the main reef via a 26 metre deep saddle. There are a lot of black coral bushes full of fish that sit on the branches like nesting birds. There are schools of yellow tailed snappers, rainbow runners and tangs, plus grey reef sharks. The other dive is on the wall which drops to 60 metres. A large depression on the reef top attracts masses of schooling fish, a real soup of species: snapper, Spanish mackerel, dogtooth tuna and juvenile whitetip sharks. Down below, grey reef sharks patrol the wall, which is coated in colourful corals. This is a good location for spotting the king of nudibranchs, notodoris minors and even a manta ray or turtle in the blue.

Temperatures rising

Although this is an unexplored country with limited tourist facilities, there are dive operations almost everywhere. Some are famous for one thing, some for another. Simply choose a dive style and go for it, you are unlikely to be disappointed.

Milne Bay, furthest east on the Papuan mainland, is credited with being the place that turned 'muck' diving into an art form.

Rabaul, on the northern tip of New Britain, has a harbour awash with shipwrecks. Some were toppled by volcanic eruptions while others went down during the war.

Madang, on the northern shore of the mainland, has highly varied reefs and is known for a great variety of fish life.

Kavieng, on New Ireland but directly opposite New Hanover island. These two islands create a barrier to the open ocean and are swept with deep water tidal currents, consequently earning Kavieng the nickname of PNG's pelagic capital.

New Britain

Kimbe Bay

New Britain island is just a 50 minute flight from Port Moresby and forms the nation's northern barrier with the Bismark Sea. This is one of PNG's best known and most spectacular dive regions. Although it's not such an emotive way to do so, the best way to describe this area is with figures – over 400 species of reef building corals have been recorded in Kimbe Bay, more than half the total number of known coral species in the world. Plus there's around 900 species of fish. And that's just a taster of what you might see.

Hoskins airport on New Britain is about an hour's flight from Port Moresby. There are two options for diving here: you can choose between being land based or a liveaboard. Walindi Plantation Resort is located in an old coconut plantation that was established in the 1930s but became a pioneer dive resort in 1969. Besides the heavy focus on the marine realm, nature conservation is paramount. Bungalows huddle beneath a tamed tropical jungle, rich with rare orchids and facing into Kimbe Bay. The Walindi Nature Centre is next door and home to the Mahonia na Dari (Guardian of the Sea) Project, which focuses on conservation and marine education. The bay is ringed by a dramatic volcanic landscape and it is beneath these that some of the more adrenaline pumping diving can be found.

There are two excellent liveaboards based here and heading off on one will take you northeast to the Fathers Islands or northwest to the Witus; both areas are equally superlative destinations. Some say the best visibility is from January to April but that seems an unnecessary statement as the comparison would be between excellent and really excellent. Currents can be strong though, a benefit to the marine life, but as there are so many dive sites avoiding these is not an issue.

Grey reef Shark, razorfish hiding amongst the whip corals and black coral bushes, all in Kimbe Bay

---

◹9 Rest Orf Island

🕐	**Depth**	18 m
◐	**Visibility**	fair to good
🌊	**Currents**	slight
⬛	**Dive type**	day boat

Just 30 minutes from Walindi, this is a true picture-postcard island with a tiny, white sand beach. The beach dips down in a semicircle to a small reef wall extending on either side to a sandy sea bed. This has patchy coral outcrops that support some brightly coloured soft corals and create homes for critters such as dendronephthya crabs. Around the base of these outcrops you can spot crabeye gobies and other tiny sand fish like flounders. Titan triggerfish nest here as well so you need to keep an eye out for them. At depth there are some really good whips and fans and different shades of black coral that flourish in the currents. The entire reef is decorated with plenty of schooling tropical fish and clownfish in their host anemones.

◹10 Susan's Reef

🕐	**Depth**	50 m
◐	**Visibility**	fair to good
🌊	**Currents**	slight
⬛	**Dive type**	day boat

Just a little way from Rest Orf Island, this incredibly pretty dive site consists of a submerged ridge that connects a small reef to a much larger one. The channel between the two is what makes it such an outstanding dive. The currents that funnel through encourage the growth of an incredible number of bright red whip corals and these coat almost every surface. One stand of whips is alive and dancing with razorfish who reflect the sun's rays as they turn their bodies this way and that, trying to remain hidden. Brightly coloured crinoids sit on the gorgonians and sponges and masses of fish hang off the walls. Longnose and pixie hawkfish are common residents as are angel and parrotfish.

Fathers Reefs

Marking the outer edge of Kimbe Bay, the Fathers refer to a group of volcanic cones protruding from the horizon. Father is flanked by his two sons and all three hover ominously over the coast. Underwater, there are sloping walls and, when the currents are running, pelagics like barracuda and even dolphins can be seen – and swum with.

⊠11 Jayne's Reef

🕐	**Depth**	36 m
◐	**Visibility**	good to stunning
🌀	**Currents**	can be strong
🌓	**Dive type**	liveaboard

This steep-sided circular pinnacle has strong currents running along on one side. There are whip corals and fans and swarms of jacks passing by. Despite the currents, it's easy to spot some minute creatures even at depth – a huge barrel sponge has sangian crabs on it and pygmy seahorses reside on a gorgonian known to the divemasters. These are as small as 4 mm so you really need that divemaster to spot them for you! The reef top is quite rubbly due to the effects of tide and currents but this is a prime area for octopus. At the right time you can even see them mating, one extending a tentacle to attract another. Eventually you will see the male inserting his specially modified arm into the female to transfer his sperm packet to her. There are small hawksbill turtles who are very friendly, swimming right up to divers. In amongst the small corals are orang-utan crabs and tiny commensal crabs living in the algae.

⊠12 Midway Reef

🕐	**Depth**	30 m
◐	**Visibility**	infinity
🌀	**Currents**	slight
🌓	**Dive type**	liveaboard

Looking down over the top of this reef is like looking through air. The visibility seems endless. The reef is circular with a small saddle and secondary pinnacle to one side. On the main section the wall drops off pretty steeply all the way around and the hard corals are pristine. At the saddle a handful of grey whalers patrol between the two sections of reef with schools of big-eye trevally and surgeonfish circling above. Napoleon wrasse hover in the shallower areas where there are incredible beds of staghorn coral with anthias, fusiliers and damsels darting in and out. Schooling snappers dance around and you'll also see several pretty anemones beneath the boat. Macro life here is very good with squat lobsters in crinoids, dendronephthya crabs, popcorn shrimp on carpet anemones and several spinecheek anemonefish. Lucky divers might even spot a boxer crab!

⊠13 Kilibob's Knob

🕐	**Depth**	18 m
◐	**Visibility**	good
🌀	**Currents**	medium
🌓	**Dive type**	liveaboard

The tops of two coral pinnacles sit at 10 and 15 metres below the surface. Between them is a cut that drops to about 25 metres. This geography often attracts sharks who patrol the channel looking for supper. Now, though, they patrol because the site is used as a shark dive. A bait bucket is attached to a mooring, which attracts both greys and whitetips. The sharks whizz between the pinnacles, ever hopeful that something will drop out of the bucket. (For those who don't approve, note that the bait bucket is sealed and the sharks are not fed.) Once you've had your fill of shark theatricals, the sloping sides of the reef are interesting with some nice corals, porcelain crabs and moray eels hiding out. Small rubble patches in between reveal minute boxer crabs – ask the divemasters to show you – but all the while the big action continues with tuna, barracuda and trevally passing by.

Large and small on the Father's Reefs: tomato clown – or spinecheek anemone – fish; fan coral and fish

Witu Islands

This cluster of small volcanic islands rises from very deep water. Garove, the largest and busiest, is actually a sunken caldera, shaped like a horseshoe and with an opening to the south. The main town and harbour sit on the edge of a beautiful inner lagoon while the outer edges are riddled by jungle-clad hills and bays.

This area has quite an interesting history, including a period when colonial Germany ruled the northern regions while Britain administered the south. Later, in the First World War, the German Navy used the bays around these islands to moor and conceal ships whilst dodging Australian forces.

The waters here are incredibly nutrient rich. There are open water reefs a short sail from the coast, which attract massive schools of pelagic fish while the many small flat bays around the islands have black sand seabeds that are a haven to weird and wacky small animals.

◰14 Wiray Bay

🕐	**Depth**	22 m
◑	**Visibility**	good
🌀	**Currents**	none
⬇	**Dive type**	liveaboard

This bay off Wiray Island feels very primeval as the surrounding jungle drips with vines and birds squawk overhead. The black sand sea bed has the odd log and coconut husks, but little coral. The divemasters hop from spot to spot to show off the critters: halimeda and sangian crabs, sand divers that puff up their necks, panda clowns, popcorn shrimp in those cauliflower-shaped anemones and masses more.

At night, there are masses of cone shells – literally hundreds. There are tiny dwarf scorpionfish and decorator crabs that cover themselves in bright green algae balls. The biggest surprise though are the huge platydoris nudibranchs, possibly the largest there is. These pair up, linking head to tail then travel at speed across the sand.

◰15 Dickie's Place

🕐	**Depth**	22 m
◑	**Visibility**	fair to good
🌀	**Currents**	none
⬇	**Dive type**	liveaboard

Local personality Dickie Doyle runs a cocoa plantation that fronts another small but perfectly formed bay. It is quite shallow and divided by a ridge. On one side is a small reef but again the dark sand sea bed is the star of the show. This is the place to see seagrass pipehorses, a tiny pipefish that wraps its tail around the blades of grass. There are also minute black mantis shrimp, the saddle back clownfish and twinspot lionfish. At night the bumblebee squid emerges from its hidey-hole along with seahares, decorator crabs and pleurobranchs. Down on the ridge the branches of an old log attract a load of squid who are mating and laying their eggs. This is quite a spectacle as the boys fight over the girls.

🐟 A double back flip to nowhere

I'm on my back, foot slung up on my bookshelf with a stomach full of codeine. I'd just done a double back flip with a half-pike onto the bottom deck. Right on the side of my left foot. Right in front of the crew. Now, Nelson the Impregnator is in charge; the infamous Digger is fixing regulators with a six-pound hammer and Elsie, the divemaster, is trying to throttle him. It is not a good time for this to happen. Our sole purpose for the next few weeks is to locate the best dive sites on the south coast of New Britain. We head off into the night to rediscover Lindenhaven, an island-studded lagoon close to the mainland. It lies straight off the Solomon Trench in the Solomon Sea, the third deepest part of the world's oceans. I already know a couple of dive sites there and purple leaffish are spotted, as well as Halimeda ghost pipefish, winged pipefish, flying gurnards – everything seemed to be going off. But I could only sit on my backside and listen to everyone rave "did you see this… did you see that…" Lindenhaven had also been home to a Japanese floatplane base station and there is plenty of war wreckage. We found one plane intact, upside down and in 60 ft of water. Digger opened the bomb bay doors and was attacked by an exotic blue ribbon eel who had been guarding two bombs which, unbelievably, were still sitting in their racks. Feeling very pleased with ourselves, we headed to Waterfall Bay, 75 miles back towards Rabaul. There we dived the Blue Hole, a magnificent place found up a freshwater river. In the hole, the depth and clarity of the blue is almost impossible to describe. As the sun comes up you can look towards the surface from about 100 ft and see the dense jungle as if it was just above you. We're starting trips to this region now. So while the Northern Hemisphere is choking on snow, if you're looking for a destination in the South Pacific that is warm and dry, I'll be there. With an operational ankle. *Alan Raabe, Captain and Owner, MV Febrina*

Witu residents include squid and sangian crabs

⭐ 16   Lama Shoals

🌀 **Depth**	45 m
👁 **Visibility**	stunning
🌊 **Currents**	can be strong
🌅 **Dive type**	liveaboard

Lama Shoals sums up the very best of diving in New Britain waters. The reef is a long oval and drops off to extreme depths and when the currents lift this dive site is revealed in all its glory. These are fairly consistent but not so aggressive as to make this a drift dive. Yet these currents bring in both pelagic fish and the nutrients that feed the corals, fans, and sponges that plaster every available surface.

As you descend below the boat, whole forests of black coral bushes are showing off, tones of gold and silver flickering in the sun. Midnight snapper, sweetlips and longnose hawkfish nestle in the bushes. A few bigeye trevally hang around them but these are obviously stragglers – as you descend further, you meet the most

66 99

It's always non-stop action on Lama, you can dive it at any time of day and there always seems to be something going on. But what really captivates is the water clarity – when we were there it seemed we were diving in air. You can just hang in the blue and watch the dramas of this prolific reef unfold.

enormous school of them. And this is just the start of the action. Further along the wall, another shoal appears above, then a third far below. Schooling barracuda stand off in the blue, possibly wary of the large dogtooth tuna cruising along the wall, or maybe it's the arrival of some Spanish mackerel, that in turn are disturbed by the passing rainbow runners.

The top of the reef is around 15 metres where plenty of smaller creatures balance out the dive. Scorpionfish and grumpy-faced false stonefish nestle amongst small

corals while lionfish hover beside fans. Schools of unicornfish and pyramid butterflies add to the colour. Good spotters may see several types of moray living behind swarms of tiny purple fairy basslets. The reef shallows also have a covering of coralliomorpharians. These rather attractive creatures look a little like anemones and are related to them but have a far more powerful sting. A school of batfish reside near the safety stop rope good entertainment for the deco-stop you are bound to have after this dive.

Papua New Guinea Dive log New Britain: Lama Shoals

Drying out

Tourism is a small industry in PNG. Right across the country, the choices of hotels are limited but nearly all coastal resorts are dive-orientated.

Papua New Guinea

Port Moresby

$$ **Airways Hotel**, Jacksons Parade, T+ 675 324 5200, airways.com.pg. Less than 5 mins from the airport. Popular, decent overnight accommodation including free airport transfers. A great roof top restaurant.

Loloata Island

Sleeping and diving

$$$ **Loloata Island Resort**, T+675 325 8590, Loloata.com. Located on a private island cum nature reserve just 30 mins from the airport, so also an option for stopovers. The bungalows are straightforward but comfortable; the atmosphere is friendly and relaxed. Rates include diving and all meals.

Tufi

Sleeping and diving

$$$ **Tufi Dive Resort**, T+675 329 6000, tufidive.com. Delightful small resort with romantic, colonial style bungalows sitting on the edge of a dramatic fjord landscape and beside a tiny, friendly village. The dive centre is at the bottom of the hill and has great shore diving. Packages include all meals and diving.

New Britain

Kimbe Bay and the Bismark Sea

Sleeping and diving

$$$ **Walindi Plantation Resort**, T+675 983 5441, walindi.com. Plantation style resort with charming, orchid strewn bungalows under tropical trees overlooking the beautiful bay. Resort packages include meals and diving. Walindi is the home port for liveaboards Febrina and Star Dancer.

Liveaboards

MV Febrina, T+675 983 5441, febrina.com. Febrina is a legend amongst liveaboards. 10-11 day schedules include Kimbe and the Witus and Rabaul to the south coast. Rates with unlimited diving US$350 per day.

MV Star Dancer, T+675 983 5441, peterhughes.com. Part of the excellent Peter Hughes Group and jointly managed by the Walindi operation. A large, luxury vessel that does 6-7 day charters. From US$350 per day.

Other options

For more PNG destinations, refer to Temperatures rising on page 212.

Wild tales from wild places

I have some very wild tales about travelling through Papua New Guinea to see her primitive and mesmerising cultures. I've been up the highlands to see the Huli Wigmen and the Mudmen of the Waghi Valley. But my favourite trip was by canoe to visit the remote villages on the Sepik River in northern PNG.

This was after 12 days of diving and an unreal contrast. The only person who would dare to come with me was my brave friend Sandy. We slept in rural villages on the river (hotter than hell and humid to match, mozzies and no breeze) and had to get really creative with the non-toilet situation. Our guide was from one of the villages and all the people knew him – but they hadn't seen white people for ages. It was fun to see how they reacted to two white girls pulling up in dug-out canoes. My aim was to search out some old and unusual handicrafts, not the copies that you can buy down in Port Moresby, beautiful though they are.

Our guide got the gist of what I was after and well after we went to sleep, people would appear from all over to show him their old pieces. Some I would not take as they were very important and ancient, regarded as spirits from their ancestors. I was amazed by my meetings with these very special people and I am so grateful that they wanted to share their past with me. I have a story from each villager about the items I bought from them so they will all be catalogued and maintain their ancestral story. Papua New Guinea is just an incredible place.

Cindi La Raia, President, Dive Discovery, San Rafael, California

Sleeping	$$$ US$150+ double room per night	$$ US$75-150	$ under US$75
Eating	$$$ US$40+ 2-course meal, excluding drinks	$$ US$20-40	$ under US$20

Papua New Guinea

Nature has taken an interesting turn in Papua New Guinea: this is the world's third largest rainforest and the jungles host as many bird and plant species as nearby Australia, with endemic species like tiny tree kangaroos, enormous Queen Alexandra Birdwing butterflies and the world's largest pigeon. Perhaps most importantly, the islands are home to 38 of the world's 43 birds of paradise. While access to very remote areas can be difficult, there are organized tours that will give a taste of the real country.

In the city…

While the centre of Port Moresby may be best avoided, there are a few attractions worth seeing. Take a trip to the National Museum & Art Gallery on Independence Hill. The building is based on traditional architecture and the displays will give you a feel for some local arts and culture. The National Capital Botanical Gardens (entry 8 kina) are equally worthy of a couple of hours as they have an extraordinary collection of tropical plants including native trees and palms, heliconias, cordyline and pandanus. Most impressive though is the display of orchids unique to Papua New Guinea. There is also a section of enclosures that contain native birds, including a few birds of paradise (but not the really flamboyant ones) and the world's largest pigeon.

…in the highlands

As most of PNG is smothered in steep mountains, almost half her population lives in the highlands. The incredibly lush vegetation and lack of roads over this steep terrain have ensured that much of this region has remained well protected from prying eyes. Conditions are simple, with some tribes still virtually unknown to westerners and white people are regarded with curiosity or suspicion. Villagers conduct their lives far removed from first-world concerns. Some areas are considered unsafe due to tribal warfare though this is mostly a cultural event and rarely affects tourism. The Southern Highlands are easily accessible and are home to the Huli Wigmen, amongst the most photographed people in PNG.

Up a river…

Often referred to as the Amazon of PNG, the mighty Sepik River is 1100 km long and up to 1.5 km wide. Flanked by mangrove swamps and flat lowlands, it is a natural highway for the Sepik people. Bordered by the Alexander Mountains and Hustein Ranges, this is a unique ecosystem for plant, bird and animal life. What attracts tourists though, is the intensely spiritual nature of the Sepik people. The Haus Tambaran (spirit house) is integral to daily life: men hide sacred objects from women and congregate to discuss village business. The Sepik's unique handicrafts (crocodile totems and legends carved on cooking tools) are a huge draw for those who sail – or canoe – up the river to visit the tribes.

…along a trail

If you are into trekking you could walk the 96 km Kokoda Trail from Port Moresby to Kokoda, then on to Tufi. This Second World War supply route was used by Australian Forces (ably helped by the Papuans) in 1942 to stop the Japanese advance on Port Moresby, a key target as an air assault could be launched from here to northern Australia. Conditions on the trail were very bad and many troops on both sides were killed in fierce fighting. Somewhat easier would be one of the half-day walks organized from Tufi. Head up the eastern ridge towards Mount Trafalgar, stopping at local villages on the way to talk with the women and children (who just adore digital cameras!) until you reach the end of the fjord. On the way are hornbills, parrots and cockatoos and spectacular scenery. Mount Trafalgar itself would take another 3 hrs and need an overnight stop. Alternatively, Baga village is 2 hours' walk along the fjord's western ridge. There are many other villages on the way and the one that's closest to Tufi, Kupari Point Village, often invites guests to join in traditional events.

A cassowary; Tufi's fjord-like vista; children from New Britain; Kupari Village celebration

Safety in numbers: swarms of bigeye trevally, *Caranx sexfasciatus,* hovering over the reef.
Barracuda Point, Mary Island

⊿1 Russell Islands ▸▸ p228

⊿4
⊿2 ⊿1
Yandina
Pavuvu
⊿3 ⊿5

⊿1 Leru Cut
⊿2 Mirror Pool
⊿3 The wreck of the Ann
⊿4 Barracuda Point, Mary Island
⊿5 White Beach

⊿2 Florida Islands ▸▸ p231

⊿7
⊿6
Nggela Sule
Tulagi ●
Savo
Iron Bottom Sound

⊿6 Tanavula Point
⊿7 Vélvia

Choiseul

PACIFIC OCEAN

New Georgia Sound

Santa Isabel
Buala ●

New Georgia

Seghe ●
⊿3

Rendova

Blanche Channel

Vangunu

Marovo Lagoon

San Jorge

SOLOMON ISLANDS

Russell Islands
Mary Island
⊿1

⊿2
Tulagi ●
Savo
Florida Island
Iron Bottom Sound

Coral Sea

HONIARA ●

Guadalca

Raeavu ●

25 km

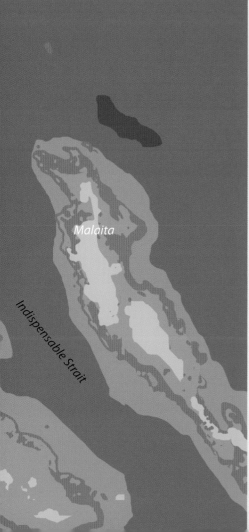

⟟3 Marovo Lagoon ⟫ p232

Seghe
Vangunu
⟟8
Marovo Lagoon
Nggatokae
⟟9
⟟10

⟟8 Lumahlihe Passage
⟟9 Wickham Island
⟟10 Who Maru 1 & 2

Malaita

Indispensable Strait

The little-known Solomon Islands are a rare treat for those who commit to discovering one of the few diving destinations in the world that has a little bit of everything. No matter what your preferred dive style, be it reefs or wrecks, caves or walls, you will find it here.

The waters surrounding this string of islands are now regarded as part of the vital Coral Triangle and as such, have high levels of marine diversity. No one knows quite what's there simply because they are less explored than some of the better known regions nearby.

The Solomons also saw some of the longest battles of the Second World War and the evidence of that is littered across the sea bed. The marine realm has engulfed this man-made detritus and reclaimed it as its own. Its presence is accepted by the animals and there are certainly plenty of them: from the smallest critters to enormous schools of pelagic fish, you will find something from almost every marine species group.

Life in the Solomons today reflects little of its history. Gone are the headhunters of ancient times, the many European colonists and over zealous missionaries, and despite some recent political turmoil, this is a country populated by laid-back and friendly islanders.

Solomon Islands rating

Diving
★★★★

Dive facilities
★★★

Accommodation
★★

Down time
★★

Value for money
★★★

Essentials

Getting there and around

There really is only one way to get to the Solomon Islands and that's from Brisbane in Australia. There are other flights but from places even more remote such as Fiji, Papua New Guinea and Vanuatu. Solomon Airlines (solomonairlines.com.au) and Virgin Blue (virginblue.com.au) fly three or four times weekly from Brisbane but bear in mind that most of their flights are operated by other carriers so the schedules change frequently. Also, the website has no online booking facility so you will need to use a travel agent or internet search engine.

Once you have arrived in the capital, Honiara, internal transport is a little more prolific. Solomon Airlines internal flights are frequent and connect all the smaller destinations. Costs are reasonable – Honiara to Seghe (for Uepi) is around US$80. There is also a network of large passenger ferries plus small motor boats, known as canoes. These are mostly fibreglass cruisers with an outboard and no shelter. They go almost anywhere but can take a very long time. For diving resorts like Gizo in the north west and Uepi Resort in Marovo Lagoon, flights are far more practical.

Alternatively, to get better coverage of the whole of the country's diving, you can make it all so much easier by hopping on a liveaboard. That way all your transfers and internal travel is sorted.

Local laws and customs

The people of the Solomons are mostly Christian, with variations from Anglican to Seventh Day Adventist. No matter where you are, the people are devout and you will be better regarded if you claim some form of Christian belief. Outside Honiara, the Solomons' way of life is based on a system of clans or families in which the headman rules. If you do go exploring independently, it is best to contact him. Just ask the first person you meet if it's "ok to be here" and if he's not the landowner, he'll take you to meet him or the chief.

Local people are open and friendly, but women should always cover their thighs and shoulders. Some other curiosities are that shaking hands is thought unnatural, as is looking directly into someone's eyes.

Tabu (taboo) is an important part of daily life and means both sacred and forbidden. There are lots of taboos that relate to male/female relationships, for instance, couples won't touch each other in public, so Western couples are better not doing so. Another curiosity is that a woman mustn't stand taller than a man. This causes some amusement in Honiara as neither sex will use the road overpass near the hospital for fear of offending the opposite sex! If you are ever unsure, just ask the closest villager what is or isn't an ok thing to do.

Solomon Islands

Location	8°00'S, 159°00'E
Capital	Honiara
Population	595,613
Land area in km²	27,540
Coastline in km	5313

The Bilikiki moored up in Marovo Lagoon

Language

English is the universal language though each village has its own local tongue (there are around 70 in all). The one that links them all together is Pijin English, an age-old amalgamation of Melanesian and English. If you can string together a few words, normally shy villagers will open up.

hello	*halo*	thank you	*tanggio*
see you later	*lukim iu*	sorry	*sorie*
yes	*ya*	how much is...	*haomas nao...*
no	*no/nating*	good	*nice tumas*
please	*plis*	great dive!	*good fella dive*

Safety

Over the last decade, the Solomons have suffered from a couple of political coups, which has naturally led to other governments advising against travel to the islands. The unrest seems to have settled since the new government took power in late 2007. Like many small nations that are undergoing constant change, crime against travellers is rare, but increasing. You are only likely to encounter petty crime if at all and, generally, only in Honiara. There is a little bit of bag-snatching and isolated reports of hotel rooms being broken into, so ensure your valuables are not left on display. Personal safety is not an issue, but note that it isn't regarded as acceptable for women to be out wandering around at night.

Health

Health care in the Solomons exists but facilities are highly variable. The bigger issue is that there are few chemist shops in the country so it's important to have a good first aid kit with you. Obviously better resorts and the liveaboards will be able to assist if anything should happen but it's best to be prepared. Having said all that, there isn't much to guard against, with the notable exception of malarial mosquitoes. Use a repellent on land.

Costs

The Solomons economy is not exactly buoyant. Both the post-colonial legacy and political instabilities mean that tourism comes at a price. It's not so much that it's an expensive place but prices can seem high for the quality you get. This is one of the reasons for going on a liveaboard – everything is included except alcohol, which is charged at US rates. Meals in Honiara are a hit and miss affair. There are a few Chinese restaurants where a meal can cost SBD$100 a head without drinks. In the hotels, a simple burger and chips with a beer will be SBD$60. Speaking of which, the hotels themselves are nothing to get excited about. The top one in Honiara charges 4-star prices for 2-star quality and that theme runs throughout the city.

 Tourist information → The government website can be found at visitsolomons.com.sb and there is some additional information at flysolomons.com/solomons.htm.

Fact file

International flights	Solomon Airlines from Brisbane
Departure tax	SBD$40
Entry	EU, US and Commonwealth – valid passport and return ticket required for stays of up to 30 days
Internal flights	Internal flights Solomon Airlines
Ground transport	Internal flights by small planes and motorized 'canoes'
Money	US$1 = 7.5 Solomon Islands dollars (SBD)
Language	English and Pijin English
Electricity	240v, Plug type E (see page 16)
Time zone	GMT +11
Religion	Various Christian denominations
Phone	Country code +677; IDD code 00; Police 911

The diversity of a Solomons wall

Solomon Islands **Essentials**

Dive brief

Diving

Presented with a nation that consists of 992 islands, and all ringed by coral reefs, you may feel a little overwhelmed by the prospect of choosing which will best suit your dive requirements. But the decision is easy simply because there's not much choice. The Solomons only get something like 5,000 visitors a year so tourist facilities haven't taken over the place and there are just a handful of options for divers.

The islands are all delightful but with resorts located on just a few, the most expedient option would be to combine several regions by hopping onto one of the country's two first-class liveaboards. This is a destination that holds the rather impressive accolade of a little bit of everything. There are walls, reefs, caves and, of course, the Second World War wrecks. Pelagic species are plentiful on some sites, macro animals on others.

However, what you won't get is huge numbers of each of these things. As the divemasters are first to admit, they have variety rather than quantity. In 2004 a scientific survey found that the Solomons also have far higher biodiversity numbers than was once thought, with nearly 500 different corals. This study led to promoting the area's inclusion in the Coral Triangle.

The Solomons also have year-round diving. Like anywhere tropical, there is a wet season, which runs from December to April, but rainfall is mostly intermittent and the water temperature is uniformly warm regardless of the season.

Snorkelling

Many reefs start just below the water line but are often murky in the shallows. Island resorts have easy access to shallower reefs but these are not always as impressive as deeper clear-water dive sites visited by the liveaboards. Strong currents are rare so you can snorkel almost everywhere, just check conditions first.

Marine life

Without doubt, whatever you might hope to see on a tropical reef, you are likely to see here. There's big stuff (sharks, rays and turtles) and schooling stuff (barracuda and jacks). At the far end of the scale, there's some great muck diving (nudibranchs, leaffish and inimicus) plus you'll find animals that have become famous drawcards elsewhere such as the pygmy seahorse.

Solomon Islands animal encounters	
Russells	white bonnet anemone fish
Mary Island	sharks, jacks, barracuda
Floridas	octopus

A lionfish checking out the alien in its world

We asked our cruise directors, Michelle and Monty, what had kept them in the Solomons for six years... that's six full years living in a tiny boat cabin, working 24/7 and showing demanding diver guests around. Their answer was pretty much what we expected: a little bit of this, a bit of that. Every dive has something a little different to the one before. By the end of the cruise, we couldn't have agreed with them more.

Making the big decision

A lot of divers are attracted to the Solomons despite knowing little about it. It's one of those places that has a certain mystique. The dive industry is small, which makes it all feel rather like an exclusive club. Others may have been and passed on the word or the reputation of one of her two liveaboards has filtered through. No matter what has attracted you, you won't be disappointed. Australians, who are on the doorstep, tend to go to the island resorts, but to get the most out of this distant island chain being escorted around by boat is the best way to go. Either way, it's the variety of diving that keeps divers happy.

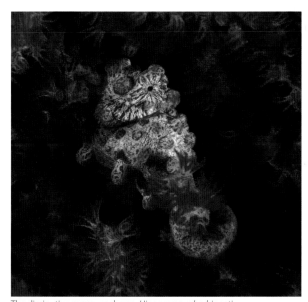

The diminutive pygmy seahorse, *Hippocampus barbiganti*

Dive data

Seasons	Diving is year round. December to April are the wetter months, May to November is drier
Visibility	5 metres inshore to 40 metres in the open
Temperatures	Air 30-34°C; water 27-29°C
Wet suit	3 mm shorty or full body suit
Training	Courses are available in the resorts at Uepi and Gizo, prebooking is advised
Nitrox	Available on liveaboards, but enquire in advance at resorts
Deco chambers	Honiara and Townsville, Australia

Bottom time

Solomon Islands	Covering about 1.4 million sq km of the South Pacific Ocean, the Solomon Islands are said to have one of the highest levels of coral diversity on the planet. Recent research has ranked the surrounding waters in the top 10 most biologically diverse, promoting their inclusion in the Southeast Asian Coral Triangle.
Russell Islands ▸▸ p228	Shallow caves, fertile reefs and a choice of Second World War – and other – wrecks.
Mary Island ▸▸ p229	Unlimited pelagic hyperactivity centred beneath the sides of an inactive volcano.
Marovo Lagoon ▸▸ p232	The world's largest lagoon, where long chains of islands and reefs combine to create a double barrier reef.
Florida Islands ▸▸ p231	Prolific and diverse reefs with exciting dives just a short trip from the capital.

Diversity   reef area 5,750 km²

HARD CORALS	68
FISH SPECIES	724
ENDEMIC FISH SPECIES	0
FISH UNDER THREAT	6
PROTECTED REEFS/MARINE PARKS	8

All diversity figures are approximate

Dive log

Russell Islands

Heading northeast from Guadalcanal, the first island group encountered is the Russells. Regarded as having 'a thousand and one islands' the largest is Pavuvu, steep-sided and covered in coconut palms. In fact, many of these islands are coconut plantations. The land is leased from the custom owners and planted with palms. The islanders then collect the fallen coconuts and take them to the main town of Yandina to sell.

The rest of the time the islanders live a traditional seabound life. Long days are spent in dugout canoes floating over the coral reefs that completely ring these small islands. Where there isn't a section of reef it's usually because there is a small cave complex. Coastal Pavuvu is riddled with small underwater caves and tunnels that lead inland then emerge on land as tiny tree-lined pools. The diving here is easy with little in the way of currents and boats can avoid any strong winds simply by sheltering on another side of an island. This is also the location of romantically-titled Sunlight Channel, a haven for the US forces in the Second World War and now a fantastic dive site.

The white bonnet anemonefish

N1 Leru Cut

Depth	20 m
Visibility	fair
Currents	no
Dive type	liveaboard

Tucked into the tree-lined coast, this dive is a little murky due to sediment and run-off but despite that, it's quite a spectacle. A deep cut in the reef wall forms a shallow cave that narrows before leading back under the island for about 75 metres. When you get to the end, you can see the pool formation above and the filtered rays of light are very moody. Inside the cavern are pretty rock formations and you ascend to see the pool is surrounded by deep green jungle. Back out on the reef, there are lots of fish hanging about: schools of rainbow runners, bumphead wrasse and midnight snapper. On the wall itself there are lots of smaller creatures, even small ornate ghost pipefish hiding in crinoids.

N2 Mirror Pool

Depth	18 m
Visibility	fair
Currents	no
Dive type	liveaboard

Almost two dives in one, this starts at another small cave with a shallow opening in the reef edge. When you swim back into it, being careful not to disturb the water too much, you see that the pool above has a fantastic mirror finish reflecting the surrounding trees and plants. Outside the cave is a maze of large coral bommies. One patch of hard coral is smothered in Paguritta hermit crabs – tiny crabs with an extended mitten on their claws that hide in old Christmas tree worm holes. A little further along is the bonnet anemonefish, thought to be indigenous to this region. It has white lines down its face and a spot for its hat. Whitetip sharks patrol along the wall, which has quite a steep drop, and part way along is a sloping rubble bed where cuttlefish hang out.

🌀	**The wreck of the Ann**	
🌀	**Depth**	36 m
🌓	**Visibility**	fair to excellent
🌊	**Currents**	mild
🌀	**Dive type**	liveaboard

Deliberately sunk just over 15 years ago, this wreck of a cargo boat is completely intact and sits virtually upright on a sandy slope quite close to the shore. The visibility here is often very good so you can see right from the bow to the stern. The decks are covered in enormous elephant's ear sponges in several different colours. The wheelhouse is full of glassy sweepers and there are several lionfish prowling around them. There is just one gaping hold which appears to be completely empty but, if you take some time, you may spot both pipefish and nudibranchs. Back on deck, there are still some mechanical winches, all covered in crusting corals. Although there are few fish, around the wreck is very impressive. When it's time to ascend for a safety stop, you can gas-off on the surrounding reef. It's a little patchy but there are several different types of clownfish and anemones. Some have cleaner shrimp and some porcelain crabs.

🌀	**Barracuda Point, Mary Island**	
🌀	**Depth**	40 m+
🌓	**Visibility**	excellent
🌊	**Currents**	mild to strong
🌀	**Dive type**	liveaboard

Due west of the Russell Islands lies isolated Mary Island, a completely inactive volcano. Although the island is ringed by steep walls and coral reefs, her star attraction lies in a tongue-shaped promontory that juts out from the coast with sloping dropoffs on either side. As you enter the water you are met by a huge ball of jacks that circle ceaselessly over the top of the tongue, then as you descend towards the point, you find another smaller ball. Continuing downwards there are lone dogtooth tuna, small gangs of chevron barracuda and then countless numbers of needlenose barracuda. Amongst it all, grey reef sharks patrol to and fro across the reef and in the evenings, hunt amongst the balls of jacks. Down at 30 metres plus, on the tip of the tongue, there are a lot of whip corals, fans and many different coloured elephant ear sponges. A few more whitetip sharks circle in to watch the divers. Back on the top of the reef, the hard corals are pristine and swarming with smaller, colourful fish as well as several Napoleon wrasse that follow divers curiously.

" " It was on our third dive here that we noticed a grey reef shark moving closer and closer to the ball of jacks. Suddenly, he whipped his tail and zoomed right into the middle of the ball. The jacks split into a million directions, like some fantasy firework, the predator accelerated away with his catch, and the jacks slid quickly back into formation. Just like it had never happened.

Solomon Islands Dive log Russell Islands

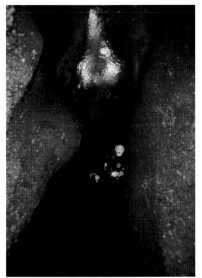

Swimming back from Leru Cut; the wreck of the *Ann*; needlenose barracuda shoaling over Barracuda Point; dogtooth tuna

★ 5 White Beach

⬡ **Depth**	45m+
◐ **Visibility**	fair to excellent
≋ **Currents**	mild
⬡ **Dive type**	liveaboard

This absolutely stunning site sits in Sunlight Channel by Mbanika Island. Diving centres around a munitions dump from a US supply base that was hidden behind the mangrove ringed coast. When the troops shipped out at the end of the war, they simply dropped everything from their base into the sea.

Once moored up, divers can come and go as they please, a fantastic option as the site has a huge amount of potential. In the shallows there are three flat topped barges that were originally lined up along shore and tied to wooden pylons. These have rotted away so now the barges are sitting partially below sea level. All the surfaces are coated in small corals and critters like blennies, nudibranchs and pipefish. There's another dive under the nearby mangroves where there are masses of juveniles and you can watch schools of archerfish shoot jets of water at the flies in the trees above. Both these areas are great for snorkelling.

At the other extreme is the deepest point of the dive where you will find the larger dumped items: there's a tractor and a crane and several other vehicles. Coming back up to the shallows you pass loads of mechanical litter – even steering wheels that are so encrusted with coral you almost don't recognize their shape. Slowly finning around you can spot old bombs, torpedos and masses of bullets. There are healthy crusting corals covering everything left from the dump plus small fish colonies, several mantis shrimp, some great gobies, weird opistobranchs, nudibranchs and pyjama cardinals.

A treasure hunt

One thing that impressed us about the Solomons was the diversity of dive sites. It seems that we encounter a 'Barracuda Point' at nearly every destination we visit, but the one at Mary Island was one of the most spectacular. When we slipped into the water, we were immediately in the presence of sharks, jacks, bumphead parrotfish, other large pelagics and yes, even some barracuda. While we love to see large things, we were thrilled by the small critters as well. Our favourite critter dive was White Beach. This site was used to distribute supplies during WWII to the US marines on Guadalcanal. All the equipment left behind by the United States was pushed into the sea, creating an artificial reef inhabited by weird and wonderful animals. This site reminded us of a treasure hunt of sorts – the treasure being scads of beautiful nudibranchs, pipefish, lionfish and several species of clownfish. A bonus for us was finding these weird and beautiful critters hiding among the abandoned jeeps, mortar shells, barges and other artefacts.

Steve and Suzanne Turek work for the Department of Fish and Game in California

Florida Islands

Closest to Honiara, the Florida Islands border the north of Iron Bottom Sound. In the Second World War, the main island of Nggela Sule was garrisoned by the Japanese who hoped to build a seaplane base. The area was liberated by US forces and became a base for their war effort.

The impact of the war meant that almost all pre-war plantations were destroyed. These were the mainstay of the local economy and little was done to re-establish them or introduce other forms of employment to the islands which are now very quiet places with little happening other than a bit of dive tourism. The diving, however, is far from quiet, for here are some of the country's most exciting and diverse reefs.

↘6 Tanavula Point

🧭 **Depth**	28 m	
🌓 **Visibility**	good	
🌀 **Currents**	mild to strong	
🛟 **Dive type**	liveaboard	

This long, sloping reef is dog-legged and from the start it's covered in fans and patches of coral. There are some huge pink gorgonians that are known homes for the barbiganti pygmy seahorse and it's possible to spot both juvenile and adult barramundi cod. As you travel around the crook in the reef, the currents pick up. You may get caught in a pressure point where the currents merge but this attracts some pelagic life – sharks are spotted out in the blue, eagle rays fly past and there are schools of rainbow runners and jacks.

↘7 Velvia

🧭 **Depth**	35 m	
🌓 **Visibility**	good	
🌀 **Currents**	mild to strong	
🛟 **Dive type**	liveaboard	

Named after the photographers' favourite film, this open sea mound has a flat top with isolated coral mounds but is mostly sand and coral rubble. However, the sides drop all around to walls rich with life and fans. The deeper you go, the more lush it becomes. Nestling in cracks and crevices are large green morays and lobsters. There are sharks off in the blue but the focus is more on small creatures – nembrotha nudibranchs, octopus and mantis shrimp plus masses of nesting fish. Damselfish are particularly active and you can see them herding newly born babes just millimetres long right up to youngsters of an inch or so. Aggressive sergeant majors also guard their eggs while clownfish couples can be spotted aerating the next generation.

🌀 Seven year itch?

We have a dive site that is consistently good for macro subjects. It's called Velvia, which will strike a chord with all the photographers out there. Nudibranchs, stonefish, cuttlefish, mantis shrimp, crocodilefish, morays, crabs, shrimps – I could go on and on. We constantly witness unusual events but with fairly ordinary creatures, which increases my appreciation and admiration for nature. It was octopus mating time and within about 30 minutes I had seen around 10 pairs. They were as bold as brass and had no fear of divers or bubbles.

I settled on the sandy bottom to watch a female play with two males. She was perched on a rocky coral head luring the boys to her, but when they approached she would slither into a crevice and just leave out a tentacle. When one male approached her, the other would chase him away. This went on for 20 minutes, until she tired of it and darted off. One followed her, but the other looked a little shell-shocked and just perched up high with his legs straight, less than a metre away from me.

I slowly moved closer – expecting him at any moment to take cover or propel away – until I got face-to-face with him. This is not how Solomon octopii normally act, they are usually shy and retiring. This made me curious, so slowly – and apprehensively I might add – I reached out and gave him a little rub between the eyes with my finger. Lo and behold, the cheeky little thing seemed to actually like it. He leaned into my finger and kind of moved his head around like a dog getting a good scratch behind the ears. My dive was soon over, but that is one encounter I will never forget.

Michelle Gaut, manager, MV Bilikiki

Octopus (left) and a spider crab, both on Velvia

Marovo Lagoon

One of the largest lagoon systems in the world, Marovo is unusual in that it has a clearly defined double barrier reef. This complex reef system, running about 100 kilometres from one end to the other, is bordered by several substantial volcanic islands – New Georgia, Vangunu and Nggatokae – and on the other by a barrier reef of several hundred islands.

Inside the lagoon there are mangrove islets and sand cays, raised reefs with extensive mangrove forests and freshwater swamp forests. Rivers and streams carry sediments off the volcanic slopes of all three islands and create a coastal plain with estuaries and deltas along the southwestern edge. The north and eastern edges of the lagoon display a string of narrow barrier islands which form a series of elevated reefs. In the south, the islands form the double barrier with the two chains of islands separated by waters up to 80 metres deep.

Much of the diving is inside the lagoon or in the channels that lead in and out. The water is shallow and highly nutrient rich so visibility is rarely fantastic, certainly not much over 20 metres. Some of the barrier islands, like Uepi, which are long, narrow islets, sit between the ocean-facing fringing reefs and lagoon-side fringing reefs. Only 20 or so islands are inhabited, with coconut farming and fishing being the main cash earners. The lagoon has been promoted as a potential World Heritage Site due to its incredible environmental diversity.

N8 Lumahlihe Passage

Depth	36 m	
Visibility	fair	
Currents	mild to medium	
Dive type	liveaboard	

This channel lies between two uninhabited islands that edge Marovo and has several dive options. You can travel along both sides and the outer walls on either the incoming or outgoing tides. The channel walls are steep sided and eventually drop to 50 metres or so on the outside of the lagoon. There are plenty of fans and soft corals making the site really colourful although the visibility can be low due to run-off from the lagoon during tide changes. Several fans have the Denise pygmy seahorse on them and there is a resident black leaffish. Travelling along the wall, small fish include longnose hawkfish and decorated dartfish. On the top of the wall is a sandy channel coated in garden eels and surrounded by small coral outcrops. Amongst them are bloodspot nudibranchs, moray eels, small bumphead parrotfish and crocodilefish.

N9 Wickham Island

Depth	28 m	
Visibility	poor to good	
Currents	medium	
Dive type	liveaboard	

Wickham is an incredibly pretty island, a classic tropical speck of white beach backed by greenery. The dive is just the opposite, a little murky and definitely 'mucky'. It starts at a small promontory that leads away from the beach and drops quite sharply to over 30 metres. The wall is covered in good fans and soft corals, crinoids and whips. It's all very colourful and pretty but the real action starts once you rise back up to the sand slope that extends from the beach. At depths of around 12-15 metres the whole seabed turns into a fantastic muck dive. There are more varieties of shrimp than you would care to name, similarly gobies in the sand and then there are harlequin crabs, seahorse, inimicus – or devilfish – and mantis shrimps. You can even spot some curious commensal relationships such as a black cucumber with two tiny fish living on it. This is a great night dive.

Life in Marovo Lagoon: a nocturnal round crab; corals on the wall of Lumahlihe Passage; roughhead blenny

⚙	**Depth**	40 m
◐	**Visibility**	poor to fair
≋	**Currents**	slight
⬯	**Dive type**	liveaboard

All Japanese warships were named after a place and tagged Maru, meaning return. The theory was that the boat would then return home safely but these two cargo boats didn't and no one knows what they were called originally. They are sitting a few hundred metres apart from each other in a section of the lagoon where the Japanese moored their supply ships. The first sits on the sand at 40 metres deep. On the bow there is an anti-aircraft gun and, just below, the anchor is still in its hawser. At the stern, there is a huge gash in the side where it was torpedoed and you can see signs of the ship's original purpose such as cable reels and winches. The wreck is covered with a lot of black coral with longnose hawkfish and small yellow damsels flitting about. On the mast, there is a circular depression that houses a coral trout and surprisingly, some Debelius shrimp.

The second vessel is similar but in shallower water. The Japanese version of a 50 mm Howitzer sits on the bow. You can see the large gash where a torpedo went through one side of the hull and then bent the other side out of shape. This structure is also smothered in lots of yellow and white black coral bushes and there are plenty of fish here too.

Longnose hawkfish; on the *Who Maru* (right)

The Solomons' war wrecks

The country's capital, Honiara, sits on the little-known island of Guadalcanal. Little known except to those who know their Pacific war history. The Battles of Midway and the Coral Sea may be more famous but the battles fought here were regarded as pivotal in the Second World War. The Japanese had been advancing through Micronesia and across the north of New Guinea. Unopposed, they made for the Solomons with the intention of building an airfield. When America became aware of this threat to a vital communications link to Australia, they decided an offensive was imperative. Guadalcanal was the first American amphibious counter-offensive of the war and highly risky as they were at the farthest extreme of their supply chain. It was also one of the longest battles in the Pacific, running for six months. Eventually the Japanese were driven off, with Imperial Headquarters privately admitting defeat and ordering an evacuation. They had been gone for some time before US operations realised what had happened. Naval losses off the north coast of Guadalcanal were so great that the area became known as Iron Bottom Sound. There are a variety of ships and planes sitting at the bottom of the sound but the largest warships are beyond safe sport diving limits. Visibility is rarely good in this area. Elsewhere, the Solomons are riddled with Second World War-era wrecks, some of which are more accessible.

Drying out

Heading out to dive the Solomons is unlikely to involve much more than an overnight stop in the capital Honiara. Accommodation is not what you would expect of a capital city. Ignore any claims of 3- or 4-star or 'international' standards. Rooms are usually shabby, but acceptable for a night or two. The staff, however, are always charming and helpful.

Honiara

Liveaboards

Bilikiki Cruises, T+1 705 363 2049 (Canada) or 677 20412 (Honiara), bilikiki.com. Canadian-owned Bilikiki Cruises run two liveaboards: the Spirit of the Solomons and Bilikiki. Both have a variety of itineraries that vary slightly by season and all their sailings link to in- and outbound flight schedules. Bilikiki has all en suite cabins, while Spirit has a mixture of en suite and shared. Both ships have spacious dive decks, unparalleled service and fabulous food – look forward to the canapés and cocktail hour.

Sleeping

$$ Kitano Mendana, T+677 20071. On the only stretch of town beach and opposite the museum, rooms are of a surprisingly low standard and pricey. Booking a beach view will get you a better room but ending up with what you book is a game of chance.

$ King Solomon, Hibiscus Avenue, T+677 21205. Up the hill behind town – cheaper rates and top floor rooms have views.

Eating

Both hotels have restaurants and snack bars where a burger and chips meal costs from SBD$55. There are several small Chinese restaurants along the main road. The Lime Lounge café opposite the main pier does a nice line in coffee, cakes and sandwiches.

Other options

Although getting on a liveaboard is by far the most practical and thorough way to see – and dive – the Solomons, there is always the option to stay at a land-based resort. There are several that are worth investigating if you are happy to stay in one place or if you prefer day diving. Consider combining two island regions to get better value out of your trip.

Florida Islands, Tulagi Dive Centre (tulagidive.com.sb), simple resort accommodation. Access to local wrecks and those in Iron Bottom Sound.

Gizo, The Gizo Explorer Hotel and Dive Gizo, T+6776 0199, divegizo.com. On the waterfront in the centre of town. Seven night packages start at US$900.

Honiara, Sunreef and Wreck Dive, T+6772 3659, sunreefdive.com. Currently the lone operator in Honiara with day dive trips to the wrecks in Iron Bottom Sound.

Marovo Lagoon, Uepi Island Resort, uepi.com. On the edge of the Marovo Lagoon, a real get-away-from-it-all resort with simple wooden bungalows. SSI-accredited dive centre onsite. Rooms start at US$160 and a dive is US$50.

❝❞ I needed to get away from my stressful city existence... Uepi wasn't easy to get to, but afterwards I realised that was its saviour. Our bungalow was simple with no mod-cons, we were surrounded by lush vegetation and there was 28-30 degree water just a few steps from the door. The snorkelling was a surreal experience with the resident reef sharks swimming alongside me, all the time. This became my best holiday experience ever. *Peter Wincott, CEO, the risk store, Sydney, Australia*

🛏 **Sleeping**	$$$ US$150+ double room per night	$$ US$75-150	$ under US$75
ⓘ **Eating**	$$$ US$40+ 2-course meal, excluding drinks	$$ US$20-40	$ under US$20

Solomon Islands Drying out

Guadalcanal

There's not much to do on the islands other than admire the lovely scenery, but there are some historical sights on the main island of Guadalcanal.

Honiara, the Solomons capital, is a small, hot and dusty city, with (as one of our American buddies says) few redeeming features. With apologies to the local people, who are always very friendly and welcoming, Honiara is worth little more than a night. Chances are you will have to stay a night due to flight schedules so while you are there, drop into the tiny museum to see the miniscule displays then wander the shops along the main road. There are a few souvenir shops with good crafts. Prices are lower than on the islands, but so is the quality.

If you are interested in Second World War history, visit the US Memorial at Skyline Ridge, with its description of the Guadalcanal Campaign, and the Japanese Peace Memorial on Mount Austin has panoramic views over the capital, Iron Bottom Sound and the Florida Islands. There is also a casino 10 minutes from the harbour back towards the airport.

Everything of note in town is within walking distance. For everything else a taxi would probably be easiest. They are unmetered so negotiate a price for a tour.

Island visits Whilst cruising, liveaboards schedule stops in local villages. These take an hour or two and are perfect for a glimpse of island life. Homes are still built traditionally with thatching and local timber and the islanders are very proud of the way their villages look: gardens have orchids much like the average English garden would have roses. You are met by children carrying flowers and the giving of small gifts such as toothbrushes and pens is appreciated. Wander the daily fruit and vegetable market, where the women sell the surplus from their own gardens, and then the displays of handicrafts by local craftsmen. Carved wooden bowls and masks are superlative but the prices aren't rock-bottom. Bartering is expected and you can take things like old snorkels and masks to part exchange for. As these people rely on fishing for their diet, old snorkelling gear is a useful swap. It's also likely that you will experience one of those traditional song and dance events as the local people are striving to keep their traditions alive by performing age-old dances for the passing tourists. It is amusing to see lengths of plumbing pipe substituted for bamboo canes to create musical instruments.

Visits from the islanders One of the joys of being on a liveaboard is the frequent visits from the islanders. No matter where you are, local people come out to visit the big ship. They paddle out in their wooden dugouts to trade vegetables and flowers, watch the divers or simply have a chat. The crew of Bilikiki take an active role in the lives of these people both personally and commercially.

Temperatures rising

A couple of hours from Honiara is another not-so-well-known island group, Vanuatu. Like the Solomons, it's familiar to those who know their Second World War history and to divers who have read about the President Coolidge. This American luxury liner was co-opted into service then sunk accidentally as she attempted to approach Espirito Santo with reinforcements for the battles at Guadalcanal. Now she is the largest, most intact diveable wreck in the world and said to make the trip to Vanuatu worthwhile despite the reefs there not being in their prime. Vanuatu is just 2-3 hours from Australia and New Zealand, vanuatutourism.com.

Bilikiki; sunset over Guadalcanal; islanders visiting the big ship; children in Marovo

Pots of gold: rainbow-toned hard and soft corals are the treasures of this reef.
The Corner, Rainbow Reef, Taveuni

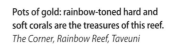

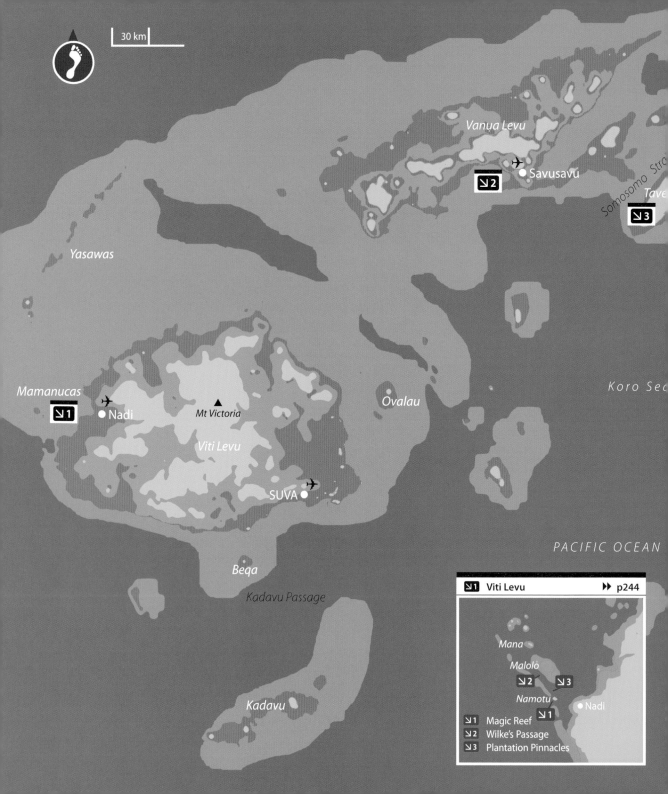

30 km

Vanua Levu

✈ ☑2 ● Savusavu

Somosomo Str

Tave

☑3

Yasawas

Koro Sea

Mamanucas

☑1 ✈
● Nadi

▲
Mt Victoria

Ovalau

Viti Levu

✈
SUVA ●

PACIFIC OCEAN

Beqa

Kadavu Passage

☑1 Viti Levu   ▶▶ p244

Mana

Malolo

☑2   ☑3

Namotu

☑1   ● Nadi

☑1 Magic Reef
☑2 Wilke's Passage
☑3 Plantation Pinnacles

Kadavu

↘2 Vanua Levu ▶▶ p246

Vanua Levu

↘5 ↘4 ↘6 ●Savusavu

Koro Sea ↘7

↘4 Alice in Wonderland
↘5 Mystery Reef
↘6 Nuggets
↘7 Goldilocks

↘3 Taveuni ▶▶ p248

Vanua Levu

↘9
↘8
↘11 Somosomo Strait
↘10

Taveuni

Koro Sea

↘8 The Corner, Rainbow Reef
↘9 Blue Ribbon Eel Reef
↘10 The Ledge
↘11 The Great White Wall

Lying across the 180 degree meridian, Fiji is where the dawn of each new day occurs, the rays of a rising sun lighting up over 300 picturesque spits of land, which hover over the world's deepest ocean.

These tiny Melanesian islands sit just outside the Coral Triangle in the southwestern Pacific Ocean and along their northern edge lies the third longest barrier reef in the world, the Great Sea Reef. This is a volcanic archipelago that is both reliant on and influenced by her maritime position.

For divers, what sets these seas and reefs apart from other favourite tropical destinations is their colour. Nicknamed the soft coral capital of the world, these display enough hues and tones to put an artist's paintbox to shame. Intensity of colour is only outdone by the profuse marine life that lives in these waters. No matter where else you have been, you won't have seen anything quite like this.

On land, the peace of the islands belies an eventful and shadowy past: a pinch of embarrassing history and a mass of multicultural intrigue means Fiji was once known to wary outsiders as the 'Cannibal Islands', yet in recent times this has become one of the friendliest nations you could ever wish to visit.

Introduction

Fiji

Fiji rating

Diving
★★★

Dive facilities
★★★

Accommodation
★★★

Down time
★★

Value for money
★★★

Essentials

Getting there and around

While the Americans and Aussies get it easy, there is nowhere that is quite so far away from Europe as Fiji, sitting right on the international date line. The shortest route from Europe is to head west via the US, taking a flight to Vancouver or Los Angeles then connecting across the Pacific. The total trip time takes about 25 hours but if you go via Asia it is closer to 30 hours. Air New Zealand (airnewzealand.com) can take you all the way or you can combine British Airways, Virgin or United with an Air Pacific flight (airpacific.com). This is Fiji's national carrier and the flight from Los Angeles takes 11 hours. They also fly from Tokyo which is around 9 hours. For Australians it's a much shorter trip: from Sydney or Brisbane you can also use low-cost carrier Virgin Blue (virginblue.com.au). If you are coming from Europe and fancy a stopover in Australia this is a good option but you'll spend longer in the air using this route.

Fiji's main airport is at Nadi and flights land there rather than at Suva, the capital. Once you have arrived in Fiji, travelling between the islands is a breeze. Pacific Sun are the internal arm of Air Pacific so book through flights with them (pacificsun.com.fj) or Air Fiji (airfiji.com.fj) whose small aircraft ensure a scenic ride to all the best diving areas. They also have a value air pass at around US$500 for four flights.

Around the islands themselves, there are plenty of transport options. Buses run virtually everywhere, although schedules are best described as 'loose'. Metered taxis are inexpensive. There are ferries, though these are time consuming. There is car rental (Avis, Hertz and so on) but unless you are on Viti Levu you are unlikely to need one.

Local laws and customs

Fiji's population consists of around 50% indigenous people, who are Christians, and 45% who are descendants from indentured Indian workers; a mix of Hindu, Muslim and Sikh. All Fijians are incredibly friendly and the usual courtesies will go a long way. However, there are a few specific rules to remember if you visit a local village: hats and sunglasses are thought to indicate disrespect for the chief; shoes should not be worn indoors and both sexes should cover knees and shoulders; avoid touching a Fijian person's head and, in very traditional villages, women may be expected to wear their hair loose. When visiting a village, it is customary to take a gift of kava root and you may be asked to drink kava with the villagers on arrival (page 251). Remember to be cautious with praise – if you admire something too much, the owner will feel obliged to give it to you. Finally, bear in mind that homosexuality is illegal here and drugs offences carry severe penalties.

Health

Fiji carries few health risks for visitors other than the usual issues of too much sun and not enough water leading to dehydration. However, there is a mosquito problem during the day and occasional outbreaks of dengue fever. If you are in an urban area use plenty of repellent. You are less likely to encounter them in coastal regions. Medical facilities are of a reasonable standard but most, including the main recompression chamber, are on Viti Levu. Make sure you have a basic medical kit with you.

Dive boat in the Somosomo Straits

Fiji	
Location	18°00'S, 175°00'E
Capital	Suva
Population	944,720
Land area in km²	18,270
Coastline in km	1,129

Language

Although almost everyone in Fiji speaks English, many Fijian terms are included in everyday use. Pronunciation is similar to English but with a few changes to the phonetic alphabet. Not that anyone will care if you get it wrong but it will help to get you to the right place if you pronounce the name correctly. Some common changes include: 'b' becomes 'mb', 'c' is 'th', 'd' is 'nd', 'g' is 'ng' and 'q' is 'ngg'. So Nadi is actually pronounced 'Nandi', and Beqa is 'Mbengga'.

hello	bula (mbula)	please	yalo vinaka
goodbye	ni sa moce		(yalo vee naka)
	(ni sa mothey)	thank you	vinaka (vee naka)
yes	io (ee-o)	sorry	lomana
no	seqa (senga)	one beer	dua (ndua) bia

Safety

Like anywhere, a dose of common sense will keep you and your possessions safe. The Fijian islands are generally crime free but in the city centres there is some small-time petty theft and occasional muggings. In a country which virtually shuts down on a Sunday – the day of rest – this upsets the older generation who are saddened by the rise in crime and what they see as a lack of respect amongst Fijian youth. Compared to western countries, crime is still minimal, but as many people live close to the bread line opportunistic theft is becoming more common. As ever, don't leave dive gear, cameras or anything of value on display, not even on a hotel balcony.

Costs

Value for money is a given in Fiji. There is a wide selection of hotels, from dirt cheap to expensive. Diving and accommodation packages in smaller resorts can start from as little as US$150 per day, add food and it might be US$200. Some of the more sophisticated resorts can be several hundred dollars a day, but you can sleep comfortably for much less. If you don't want to be limited to staying, diving and eating in only one place, you can always use the closest resort's dive centre. Small, local restaurants are simple and cheap and you'd be hard pressed to spend over FJD$30 a head on a meal. A local Fiji Bitter will be around FJD$3. Chinese food is common on the smaller islands, Indian food on Viti Levu. Getting traditional Fijian food is more difficult but resorts will do a 'lovo night' when a meal is cooked over hot stones. Apart from Nadi and Suva, there won't be a huge selection of shops or restaurants. Tipping isn't customary in Fiji, although you may find it's expected in the more expensive resorts and some will have a special staff fund. For liveaboard dive crews, see page 12.

 Tourist Information → The government website can be found at bulafiji.com. This informative site runs in several languages, including Korean and Japanese.

Fact file

International flights	Air New Zealand, Air Pacific, Qantas
Departure Tax	FJD$30
Entry	EU, US and Commonwealth – valid passport required for stays of up to 4 months
Internal flights	Air Fiji and Pacific Sun
Ground Transport	Taxis, buses and ferries
Money	US$1 = 1.5 Fijian dollars (FJD)
Language	English
Electricity	220v, plug type E (see page 16)
Time zone	GMT +7
Religion	Christian, Hindu, Muslim, Sikh
Phone	Country code +679; IDD code 00; Police 911

Hanging over a Fijian Wall

Dive Brief

Diving

Fiji's reefs have earned more elaborate, flowery descriptions than appears logical – until you get there. Terms like underwater rainbows, technicolour wonderlands and kaleidoscopic colours are used and over used to exhaustion.

Despite that, this tiny country has been nicknamed the 'soft coral capital of the world' and in that sense, it deserves every fancy description that comes its way. Yes, divers and writers do tend to over-enthuse but it will only take one dive amongst this most incredible array of rainbow-hued soft corals and you will understand. It's not just that the colours seem extraordinarily bright in amongst the clear waters, it's the sheer range of colours that clash with each other. Sometimes gaudy might be a better tag.

But it's not only about the colourful corals. Like much of the South Pacific, Fiji diving is varied and exciting with shallow reefs and sheer walls, narrow tunnels that lead through caverns with overhangs and small caves to explore. Small schooling fish continually paint the reefs with ever more colour and pelagic life is plentiful. Yet somehow it still comes back to the corals which can be found all over, from huge fans close to the surface to fragile black corals found well below normal diving limits. All this is possible thanks to the 30 metre-plus visibility that keeps the depths well lit. Plankton blooms during April and May or November and December can reduce the visibility a little but they bring in filter-feeders and pelagics. Conditions are fairly easy, there is some current but drift diving is straightforward and water temperatures are consistent.

Snorkelling

Protected lagoons around many of the islands mean that snorkelling can be very rewarding. However, these spots are not always in the same places as the best diving. Taveuni would be one of the better exceptions to that, as would the tiny, sandy islands of the Yasawa Group, off Nadi. Viti Levu has few easily accessible snorkelling areas but resorts arrange trips to offshore reefs where the snorkelling is much better.

Marine Life

Did anyone mention the mass of incredible technicolour soft corals? All reef species are well represented here – although maybe not in such great numbers as in the countries of the Coral Triangle – but there is everything from reef sharks to crinoids. Look out for the blue ribbon eels.

Fiji
animal
encounters

Viti Levu	barracuda
Vanua Levu	soft corals
Taveuni	blue ribbon eels

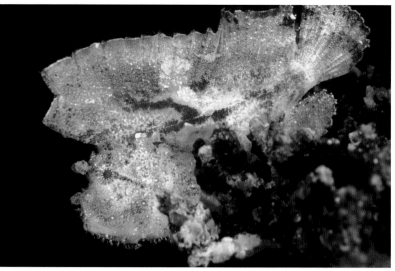

Camouflaged and motionless, the ever-patient leaf scorpionfish

We discovered Fiji while crossing the Pacific on a round the world flight. What a contrast to the stops one either side – Hawaii and Australia! There are so few places in the world these days that manage to live in the 21st century yet still remain 'unspoilt'. Of course everyone's idea of unspoilt varies, but there is little in Fiji to taint the experience. It's calm, it's quiet, it has welcoming people and amazing diving. And yes, we would go back.

Making the big decision

The biggest issue for many divers is the distance to Fiji and it cannot be denied that this country is a little out of the way for most. Unfortunately, flights are not so cheap that they are too tempting to ignore. What is tempting though is the quality of what you will see and do underwater. This marine area seems removed from many of the problems facing our planet's seas. There is tourism, and marine tourism, but it doesn't engulf the country or its personality. There is fishing but the industry isn't overwhelming. Because of the sea conditions, events like El Niño have had less of a detrimental effect than in other oceans. You may only go once but it will be a once-in-a-lifetime experience.

Whitetip reef shark taking advantage of some pristine hard coral

Dive data

Seasons	Summer (wet season) November to April, subject to occasional cyclones. Winter (dry season) May to October
Visibility	20 metres (summer) to 50 metres (winter)
Temperatures	Air 20-31°C; water 25-30° C
Wet suit	3 mm full body suit. 5 mm in cooler months
Training	Generally available, look for PADI or NAUI affiliated schools
Nitrox	Generally available
Deco chambers	Deco chambers Suva

Bottom time

Fiji		2,700 kilometres due east of Cairns in Australia and around 10 hours flying time from the west coast of America, each of the Fijian islands emerge as the epitome of a South Pacific idyll. Of the 300 islands that make up this small nation, only 100 are occupied; however, there are reefs around almost all.
Viti Levu	▸▸ p244	Fiji's main island is ringed by many others – including the western Mamanucas and Yasawas. These exotic names reflect exotic locations and their varied diving options.
Vanua Levu	▸▸ p246	Fiji's second largest island lies to the north east and borders the top edge of the Somosomo Straits. The rushing waters there contrast strongly with the more sheltered sites in Savusavu Bay.
Taveuni	▸▸ p248	Sitting along the bottom edge of the dramatic Somosomo Straits, these dives are the ones that gave the country the title 'soft coral capital of the world'.

Diversity   reef area 10,020km²

HARD CORALS	56
FISH SPECIES	895
ENDEMIC FISH SPECIES	3
FISH UNDER THREAT	10
PROTECTED REEFS/MARINE PARKS	12

All diversity figures are approximate

Viti Levu

Fiji's largest island is home to Suva, the political capital and Nadi, her second city, which is where all international flights land. Off the western side of the island there are many coral reefs and handfuls of tiny, delightful islands.

Many divers head straight out to one of the more distant island groups to find the best diving in Fiji; however, there is pleasant diving around Viti Levu. Just off Nadi's shoreline are two chains of islands that are classically pretty cays. The Mamanucas are the nearest group, the Yasawas a little further north. The Mamanuca Islands are riddled with small resorts and dive centres and some of the sites along the outer barrier reef can be quite exciting. Quite a few of these resorts are targeted at budget travellers so courses are good value.

There is more diving off the southern coast of Viti Levu, also known as the Coral Coast. Beqa Lagoon is popular and hundreds of divers come to this area as access is easy and facilities are good. Over 10 miles across, the lagoon is actually the crater of an extinct volcano. There is a very popular shark feed dive at Shark Reef, where you have a good chance of coming face to face with reef, bull and tiger sharks.

Conditions around Viti Levu are good but less so than the outlying islands as this area is prone to cyclones. Visibility is about 30 metres at best as all that lovely, white sand does muddy the water when the winds are up. At the same time, the surface conditions can be rocky and while reef conditions are pretty good, they are nowhere near as impressive as elsewhere.

⌖1 Magic Reef

Depth	20 m
Visibility	fair to great
Currents	mild
Dive Type	day boat

Magic Island, more properly known as Namotu, is little more than a small cay ringed by sand. The reefs around her perimeter can be dived either from Nadi or from one of the many local island resorts. Diving the passage between this island and nearby Tavarua can be highly exhilarating. The coral life takes second place to the incredible numbers of fish. As you near the wall, you will encounter some schooling barracuda, turtles and perhaps a shark or two. Back in shallower waters, it's small colourful fish like lions or butterflies and black and white banded seasnakes feeding in the corals.

Underwater rainbows, technicolour wonderlands, kaleidoscopic colour: Fijian soft corals

N2 Wilke's Passage, Mamanuca

🕙	**Depth**	22 m
◐	**Visibility**	very good
🌊	**Currents**	mild to strong
🚤	**Dive Type**	day boat

It's unusual for an open water dive site to be good for snorkelling, but this one is. It's also a favourite for surfers. Northwest of Magic Island, Wilke's Passage cuts through the outer edge of the barrier reef. The flow of water on the outside creates decent waves for the surfers and there are frequent dolphin sightings too. The inner lagoon is good for snorkelling while below the water these conditions create an interesting drift dive. The currents can be strong but not so fierce as to make dives difficult and they attract schools of barracuda and trevally. Corals flourish in the nutrient-rich waters.

N3 Plantation Pinnacles

🕙	**Depth**	24 m
◐	**Visibility**	good
🌊	**Currents**	can be strong
🚤	**Dive Type**	day boat

A little further north is Mamanuca Lagoon, where three pinnacles protrude from the seabed. Conditions here are usually easy – you can do several circuits, some swim-throughs then slowly ascend up the sides. At the base there are black coral trees with resident longnose hawkfish and small fans and soft corals coat the sides. At the top, the macro life is particularly interesting with nudibranchs and starfish, masses of anemones and clowns, leaffish and morays.

Clown triggerfish with wacky skin patterns

Fish tales

In Beqa Lagoon there's an innocuous site where shark feeding takes place. Every diver that visits Shark Reef must pay FJD$10 which goes to two local villages to compensate them for not fishing the reef and for protecting it from other fishing and diving boats. After an extremely thorough brief, our four dive guides, together with two huge sealed bins full of dead fish, dropped into the water. The guests followed, taking up positions behind a constructed one-foot-high coral wall. With metal mesh gloves covering his hands, one guide began hand feeding. Soon a huge ball of snapper and trevally was joined by half a dozen grey reef sharks. Shy at first, they slowly circled ever-closer before taking food from the guide's hand. Behind us, white and blacktip reef sharks buzzed back and forth, excitedly waiting their turn. After about ten minutes I got my first sight of a bull shark, a full size pregnant female. Then as we started our ascent, a very swift-moving and impressive silvertip shark passed by overhead in search of food. During the briefing for our second dive, one of the guides commented that this is normally when the tiger sharks make their appearance. "Yeah right, I've heard that one before" thinks I, quite immune to exaggerated marketing speak. Within minutes, I saw several large bull sharks, then I thought it was another in the distance. But the stripes were plainly visible… just a few metres above was the legendary tiger. I saw her circle five times, then she passed straight over my head, easily within arm's reach. At this stage I was doing my best to melt into the boulder behind me. It was so close I could have smelt her breath! What a truly awesome moment! *Sheldon Hey*

Later, we steamed up to the Namena Marine Protected Area, south east of Savusavu. This region can only be reached by liveaboard and is generally regarded as having some of the best sites in Fiji. It certainly did not disappoint. Chimneys is a dive with pinnacles and ridges all covered in a glorious blanket of soft corals (among other things) with plenty of fish life and the occasional shark too. The colour and sheer health of the reefs were breathtaking. Ned's Head was similar, if a slightly poorer cousin of Chimneys, yet there was still a riot of colour and a remarkable amount of marine life here too. North Save A Tack was the unlikely name for our next dive site and deserves special mention. Not only did it serve to break up the pinnacle diving (there are a lot of pinnacle dives in Namena) but it also really helped to hit home that some of these sites are truly world class. Here the first half of the dive was on the lip of a deep wall with huge schools of jacks, yellow tail barracudas, chevron barracudas, a few meaty grey reef sharks and even a manta before the dive entered its second phase. This entailed swimming though a large archway festooned with gorgonians, whip corals and sponges, before taking in a series of ridges providing the base for an impressive array of sessile life which is enough to make you forget that there are a lot of fish nearby including schooling needlefish, Achilles tangs and plenty of snapper. Surfacing from this dive it was difficult to know where to begin to discuss the highlights. *Gavin Macaulay*

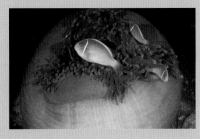

Sheldon Hey and Gavin Macaulay are directors of dive-the-world.com

Temperatures rising

The Kadavu group of islands lies about 100 kilometres south of Viti Levu and marks the position of the world's fourth largest barrier reef. The Great Astrolabe Reef encloses a lagoon containing a handful of islands and is said to have some of the best hard corals in the country. Although the islands are only 35 minutes flight from Nadi they are still remarkably remote, untainted by modern tourism. This is in part because weather conditions in some seasons mean flights are cancelled, and because there are no roads – Vunisea, the main town, has just a few but apart from these, it's walking trails and boats.

Vanua Levu

This is the second largest island in Fiji yet it is incredibly undeveloped, except around the capital, Savusavu. While both infrastructure and services are limited, you can get an insight into multi-cultural Fijian daily life. There's not a lot of sightseeing to be done but who needs that when you have some of the best diving just moments from shore.

There are sheer walls for drifting over and caves to explore; the fish life is varied and sightings of pelagic species are reasonably common. However, one of this area's best features is her ability to provide dives for everyone. There are sheltered dives inside Savusavu Bay while the more exhilarating Somosomo Straits are still close enough to enjoy in a day. The diving season is year round but from April to October it's dryer, with visibility best from July to September when the surface can also get quite choppy. During the summer months of November to April water temperatures reach 30°C and it's calm.

N4 Alice in Wonderland	
Depth	22 m
Visibility	good to stunning
Currents	mild
Dive Type	day boat

Located towards the outer reaches of Savusavu Bay, the story goes that this dive was named after the huge mushroom-shaped coral heads that cover the wide patch reef. The area is exposed to currents flowing from the south and east so there are lots of schooling fish. Small whitetips cruise in to feed and lurk about beneath the 'mushrooms' which are in impeccable condition. There is some interesting macro life with plenty of cleaner shrimp hopping around tube anemones and coral banded shrimp under sponges. An unusual find is the juvenile rockmover wrasse whose spiky decorations make it hard to spot while it flits about in the surface rubble.

⬇5 Mystery Reef

🌀 **Depth**	20 m
◐ **Visibility**	good
🌊 **Currents**	medium
🌓 **Dive Type**	day boat

This isolated reef is half an hour or so from shore at the edge of Savusavu Bay and just a little past Alice. The sea floor here is also scattered with hard coral heads but these are painted with a huge number of multi-coloured soft corals. There are plenty of fish too as the whole reef seems to be a breeding ground. There are clownfish with their babies, moorish idols chasing each other in mating games while newborn damselfish hide behind their parents. Even tiny scorpionfish sit on the seabed. Coral trout, Spanish mackerel, angels and parrotfish are also in residence.

⬇6 Nuggets

🌀 **Depth**	18 m
◐ **Visibility**	excellent
🌊 **Currents**	medium
🌓 **Dive Type**	day boat

On the southern edge of Savusavu Bay, the Nuggets are two coral heads. The main pinnacle has a base about 50 metres around, at 18 metres deep, and rises to just below the surface. It's a tiny area but a whole world resides there. There are myriad soft corals surrounded by schools of fairy basslets, from the tiniest babes to adults. Masked bannerfish and damsels flutter about the steep walls and young angels seem to pop out of tiny caves every few seconds. Leaffish are spotted nestling in crevices and occasional jacks circle above. On the surrounding sandy sea floor titan triggers nest. They can be very aggressive while guarding their eggs so it's best to watch from the safety of the pinnacle. The second, smaller bommie is covered in golden soft corals with lionfish, scorpions and moray eels poking about while giant pufferfish hover nearby.

⬇7 Goldilocks

🌀 **Depth**	20 m
◐ **Visibility**	good to stunning
🌊 **Currents**	mild to strong
🌓 **Dive Type**	day boat

Heading south and around the outer edge of Vanua Levu, but still only half an hour or so from town, you reach the Koro Sea. Away from the protection of the bay, currents here are much stronger and consequently coral growth is thicker and more lush. As you descend over the reef you encounter a vast carpet of hard corals. There seems to be a huge variety in a very small area. Swimming around the edge of the reef you reach a large bommie that is thronged by tropical fish, while beneath are several small rays. A little further on, a second bommie stands out from a distance. It is completely smothered in bright yellow soft corals, hence the name of the dive site. Bright yellow plumes seem to drip from every crack and crevice. Of course, there are plenty of other corals plus nudibranchs, unicornfish and many damselfish couples guarding their eggs.

Fiji Dive log Vanua Levu

Leopard shark resting on the seabed

Taveuni

This 'small but perfectly formed' island is opposite Vanua Levu. Its steep hills are shrouded in riotous flora which earned it the title of 'Garden Island' and although the scenery is simply awe-inspiring, it pales in comparison to the beauty of the diving in the Somosomo Straits.

This stretch of water separating Taveuni from Vanua Levu almost single-handedly earned Fiji the title of soft coral capital of the world. The narrow channel funnels water from south to north and back again, supplying nutrients, stimulating growth and ensuring the health of reef-building animals. The currents are constant, not always strong but ever-present. In the continual flow the corals are always out feeding, revealing the multiple tones for which it was christened 'Rainbow Reef'.

All this activity attracts plenty of fish too, while pelagics hover over the deep blue channels. Diving is best from April to October, when the water is clearest with visibility up to 50 metres, but it can be chilly. In the wet season, the water is warmer but visibility is around 30 metres.

On land, Taveuni is a rural sort of place. There are some small villages, the biggest being Somosomo, but her real attractions are the lakes and waterfalls, rare birds and indigenous flowers of the inland Bouma National Heritage Park

↘8 The Corner, Rainbow Reef

Depth	18 m
Visibility	good
Currents	medium to strong
Dive Type	day boat

Rainbow Reef was obviously named after the immense profusion of multi-coloured soft corals that envelope this entire reef. The topography is highly varied with walls, caves and many swim-throughs while the Corner is a popular dive area with shallow coral gardens on the inner edge of the reef interspersed with sandy channels. There are young whitetip sharks hiding under table corals living alongside groups of giant clams. The bommies that grow upwards towards the surface are covered in masses of anemones, with anthias dancing amongst the soft and hard corals. This a great site for spotting nudibranchs.

↘9 Blue Ribbon Eel Reef

Depth	20 m
Visibility	fair to good
Currents	slight to strong
Dive Type	day boat

This drift dive is just a few minutes boat ride from shore. As you drop over the reef you are met by patches of purple soft corals that make it easy to bypass the main attraction – the blue ribbon eel. This is one of those sites where they are almost guaranteed though few people spot them first time round. These elusive creatures retreat rapidly into their holes in the sand as soon as they feel threatened. However, the dive guides know where they are and wait for a few minutes nearby until they pop out again. Although they are a couple of feet long you usually only see about a hand's length. This is enough to admire the vivid bands of blue and yellow on a young male. All yellow ribbon eels are female and adult, while black ones are the juveniles. The males change to female on maturity. There are plenty of fish, too, swarming around the corals.

↘10 The Ledge

Depth	25 m
Visibility	fair to good
Currents	mild
Dive Type	day boat

Located only 10 minutes from shore this pinnacle rises from the seabed at about 80 metres to about five metres below the surface. While the current can be quite strong in the shallows, as you descend it drops right off. The pinnacle is isolated from nearby reefs so many fish are attracted to it and pelagics shelter in its overhangs and crevices. There are plenty of lionfish, moorish idols, butterflies and damsels. Trevally school around the edges and there are plenty of beautiful soft corals. As this site is so close to shore it also makes a great night dive.

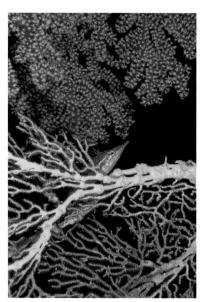

Crinoid in buttercup yellow; longnose hawkfish on the lookout

The Great White Wall

11

Depth	31 m
Visibility	stunning
Currents	medium to strong
Dive Type	day boat

Arguably Fiji's most famous site, diving on the Great White Wall means diving with a current and if, for some reason, it has dropped off completely, there is really no point in going.

The start of this dive involves a descent over the reef edge then swimming down through a tunnel which has two exits. The first exit is at 10 metres and you might find a moray here but the more exciting exit is at 30 metres. Emerging onto a sheer wall that plunges to unfathomable depths, you then find yourself surrounded by a fantastic

swathe of pure white. The water running over the wall has encouraged all the soft corals tentacles out to feed. The effect is luminescent, almost like snow on a hill which glows when the sun's rays bounce off it. There are huge quantities of these small soft corals which are actually a pale pink or mauve though you can only see that if you shine a torch on them.

A few whip corals and fans sprout from the wall, so you may spot some gobies or longnose hawkfish sheltering.

Meanwhile, off the wall, several large humphead wrasse swim along in tandem with the divers, and reef sharks are seen hanging around in the shallows, but their attraction pales in comparison to the overall effect of the landscape.

Fiji Dive log Taveuni: The Great White Wall

66 99 The vision of these same-coloured corals, after several days of gaudy, multi-toned reefs, is really quite breathtaking. The light they reflect back from the reef is a little ghostly, definitely a bit other-world.

Drying out

Coastal and offshore island resorts on the western side of Viti Levu are less than an hour from Nadi airport, while transfers to Beqa Lagoon and the Coral Coast take around two hours. To the northern islands, scenic flights in small aircraft take around an hour. The hop between Vanua Levu and Taveuni takes 15 minutes.

Viti Levu

Dive centres

Subsurface Fiji, T+679 666 6738, fijidiving.com. This large, efficient dive company works with around 18 resorts in Nadi and the Mamanucas. They organise good value packages including diving and accommodation from backpacker to top class. Courses available.

Liveaboards

MY Nai'A, T+679 345 0382, naia.com.fj. Nai'A sails around the central Fijian area. This boat is expensive but is the one with 'the' reputation.

Sleeping

$$ First Landing Resort, T+679 6666171, firstlandingfiji.com. Just north of the airport, this mid-range hotel is ideal for stopovers or short breaks before heading further afield. Lovely rooms on a good beach. Easy access to offshore dives using Subsurface Fiji.

Other options

$$$-$ Lagoon Resort, T+679 345 0100, lagoonresort.com. Near Beqa Lagoon; Beqa Adventure Divers (fiji-sharks.com) on site.

$$$-$$ Malolo Island Resort, T+679 666 9192, maloloisland.com. A delightful resort on a beautiful island. Rooms are spacious and facilities include a spa and diving with Subsurface Fiji.

Eating

All resorts have onsite restaurants. In Nadi town there are international, Indian and Chinese restaurants and for the biggest pizza you will ever see head for Mama's Pizza on Queen's Rd.

Vanua Levu

Sleeping and diving

$$$ Jean Michel Cousteau Fiji Islands Resort, T+679 885 0694, fijiresort.com. Upscale resort with large traditional bures (bungalows) and landscaped gardens. This is not a cheap option but it is a beautiful location and L'Aventure Divers are on site.

$$ Savusavu Hot Springs Hotel, T+679 885 0195, savusavufiji.com. Comfortable, central hotel with views of the bay and town. Now working with Reef Safari who are below the hotel. Good value dive and stay packages.

Eating

$$ Captain's Café Restaurant, T+679 885 0457. Great steak, fish and pizzas served on the deck of the Copra Shed Marina.

Taveuni

Sleeping and diving

$$-$ Garden Island Resort and AquaTrek, T+679 888 0286, aquatrek.com. This comfortable resort is near the village of Somosomo, 20 mins from the airstrip and minutes from the Meridian line.

Eating

Restaurants on Taveuni are mostly linked to one resort or another so unless you have transport getting around at night is difficult. Most divers book meal packages at their resort.

Other options

Maravu Plantation Resort, maravu.net
Paradise Taveuni, paradiseinfiji.com

Kadavu

Options for diving on the remote Great Astrolabe Reef include:
Mai Dive, maidive.com
Matava, matava.com

 Sleeping   **$$$** US$150+ double room per night   **$$** US$75-150   **$** under US$75

Eating   **$$$** US$40+ 2-course meal, excluding drinks   **$$** US$20-40   **$** under US$20

Viti Levu

Fiji's main island has the highest levels of sports, activities, some colonial history and a few museums.

Nadi Not a very pretty place but there is some decent shopping. Day tours that include the centre also head to the Vatukoula Gold Mines near the market town of Tavua and Viseisei Village, which is regarded as the 'foundation village' of Fijian heritage and culture.

Koroyanitu National Park Located 10 km east of Lautoka, the park has beautiful bush walks, waterfalls, archaeological sites and lush native rainforest.

Ba and Rakiraki Ba is an Indian town known for its mosque and colourful bazaar. Rakiraki is the home of Ratu Udre, Fiji's last known cannibal. His tomb at the town junction is surrounded by 999 stones, which represents the number of people he ate.

Sigatoka A small town on a river mouth with markets and access to archaeological sites on the south coast sand dunes. Digs have uncovered skeletons and artefacts dating back to 15 BC.

Suva The political capital has markets, shopping and nightlife, a few museums and the governmental buildings. Like Nadi, there is little to hold you here for more than a day.

Ovalau Island Northeast of Suva, this tiny island is home to Levuka, Fiji's first capital, and most historic location. A national heritage site, it's well worth a visit to see its gloriously faded main street.

Vanua Levu

Downtown Savusavu With the feel of a Wild West staging post, there's just one road with banks, ATMs, a post office and an internet outlet. There are two marinas: the Copra Shed is an old warehouse that has some tourist shops and a café. A bit further along is Waitui Marina, where you can chill out on the decks over the bay.

Salt Lake Kayaking Drive up the Hibiscus Highway to a salt water river that leads to a salty lake, the island's largest.

Waisali Rainforest Reserve A gentle walk through dense rainforest with the cooling spray of the waterfall at the end.

Tunuloa Peninsula Said to be the island's best birdwatching spot, including the chance to see a rare silk-tail.

Waivunia Village Take an organized excursion to see the village, homes, church and meeting hall. The villagers display arts and crafts and hold kava ceremonies for the uninitiated.

Taveuni

Bouma Falls In the National Park, these 3 waterfalls are in a remote area but are fairly easy walks. And you can swim beneath them to cool off once you arrive.

Lavena Village A picturesque, traditional village where you can meet some of the villagers. The spectacular beach is a great snorkelling spot.

Lake Tagimoucia This old crater lake, which is filled with floating plant life, is just below Des Voeux Peak, the second highest spot on Taveuni. The hike is strenuous, 3-4 hours each way, but the views are amazing. You may spot Fiji's most famous flower, the tagimoucia, subject of local legend. Bird watching is said to be excellent.

Kava Ceremonies It's a great honour to be invited to join a kava ceremony, the ritualized drinking of a bowl of muddy brown water, with the village elders. Kava is a root from the pepper family and when ground and soaked in water, has a very faint narcotic effect. Expect numb lips at least. Ceremonies are held constantly to celebrate all sorts of events, even a local sports day. It's generally a male preserve but female tourists will be tolerated. If you are invited to attend, it's bad form not to.

Wairiki Mission This old Catholic mission overlooks the site where local warriors once defeated thousands of Tongans then celebrated their victory by cooking them in a lovo oven and eating them with breadfruit! The priest who advised the warriors was 'rewarded' for his help by the building of the large mission.

Fiji Drying out

Dive boat and beach on Taveuni; the view over Savusavu; Kava ceremony; Levuka high street

Galápagos

Play with me: the mischievous antics of the Galápagos sea lion, *Zalophus californianus wollebacki*. *Cousins Rock, Bartolomé*

90 km

Darwin

⊿2 *Wolf*

The Galápagos

⊿3

⊿1

Isabela

Santa Cruz

San Cristóbal

PACIFIC OCEAN

⊿1 Central zone ▶▶ p260

Pinta

Marchena *Genovesa*

⊿2

⊿3

Santiago

⊿1

● Puerto Ayora

⊿1 Gordon Rocks
⊿2 Cousins Rock
⊿3 Bartolomé

⊿2 Northern zone ▶▶ p262

Darwin

⊿4 *Darwin's Arch*

⊿4 The Arch
⊿5 The Caves
⊿6 Rockslide

⊿5

⊿6

Wolf

⊿3 Western zone ▶▶ p264

⊿7 Roca Rodonda
⊿8 Punta Vicente Roca
⊿9 Cape Marshall

Pinta

⊿7

⊿8 ⊿9

Santiago

Fernandina

Isabela

Introduction

Nearly a thousand kilometres west of mainland Ecuador, and lying right on the Equator, the Galápagos Islands are home to some of the most intriguing and unique wildlife on earth. This ancient archipelago of harsh volcanic landscapes is ruled by animals while human visitors are reduced to the role of voyeur. Both above and below the waterline, sit back, wait patiently and allow the animals to come to you. They nearly always do.

While biodiversity figures may not be as high as in some other countries, the number of endemic species is unparalleled. Beneath the incessant waves, there are – still – vast numbers of sharks: from the sleek silky to the ever gentle whaleshark you'd have to be asleep not to see half a dozen different species. Huge hammerhead schools are the most common, often obliterating the sunlight, yet they also appear solo sitting by your shoulder.

On land you can immerse yourself in another world. Sit beside newborn sea lion pups and their parents will simply lift their heads and give you a cursory glance. Marine iguanas bask by your toes while birds pause on their backs doing daily clean up duty.

Despite their relative isolation and the cost of getting there, these islands are a popular destination. A steady stream of people flies in daily, passing along well trodden routes to witness the spectacular wildlife show.

Galápagos rating

Diving
★★★

Dive facilities
★★★

Accommodation
★★★

Down time
★★★★

Value for money
★★★

Essentials

Getting there and around

If you live in America, finding a flight to Ecuador is easy enough. If you are further away it's more about finding one that will take you there in a modicum of comfort. The most obvious route is via major US hub cities, Houston and Miami. Both have daily connections to the capital, Quito, and port city of Guayaquil but avoid stopping in Guayaquil as it has little to recommend it. Several American airlines also fly from further afield but a downside is that their in-flight service leaves a lot to be desired. The upside is that most do have more generous baggage allowance. All the same it may be worth looking at options such as Qantas (qantas.com), British Airways (ba.com) or Virgin (virginatlantic.com). If you can get to Miami, there are connections with American Airlines (aa.com), who have the most economy legroom but charge for alcoholic drinks.

Many flights arrive in Quito either early in the day or very late at night. If you're stopping over and don't have a hotel courtesy transfer, head straight for a bright yellow cab, which will cost US$5 to the 'New City'. Avoid unlicensed "taxi amigos" which will cost extra.

Getting around in Quito is easy. The city is divided into the New City, where most of the upmarket hotels, bars and restaurants are located, and the colonial Old City. There are plenty of taxis and they mostly charge US$2-3 for trips within the city. There is also a good network of trams and buses but if time is short stick to taxis.

From Quito you then connect to either San Cristóbal or Baltra for the Galápagos. Baltra is closest to Puerto Ayora, the largest town on the islands, but San Cristóbal is where all the liveaboards are based. Flights with AeroGal (aerogal.com.ec) and TAME (tame.com.ec) can cost as much as US$500 depending on season. There are also flights between the two islands, or you can fly in to one and depart from the other. These bookings are likely to be handled by your Ecuadorean agent who will ensure you reach your boat or island on time.

When you arrive in the Galápagos, as everything is so highly controlled, all arrangements will be made in advance by your dive operator.

Local laws and customs

Ecuador is an overwhelmingly Catholic country with just a small minority following alternative forms of Christianity. Some indigenous Ecuadoreans have adapted their Catholicism to incorporate traditional beliefs. Dressing modestly and behaving with courtesy and respect, especially inside Quito's historic churches, is advised at all times. Losing your temper in public is regarded as very bad form.

Ecuador	
Location	2°00′ S, 77°30′ W
Capital	Quito
Population	14,573,101
Land area in km²	283,560
Coastline in km	2,237

Arriving at Darwin's Arch

Language

Spanish is the universal language although some indigenous ones are still used in remote areas. English is only spoken in upmarket hotels, restaurants and tour agencies. Taxi drivers speak just enough English to understand where you are going. Some basic Spanish is on page 273, just a few words will work wonders.

Safety

Most Ecuadoreans are very friendly and helpful but, as in any large city, care should be taken in Quito and common sense should prevail. Avoid walking in dark areas at night, don't display expensive cameras or flashy jewellery and take only what cash you need. The Old City is virtually dead at night and best avoided, especially around the bus terminal, but stepping out in the New City is generally OK. Guayaquil, on the other hand, has a reputation for petty crime and is subject to frequent civil disturbances.

Health

If you are going to get sick it's only likely to be a bit of altitude sickness in Quito. The city is 2,800 metres up and the air is thin. It's usual to feel a little more tired than you would normally and perhaps a bit breathless. Quito doesn't seem to have any vehicle emission laws, which exacerbates things a little. Some people also report stomach upsets and sinus problems. And take care when eating in seafood restaurants; try to get a recommendation. Down at sea level, in the Galápagos, mosquitoes can be a problem at dusk and, depending on the time of year you visit, the sun can be very strong (remember you're sitting on the Equator). There is no malaria in or around Quito or in the Galápagos but there is said to be some risk in Guayaquil and the Pacific Lowlands.

Costs

As a liveaboard is the best option for diving the Galápagos this may seem like a costly trip. There is also a hefty US$100 per person National Park tax, which is collected at the airport on arrival. That aside, there is little extra to pay for except the odd souvenir or drinks. If you want to spend a few days on land, there are plenty of hotels and restaurants at all budget levels. Mainland Ecuador is particularly good value. There are masses of hotels at all levels, though standards are variable. Hotels rated 5 star can be more like a 3 star back home, while a 3 star may actually be perfectly adequate. Eating out in Quito is a pleasure. There are trendy fusion restaurants where a fabulous two-course meal with a bottle of wine costs just US$15 a head. If that's too much, snack bars are cheap and ubiquitous. There is a 10% service charge on bills but adding a bit extra is usual. Add a little for cab drivers and a dollar for porters. Dive boat crews will expect a tip, see page 12.

Fact file

International flights	Virgin or British Airways to Miami, American or Continental to Quito
Departure Tax	US$25
Entry	EU, US and Commonwealth – valid passport required for stays of up to 90 days
Internal flights	AeroGal or TAME for the Galápagos
Ground Transport	Countrywide bus and train routes
Money	The US dollar is the official currency
Language	Spanish
Electricity	110/220v, plug type A (see page 16)
Time zone	GMT -5
Religion	Catholic
Phone	Country code +593; IDD code 00; Police in Quito 911. Police elsewhere 101.

New versions on old themes: King angelfish, Mexican hogfish, giant hawkfish

Tourist Information → Government websites can be found at vivecuador.com and ecuadortouristboard.com; the Galápagos National Park site is at galapagospark.org.

Dive brief

Diving

More than almost any other destination, planning a trip to the Galápagos requires a high level of understanding of local diving conditions. This is not diving for the faint-hearted: the water can be icy, it's rarely dead calm and currents and surges are an every-dive occurrence. Plus there are substantial seasonal differences from summer to winter and hugely varying sea current patterns. Then add in the fact that each island has its own microclimate.

Of course, the attraction is the likelihood of seeing large pelagics and there certainly are plenty. The marine life is big with a capital B. You can swim with a hundred hammerheads or do your safety stop surrounded by 20 silky sharks. If that's your thing you won't leave disappointed. The best time for the biggest animals is the winter as they are attracted by cool water. Whalesharks start to appear at the end of May, when the water temperature drops down to around 15°C. As the water warms up again, rising to 28°C, the chance of seeing mantas improves. But no matter what time of year you come, thermoclines are a serious issue. One minute you can be in water that's 25°C then, within seconds, it will drop to 14°C. No joke! This also plays havoc with visibility so it's hard to predict when the best time to visit would be.

Generally speaking, though, the most favourable periods are those around the change of seasons; ie, April-June and November-December. December to May are warmest and the weather could be regarded as sub-tropical to tropical in the north. June to December is cold and sees some unusual anomalies such as huge banks of mist around Roca Rodonda.

Snorkelling

Although there are shallow bays around some of the islands, liveaboard dive trips head out to better dive sites around submerged pinnacles where the surge is rough. If you only want to snorkel, book onto a naturalist trip instead.

Marine Life

Hammerheads are seen on almost every dive. Galápagos, whitetip and silky sharks are common companions. Turtles, eagle rays and marble rays are everywhere as, of course, are curious and playful sea lions. Other large animals tend to be seasonal. There are small creatures as well - morays, seahorses and even nudibranchs - which may seem familiar but these have regional differences. It really is worth looking down for some of the dive, not just out into the blue. There is, however, very little in the way of coral so the reefs are not classically pretty like somewhere in the tropics.

Diver safety

It should be noted once again that this is not easy diving. At certain times, entries can be in huge swells and getting back on the RIB then onto your boat is no fun. Currents can be so strong you have to grab hold of the nearest rock with two hands (bring gloves!) and washing machine conditions occur regularly. Most dives are within normal depth limits but some are very deep and neither decompression nor solo diving is allowed. Only do what you know you are capable of and obey your computer. All this might seem a little over the top, especially when the sun is shining and the sky is blue, but this is not a place to underestimate the power of nature.

Pufferfish nestled on a wall

Galápagos animal encounters

Central zone	sea lions and turtles
Northern zone	eagle rays
Western zone	hammerheads

Darwin said: "It is not the strongest of the species that survive, nor the most intelligent, but the one most responsive to change". That hits the nail right on the head for the Galápagos. This is a place where you can't even hope to accurately predict what conditions you will find or animals you will see. We thought we were going to see mantas and whalesharks but got hammerheads and whales; we were told it was the warm season and we got ice-cold thermoclines. Everyone on our boat said the same thing... expectations were not always met, but often exceeded. Go with an open mind, adapt to the conditions and you will enjoy it.

Making the big decision

The Galápagos islands are on almost every diver's hit-list but before rushing out to book, consider a couple of things: are you experienced – and adaptable – enough to cope with rough and unpredictable surface water conditions and equally unusual ones below? Are you picking the right boat? Changes in local policies have left very few liveaboards with valid dive permits. Those currently running are very professional and 100% diver focussed so you will want some time on land to see the animals. Although this is an extraordinary experience, it is not an easy one, so plan carefully to get the most out of your time.

An encounter with a diver for a playful sea lion

Dive data

Seasons	Roughly, December to May – warm
	June to November – cold
Visibility	10-40 metres
Temperatures	Air 30-34°C; water 13-28°C
Wet suit	5 mm full body suit summer minimum
	7 mm semi-dry winter minimum
Training	On land
Nitrox	Can be pre-booked
Deco chambers	Puerto Ayora; there are no airlift facilities

Bottom time

The Galápagos	Created some 5 million years ago by a series of volcanic eruptions, the Galápagos sit 1000km west of South America straddling the equator. Still one of the world's most active volcanic regions, the Galápagos are also at the crossroads of seven major ocean currents. Most influential are the Equatorial (Cromwell) current which sweeps in cold water from due west, the warmer Panama current from the northeast and the cold Peru (Humboldt) from the south. Each brings in its own particular species, resulting in a rare mix of tropical, subtropical and temperate sea animals.
Central zone ▸▸ p260	Calmer, warmer and prettier, this area is protected from the harshest currents and conditions by Isabella, the largest island.
Northern zone ▸▸ p262	Rock-your-dive-boots off with countless eagle rays and hammerheads at two isolated outposts, the Wolf and Darwin Islands.
Western zone ▸▸ p264	Open to the Pacific and influenced by all the equatorial currents; an area of wildly varying conditions and diverse marine life.

Diversity   reef area 7,665 km²

HARD CORALS	
	517
FISH SPECIES	
	474
ENDEMIC FISH SPECIES	
	32
FISH SPECIES UNDER THREAT	
	9
PROTECTED REEFS/MARINE PARKS	
	15

All diversity figures are approximate

Galápagos Dive brief

Central zone

Most divers fly to San Cristóbal on the eastern side of the archipelago as this is the departure point for all main cruises and liveaboards. From the airport to the small port is just a five minute drive and it's here that you get your first taste of Galápagos wildlife. The dock is surrounded by tiny boats and masses of sea lions sitting on every available surface.

Thirty minutes flight away is the Galápagos' second entry point, Puerto Ayora on Santa Cruz. This rather pretty little port town is also the economic hub of the islands. If you are going on a liveaboard this will probably be your last stop. It also makes a great base for those who prefer to day dive or would like a few days on land. There are several good dive centres that have small, fast boats to take you to local reefs.

Either way, both islands sit in the centre of the Galápagos which is the best place to start diving, allowing you to acclimatise to local conditions. The waters here are some of the easiest, a little shallower and a little warmer than elsewhere plus dive sites tend to be in protected coastal bays. The best aspect of this region though is that, post diving, you can take trips ashore to see the landscape and wildlife as the islands have "pedestrian access".

S1 **Gordon Rocks**	
Depth	19 m
Visibility	good
Currents	medium to strong
Dive Type	liveaboard

Not far from Santa Cruz island, two large rocks about 100 metres apart protrude above the water, indicating the remains of an ancient volcano. The sunken caldera is marked by half-moon-shaped rocky masses on each side, the top is open to currents and the bottom has three large pinnacles dividing the space. A central pinnacle is thought to be the point of eruption. You can dive right around the site, inside and out, but beware - the dive is also known as 'La Lavadora' (the washing machine) as currents can be fearsome. Large schools of eagle rays fly past, along with a green turtle or two. If you head out through one of the channels the strong currents attract large schools of king angelfish and, on the outside edge, several hammerheads. The outer walls are absolutely sheer and full of bubble-shaped holes – erosion, evidently – and each is inhabited by a pencil urchin or fish while gangs of young sea lions race up and down the walls playing with each other. These walls are also good locations for spotting bright red Barnaclebill blennies and giant hawkfish.

Razor surgeonfish by the hundreds; the tiny, indigenous Galápagos penguin

◲2 Cousins Rock

⏱ Depth	19 m
◑ Visibility	good
≋ Currents	medium to strong
⏏ Dive Type	liveaboard

North of Bartolomé, this exposed rock is home to passing birds and sea lions. These slide down the walls to meet divers then swim away over a series of terraces which are smothered in black corals displaying tones of gold. Longnose hawkfish and the giant Galápagos seahorse can be spotted amongst the corals along with the unusual blue-eyed damsel. Sandy bottomed ledges house impressive starfish and gangs of whitetip sharks. Descending to the base of the wall, a tongue of land pokes out into the current where several types of ray are surfing along with a very large school of pelican barracuda. Meanwhile, the sea lions are still darting around divers as they chase schools of tiny snapper, their favourite food.

◲3 Bartolomé

⏱ Depth	19 m
◑ Visibility	good
≋ Currents	medium to strong
⏏ Dive Type	liveaboard

No, it's not a dive, it's a snorkel, but worth it – even for hardened tank-suckers – as it is one of the few colonies of Galápagos penguins. Sadly, their numbers are in decline. At just about a foot tall, they zip past underwater at the speed of light. You are more likely to see them sunning on the rocks, where they stand proudly over inferior snorkellers, although quite a way apart from each other as they have a strong sense of personal space. Other marine life includes massive starfish, blennies and small schools of butterflyfish. Snorkellers slip into the water beside a pointed rocky pinnacle that soars into the sky and neatly divides the island.

The Barnaclebill blenny

Northern zone

There's very little point in going all the way to the Galápagos and not seeing the two northernmost islands – Wolf and Darwin. They are regarded as the ultimate in diving in this archipelago as well as being the most isolated islands. Only reached by liveaboard boats, Wolf is an overnight sail north of the central islands, with Darwin another four hours or so on.

These sheer-sided, rocky landmasses are home to birds such as red-footed boobies and frigates, but little else. You cannot make landfall on the islands nor, for that matter, can the other animals. Even the sea lions struggle to find resting spots.

Because both islands are a long way north and protected by others to the south, the Humboldt current has a lesser effect here and the water is just a little warmer. But even when the surface temperature is 28°C, the thermoclines at depth can still be icy. Despite this there is one big attraction – hammerhead sharks. No matter what time of year you come, these two outposts are famous for attracting enormous schools of them. At certain times of year there are whalesharks too but most divers come here to immerse themselves amongst these strange, prehistoric-looking creatures.

⊠4	The Arch, Darwin	
⏱	**Depth**	35 m
◑	**Visibility**	poor to fair
≋	**Currents**	ripping
◓	**Dive Type**	liveaboard

One of the archipelago's most impressive landmarks is Darwin's Arch. The eroded remains of a forgotten eruption mark an oval-shaped reef that drops away to great depths. A gradual slope is covered in huge boulders and currents sweep up from who knows where to hit the rocky reef broad side and then veer off in all directions. No matter where you enter the water, you seem to catch both surge and current so it's a case of dragging yourself down over the boulders – admiring some morays and lobsters as you go – then making your way to the sandy channel. Moving forward you slowly become aware of the silent wave of hammerheads above. Some are curious and move in closer, while others watch from a distance. Visibility over the channel is not always all that good as the currents lift the sand but your reward for peering into the blue may be a bottlenose dolphin – a frequent visitor – and, it is said, whalesharks in the winter months.

⊠5	The Caves, Wolf	
⏱	**Depth**	28 m
◑	**Visibility**	poor to good
≋	**Currents**	slight to ripping
◓	**Dive Type**	liveaboard

Sitting at the base of Wolf's sheer cliffs and beside a protruding pinnacle, you look at the water and know that the currents are absolutely fearsome. The clue is in the rapidly swirling surface movement. The site, however, is marvellous: a wall of very large boulders interspersed with several caves. You drift quickly along to the first which has a swim through, although it is better described as a suck through. The second is protected by some big boulders at the front which create a break. Butterflies, snappers and divers take advantage of the calmer water and hover behind the boulders while a few whitetip sharks rest inside. Back out on the wall, there are a lot of morays while several Galápagos sharks pass by in the blue. Some are over two metres long and swim along with a few hammerheads while marble rays flit along the sea bed. Near the end of the wall you can divert to a nearby underwater pinnacle but at this point you are likely to encounter some fierce washing machine currents so it may be safer to ascend.

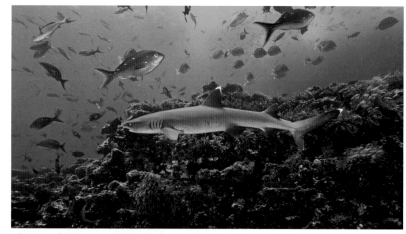

Whitetip reef shark surrounded by Pacific creolefish at the Caves on Wolf

Rockslide, Wolf Island

Depth	35 m	
Visibility	fair to good	
Currents	slight to ripping	
Dive Type	liveaboard	

Sometimes known as Landslide, this site is on the eastern side of Wolf Island. Way back when, violent geological activity resulted in a rockslide that in turn created a gently falling slope. Starting just beneath the surface at the base of Wolf's steep walls, there are masses of enormous boulders that have been shaped and smoothed by centuries of surge. Traversing these often requires a crab walk, hand-over-hand, to take you down to the open channel.

This is a dive where currents are all important, not only for safety reasons but also because no current means no animals. However, when the currents are running the pelagic life is incredible.

Stopping at 20 metres, you can watch the schooling hammerheads come in. There are at least thirty in the blue, often very many more. It's worth descending a little further to watch them hover above your head but be aware that the deeper water can be like ice. Glancing back up the slope, the resident school of eagle rays pass by. They pause and take a look at the divers, dropping a little to let the exhaust bubbles caress their tummies. Behind, and

up in the shallows, Galápagos sharks cruise by and enormous green turtles hide in the crevices. The ascent to the surface takes you through a school of pompano so huge they block out the sun rays. As you glance back down during your safety stop, you realise there are a lot of silky sharks approaching. These beautiful creatures disperse the pompano but hang around to admire your fins as long as you stay to gas off.

❝ ❞ I was a little scared sometimes. We would be going up and down in the surge so often. I am not experienced enough to feel completely secure. But I never thought I would see the hammerheads so close. It was amazing. *Inés Yturbe, Mexico City*

Western zone

Isabela is the largest island in the group and creates a barrier between the open Pacific Ocean and the remainder of the Galápagos archipelago. She is shaped a bit like a seahorse – which is appropriate as the islands have their own indigenous version – and most diving takes place around the seahorse's head.

Isabela's other claim to fame is that her position divides current patterns in such a way that diving in her waters can be like stepping into a tub of ice water. The cold Cromwell current sweeps in from the west, hits Isabela and Fernandina and then is directed north to Cape Marshall and on to Roca Rodonda. This, along with the fact that the region's volcanoes are highly active, creates yet another mini-ecosystem.

↘7 Roca Rodonda	
Depth	35 m
Visibility	poor to fair
Currents	slight to strong
Dive Type	liveaboard

Heading south from Wolf, the first real land mass you come across is the isolated Roca Rodonda, the tip of a still active volcano. Descending over a landscape of barnacle covered boulders, you notice gangs of small fish hunkering down in the cracks and crevices. Actually, they're basking in water which has been warmed by streams of hot volcanic gases fizzing up through the sea bed. You would think they were bubbles in a glass of champagne except for the hint of sulphur. Cold water thermoclines here are extremely uncomfortable, probably due to the contrast with the naturally warmed water. There are also some serious down currents on this site so dives can be called off or aborted, which is a shame as the life is impressive and includes hammerheads, king angels and schooling surgeonfish.

↘8 **Punta Vicente Roca**	
Depth	35 m
Visibility	fair to good
Currents	medium to strong
Dive Type	liveaboard

Just west of the seahorse's nose, this dive lies beneath a pretty cove which is itself beneath the eroded remains of a volcanic cone. The geography of the dive mirrors the landscape above with hills and gullies, walls and lots of tumbled boulders. There is a lot of coral, the mola-mola, or oceanic sunfish, is seen occasionally and green turtles are common. An unusual fish is the harlequin wrasse which is consistently inconsistent in appearance and comes in various shades of orange, white or black. It's a colourful dive but the water can be breathtakingly cold so it's a relief to ascend into warmer shallows where there are schools of native salema, a small member of the grunt family and the favourite diet of fur seals and sea lions.

Coral clad walls at Cape Marshall

Galápagos Dive log Western zone

⑨9	Cape Marshall	
⬥	**Depth**	35 m
◉	**Visibility**	poor to fair
⬨	**Currents**	ripping
⬭	**Dive Type**	liveaboard

This long sharp wall sits almost exactly on the Equator. It's covered in tiny yellow gorgonian corals, which are rarely more than about 20-25 centimetres long, their growth stunted by the surge and currents. The effect is very pretty though, looking like heather on the rocks. As you enter the water you see quite a lot of life out in the blue – a small school of hammerheads, maybe a couple of turtles and even golden cow rays. There are some unusual puffers like the yellow spotted burrfish and guinea fowl puffer. Thermoclines can lower the temperature down to 15°C and the visibility drops as you pass through them. If you make it around the point and into the nearby bay, there is a bit more protection for the animals and some interesting smaller fish are seen, especially at night.

Pacific spotted scorpionfish

🌐 Nothing but animals...

The first time I saw the Galápagos Islands was way back in 1969. My friend and I had heard about a navy ship going down there to do some research and that they were willing to take a few passengers. So we signed up. The trip across was awful, terrible weather and very rough, so we spent most of the crossing outside staring at the horizon. We finally arrived and, of course, back then, there was nothing there except the animals. Tourism visits had not yet been organized, so we had no guides nor anybody to look after us. The crew would drop us off on an island during the day with some water and mandarins. We were free to spend the day just wandering around, getting as close to the wildlife as we wanted. At dusk the ship would come back and collect us. We had no idea what they were doing all day but it was quite an experience for us. I never forgot it and when my husband and I decided to start a business together, it seemed the obvious thing to do, to work with these unique islands.

Dolores Diez, vice president, Quasar Nautica Expeditions.

The Galápagos giant tortoise and a marine iguana

Drying out

The Galápagos

Dive centres

Nauti Diving, Av Charles Darwin, Puerto Ayora, Santa Cruz, T+593 (0)525 27004, nautidiving.com. 4 day packs from US$599.

Scuba Iguana, Av Charles Darwin, Puerto Ayora, Santa Cruz, T+593 (0)525 26497, scubaiguana.com. Day trips from US$110.

Liveaboards

Liveaboard diving permits are restricted and constantly under review (see Undercurrents, right) but the following boats had them at the time of publication:

M/S Alta, quasarex.com
Deep Blue, deepbluegalapagosdiving.com
Estrella del Mar, explorerventures.com
Sky Dancer, peterhughes.com

Sleeping

$$$ Finch Bay Eco-hotel, T+593 (0)525 26297, finchbayhotel.com. They also have an on-site dive centre.

$$ Silberstein, T+593 (0)525 26277, hotelsilberstein.com. A short walk from the Darwin Research station and with an on-site dive centre.

Eating

$$$ Angermeyer Point, T+593 (0)525 26452. Across the bay from Puerto Ayora, this is the former home of Galápagos pioneer and artist Carl Angermeyer. Gorgeous setting and excellent, innovative and varied menu.

Quito

Sleeping

These hotels are located in the New City where facilities and access are better, especially in the evening.

$$ Grand Hotel Mercure Alameda, T+593 (0)225 62345, accorhotels.com. Decent rooms with international standards and free internet access in the lobby.

$ La Cartuja, T+593 (0)225 23577, hotelacartuja.com. In the former British Embassy, spacious comfortable rooms set around a lovely garden.

Eating

$$$ Café de la Roca, T+593 (0)225 65659. Open Mon-Fri only. Stylish, small restaurant serving modern Ecuadorean food and with great staff.

$$$ La Sala, T+593 (0)225 46086. A few minutes' walk from the main hotels, a superb, eclectic mix of Ecuadorean and international food.

$$$ Tianguez, T+593 (0)229 54326, sinchisacha.org. Local specialities and a great location right on Plaza de San Francisco for people watching.

Touring

Quasar Expeditions, T+593 (0)224 46996, quasarex.com. One of the biggest tour organizers in Ecuador and responsible for several specialist boats with either diving or naturalist cruises in the Galápagos. Also land tours throughout Ecuador.

Safari Tours, T+593 (0)225 52505, safari.com.ec. Great source of diverse travel information, day trips and activity tours – mountain climbing, cycling, rafting, trekking and jungle trips.

Otavalo market and handicrafts; Galápagos hawk

Undercurrents

Politics and diving shouldn't be mixed but too often they are. A political stance may change the way dive, cruise and fishing operations work in national parks or World Heritage sites. In some countries fishermen are encouraged to swap their permits for dive ones. The concept is to help protect an already fragile ecosystem as well as depleted fishing stocks by re-employing them in the tourist industry.

In the Galápagos recently, this strategy seems to have happened in reverse and many dive boats lost their permits, ostensibly to fishermen. This is a very confused situation that originally developed out of concerns over the growth in tourism and a desire to ensure that operators were kept in check. Many were applying for one permit then doing something completely different. From a diving point of view, it still doesn't quite make sense: the situation seems to be in a permanent state of flux and no doubt will change again. Before booking any liveaboard dive cruise check that the operator has the correct permits.

	Sleeping	$$$ US$150+ double room per night	$$ US$75-150	$ under US$75
	Eating	$$$ US$40+ 2-course meal, excluding drinks	$$ US$20-40	$ under US$20

The Galápagos

All cruise boats, whether nature or dive orientated, will ensure that you see a good variety of wildlife on the islands.

Isla Lobos A short sail from San Cristóbal, this island makes a fantastic late afternoon stroll. Walk across the sandy beach within inches of blue-footed boobies, get an evil look from a marine iguana who is definitely not moving from your path and admire a herd of sea lions snoozing under a tree. You will be advised to be quiet and not disturb the mums with new pups but it would be hard to compete with the noise of those babes suckling.

Puerto Egas on Santiago is a well trodden nature trail but perhaps the highlight of any trip. The large natural bay requires a wet landing (jumping into the surf from your tender) but after that the walk around the coast is easy. Fur seals and sea lions live in rocky, lava-ringed pools and are curious enough about their human visitors to approach them. Marine iguanas bring their body temperatures back up to normal after a hard day's fishing by wiggling into sun-warmed crevices and, if you are lucky, you might spot the endemic Galápagos Hawk guarding a kill. Bright red Sally Lightfoot crabs skitter about in the rock pools and indigenous mockingbirds peck at berries on scrappy Palo Santo trees. Herons stalk the rocks beside the tourists while lava lizards run away at the slightest footfall.

Puerto Ayora, capital of Santa Cruz, is a lively town with a cosmopolitan feel. There are lots of hotels with restaurants on site,

restaurants with dive centres attached and a healthy selection of cafés, bars and dive facilities. And of course, this is the location of the Charles Darwin Research Station, a facility with educational exhibits in a zoo-like setting. Here you can see several age-old Galápagos tortoises.

Ecuador

While the Galápagos is all about nature, mainland Ecuador has amazing culture and history. It's well worth extending your trip to spend some time there.

Quito, the capital, was declared a World Heritage site in 1978 and is worthy of the title. Much of the colonial Old City dates from the early 1500s although there were settlements here long before. Sadly, the colonists wiped all traces of the Inca past.

Take a taxi to the Plaza Grande – also known as the Plaza de la Independencia – in the Old City. Admire the four sides of the square. On each a building represents varying governing bodies: the Cathedral on the west was consecrated in 1572, the Archbishop's Palace is opposite, the 18th century Government Palace is north and the modern Municipal Palace is on the south side. Get a walking tour map (from the Cathedral) and head down the Street of the Seven Crosses, where every other building is something of interest: churches, galleries and museums – even one that explains the history of currency in the region, from Inca times to the present.

Next, divert to the Plaza San Francisco, a few minutes away. This colourful square was built over an indigenous trading market. The restaurant, Tianguez, right on the square is a perfect spot for people

watching. While away a couple of hours with an icy beer and some lunch. Once refreshed you can view the overwhelming interior of the Franciscan church, convent and museum and then continue exploring more of the Old City's cobbled streets. Many attractions are free while a few want just a dollar or two. At the end of the day stop by the Artisans' Market, at Jorge Washington and Juan Leon Mera, in the New City, to choose from a good range of local crafts at reasonable prices.

Otavalo If you are in Quito on a Saturday, book a day trip to see the Otavalo markets. This town is a haven for all sorts of artisans, plus a day tour will also give you a taste of the Ecuadorean countryside. Tours depart the city to the north then drive through the Andes past several points of natural beauty. Stops are made at the San Pablo lake and Imbabura volcano, and in the valley of Guallabamba where the major industry is flower-growing. Stops are also made at several local cottage industries that are hidden away in small towns you wouldn't know existed. There is no pressure to purchase anything, this is just about displaying local talent and traditions.

Otavalo itself is both a shopaholic's and photographer's dream. Indigenous handicrafts jostle for space with fresh fruit, vegetables and local spices. The local artists and crafts people sell their work at very reasonable prices. It is all amazingly colourful and lively. The return route to Quito goes via the nature reserve at Cotacachi-Cayapas, which surrounds a sunken caldera and is backed by the volcano itself – though it's often hidden in the cloud layer.

Plaza Grande in Quito; local handicrafts, Plaza San Francisco in Quito

Mexico

Hello, my precious: getting up close and personal with an adult whitetip reef shark, *Triaenodon obesus*. *Roca Partida, Islas Revillagigedo*

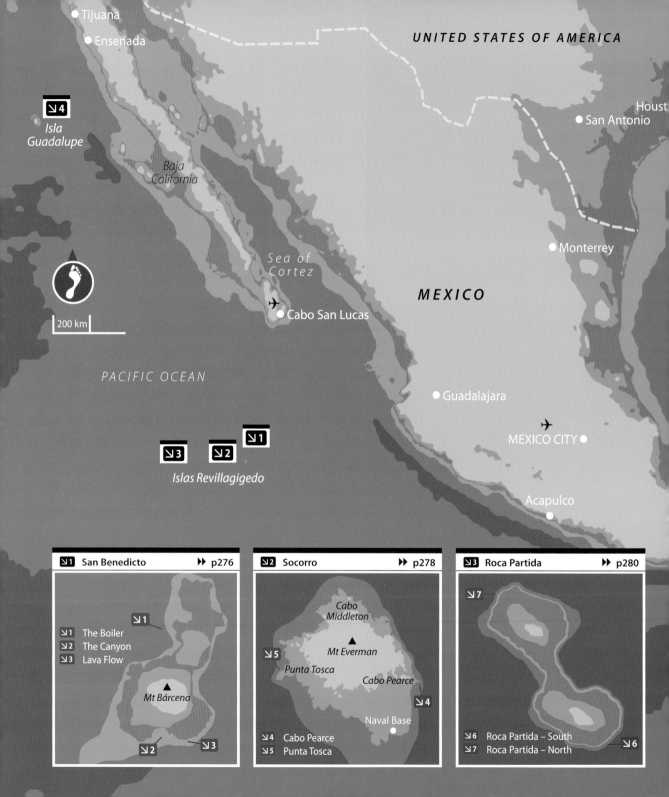

Tijuana

Ensenada

UNITED STATES OF AMERICA

Houst

San Antonio

⬂4

Isla
Guadalupe

Baja
California

Sea of
Cortez

MEXICO

Monterrey

Cabo San Lucas

PACIFIC OCEAN

200 km

⬂3 ⬂2 ⬂1

Islas Revillagigedo

Guadalajara

MEXICO CITY

Acapulco

⬂1 San Benedicto ▶▶ p276

⬂1
⬂1 The Boiler
⬂2 The Canyon
⬂3 Lava Flow

▲
Mt Bárcena

⬂2 ⬂3

⬂2 Socorro ▶▶ p278

Cabo
Middleton

⬂5
▲
Mt Everman

Punta Tosca

Cabo Pearce

⬂4

Naval Base

⬂4 Cabo Pearce
⬂5 Punta Tosca

⬂3 Roca Partida ▶▶ p280

⬂7

⬂6 Roca Partida – South
⬂7 Roca Partida – North

⬂6

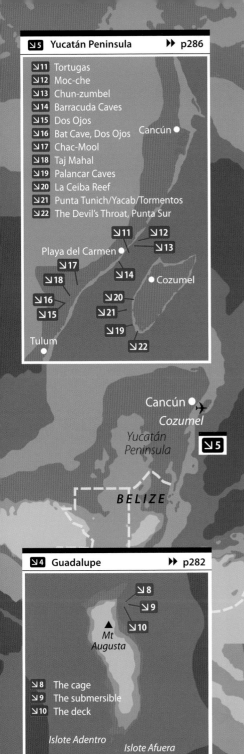

Introduction

Mexico

Mexico is a land of contradictions: it is both a burgeoning commercial nation rife with busy industrial cities and a natural paradise where crisp white-sand beaches act as a foil to cartoon-like landscapes of cactus bushes bursting from scrubby soil.

The country's rich, ancient and colonial past is often completely neglected in the rush to compete with (or serve) her mighty neighbour. Yet the inhabitants of this vast land were once a superpower in their own right. Back then, it was a world where people were sacrificed in gruesome rituals or left to drown in deep water cenotes with no hope of escape. These sinkholes are now modern-day dive sites, a unique and captivating underwater experience.

However, because Mexico has two oceanic borders, the cenotes must compete with an impressive array and variety of diving styles. The Yucatán's coastal waters edge the Caribbean Sea and reveal both unexpected marine life and curious underwater geography. There are gentle reefs but also some of the fastest drift dives you will ever participate in.

Meanwhile across in the Pacific, the deeper waters of the Ring of Fire teem with large animals. Most divers only dream about an encounter with pelagics like those that are seen here on a regular basis.

Mexico rating

Diving
★★★★

Dive facilities
★★★★

Accommodation
★★★★

Down time
★★★★

Value for money
★★★★

Essentials

Getting there and around

Flying to Mexico is all about options – and there are plenty. Wherever you commence your trip, getting to this vast nation is easy enough although you probably will end up transiting through the US. Check out a reputable flight website like Expedia or Travelocity for ideas as almost any airline you can think of will get you there. Base your flight plan on whichever route is the shortest, or whether you fancy a stopover in the hub city you transit through. Choose your destination first though as the two main dive regions – on the Caribbean and Pacific coasts – are a long way apart.

There are two major airports on the Caribbean Yucatán Peninsula: Cancún and Cozumel. These are close together and either one will give access to the various dive areas nearby. Both get charter flights from some countries if you are willing to give up the comfort of a scheduled carrier.

Dive trips on the Pacific side are not in such close proximity to each other. The most popular are to the islands loosely termed as Socorro, but more properly known as Islas Revillagigedo. Liveaboards

leave from Cabo San Lucas on the very southern tip of the Baja Peninsula; the airport is at San José del Cabo. Guadalupe trips, however, are accessed from Ensenda in the north so operators usually collect guests from San Diego and take them over the border by bus. It's just a couple of hours drive away.

You could also travel via neighbouring Belize or Honduras if you want to dive a second country or do some sightseeing. TACA (taca.com) flies between all Central American countries but its routes often require an extra transit point.

Once you have arrived, transfers and transport options are as numerous as flights. However, not all hotels and dive operators will collect you, but may help arrange for someone to do so. Or go to an online service to prearrange a taxi. Touring is also relatively straightforward. Car hire is cheap (from US$30 per day) and very popular in Baja, buses go everywhere, ferries link the Yucatán's offshore islands and there are masses of organized tours.

Language

Although there are regional indigenous languages in Mexico like Mayan and Nahuatl, you are unlikely to encounter them. In busy Cancún, Cozumel and Cabo almost everyone will speak English. In smaller resorts you might meet someone who prefers to use Spanish but it's unlikely in the tourist industry. It's always worth trying a few words:

hello	hola
goodbye	adiós
yes	sí
no	no
I don't know	no se
okay	vale (like ballet)
please	por favor
thank you	gracias
I'm sorry	lo siento
good	bueno
how much is... ?	¿cuánto es... ?
a beer/water	una cerveza/agua mineral
great dive	una buceada fantastica

Giant Pacific manta at San Benedicto

Mexico

Location	23°00'N, 102°00'W°
Capital	Mexico City
Population	109,955,400
Land area in km²	1,923,040
Coastline in km	9,330

Local laws and customs

Mexico is a land full of rich history and vibrant customs. Her influences range from ancient Toltec, Aztec and Maya through Spanish colonialization and Catholicism right up to the present day trade agreement with the US. The coastal regions have become incredibly Americanized in recent years so it's unlikely that you will upset anyone providing you apply the usual rules of courtesy and politeness.

Safety

The Yucatán is a fairly safe place to be, whether you are in raucous Cancún, casual Playa del Carmen or over on busy Cozumel. The pace is similar in Baja: Cabo San Lucas is lively and San José del Cabo more laid back, but like anywhere, walking about at night showing off your expensive jewellery or with a wallet in your back pocket is an invitation for trouble. One of the more reassuring aspects of travelling here is that the police presence is strong with special Tourist Police booths dotted about many resorts. They are manned by a multilingual force and will help with maps, directions and advice. Go to them if you have a problem.

Health

Healthcare facilities in the Yucatán are best described as being in a state of flux. As the area has expanded, medical facilities have struggled to keep up. The best are said to be on Cozumel while in Cancún they are regarded as questionable. Playa del Carmen sits somewhere in the middle. If there was a medical emergency, Mérida, the capital of Quintana Roo state, has superlative medical services. Across in Baja though, it's all very Americanised – this state is a geographic extension of California and sometimes you will think you are still there as the lifestyles and facilities seem so similar. Providing you have all the right inoculations and stay hydrated chances are that little will go wrong beyond a case of Montezuma's Revenge.

What is more interesting though is that you can buy almost any prescription drug your heart desires... even the infamous little blue pill. Frequent travellers may find malaria tablets or antibiotic ear-drops are cheaper here than at home but be sensible and only buy what you know your doctor has prescribed in the past.

Costs

Mexico is not the cheap destination it once was. As the economy becomes more and more closely aligned with the US, so prices rise. The Yucatán was once principally rural until Cancún was built as a tourist city. Development has spread right along the coast with many large resort complexes. In Playa del Carmen and on Cozumel, it is possible to stay in a B&B or mid-range hotel but

Fact file

International flights	Mexicana, Continental, BA, Virgin, TACA
Departure tax	Included in your ticket, or US$46
Entry	Visas not required for most nationals for stays of up to 180 days
Internal flights	Aeromexico and subsidiaries
Ground transport	Countrywide buses, ferries, taxis, car hire
Money	US$1 = 14 Mexican pesos (MXN)
Language	Spanish but English is common
Electricity	110v, plug type A (see page 16)
Time zone	GMT -5
Religion	Catholic
Phone	Country code +52; IDD code 00; Police 066

four star hotels are more common. The Baja region is similar. The once charming harbourside village at Cabo San Lucas is now brimming with top class resorts and timeshare complexes. Head north back towards the airport and the coastline is being steadily developed, but smaller San José del Cabo still has several lovely hotels sited at its historic heart. Across the country, you can pay as much or as little as you want and deals are easy to come by.

This is also reflected in food and drink costs as you can go trendy or traditional. There is never any reason to pay full price for a beer (30-40 pesos) when you can almost always get two-for-one. The US dollar is interchangeable with pesos and often a restaurant will give you a better exchange rate than a bank. One thing to be aware of though is that you may find your budget takes a hammering in high season, when costs are often doubled.

There are also a lot of scams that involve being served with a dish or drinks you didn't order and then being charged extra. Always check your bill before paying. Another scam involves transport. For example, if you buy a return ferry ticket between Playa del Carmen and Cozumel, ensure it is a return and not just one way. That said, Mexico is a good value trip as long as you keep an eye on things.

A Spotted Cyphoma shell crawling on an Angular sea whip in Cozumel

Tourist information → Local government websites can be found at visitmexico.com, discoverbajacalifornia.com and mayayucatan.com.mx

Dive brief

Diving

With two different coastlines, one edging the Pacific, the other on the Caribbean Sea, Mexico has two very distinctive dive styles. The Caribbean grabs the most attention with its warm tropical waters and pretty coral reefs. Mexico's Yucatán Peninsula sits on the world's second largest barrier reef which runs 300 kilometres south through Belize then on to Honduras. Now referred to as the Mesoamerican Barrier Reef (to distinguish it from that other more famous barrier reef) this extensive marine system is regarded as unique due to its length and variety of habitats.

You would think that conditions would be fairly similar in this whole region and, while you might see similar things, this northern end of the reef has its own dive personality. It's all to do with currents. The Caribbean is a shallow basin into which water floods from the Atlantic Ocean. The Caribbean Current moves across the top of the South American continent, travels counter clockwise and northwest towards the Yucatán coast, where it becomes the Yucatán Current. The water then has little choice but to force its way through the comparatively narrow Yucatán Channel between Mexico and Cuba. From there it eddies around the Gulf of Mexico before heading off around Florida and up the US east coast. This is what gives the Yucatán its dive character. The currents created can

be fierce. It's rare to be able to stay still on a dive when the water regularly rips along at over two knots. It also means that the reef animals are only the ones capable of living in this environment. Some people may be disappointed by the lack of animal encounters. There are some pelagics and schooling fish but as there is a dearth of lush corals, smaller creatures are not so prolific. However, the underwater terrain is fabulous, with plenty to explore both at sea and inland in underground, freshwater caverns and rivers.

Across on the Pacific coast, the marine world is tailored by a very different, but equally dynamic, set of conditions. Sitting firmly along the Pacific Rim of Fire, this coastline and nearby offshore landmasses were formed by aeons of volcanic activity that continues to this day. Diving focuses on the offshore islands where, beneath the water, rugged geology and harsh landscapes reflect the desert terrain of Baja California. Current patterns play a strong part too, in much the same way as they do in the Galápagos. In fact these isolated islands look much the same and have such similar marine life they are often referred to as the mini-Galápagos. On dry land there is little flora and almost no human habitation yet the marine realm is a magnet for big animals: Isla Guadalupe is known for Great White sharks while the Revillagigedo Islands are best known for their giant manta populations. This is definitely big fish territory.

Marine life

On the Yucatán side, reefs are typically Caribbean with pastel toned corals and plenty of fish to admire. Small creatures like arrow crabs and shells are common but there are enough turtles and tarpon to keep everyone happy. Across in Pacific waters the balance alters. Bigger animals take first place. There are encounters with mantas and sharks while smaller animals recede into the background. They are there though if you take your time to look for them.

Mexico animal encounters

Caribbean coast turtles and crabs
Baja Coast dolphins, mantas and Great White sharks

Approaching the Yucatán coast

We have spent a lot of time in Mexico – the diving is consistent, and lots of fun. But what makes it really worth the trip are the differing dive styles, from face-to-face encounters with marine giants to wild drifts and the bizarre world of the cenotes. Mix it all up and you get something really special. The ultra-modern coastal resorts are absolutely no reflection of the country as a whole which is far more complex and varied.

Snorkelling

Cozumel's marine reputation was based on its shallow-water reserves, many of which are now family-orientated theme parks. The mainland coastline is more exposed and the surf stirs up the sand on the patchy reefs closer to shore. You can snorkel in the cenotes and at certain times of year you can also head up to Holbox to see migrating whalesharks. There are many motorized watersports in this region so get advice on safe areas. The Pacific areas are not really appropriate for snorkellers as they are subject to strong currents and surge.

Making the big decision

The Yucatán is more about what type of holiday you want rather than the type of diving. Its entire being is devoted to the pleasures of a sojourn in the sun with endless activities, theme parks and great nightlife as well as a dash of history. It is great for families – especially those with teenagers – though in high season, it may be all a bit too hyperactive. Underwater there's some unusual diving, the different styles adding a certain novelty to the experience. The Pacific, however, is a mostly dedicated divers destination. Once you head offshore there is nothing but sea and the promise of a pelagic encounter.

Redtail triggerfish with Clarion angels at San Benedicto Island

Dive data

Seasons	For Isla Guadalupe the season is restricted to August to October; for Islas Revillagigedo, November to May. In the Yucatán, the best visibility is from April to October
Visibility	10 metres inshore to 40 metres+ in open water, occasionally 60 m in Cozumel
Temperatures	Air 20-34°C; water 24-30°C
Wet suit	3 mm full suit; 5 mm+ for the cenotes & Pacific
Training	Available in the Yucatán and mainland Baja. Look for accredited training agencies
Nitrox	Available nearly everywhere, but quantities may be limited, pre-booking advised
Deco chambers	Cozumel, Playa del Carmen, Cabo San Lucas, La Paz

Bottom time

Baja California	**Sandwiched between the Sea of Cortez and the Pacific Ocean, Baja is a dry desert peninsula loaded with spectacular scenery that quickly fades into insignificance beside the indigo oceans that surround it.**
Islas Revillagigedo ›› p276	Travel nearly 400 kilometres south of Baja's most southerly point to find nothing but open ocean and masses of massive pelagic fish around Socorro and her sister islands.
Isla Guadalupe ›› p282	Lying off the shores of northwestern Baja is the world's most watched population of Great White Sharks.
Yucatán Peninsula	**Mexico's liveliest resort areas, with equally lively diving.**
Playa del Carmen ›› p286	Calmer conditions and gentler reefs wander along the Yucatán coast.
The Cenotes ›› p288	Eerie diving in ancient underground freshwater rivers and limestone caves.
Cozumel ›› p290	Clear water and lightning-speed drift dives over tortuous topography.

Diversity
reef area 1,780 km²

HARD CORALS	25
FISH SPECIES	1,848
ENDEMIC FISH SPECIES	222
FISH UNDER THREAT	119
PROTECTED REEFS/MARINE PARKS	9

All diversity figures are approximate

Islas Revillagigedo

Sail for 24 hours across 386 kilometres of open ocean southwest from Cabo San Lucas on Mexico's Baja Peninsula to reach the isolated Revillagigedo islands. Sitting firmly on the Pacific Ring of Fire, these are the location of a unique marine ecosystem.

This lonely archipelago consists of four specks of land: San Benedicto, Socorro, Roca Partida and Clarion islands. Each is the tip of an ancient volcano and it is regarded as one of nature's most unusual environments. The islands are often nicknamed the mini-Galápagos as the landscapes of these island groups are similar. Revillagigedo land animals are less distinctive than those of the Galápagos but there are many indigenous species including a dove, a mockingbird, a spider and a tree lizard. The islands attract masses of seabirds but sadly, you will see little of this as no one is allowed to land apart from the Mexican navy.

The marine life is closely aligned to that of the Galápagos with sharks and mantas, dolphins, whales and whalesharks but where this destination differs is that it is all about interaction. The mantas are so friendly they swoop in to see visiting divers. The dolphins come to play, the sharks approach the boat to see what is happening. Wishful thinking? Perhaps. Guaranteed? As much as it can be. No one really knows why, but this is one part of the ocean where the pelagics are always in residence.

Conditions on the islands can be challenging, but again as a comparison to the Galápagos, this diving is far easier and the water temperatures are warmer.

San Benedicto

Usually the first stop on any dive trip, sunrise over still active Bárcena volcano reveals a rugged landscape. The island was deeply scarred by the last eruption in 1952, which wiped out all flora and fauna. Beneath the surface, all this is evident in the scenery of strong rocky walls and volcanic boulders. Dive conditions are changeable: you can arrive to find calm waters and very little current but sometimes the wind will whip up the surface and the boat will retreat to a calmer bay where you can dive in peace.

⌖1 The Boiler

Depth	32 m
Visibility	good
Currents	moderate but variable
Dive type	liveaboard

The most anticipated dive is The Boiler as this is 'the' manta site. A short surface swim takes you to a circular pinnacle. The top sits at about six metres, with several other pinnacles to the sides. You fin past sheer walls made up of millions of thin layers, almost like stacks of paper, and get a first glimpse of the indigenous Clarion angel. Finespotted, green and zebra morays weave in and out of crevices. Around the bend, and up over a plateau, you come face-to-face with the giant Pacific manta. Hanging about, flapping to and fro, this graceful creature is more than interested in being interactive. As more divers arrive she works the group, sliding from one diver to the next, seeming to say hello to each in turn. It's hard to ascend (watch your air!) but a second dive here just gets better as two mantas arrive. Both are female with very distinct differences in their body patterns.

⌖2 The Canyon

Depth	26 m
Visibility	good
Currents	moderate but variable
Dive type	liveaboard

On the south of San Benedicto, this dive is meant to be the hammerhead site. It's also meant to have some strong currents – typically, it's current one dive and not the next. Sometimes even current one minute and not the next. Descending beneath the boat, you swim to the anchor chain then head east until you hit a barrier reef of tumbled rocks. It's a long way from pretty but there are lots of fish: Clarion angels, Redtail triggerfish in big groups, juvenile king angels, guinea fowl and porcupine puffers and the giant electric ray. There is a special spot where divers are told to wait for the hammerheads to appear, but as is the way, they were not there. And that's because they were sitting just over our shoulders watching us. Sadly, as soon as we turned we scared them off. On repeat dives they proved to be equally skittish, always there but never close.

⌖3 Lava Flow

Depth	32 m
Visibility	good
Currents	moderate but variable
Dive type	liveaboard

Weather conditions in this area dictate where and when you can dive. One site directly under the huge lava flow is well protected. The topography is naturally rockier, with swim-throughs in the shallows. As you drop in you meet a green turtle, but within milliseconds a manta appears. She is completely black, unlike the Boiler's chevron mantas (which have the arrow-shaped white collars across their wings) and look like sleek stealth bombers. More appear, smaller juveniles who are a little less curious and stay behind the adult. Redtail triggerfish arrive in clusters, there are spotted boxfish and some of the biggest scorpionfish ever seen: the stone scorpion is 18 inches long and quite flat. Clarion angels dance around the area's other indigenous fish, the Clarion damsel, then at the end of the dive a very friendly octopus moves across the rocks.

The Clarion angelfish (top) and Clarion damselfish (bottom) are indigenous to the islands; divemaster Buzz greeting a friend

An overnight sail takes you to Socorro, the largest island in the group. Again, arriving at dawn, you watch the sun rise over sloping Mt Evermann which last erupted in 1993. After checking in at the Naval station, the only community on these islands, it's off to Cabo Pearce on the eastern coast. The divemasters build this site up as having ripping currents yet the bay is often calm with just a little surface swell.

⊠4 **Cabo Pearce**	
🧭 **Depth**	34 m
◑ **Visibility**	good
🌊 **Currents**	moderate but variable
🌊 **Dive type**	liveaboard

Descending the line from the surface buoy, you reach the centre of a narrow tongue-shaped promontory which leads down to an area at its tip where sharks are often seen – but at times there will not be a single one. Instead, there are mantas, one female and one male who has the hugest remoras hitchhiking on his back. The rest of the dive is lost to admiring these majestic and very friendly beauties.

A second dive is spent exploring the rocky surfaces of the promontory, where there are lobster, slipper lobsters and an octopus. Unfortunately for the smaller critters, it's not long before the sunlight fades again, forcing you to look up. Yet another manta is hovering overhead and demanding all your attention even while you are being mobbed by massive schools of Clarion angels and creole fish.

By late afternoon, the currents have picked up and the final dive of the day is done beneath the sheer, vertical island wall. Towering overhead, the rock is carved with patterns more sculptural than any piece of modern art. Beneath the waterline lies a bed of huge, rounded boulders, all coated with a furry carpet of algae. Poking between them, you find octopus in the throes of a romantic moment. You soon find several others who are far more interested in reacting to the divers than each other.

The common octopus, *Octopus vulgaris*, is anything but vulgar

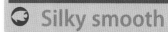

Silky smooth

An activity that will certainly not be to everyone's taste is the opportunity to go snorkelling with silky sharks. In the bay at Cabo Pearce, once the sun goes down, the lights from the boat attract flying fish to hunt across the surface of the water. Their arrival then attracts the silky sharks who hunt them but these sleek creatures soon get diverted to swim around and under the boat, curious to watch the activities on board.

On our trip, there were only three, but the crew say that sometimes there are as many as ten in attendance. After watching the sharks from deck for a short while, it's time to slip into the water – no splashing allowed – to see them at close range. Silky sharks grow to 3.3 metres and are renowned for their 'silky' smooth skin which is a light beige-grey on top and white on the tummy. It can be hard to see them as all your excited buddies get in the way and the torches attract quite a lot of planktonic matter.

A mother and baby dolphin came to join the party, then one of the divemasters noticed a tiny seahorse floating in front of his mask. What this poor creature was doing so far up the water column, no one knows, so he was gently scooped into a plastic bucket and taken away from all the activity for fear he would become a snack for the sharks. This was the first seahorse seen in Socorro by the crew.

⬛5 Punta Tosca

⏱	**Depth**	30 m
◑	**Visibility**	good
❋	**Currents**	moderate but variable
⬭	**Dive type**	liveaboard

Lying almost directly opposite Cabo Pearce but on the west coast of Socorro, this site is another submerged tongue that extends to depth. However, the topography is a little more interesting with several diverse sections to explore. Surface currents can be strong but they drop away as you reach the reef and are easy to avoid by moving to the opposing side of the ridge. One side is an almost vertical wall made of huge rock slabs stacked on top of each other like some ancient Aztec fortress. The wall is covered in small green sponges and tiny feathery corals. Legions of lobsters, the hugest you think you will ever see, crawl across the surfaces, disturbing more giant hawkfish. At 30 metres, the ridge is broken by sand and beyond that there are several more rocky outcrops. This area attracts sharks and you can hear whale song reverberating through the sea.

On the other side of the ridge, sandy patches are broken by pinnacles and carved rock formations. The mountainous scenery is dramatic and giant electric rays and large grey rays hover over the seabed. Another dive can be done closer to shore, but the surge means the visibility isn't as good. A mix of sheer walls and boulders are interspersed with mini caves. A green turtle sits in one and stays completely still even when a lobster comes running right up to his tail, touching him, then hightailing it out of the cave. There are many tunnel-like holes in the sand which house odd, furry little crabs.

The giant electric ray is only 60 cm long; the underwater landscape at Punta Tosca; green turtle with his barnacle.

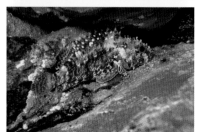

Trumpet fish and cup corals; stacks of whitetips; rainbow scorpionfish

Roca Partida

The smallest of the Revillagigedo Islands is an exposed twin-pinnacle of rock that explodes up from the ocean. Just 100 metres long and much less wide, beneath the surface it falls equally dramatically down to the depths of the Pacific. Roca Partida is a small site and can easily be circumnavigated in a dive. However, if you did this you would miss a lot as there is something on every surface and always in the blue, just waiting to be seen.

The conditions can be a little tougher here: there is surge close to the walls, but as these slope away, you rarely end up in the surge zone. There is always some current too, which hits the two ends of the island, north and south. Again, it's never so strong that you can't swim through it and it's the current that makes this dive the spectacle that it is.

↘6	Roca Partida – South	
🕐	**Depth**	39 m
◑	**Visibility**	good
🌀	**Currents**	moderate but variable
⬤	**Dive type**	liveaboard

Dropping in by the rock's curved south point means divers might have to swim through current to find calmer waters – and might encounter mantas doing much the same. They whizz effortlessly around the point, see the divers and greet them with a belly roll before taking off again. After laughing at the precocious show-off, you can admire the steep walls where every crack and crevice is home to an animal. There are twice-spotted soapfish, the Panamic fang blenny, minute rainbow scorpionfish and sally lightfoot crabs. The frustrating thing about these dives is that just as you start to discover more unusual small creatures another manta ray appears. These sadly endangered animals are so playful you just have to desert whatever else you were looking for. After they flap away you can return to the walls where several wide shelves are stacked with whitetip sharks. Smaller caves have two or three juvenile sharks nestling with a giant green moray who appears to be acting as a surrogate mother, keeping the young sharks cosy by wrapping her sinuous bodies around them.

❝❞ The smallest dolphin paused by my side, moved away a little, then paused again. It was an invitation to play so I joined in, until I realised the cheeky creature had taken me down past 40 metres!

7 Roca Partida – North

Depth	45 m
Visibility	good
Currents	moderate but variable
Dive type	liveaboard

Crossing from the main ship to dive Roca's northern point you might be met by a pod of bottlenose dolphins – a tantalizing taste of things to come. As you roll in you find you have dropped right into the centre of the pod! One youngster approaches: he hangs perfectly vertically, just waiting until everyone is in the water. Then he rapidly flips his tail and takes off to collect the gang, bringing them back to play. The dolphins do what you always hoped they would – they spend time with you, darting to and fro, returning to your side. The encounter takes you way too deep but there is no way you can resist swimming with them.

Moving back up to a sensible depth near the northwestern tip, you run straight into a heaving mass of jacks, giant trevally and creole fish.

There is a shelf at 33 metres which is a good place to look for sharks on a second dive. You find you don't move far as they keep passing by at this level. There is a lone hammerhead that hovers just at the edge of vision but a group of silvertips spin in quite closely, then a Galápagos shark just about kisses your fins.

This corner is very active and as you ascend, you see more hammers (sadly still too far away) and a passing silky shark. Moving up to about 15 metres to start gassing off, you can visit the two small caves that are always loaded with whitetip sharks. Ten or 12 at a time sit piled on top of each other, adults on top of babies on top of adults. A few flashes from the camera and they take off, circle for a moment then descend again for another photo session.

Roca Partida residents: the guinea fowl pufferfish; Galápagos shark; leather bass (the juvenile uses the spiny urchin to its side as camouflage); a trio of silvertips; giant damselfish; clusters of whitetips and Bruce (non-resident)

Isla Guadalupe

Southwest of the city of Ensenada and 240 kilometers off the western coast of the Baja California peninsula lies another isolated island, Guadalupe. Scarred by ancient volcanic activity, devastated in modern times by imported animals, this ecosytem is still one of vital importance.

It may seem surprising when you see the barren, volcanic rock walls, but Guadalupe's ecology is actually far more closely aligned to that of American California than Baja, the landscape reflecting those woodlands to the north. Guadalupe tree species included a palm, cypress, island oak and pine. Only sporadic specimens of these remain and the California Juniper has disappeared. There were indigenous birds too, long since extinct and it was all due to goats which were imported as a food source by early 19th century whalers. In recent years, actions have been taken to remove them and conservation projects are working to re-establish the fauna.

There are two volcanoes on Guadalupe but neither has erupted in modern times. All the same, the landscape as seen from sea level is harsh with long layers of coloured rocks describing the volcanic past. You are unlikely to set foot on the island as there are no land facilities, only a couple of research stations and a small fishing village that is deserted part of the year.

Likewise, diving off Guadalupe is rare, a great pity as the underwater realm is reminiscent of California's Channel Islands. And while the land based flora and fauna suffered terribly, the sea creatures thrived. Guadalupe is a refuge for the Northern Elephant Seal and the Guadalupe Fur Seal and it is now a sanctuary for all the seal species that rest on its rocky shores.

It's because of the seal populations that Guadalupe has become one of the best places in the world to see Great White Sharks. Face-to-face, up close and personal.

Conditions

This is a highly regulated affair. An official joins all boats to ensure it's done the right way: chumming is not allowed; instead, chunks of tuna are placed inside hessian 'teabags' and floated just below the surface. The smell attracts the animals but they can't access the goodies inside. The crew do throw tuna tails out on ropes but try to haul them back in if the sharks try to snatch them. This activity continues for the entire time you are moored up.

Divers can enter the cages at will, and stay in as long as they like as the depth is just three metres. The only restrictions are not being a hog if others are waiting and the water temperature, at a chilly 19ºC. Visibility is usually good, with the deep blue water only muddied by the smaller fish also attracted to the smell of the bait. You are also briefed not to lean out of the cages as "it's not the shark you're watching that will get you but the one behind you". Guess how many people follow that rule?

❝❞ I never thought I would say this but cage diving was nothing like I expected. I would have said it was totally unnatural, but now... well, I have a whole new outlook on Great Whites. I feel I have more of an understanding of the animal and far more appreciation.

🌀 Did I mention I'm afraid of the water?

My last boat ride took two hours – toured Manhattan. Fun. I don't fear boats...
I DO fear water. Drowning mostly. I get disoriented in my pool. I'm not sure why
I chose to cage-dive with Great White Sharks. Oh, I remember... I'm *obsessed* with
sharks. Seeing a Great White has consumed me my whole life. A friend steered me
towards Isla Guadalupe, Mexico. She said "it's close (I'm in Northern California) and
you *will* see Whites."

Found The Nautilus Explorer. Five days on the boat, three days in the water.
Did I mention I'm afraid of water? And not SCUBA certified?

DAYS 1 and 2: Board and think about sharks for 20 hours. That's how long it takes to
get to the island.

DAY 3: Wake up, (ok *bolt* up) run to the back deck to see MY FIRST GREAT WHITE!
I thought it was two sharks then realized it was the dorsal and tail of *one*. Put on my
wetsuit. Ever tried to *rush* putting on a wetsuit? It doesn't work. Time for my first
dive. The crew and divers on board were betting how quick the novice would get
eaten. Down I go. Within a minute I'm seeing a 15 foot shark – *three feet from me!*

I jump back. Everything slows down... It doesn't seem real. I relax and get some
amazing pictures. "This is awesome." "That's a Great White!" "I have to pee." "Diver up!"
My adrenaline is pumping. I fling my mask into the ocean. Whatever! It's not every
day I see something that I'd never seen before.

DAYS 4 & 5: See day three.

I'll be certified soon and will go to the Socorro Islands to dive with manta rays and
reef sharks. Can't wait! But it won't be long before I see the Great Whites again.

Rich Rubin, imaging director/afternoon drive DJ, Sacramento, California

Images of Rich's day: the crew dropping the cages into the sea; Sten throwing out a tuna tail at dawn;
Buzz spotting a dorsal fin as he lowers the boom cage; diver down again; Rich and Sheri finally leave
the cages to warm up, but not for long; and hanging out of the cage to get closer!

↘8 The cage	
🧭 **Depth**	3 m
🌓 **Visibility**	good
🌊 **Currents**	none
🌀 **Dive type**	liveaboard

At dawn, the most curious of divers are up and waiting on the back deck. The cages have been floating at surface level since the previous night and the teabags of tuna are dropped into the sea as the first cups of coffee are poured. Anticipation is rife and before the sun breaks over the horizon, a black fin breaks the surface. You will never see so many divers move so fast to be the first in. No more vaguely cynical comments about this not being proper diving; the crew smirk (they've seen it all before), cage lids are raised, hookahs grabbed and divers drop. And there, right in front of your face is a Great White. A five metre long beastie swims right past you, the nose here, the tail way back there. As time goes on there will be more. Some are full grown adults, some are smaller. A few are tagged and you begin to recognise individuals. They swim around and below the cage, vanish beneath the boat and circulate back. After an hour, they disappear from view and it's time to get out, drink something hot, visit the bathroom, then get back in again.

↘9 The submersible	
🧭 **Depth**	15 m
🌓 **Visibility**	good
🌊 **Currents**	none
🌀 **Dive type**	liveaboard

For qualified divers only, the next trip into the water is in a submersible cage. This is fed with hookahs to the surface too, so no need for any dive kit. This cage only takes two divers and a divemaster with extra safety equipment. It is winched down into the blue from a boom arm, stopping at around 15 metres. The water temperature

is a bit cooler and the view surprisingly different. At depth you are really in shark territory, down here they swim faster and far more freely, swooping to and fro. You can watch them pause as they approach the cages above, monitoring the activity curiously before swimming off then fading away in the distance. Next thing you know they are barrelling towards you again at speed, spinning past with a friendly grin (or menacing grimace depending on your personal state of mind) then heading up again. You ascend and re-enter the shallow cage where it all happens again.

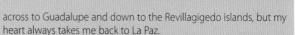

❽ Temperatures rising

The Sea of Cortez

In 2002, I was searching for a new place to work. I had been in the Caribbean for a very long time but hadn't been diving on the Pacific coast of Mexico. I remembered a story I had read as a kid, so travelled across the country then caught a ferry across the Sea of Cortez to La Paz on the coast of Baja California Sur.

There wasn't a lot of work when I arrived. It wasn't long after 9/11 and business was slow, so I went down to Cabo San Lucas but turned back the same day. It wasn't my sort of place. A little while later I was talking to some guys at a dive centre in La Paz, who took me out with their snorkellers for a day to see what I thought. We were only about 10 nautical miles from shore when we came across a school of dolphins; a little further on we met a pod of pilot whales, then about two hours from shore, we found the mobula rays. There were hundreds – maybe four or five hundred – in the water all around us. Next we reached Los Islotes and we were in the water again, this time with sea lions.

From that moment on I decided I was staying in the area. I took my first job at a small dive centre in La Paz and stayed for a year before moving over to liveaboards. This allowed me to explore so much more of this region. I love heading

across to Guadalupe and down to the Revillagigedo islands, but my heart always takes me back to La Paz.

The Sea of Cortez is famous for it's large animal encounters but really its a place to go and sit and study the marine life behaviour. It's a bit like a safari as you never know what you will see. Some days we see orcas, sometimes a blue whale will surface just 20 metres behind boat.

Underwater it's not so pretty, it's not coral reefs with sea fans and bright colours, it's more like being in a Norwegian fjord. The vegetation is minimal and the colours are a bit monotone, but the life is incredible. Sometimes the density of scads or grunts that surround you is so thick that you lose your orientation.

The topography fades away behind the fish. The cleaning stations can be fascinating, you can see a colony of sea lions as they come in to feed on the fish but are still very playful with the divers. Groupers and snappers follow behind and sometimes you even catch a glimpse of a cormorant as it dives into the grunts trying to catch them.

Sten Johansson, cruise director and divemaster, La Paz, Mexico

The deck

🕐	**Depth**	0 m
◑	**Visibility**	good
🌊	**Currents**	none
🌀	**Dive type**	liveaboard

Stepping outside the box (or cage) for a moment... no, being on deck is not a dive, but this is part of the experience that should not be ignored. The best position to appreciate just how enormous this apex predator is, is from the rear of the upper deck. It's from here that you can judge the size and scale of an adult Great White as it passes by the cages tethered to the stern of the boat. The sharks average four to five metres long but have been known to grow to over six. Whatever the size of the one you are looking at, you have to move your head to see its nose at one side of the boat and its tail fin near the other. The levels of excitement on the back deck are profound as people feeds other's experiences: every person has a unique tale and it is a lot of fun sharing them – an adrenaline rush of a very special nature.

A shark swimming below the submersible cage

🌊 It's not going to last

There are few places in the world where you can have dive experiences like those around Baja California. We came face-to-face with the ocean's apex predator, the Great White shark. We played with dolphins, we danced with giant mantas. We saw five different shark species on a single dive. They are all endangered. It's not going to last.

We travelled on Nautilus Explorer and at the end of every trip there is a talk about the animals you have seen. It's a sad talk that almost brings the adrenaline rush of these encounters crashing around your ears. Last year, on their first trip to San Benedicto, the divemasters removed hundreds of metres of fishing nets from the rocks around the Boiler. On another trip they came across an illegal fishing vessel called in the Navy. A patrol boat was sent from the mainland but it was too late. At least the authorities did – and do – act. Because of all this, the owners of Nautilus have started special conservation funds to help.

Owner Mike Lever says: "It was incidents like those that triggered the setting up of the Nautilus Foundation. I am passionate about our support of the Guadalupe and Socorro Conservation Funds as they are the only bastion against illegal fishing of sharks and mantas in the areas that we have the privilege of visiting and diving. Both are sub-funds of the International Community Foundation in San Diego whose CEO is dedicated to helping us and the Mexican authorities. In fact, he and his son were on a Guadalupe trip with us last year. Nine-year-old Danny promptly started up another sub-fund called kids4sharks as soon as they got home.

The momentum building on this is heartening. Over the last 2½ years we have raised US$64,000 for the Guadalupe Conservation Fund, out of which US$25,000 has been disbursed to support scientific efforts. There are no paid staff or expenses coming out of the fund and all donations are used for research. One current objective is to census the Great Whites and gain more understanding of what is going on. It is impossible to protect them if we can't quantify their numbers and the decline in their population. A larger goal is to establish and support a full-time Marine Biological Station on Guadalupe. Our hope is that the full-time presence of biologists on the island will help deter poachers.

The Socorro Conservation Fund is still developing. Donations to date have been around US$15,000. The objectives are to support scientific endeavours regarding the shark and manta populations – we really need to know what's going on with these animals if we are going to make a difference. We can see with our own eyes that numbers are declining but to be effective, we need to quantify the figures. The second and far more challenging goal is to deter illegal fishermen from stripping out the mantas and sharks from what is a protected Biosphere Reserve. Kudos to the Mexican Navy for their efforts in patrolling the islands, but there is a big area to cover and a limit to their resources. We hope to assist them by operating volunteer aerial patrols with the direct costs covered by donations... US$2,000 buys one patrol but if we could raise US$50,000 per year, that would fund 25 aerial patrols and we believe that is enough to make a very significant deterrent to the illegal fishermen."

It would be great to know that ecosystems as unique as these were given every available opportunity to survive.

 Conservation information → visit the international community foundation website at icfdn.org and type Socorro or Guadalupe into the search box for news or go to socorroislandconservation.org

Yucatán Peninsula

The Yucatán an is incredibly diverse area, marked by centuries-old colonial Spanish cities, ancient Maya ruins, fabulous natural resources and miles of perfect white sand beaches stretching along the coast. So it's no surprise that a few decades ago some bright spark decided to turn it into a tourist region. The city of Cancún was chosen as its centre.

Today, this is the country's top tourist region and a major dollar earner, no doubt due to the stylish international airport, an efficient transport infrastructure and mega-hotel after mega-hotel marching down the coast. The Mesoamerican Barrier Reef has almost petered out by the time it reaches this northern point but there are some exciting and unusual diving experiences to be had.

Playa del Carmen

Those who visited the area before the boom might wince at the rampant development near Cancún but head down to Playa del Carmen, an hour south of the airport, and you will still find some of the old Mexico – mixed with enough modern amenities to keep most people happy.

Head a little away from the blindingly white coastal beaches to dive flat reef top plateaux swept by strong currents. Despite that, these are still fairly easy dives, far easier than those near Cozumel. The currents attract a fair number of pelagic species and visibility is better than the sites closer to shore. The shallower, inshore reefs are fairly protected but the surf stirs up the sand and visibility drops. This area is hit by hurricanes every other year or so yet always appears to recover quickly.

⛵11 Tortugas	
🕐 Depth	19 m
◑ Visibility	good
🌊 Currents	medium to strong
🌀 Dive type	day boat

At first glance, this incredibly flat plateau appears to have very little life on it. The current is fairly strong and whips divers across the reef even as they descend. The corals grow to just a few centimetres and even seaplumes are only 30 centimetres high. There's little time to do more than focus on the blue vase and other small sponges that pepper the surface. Then you start to notice the masses of turtles (tortugas) feeding on them, many of which are quite old and studded with barnacles. Near the end of the plateau, you run into the big surprise: a resident school of tarpon. These are BIG fish, nearly two metres long, with metallic silver scales and a very grumpy expression. There seem to be hundreds of them hovering effortlessly over the reef. If you look beneath them you might spot a small nurse shark.

French angelfish: pale bands indicate he is at intermediate – or teenager – stage; a turtle eating the sponges on Tortugas

◼12 Moc-che

Depth	14 m
Visibility	fair
Currents	mild to strong
Dive type	day boat

Descending to this small reef, you find a submerged mound just a metre or two high that is covered in typical Caribbean corals. It is a classic example of the dives here. Small fans and seaplumes decorate the surface, all in shades of brown and beige with pale purple ones interspersed between them. Although at first glance the reef may seem a bit uninteresting, the fish life is a surprise. There are lots of schooling snappers, grunts and porkfish hanging about the various corals in mixed groups. Nestling inside tiny overhangs you find soapfish and lobster, huge green morays, small, black and white blotched morays, masses of arrow crabs and many periclimines shrimp living inside corkscrew anemones. There are a lot of conch shells scattered over the sand that encircles the mound while small stingrays and electric rays bury themselves there.

◼13 Chun-zumbel

Depth	10 m
Visibility	fair
Currents	slight to medium
Dive type	day boat

Just a few minutes off the beach at Playa del Carmen, this site is relatively shallow. Visibility can be low, as it is ringed by so much sand. The reef is bordered by low walls, just a few feet high, with an almost flat and patchy reef top. The undulating surface is covered in a fair number of pastel-coloured sponges and fans which add splashes of colour and often have flamingo tongue shells living on them. They are also surrounded by small schools of grunts – including the cutely named Sailor's Choice. There are various angelfish with their tiny offspring: blacklipped, grey and French. The reef edges are defined by small overhangs beneath which you can find porcupine puffers, arrow crabs and shrimp in every nook. There aren't a lot of anemones but if you spot one it's likely to house a porcelain crab. An occasional great barracuda hovers over the sand.

◼14 Barracuda Caves

Depth	14 m
Visibility	fair
Currents	mild to strong
Dive type	day boat

To the south of Playa del Carmen, beyond the Xcaret eco-park, this comparatively shallow reef is surrounded by low walls with overhangs and mini caves. The upper surface of the reef is covered in a gentle garden of soft corals and a substantial variety of sponges. Around the edge of the reef there are a few small caverns that you can enter. One is particularly good for spotting lobster and in late summer you are likely to see adults that have reached quite a size. There are lots of little critters such as arrow crabs and coral banded shrimp on the walls. Another cave, a little further along, has a resident green moray who is quite accustomed to having visitors. The great barracuda is also a resident, hence the site's name. Although normally solitary, they are sometimes seen in groups of three or four around the reef, although not in the caves, despite the name.

Arrow crabs are common and often live inside sponges; gently undulating topography at Moc-che

The Cenotes

The Yucatán Peninsula is a limestone platform several million years old. The landscape was shaped by an eternity of changing weather patterns. Over the centuries, the bedrock literally dissolved leaving a vast network of subterranean rivers, underground caverns and sinkholes (cenotes) that extend miles inland. After the last ice age ocean levels rose and flooded the caverns that lay closest to the coast with sea water while those further inland filled with rainwater.

These were used by the ancient Maya as a source of fresh water. The cenotes were an inherent part of their daily life, mythology and religion. They believed the underworld gods lived in their depths and people were sacrificed to appease them.

Now, these geological peculiarities, many of which are full of stalactites and stalagmites, form a series of unique dives. Less than an hour from Playa del Carmen, these vary in difficulty from those that are for experienced cave divers to some that are shallow and easy. The simpler ones have guide ropes to lead the way through. Light floods in from fissures in the earth above or from small, secondary cenotes along the river. Although the dive plan is quite straightforward, you will never get to dive solo as there are too many unexplored passages and many 'warning – keep out' signs. Even in the more complex cenotes, conditions are not difficult – but you will be well briefed on being especially careful with buoyancy and to use a special finning technique.

One of the most fascinating aspects is when you pass through a halocline – this is a phenomena created by the meeting of sea water and fresh. The freshwater sits over the salt and forms a bizarre, mirror-like layer. Although most are shallow, the cenotes usually involve a lot of multilevel movement so be careful with your ears. Bear in mind that the water is pretty chilly compared to the sea.

⌖15 Dos Ojos	
Depth	8 m
Visibility	crystal clear, but dark
Currents	none
Dive type	shore

Dos Ojos, meaning two eyes, refers to two circular cenotes that sit beside each other. Entry is via a wooden platform built under the overhang of a small cave between the two eyes. The water feels icy as you jump in, especially as the surrounding jungle is so humid. And it is mosquito heaven! The system has guidelines to follow but entry without a dive guide is not allowed. The first descent into an enormous yawning cave is breathtaking then you are quickly led into a dark and gloomy passage past fragile rock formations. The first part of the system leads off towards one of the 'eyes' and is quite open, with shafts of daylight shining through. You'll even see snorkellers swimming above you. The experience becomes far more surreal once you enter tunnels that are completely black, lit only by your torch beam. You round corners to discover weird and wonderful formations, swim past rocky towers that glitter with minerals then into cathedral-like chambers.

⌖16 Bat Cave, Dos Ojos	
Depth	11 m
Visibility	crystal clear, but dark
Currents	none
Dive type	shore

The second 'eye' inside Dos Ojos is in the opposite direction from the cave entrance, and leads away from the busier areas. Once past the gaping opening, the system drops into a mass of narrow tunnels. Exploration of these is restricted to professional divers while the sport diver route passes more beautiful limestone formations with arches and doorways leading to huge, cavernous rooms. Stunning stalactites seem to hang from every available space on the ceiling, sometimes converging to form thick columns. The depth is shallow all the way but there is very little daylight. At the furthest point from the entry, you finally reach the Bat Cave where you can surface. Above the waterline the limestone cavern roof reveals colours and minerals that sparkle like jewels, and tiny bats hanging from crevices. As you return to the cave entrance, the dive guides like to instruct you to turn off your torch. Wait for your eyes to adjust – it's an eerie experience!

Inside Dos Ojos; an ancient fossil buried in stone; a cenote from inside the forest.

⬎17 Chac-Mool	
Depth	13 m
Visibility	good
Currents	none
Dive type	shore

Hidden further into the jungle, this cenote feels less touristy than popular Dos Ojos – providing you arrive early enough to avoid the bus loads of day divers from Cancún. Entry is through the natural rock pool of Little Brother cenote, where you descend through a school of black catfish into a large cavern. There are several haloclines so as you descend, the visibility decreases and the water seems to be like jelly. Below the halocline, it's a few degrees warmer. Again, there are two directions you can go – one leads to an air dome where you ascend to see the dome edges covered in stalactites that extend down into the water.

⬎18 Taj Mahal	
Depth	14 m
Visibility	good
Currents	none
Dive type	shore

This far less busy site is one of the most interesting with a variety of features. The river system runs in a straight line away from the entry. The opening cavern drops down to the jelly-like layers of 'Halocline Tunnel' and past the impressive limestone formations of 'Close Encounter' then on to 'Cenote Sugarbowl'. Rays of light illuminate massive tumbled boulders (the sugar cubes) and an old tree stump dripping in detritus from the jungle above. A little further on you make a U-turn and head back to 'Bill's Hole', another tiny cenote where you can ascend into the daylight. There's a lot of decaying plant matter so good buoyancy is imperative here. The route back parallels the start but leads past even more fanciful limestone formations, such as 'The Candlestick', until you reach 'Points of Light', a tiny fissure in the ceiling, which shines a sharp beam onto a pile of rocks.

66 99 The very first time we stepped into that cool water it felt like we were entering into the secrets of the Earth. Every moment was a surprise: we passed from brightness to obscurity, catching the light's effects dropping through the jungle right on to a fossil, seeing the sun's rays expose ancient mysteries, slaloming stalactites and stalagmites, tracing roots sneaking out of earth from the Maya's sacred underworld.
Sophie and Patricio Durante, Go Cenotes, Playa del Carmen

Cozumel

Mexico's largest island, Cozumel is just 12 miles off the Yucatán Peninsula. At 28 miles long and 10 miles wide, the island is separated from the mainland coast by an extremely deep oceanic trench. This, along with the island's location, creates a funnel for the strong currents that flow up from the south and are then squeezed out into the Gulf of Mexico.

Cozumel was a sleepy place until Jacques Cousteau visited in the 1960s and made it famous. Since then diving has become a huge part of the island's life and it is an incredibly popular dive destination. There are something like 180 dive centres spread about, mostly catering for Americans who arrive at the island's international airport to take a quick weekend break, or the passengers from the many cruise ships that dock daily. You are rarely on a reef on your own, sometimes there can be four or more boat loads of divers all jostling for space. It has been said that the cruise ship activity has damaged the reefs but in reality it's not the ships, just the sheer numbers,

that may spoil your diving days here. Either way, these reefs were never all that pretty, but, to be fair, that's as much to do with environmental influences.

Cozumel's west coast is bordered by a double row of parallel reefs and, unless you are in a protected cove, the waters are never still. Move just a short way into the ocean and you will meet currents that often hit five knots – even as much as eight at times! You can descend on one dive site and ascend on a completely different one. It may sound a bit scary but it can be a highly exhilarating experience.

This aggressive movement has sculpted these long reefs by eating away at softer core materials, leaving a highly varied and complicated terrain. The area is riddled with so many tunnels, channels and grooves that at times the reefs feel like a giant maze. Inside the caverns and overhangs, smaller marine creatures take a break from the activity, while the rushing waters attract some bigger pelagics. Of course, the corals here are not prolific, the delicate structures of soft corals in particular just don't cope well with these conditions.

☒19 Palancar Caves	
🕑 **Depth**	31 m
🌓 **Visibility**	can be breathtaking
🌊 **Currents**	slight to ripping
🛥 **Dive type**	day boat

This very popular dive starts with a quick descent down over the reef edge to 30 metres. From there, and rising up to about 18 metres, the wall becomes a tortuous maze of tunnels. There are architectural spires and buttresses, gullies and canyons all winding to and fro between the outer wall and the inner reef. At the base of the wall, a sandy slope disappears into the depths. Although there are countless caves and caverns along this stretch there is not as much marine life as you might expect. There are schooling grunts and snapper, and lots of small fish, several types of morays and crustaceans in the tunnels but you are likely to be far too busy having fun swimming through the labyrinth to really notice them.

☒20 La Ceiba Reef	
🕑 **Depth**	12 m
🌓 **Visibility**	good to great
🌊 **Currents**	slight to medium
🛥 **Dive type**	shore

Just offshore from the La Ceiba Hotel and beside one of the cruise liner piers, this small beach and cove makes a great dive for novices, critter-hunters and night dives. The wreck of a DC3 passenger aeroplane sits to the south of the bay. The plane, sunk deliberately as a film prop, is fairly broken up but the scrap metal provides shelter for a range of fish. A current often sweeps the bay – not too strong – and pushes divers along towards the next pier. You pass over small coral heads that are smothered in multi-coloured Christmas tree and feather duster worms. At night there are parrotfish hiding in their mucous bubbles and small morays nestled in the rocks. Octopus hunt in the rubble, looking for hermit crabs, shrimps and other morsels.

One of the many reef crevices that define Cozumel diving; a baby French angelfish

ⓈⒿ21 Punta Tunich/Yacab/Tormentos

🕐	**Depth**	28 m
◐	**Visibility**	good to excellent
🌊	**Currents**	unbelievable
🌙	**Dive type**	day boat

While each of these dives is individually quite satisfying, what defines this stretch of reef – and Cozumel diving generally – is what happens when the currents pick up. And they often do, extending an invitation to a triple-value dive. Dropping over the wall at Punta Tunich, it's not unusual to hit the water and find the current is moving faster than three knots. At that level you can drift along, stopping every now and then to admire something you have spotted on the reef. However, when it's over five knots, there is no option but to move away from the wall and enjoy the passing show as you are swept along over Tunich, past Yucab Reef and onto the next section, known as Tormentos. You're not likely to see anything much in detail but riding the stream is quite a rush. The ever-present schools of grunts will accompany you and there are sometimes a few creole wrasse. As you fly along you can also spot angelfish or lobster on the wall or a grey ray below, who is taking it all in his stride.

ⓈⒿ22 The Devil's Throat, Punta Sur

🕐	**Depth**	38 m
◐	**Visibility**	can be breathtaking
🌊	**Currents**	strong to ripping
🌙	**Dive type**	day boat

Although this dive is one of the most popular here, it can only be done when conditions are just right and is restricted to advanced divers (although the definition of 'advanced' is often loose). Punta Sur is at the very southern tip of Cozumel and is washed by currents, surge and some surf. The first stage of the dive involves finning into a cave system at 26 metres, which turns into a descending tunnel. Lobster and morays often lurk along the passages in the dark. You continue through the tunnel until you emerge on the reef wall, before quickly re-entering another cave that leads to a second complex of tunnels. About four metres in, the tunnel narrows significantly and you enter the 'Devil's Throat'. There are several passageways including one that exits on a sheer section of wall at 37 metres. Another leads to the 'Cathedral', a vast cavern lit by beams of sun filtering through fissures in the reef. There aren't that many fish as the point is so exposed, but you still see angels and butterflyfish swimming along the reef edge and some black corals at depth.

🌀 Playing with Flipper

In many of the world's more commercial resort areas, organized animal encounters are becoming quite commonplace. Settle on the bottom of the sea to watch a chainmail-clad divemaster feed some over-excited whitetips that are only there as they know they will be fed. Join an organized dolphin experience where 'rescued' animals are trained to entertain divers who pay humungous rates for the privilege of seeing creatures they think they will never see in the wild.

There are two sides to this argument. Do you encourage an animal that should be in the wild to do something outside its remit? Do you save some of these creatures for future generations by ensuring their survival, even if that means hemming them in? Remember that pandas may have been saved by zoo breeding programmes, while the Tasmanian Devil is no more.

Not long ago an American aquarium purchased two young whalesharks. The response to outraged conservationists was that they had saved the whalesharks' lives. Whilst that may be true in the short term, no one can predict the effect of captivity on these gentle giants. Is it even possible to provide a suitable, contained habitat? Perhaps the answer lies in their deaths a short while later. Few zoos live up to the ideals we would like them to have and even fewer truly understand the impact on marine species. Only you can decide if you think that this type of activity is a good thing and whether you want to support it.

Drying out

Baja California

Baja California's principal dive areas are reached by liveaboard. Isla Guadalupe departures are from San Diego, where you are likely to need an overnight stop. Transfers are by bus to Ensenada in Baja California Norte and take 2-3 hours. Islas Revillagigedo liveaboards leave from Cabo San Lucas in Baja California Sur.

Islas Revillagigedo
Liveaboards

Nautilus Explorer, T+01 (604) 657 7614, nautilusexplorer.com. This recently built vessel operates cruises to Guadalupe, Islas Revillagigedo and the Sea of Cortez. She is spacious, comfortable and stable – an important consideration for long crossings to these destinations. On-board facilities include nice touches like hot water deck showers and on-tap fresh cookies. The crew are some of the best you will ever meet. Schedules take advantage of local seasonal conditions. Nautilus also runs diving trips as far north as Alaska.

Other options

Solmar V, solmarv.com
Don Jose, bajaex.com

San José del Cabo

About half an hour from the airport, San José del Cabo is a far more peaceful place to stay than along the coastal strip that runs from there to Cabo San Lucas (one hour) where the liveaboards are moored. But if lively restaurants and even livelier bars are your preference, Cabo San Lucas has many of those and plenty of hotels in most price ranges. Your operator will make some recommendations.

Sleeping

$$$-$$ El Encanto Inn, T+52 (624) 142 0388, elencantoinn.com. This small hotel is situated in the heart of historic San José del Cabo, right in the artists' quarter. Each room is decorated with an eclectic mix of local crafts and antiques which reflect the tone of the town's focus on the arts. The hotel is quiet and peaceful with a spa, a pool and a chapel (should you decide a wedding is on the cards) and it's about 20 mins walk to the beach.

La Paz

If you have time to visit La Paz and dive in the Sea of Cortez, Baja Expeditions, has day trip and liveaboard diving – bajaex.com.

Isla Guadalupe
Liveaboards

Nautilus Explorer, T+01 (604) 657 7614, nautilusexplorer.com. Details as left.

San Diego
Sleeping

$ Dolphin Motel, T+1 (619) 758 1404, dolphin-motel.com. Small, simple and spotless, this comfortable family-run motel is on San Diego bay right beside the pick-up and departure points for liveaboards to Guadalupe. Far better value than some of the bigger chain hotels nearby.

Eating

The waterfront near the Dolphin is lined with small and sometimes famous seafood restaurants. The style tends to be casual so if you fancy something a little classier head across the bay to the Gaslight Quarter.

San José del Cabo – restaurant or work of art?
Roca Partida at sunset

	Sleeping	$$$ US$150+ double room per night	$$ US$75-150	$ under US$75
	Eating	$$$ US$40+ 2-course meal, excluding drinks	$$ US$20-40	$ under US$20

San Diego

An added bonus of going to Guadalupe is having an excuse to stopover in one of America's nicest small cities. Central San Diego is compact and easy to get around with a very good public transport system.

Old Town San Diego A State Historic Park, a short distance from the bay, this is a recreation of how San Diego looked in the 1800s. With 'olde worlde' shops and museums, it is free and worth an hour.

The Gaslamp Quarter In the 1860s, Enterpreneur Alonzo Horton purchased this land as a 'better location for a major city' then set about developing it. Most buildings were erected in the late1800s – along with the famed gaslamps – and are haunted by tales of gambling, wild saloons and wilder bordellos. The area was redeveloped in the 1970s and is now full of vibrant galleries and restaurants.

Balboa Park Promoted as America's largest urban cultural park, this expansive green space houses 15 museums (some free), many performing arts venues and its most famous attraction, the zoo.

SeaWorld and San Diego Zoo Not located together (SeaWorld is half an hour north of Balboa), these two animal attractions are done with typical American finesse and glamour. Well-organised and somewhat theatrical, both run respected conservation programmes. If you have kids, you have to go. If you don't borrow some or go anyway. From US$35

USS Nimitz San Diego is also a major US naval base and is the home port of the supercarrier *USS Nimitz*. This imposing vessel is one of the largest warships in the world. It hovers over the waterfront and while Naval warfare may not be your favourite subject, it is worth touring a vessel of such a tremendous scale.

San José del Cabo

Anyone who has ever travelled through the heart of Mexico will be delighted to see that the centre of this small town still retains a traditional air. If you have a day or two to spare, it's a relaxing town. Prior to colonization it was a provisioning stop for Spanish galleons and famous pirates like Sir Francis Drake.

The Mission In 1730, a Jesuit fort and mission was built on what would become the main town square. The imposing exterior has an ornate ceramic mural of native Indians on the front, and contrasts stongly with its simplistic interior.

The Plaza Lying in front of the Mission, this lovely cobbled square is edged by Spanish colonial buildings including the city hall. At night the plaza has buskers and acrobats, musicians on a bandstand or dancers on the stage. The enormous fountain is ringed by sculptures of famed local dignataries.

The Artists' Quarter The quiet streets that lie behind the plaza have attracted both artists in residence and art galleries showing the works of many well-known Mexican artists. Well worth touring, well worth leaving your credit card behind.

The coast Despite its history, the coast near San José has become developed. However, you can still commune with nature at the nearby river estuary, go horseriding or visit a turtle nursery.

Cabo San Lucas

Highly developed and highly touristy, this once idyllic, small fishing harbour is now a busy marina that is swarmed almost daily by the occupants of visiting cruise ships. Touts for game-fishing trips, beach trips, snorkelling, paragliding and so on, attack anyone walking around the marina. Beyond the pier, and at night, it calms down somewhat and you can sit at a marina-side restaurant to enjoy the view. Shops, restaurants and nightlife are all on tap, if you like a busy stopover.

Mexico Drying out

Clockwise: San Diego's Gaslamp Quarter; the *Nimitz*; Cabo San Lucas marina; San José del Cabo Plaza; El Encanto Hotel

Yucatán Peninsula

Choosing where to stay in the Yucatán should be based on what type of diving you want to do the most. Whether you are on the coast near Playa del Carmen or over on Cozumel island, there is a huge variety of accommodation options, almost as many dive centres and far more restaurants than you could ever try in a lifetime.

Playa del Carmen

Dive Centres

GoCenotes, T+52 (01)984 803 3924, gocenotes.com. Well-structured, daily dive programmes right across the area. Modern equipment and multi-lingual guides.

SeaLife Divers, T+52 (01)984 803 0809, sealifedivers.com. Located right on Mamitas Beach, this flexible and friendly dive centre has various good value dive packs which include all local reefs, trips across to Cozumel and fully escorted cenote diving. Partners to **SeaMonkey Business**, seamonkeybusiness.com for advice on hotels, transfers and touring.

Sleeping

$$$-$$ Condo Ali, Nueva Quinta Building, Av 5 y Calle 28. Luxury 2-bed villa with a rooftop jacuzzi and view of the sea. On the lively main road with good access to both the beach and all nightlife. Book through SeaMonkey Business.

$$ Villa Amanecer, T+52 (01)984 873 2716, villa-amanecer.com. Small, friendly hotel in a quiet location just back from the beach and near GoCenotes. Some rooms have sea views.

Eating

Playa del Carmen restaurants can supply virtually every cuisine known to man.

$$ La Vagabunda, T+52 (01)984 873 3753. Decent Mexican food. Open all day and perfect for a traditional Mexican breakfast or just an afternoon drink.

$$ El Sazón, next door to La Vagabunda on Av 5 between Calle 24 y 26 this tiny Mexican bistro is more upmarket and has delicious fish dishes as well as some stable fare but often with a twist.

Cozumel

Dive centres

Deep Blue, T+52 (01)987 872 5653, deepbluecozumel.com. Custom packages for more experienced divers. Accessible location just back from the town square.

Del Mar Aquatics, delmaraquatics.net, T+52 (01)987 872 5949. At the Casa del Mar hotel. Good value accommodation and dive packages, see below.

Sleeping

$$$-$$ Casa Mexicana, T+52 (01)987 872 9090, casamexicanacozumel.com. In the centre of town opposite the waterfront, this hotel is surprisingly good value if you prefer a lively environment and are happy to walk to a nearby dive centre.

$$ Casa del Mar, T+52 (01)987 872 1900, casadelmarcozumel.com. This resort-style hotel is a little north of town on a more peaceful section of the coast. The hotel is often full but it is highly diver-focussed with Del Mar Aquatics across the road and shore diving available.

Eating

$$$ Pepe's Grill, T+52 (01)987 872 0213. Upmarket fare – steaks, lobster and seafood – opposite the sea front and piers.

$$ La Choza, Calle Adolfo Rosado Salas 198, T+52 (01)987 872 0958, Genuine Mexican home-style cooking served all day, probably the most authentic dishes on the entire island.

Chichén Itzá on the Yucatán Peninsula; Mexican child selling balloons; dive centre on the beach, Cozumel waterfront

Sleeping	$$$ US$150+ double room per night	$$ US$75-150	$ under US$75
Eating	$$$ US$40+ 2-course meal, excluding drinks	$$ US$20-40	$ under US$20

Yucatán Peninsula

Mexico is a vast and fascinating country with more to see than you could ever cover in a two week holiday. Unless you are willing to include internal flights, it would be best to restrict sightseeing to around the Yucatán Peninsula.

Fortunately, no matter where you are staying, all the following sights are easily accessible. The ferries that link Cozumel to Playa del Carmen only take 45 minutes and leave hourly. Apart from what is listed here, there are numerous other traditional holiday activities like skydiving, kayaking, golf and jungle treks. As a purpose-built tourist city, Cancún is the place to go for staged bullfights, dolphin shows and to shop-till-you-drop. The town is a highly commercialized place, which may not suit everyone so details are not included. All prices quoted are generally for tours that start on the coast; allow an extra US$20 if you are on Cozumel.

Chankanaab National Park, Cozumel
The original marine park in this region. Its shallow lagoon is a great place to get your toes wet if you're not a diver, but you can dive here as well – it's good for novices. There are good snorkelling facilities and shallow marine pools for children. The botanical garden has hundreds of tropical plant species and many iguanas. There is also the option to join in a man-made "dolphin experience". Only you can decide if that's a good thing. Entrance is US$10.

Chichén Itzá
West of Cancún, this sacred Maya city is the best known in the area and its pyramid is something of an icon. It has 91 very steep steps to the top and if you climb it, your calves will be sorry. There are many other buildings around the complex, including an observatory and a ball court. Here an ancient Olmec ball game was played, which gave a whole new meaning to the term 'sudden death'. The winners (or losers, no one really knows which) were decapitated after the game. Tours from US$60.

Tulum
An hour's drive south from Playa del Carmen, this ancient site was both a Maya seaport and an astronomical centre. It's not as substantial or impressive as many others in Mexico; however, it sits in the most breathtaking location facing the rising sun and looking over the sea. As it's very easy to reach, the site gets busy in the late morning when tour buses arrive. You can take one of these (US$60) or go independently but get there early.

Xel-há
A little further north from Tulum, this once natural complex of waterways and mangroves is now a themed park and aquarium. There are swimming lagoons, cenotes, ancient caves and organized activities like swimming with dolphins and jungle walks. A good day out for those with young kids and non-divers. Entrance fees with limited access range from US$15 (children) to US$29 (adult) up to an all-inclusive day pass at US$28/56 respectively.

Xcaret
Just south of Playa and a little like Xel-há, this centre is promoted as an eco-archaeological park. Inside the complex are some marine-based activities plus a Museum of Culture and Archaeology, a replica Maya Village and special evening events like recreations of ball games and dance extravaganzas. You can even get married here! At US$80 (adult) and US$60 for children it's quite pricey, but there is lots to do.

Sian Ka'an Biosphere Reserve
Further south towards the border with Belize, this UNESCO World Heritage Site covers an area of rare coastal wetlands with over 20 archaeological sites, 100 or so mammal species and 300 bird species. It is also a nesting site for two species of endangered sea turtles. The management of the reserve is much more heavily biased towards eco-tourism and the natural world. Day tours cost US$68 or you could join conservation group, Global Vision International (gvi.co.uk) and assist in their coral, fish and crocodile surveys.

Holbox
On the very northeastern tip of the Yucatán, tiny Holbox sits just off the coast. This island still reflects life in the region before mass tourism hit and for that alone it's worth a trip. However, that is unlikely to last as the seas close by are also a known whaleshark highway. Between late June and August, it is said you can snorkel with more whalesharks than you can count on all your digits. In reality, you are just as likely to spend a long, hot day on the water and see only one or two. Ask about most recent numbers of sightings before booking. Day trips by bus run from US$100 or you could go by private Cessna for US$280, aerosaab.com.

Playa del Carmen beach and market stalls; a mural by Diego Riviera, Mexico's most revered artist.

Central America

Smile for the camera: an encounter with the great barracuda, *Sphyraena barracuda*, on Lighthouse Reef.
Tarpon Cave, Belize

● Orange Walk

25 km

Ambergris Caye

Caye Caulker

↘1

BELIZE CITY ●

Turneffe Atoll

Lighthouse Reef

↘2

B E L I Z E

Dangriga ●

▲
Richardson Peak

Caribbean Sea

● Punta Gorda

● Puerto Barrios

San Pedro Sula ●

G U A T E M A L A

Roatan

West End ●   ↘3

Utila   ↘4

● Utila Town

Cayos Cochinos

● La Ceiba

▲
Pico Bonito

H O N D U R A S

↘1 Inner Reefs & Turneffe Atoll ▶▶ p304

San Pedro ●   *Ambergris Caye*
                     ↘1

BELIZE
CITY ●   ↘5

            ↘2   ↘6

                  ↘3   *Turneffe
                       Atoll*

                  ↘4

↘1 Hol Chan Marine Reserve
↘2 Canyons II
↘3 Sandslope
↘4 Sayonara Wreck
↘5 Rendezvous Point
↘6 Tubular Barrels

⬊2 Lighthouse Reef ▶▶ p307

Northern Caye

⬊14

⬊10
⬊11
⬊7 ⬊12
⬊9 Half Moon Caye
Long Caye ⬊8 ⬊13

⬊7 Long Caye Wall
⬊8 East Cut
⬊9 Uno Coco
⬊10 The Aquarium
⬊11 Cathedral
⬊12 Tarpon Cave
⬊13 Half Moon Caye Wall
⬊14 The Blue Hole

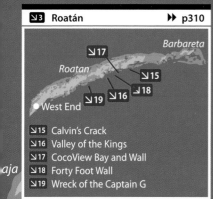

⬊3 Roatán ▶▶ p310

Barbareta

⬊17
Roatan
⬊15
⬊18
⬊19 ⬊16

West End

⬊15 Calvin's Crack
⬊16 Valley of the Kings
⬊17 CocoView Bay and Wall
⬊18 Forty Foot Wall
⬊19 Wreck of the Captain G

⬊4 Utila ▶▶ p312

⬊20 ⬊21

Utila
Town
Roatan
⬊24 ⬊23 ⬊22

⬊20 Great Wall
⬊21 Aquarium I & II
⬊22 Ted's Point
⬊23 Halliburton Wreck
⬊24 Silver Garden

Introduction

Shaped by the ice age, the small sea that is now known as the Caribbean developed in isolation from the world's other oceans. It's almost as if it was at the back of the queue and missed out on its fair share of marine species. However, it did inherit the world's second largest barrier reef, which now defines the eastern coastlines of Central American Belize and Honduras.

Like elsewhere in the region, diving from these countries is not a mind-numbing assault on the senses, but rather a far more subtle underwater experience. Pastel-coloured soft corals and neutral-toned hard corals create a delicate backdrop for a marine realm that never demands attention but waits patiently for observant divers to appreciate its unique features.

That isn't to say there aren't some truly unusual diving experiences, including one of the world's most famous, the Blue Hole on Belize's Lighthouse Reef. Or if you simply want to go critter hunting, you can do that on a quiet and laid-back Honduran island.

Although these countries edge the western side of the Caribbean, their personalities are more Latin American; their histories shaped first by the Maya, then by colonial invaders and later pirate exploits. There are some cultural diversions but, in reality, the landside charms lie with the many gifts from nature.

Central
America rating

Diving
★★★

Dive facilities
★★★

Accommodation
★★★

Down time
★★★

Value for money
★★★

Essentials

Getting there and around

At a time when air travel couldn't be easier, it seems bizarre to find a region that needs more than the usual amount of planning. Unless you are in the US, you are likely to need several flights to reach either Belize or Honduras.

Because **Belize** doesn't have a national carrier, you will need to fly via the USA. American, Continental, US Airways and Delta all fly to Belize City. Alternatively, fly with any other carrier (say BA, Virgin or Qantas) and then connect to a shorter flight with Central American airline TACA (taca.com). TACA also have flights from other US cities but these may entail flying via another Central American country.

Once you have arrived, liveaboards depart from the dock at Fort George in the city or, if you choose to visit one of the islands, there are two local airlines, Tropic Air (tropicair.com) and Maya Island Air (mayaairways.com), that shuttle people around in fleets of small aircraft. Water taxis head to the various cayes and on land there's a good public bus system that covers the whole of the country. Fares are cheap although the buses are somewhat rickety. Wherever you are going, your dive operator will advise on transfers.

There are several airports in **Honduras** – in the capital, Tegucigalpa, second city, San Pedro Sula and coastal La Ceiba – so it's something of a surprise that it's not always straightforward to get there either, at least not without several transit stops on the way. For diving it is best to head straight to the international terminal on Roatán from Houston or Miami. Several small airlines then link Roatán to the other islands via the hub at La Ceiba: Atlantic (atlanticairlines.com.ni), Isleña (flyislena.com) and SOSA (aerolineassosa.com) flights are only 20 minutes or so per hop and are generally quick and efficient. There are also ferries linking the islands.

Hotels normally collect their guests on arrival in Roatán but taxis from the airport are reasonably priced and meet arriving flights. On Utila you will be met at the airport by whoever you booked with.

The Bay Islands are so relaxing you may not feel the need to go anywhere else, but it is easy to reach the mainland and spend a few days in the cloud forest coastal region or head across to the Maya ruins at Copán, near the border with Guatemala.

After you have absorbed all that, there is one more thing to note. It may seem like a good idea to combine these countries into one trip but in reality it's not easy. You would expect to find a short air hop from say, Cancún to Belize City, or from there to Roatán, but the flights simply don't exist. You can travel overland: from Mexico to Belize there are buses that connect on the border but the total journey time, including border crossing, is around 12 hours and you are likely to need to stop overnight. And you could go from Punta Gorda on Belize's southern coast through Guatemala to Honduras. However, the best advice on that one is don't even think about it unless you have days to spare. If you do want to combine two countries, it might actually be quicker to go back via Miami.

Belize	
Location	
17°15'N, 88°45'W	
Capital	Belmopan
Population	307,899
Land area in km²	22,806
Coastline in km	386

Honduras	
Location	
15°00'N, 86°30'W	
Capital	Tegucigalpa
Population	7,792,854
Land area in km²	111,890
Coastline in km	820

Arrow crab hiding amongst the corals

Language

In Belize, the official language is English. There are others, including two versions of Mayan, but here people seem to swap between English and Spanish with hardly a thought. Down in Honduras, the balance swaps: Spanish is the official language and is spoken across the country, though English remains the most common language on the islands. See page 272 for a few Spanish words.

Local laws and customs

A rather informal place, **Belize** has a laid-back lifestyle with serious Caribbean overtones. There are traces of the ancient cultures but about half the population is Catholic and the remainder is a mix of other Christian religions. **Honduras** is also principally Catholic although a few indigenous religions are still practiced. The people can be more reserved but you may only notice if you head inland.

Health

The appearance of things in **Belize** might make you think that standards are low but the country actually has a good health record with a clinic in most villages and good hospitals in Belize City. In **Honduras**, medical facilities are a mixed bag. On the islands you will find an English-speaking doctor easily but not on the mainland, where pharmacists are seen as a first line of defence. They are all well trained and will treat any minor ailment. Generally health risks are low and apart from sun block and insect repellent you aren't likely to need much. However, on the insect front there is one noteworthy nuisance: the no-see-um. These biting midges live in the sand and are a real problem. Although they don't spread disease they do cause plenty of discomfort for their victims. Protect yourself as you would for mosquitoes or simply stay off the sand. They'll still get you but perhaps a bit less often.

Costs

Both these countries can be as expensive or cheap as you want them to be. In **Belize**, you can easily find a decent guesthouse for around US$40 a night and eat in one of the local restaurants for less than US$10. Seafood is good, unless you go in conch season when it's conch curry, conch burgers and conch and chips. Of course, you can also spend much more on private island resorts or upmarket eco-lodges owned by the rich and famous (Francis Ford Coppola runs a group of very expensive hotels). A beer in a local bar will be around US$1.25, or up to US$2.50 in a resort. A 10% service charge might be added to your bill, especially in Belize City but if not, then tipping is at your discretion. Small change on a small bill or 10% is acceptable.

Things are similar in **Honduras**, but if anything it is cheaper in some places. Utila is regarded as one of the most economical

Fact file

Belize

International flights	Continental, TACA, BA, Virgin, Qantas
Departure tax	US$35, but usually included in ticket
Entry	Visa not required for EU, USA, Canada, Australia and NZ. Other countries' citizens should check.
Internal flights	Tropic Air and Maya Island Air
Ground transport	Countrywide buses, taxis, water taxis
Money	US$1 = 2 Belize dollars (BZD)
Language	English officially, Spanish is common
Electricity	110v, plug type A/B (see page 16)
Time zone	GMT -6
Religion	Christian
Phone	Country code +501; IDD code 0; Police 916

Honduras

International flights	TACA, Continental
Departure tax	US$30 in cash only
Entry	30 days entry for most nationalities
Internal flights	TACA, SOSA, Isleña, Atlantic
Ground transport	Countrywide buses, island buses, taxis
Money	US$1 = 20 Lempira (HNL)
Language	English and Spanish
Electricity	110/220v, plug type A (see page 16)
Time zone	GMT -6
Religion	Christian
Phone	Country code +504; IDD code 00; Police119

places on the planet to learn to dive. Costs in most resort style hotels on the islands don't necessarily reflect the cost of living in the country. Many are US-run with US or European staff. All the same, Honduras is great value with resorts that are completely focussed on dive tourism – packages include everything except your nightly cocktails. A beer in a local bar will be around US$1.50, but up to US$5 in a resort. Service charges are added to some bills; where it isn't tipping is the done thing – between 10% and 15%.

For more information on tipping, especially for dive guides and crews see page 12.

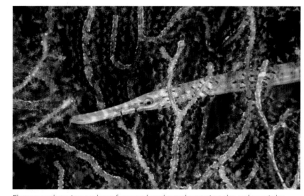

Flutemouth trying to be a fan coral and nearly getting the colour right

 Tourist information → The Belize government websites can be found at travelbelize.org and belizetourism.org. For the Bay Islands in Honduras, roatanonline.com and aboututila.com.

Dive brief

Diving

The world's second largest barrier reef runs for 300 kilometres down Mexico's Yucatán coast, south through Belize then on to Honduras. Referred to as the Mesoamerican Barrier Reef – to distinguish it from that other more famous barrier reef – this extensive system is regarded as unique due to its length and variety of habitats. Because the Caribbean Sea developed in isolation from the others on the planet, it has far lower biodiversity levels than those in Asia or the Pacific. You might think this means the diving isn't so hot here – and comparing diversity figures, you will see that the area does lag behind – yet this reef has the highest levels of marine life in the region. There are around 430 species of fish in the Caribbean Sea and more than half are found along this reef.

Its geographic structures have been carved by a variety of current patterns and these give each country special features both on land and underwater. Mexico's segment of the reef is influenced heavily by the currents, but as you travel down the coast towards **Belize** the currents lose their aggression and the diving is a lot calmer. Diving near the small cayes just off the coast is always easy. Further out to sea there are two impressive and challenging atoll groups: Turneffe is closest to shore then next is Lighthouse Reef, regarded as the best in Belize and location of the Blue Hole. Dive sites are, in the main, a mix of gentle, open mounds and steeper drop-offs, all characterized by sharp channels that cut through the reef rim – the best habitats for fish and richer coral growth.

Further south in **Honduras**, levels of marine diversity are at their highest, due to its location at the very bottom of the reef and the influences of Central America's volcanic geography. Divers target the Bay Islands, which sit 30 or more miles offshore. Roatán and Utila are the most attractive while Guanaja and the Hog Islands (Cayos Cochinos) have some good diving but are less visited. Conditions are fairly easy with consistent temperatures and not too much in the way of currents.

Marine life

These reefs mostly consist of a rocky strata covered by layers of soft corals, referred to as sea plumes. These look like twiggy tree branches until currents bring out polyps to feed, creating soft and furry feathers. As the variety of corals are less prolific than in other oceans you seem to see more pelagic life. Strange but true... eagle rays, schools of jacks and snapper and the most enormous tarpon. Not that these outdo the smaller creatures: the indigo hamlets, indigenous bluebell tunicates and some very sexy seahorses.

Central America animals encounters

Belize	eagle rays and barracuda
Honduras	the cryptic teardrop crab

Half Moon Key on Lighthouse Reef; rare bluebell tunicates live in a colony

We first travelled Central America as trekkers, not divers, and always enjoyed the pace of life in these countries. It's odd how they are so close with many similarities and yet each feels a little different. But no matter where you go, you feel completely immersed in that distinctive style of island life: hammocks under palms, rum cocktail in hand, the sun setting fiery red over cool turquoise...

Snorkelling

Those who prefer not to submerge will find some great places to snorkel. In the Bay Islands there are many artificial reefs, including some small boat wrecks, that sit close to shore. And if you are in Utila at the right time, there are excursions to find migrating whalesharks as they pass by. Belize's shallow seagrass beds attract large bottom feeders while reefs around the outer atolls come in close to shore, so it's easy to see the 'big stuff'.

Making the big decision

Choosing where to dive can be a little confusing as you first have to choose between Belize and Honduras. More serious divers will go for a Belize liveaboard as they have easy access to the Blue Hole, famously lauded by Jacques Cousteau as one of the world's 'must-dives'. Sailing out is also more comfortable and gives the chance to tour the best of the atolls on the way. There are still plenty of resorts across all the islands for those who prefer to be land based.

Honduras, however, has the advantage of being the most diverse marine region within the Caribbean Sea. The hardest decision will be where to go as each of her small islands has its own personality – at least they are all close enough together to organize a multi-centre trip.

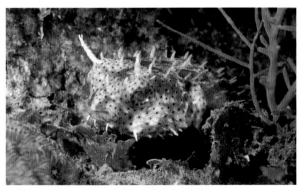

Pufferfish are sometimes called burrfish in the Caribbean

Dive data

Seasons	Year round diving. Belize is driest from February to March and can be very windy in September; Honduras is wetter from October to January; Chances of hurricanes from August to October
Visibility	10 metres inshore to 40 metres+ in open water.
Temperatures	Air 20-34°C; water 24-30°C
Wet suit	3 mm shorty or full suit, 5 mm+ for the cenotes
Training	Available everywhere. Cheapest on Utila but look for accredited training agencies
Nitrox	Available in resorts, but quantities may be limited, pre-booking advised
Deco chambers	Cozumel, Playa del Carmen, Ambergris Caye, Roatán and Utila

Bottom time

Belize		Lying at the heart of the Mesoamerican Barrier Reef, Belize borders the central section of the world's second largest continuous reef system.
Inner barrier reef	▶▶ p304	Within minutes of the capital, the reefs that parallel the coast and her offshore islands are surprisingly active.
Turneffe Atoll	▶▶ p305	A gently shelving, oval-shaped reef system with curious topography and varying conditions.
Lighthouse Reef	▶▶ p307	The location of the planet's most famous underwater cavern, the Blue Hole, as well as many other excellent sites.
Honduras		Charming islands that play host to the highest regional levels of marine diversity in the entire Caribbean Sea.
Roatán	▶▶ p310	Great shore dives inside the lagoons and exciting walls on the fringing reef.
Utila	▶▶ p312	Gentle slopes and craggy shores in the south contrast with steep walls around the north of the island.

Diversity

combined reef area 2,140 km²
Belize | Honduras

HARD CORALS

24 | 25

FISH SPECIES

575 | 938

ENDEMIC FISH SPECIES

2 | 2

FISH UNDER THREAT

22 | 18

PROTECTED REEFS/MARINE PARKS

9 | 3

All diversity figures are approximate

Belize

Inner Barrier Reef

Belize's barrier reef is less than an hour from Belize City and only a mile from the popular islands of Ambergris Caye and Caye Caulker. Just to the south these is a series of smaller cayes and reefs with evocative names like Drowned Caye and Spanish Lookout Caye, all a reflection of their illustrious pasts.

East of these small islands, a deep marine trench separates the inner reef from the distant, deeper atolls of Turneffe and Lighthouse Reefs, which in turn protect the lagoon like area inside the coastal reef. Shallow and well protected, there's good diving and snorkelling in the marine parks plus strict restrictions on fishing. Several different ecosystems support a wide diversity of species. There are coral reefs, seagrass beds and mangroves: the mangrove trees are habitats for seabirds while fish, shellfish and marine organisms begin their lives protected by their roots. Coral cayes, recognized by their palm trees, are ringed by reefs, lagoons and occasional seagrass beds.

◹1 Hol Chan Marine Reserve

Depth	12 m
Visibility	fair
Currents	unlikely
Dive type	day boat

This small marine reserve, which lies just off Ambergris Caye, is a favourite destination for both divers and snorkellers. It's not that the site is particularly challenging diving, and it can be very crowded at times, but it is a good example of an inner Belizean reef. The structure runs east-west, creating a long, winding ridge with cuts, fan corals and hard coral outcrops. The outer side gently slopes down to about 12 metres then heads off to the distant reef edge. There are a lot of large pelagic fish as this is a no fishing zone. You can see barracuda and grouper plus angelfish and masses of bluestriped grunts. Spending some time up in the shallow seagrass beds is well worthwhile as snorkellers may encounter gentle nurse sharks, rays and morays – and often in just waist-deep water.

◹2 Canyons II

Depth	25 m
Visibility	fair
Currents	can be strong
Dive type	day boat

Spanish Lookout Caye is less than an hour by speedboat from Belize City, yet this has to be one of the more interesting dives in the inner reef area. Within seconds of hitting the water you are likely to see eagle rays, groupers and lobsters. Smaller animals nestle into the reef's cracks and crevices and include arrow crabs, cleaner shrimp, coral banded shrimp and morays. Off over the edge of the wall there are barracuda and tuna watching curiously. An area of mangrove swamp is a fantastic nursery ground for lobster and molluscs and, if you are lucky, you may even see manatees feeding on the seagrass beds.

The indigo hamlet is common in the Bay Islands in Honduras but is less frequently seen in Belize

Turneffe Atoll

As you sail east from Belize City, passing over the barrier reef, you meet a series of atolls divided by deep water marine trenches. Turneffe Atoll sits on the first, and shallower, of two submarine ridges.

Turneffe is the largest of the country's atolls and the closest to the mainland at about 20 miles to the east. The Turneffe Islands are dotted about this scenic atoll and are quite different from those on Lighthouse Reef (further to the east) and Glovers Reef (due south) in that many of the islands are covered in mangroves. There are 200 or so small cayes dotted around and these all provide shelter for a range of marine animals, as well as being nursery grounds for all sorts of birds and land-based creatures. The tides and winds distribute nutrients around the atoll so fish populations are fairly substantial.

Each side of the atoll has a differing set of weather conditions that affect diving. The north and west can be choppy while the eastern side drops off to greater depths. There are dive sites all the way around the perimeter, although shallow lagoon waters and numerous islands make navigating through the centre a risky business.

↘3 Sandslope

🕐	**Depth**	36 m
◑	**Visibility**	fair to good
🌊	**Currents**	none to medium
🌐	**Dive type**	day boat/liveaboard

This oval-shaped reef consists of lots of small bommies with coral patches dotted around them. There is good coverage of seaplumes, rods and whips and even some fan corals that are several feet high. These thrive in the currents created by the atoll's tidal flow. The very pretty indigo hamlet is a resident as is his cousin, the shy hamlet. These small skittish fish are easy to miss, unlike the lobsters that settle anywhere they find comfortable sometimes even inside really tall vase sponges. As the atoll is so far away from the coast, you are likely to see some of the more unusual Caribbean fish like the white sargassam triggerfish and highly patterned diamond and quillfin blennies – check the male's dorsal fin. There are also plenty of cleaner shrimp residing in corkscrew anemones and spinyhead blennies squatting in holes made by tube worms, spotted morays and arrow crabs in sponges and lots of jawfish living in burrows in the sand.

↘4 Sayonara Wreck

🕐	**Depth**	33 m
◑	**Visibility**	good
🌊	**Currents**	none to mild
🌐	**Dive type**	day boat/liveaboard

Off the southwest of Turneffe Atoll, this long, sloping wall drops to a depth of over 40 metres and has a pure white sandy seabed with seaplumes and large barrel sponges scattered across it. Finning along the reef ridge you encounter a series of cuts and gullies, which create nice swim-throughs for divers and shelters for the fish. Mackerel pass overhead in small groups and always appear to be followed by a solitary oceanic triggerfish, a fish that never seems to have a mate. Heading back towards the mooring you come to the wreck of the Sayonara, a cargo boat that was deliberately sunk in 1985. There's nothing much left of its wooden hull save for a few planks and a lot of mechanical detritus but there is an incredible number of indigo hamlets, and just as many spotted trunkfish. The rare toadfish is known to live on this reef so if you want to see this elusive creature stick closely to your dive guide!

Central America Dive log Belize: Turneffe Atoll

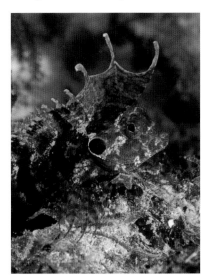

Only in the Caribbean and not all that common even there, the male quillfin blenny; the pastel tones of a tranquil underwater garden in Belize

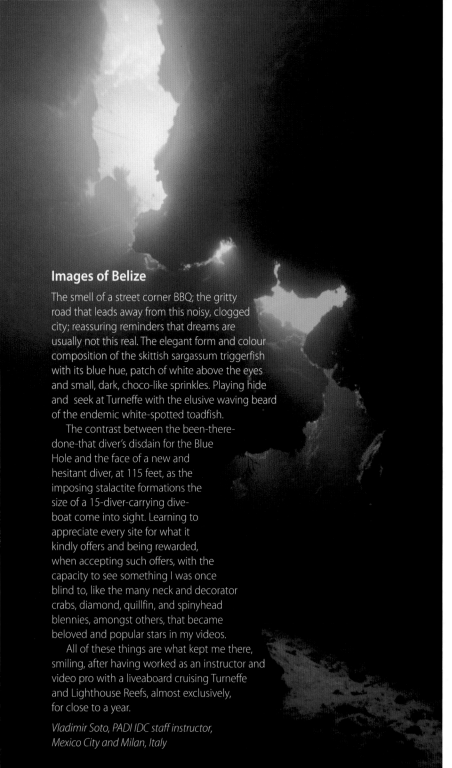

Images of Belize

The smell of a street corner BBQ; the gritty road that leads away from this noisy, clogged city; reassuring reminders that dreams are usually not this real. The elegant form and colour composition of the skittish sargassum triggerfish with its blue hue, patch of white above the eyes and small, dark, choco-like sprinkles. Playing hide and seek at Turneffe with the elusive waving beard of the endemic white-spotted toadfish.

The contrast between the been-there-done-that diver's disdain for the Blue Hole and the face of a new and hesitant diver, at 115 feet, as the imposing stalactite formations the size of a 15-diver-carrying dive-boat come into sight. Learning to appreciate every site for what it kindly offers and being rewarded, when accepting such offers, with the capacity to see something I was once blind to, like the many neck and decorator crabs, diamond, quillfin, and spinyhead blennies, amongst others, that became beloved and popular stars in my videos.

All of these things are what kept me there, smiling, after having worked as an instructor and video pro with a liveaboard cruising Turneffe and Lighthouse Reefs, almost exclusively, for close to a year.

Vladimir Soto, PADI IDC staff instructor, Mexico City and Milan, Italy

---

⑤ Rendezvous Point

🕐 **Depth**	21 m
◐ **Visibility**	good
🌀 **Currents**	mild to strong
⚓ **Dive type**	liveaboard

Sitting on the northwestern side of the atoll, this dive marks the edge of one of the few safe entries to the inner lagoon. The wall begins at 15 metres and slopes down to a series of canyons. The topography is quite gentle with fewer tunnels than in the south of the atoll. However, even these shallow grooves through the reef are full of life with swarms of glassfish, small neon gobies and arrow crabs sheltering inside. The sloping wall has a variety of sponges and plenty of schooling fish, plus you may glimpse a blacktip shark, eagle ray or turtle.

---

⑥ Tubular Barrels

🕐 **Depth**	22 m
◐ **Visibility**	good
🌀 **Currents**	mild to medium
⚓ **Dive type**	liveaboard

Another charming site, but on the eastern side of the atoll. The wall is shallow but covered in an amazing array of sponges – yellow tube sponges, azure vase sponges and huge barrel sponges that stand proud of the surrounding pastel-toned soft corals. All are ringed by small shoals of fish, plenty of flamingo tongue shells and arrow crabs. There are cleaning stations and a surprising number of boxfish. Bottlenose dolphins are regular visitors here and can also be seen at Wonderland a little way north.

Yellow tube sponges on Tubular Barrels

Lighthouse Reef

The reason most people give when asked why they want to dive Belize is to witness the spectacle made famous over 30 years ago by one Jacques-Yves Cousteau: the Blue Hole at Lighthouse Reef.

Just 50 miles southeast of Belize City yet the most distant of her atolls, Lighthouse Reef is only 30 miles long and eight miles wide but, despite its size, this is where you'll find the best diving in Belize. Apart from the Blue Hole National Monument,

there are great dive sites at Half Moon and Long Cayes, which are some distance away from the Blue Hole. Both cayes are ringed by impressive reefs with sharp walls cut by deep grooves and channels, caves and caverns. The sites all have a similar profile although some are backed by shelves with seagrass beds, which are perfect for stingray hunting.

The diving at Lighthouse is subject to prevailing weather conditions but even if the winds pick up from one direction, you simply move to the opposite coast. What's

more, the Blue Hole is smack-bang in the middle of it all so you'll never miss out on diving that.

Another feature is the Half Moon Caye National Monument. This small island is protected as one of only two Caribbean nesting areas for the red-footed booby: there are said to be 4,000, along with frigates and around 90 other bird species plus iguanas, lizards and loggerhead turtles. You can wander the beaches or head along the narrow nature trail to a bird-viewing platform.

↘7 Long Caye Wall	
Depth	33 m
Visibility	good to excellent
Currents	slight
Dive type	liveaboard

This reef is covered in very pretty corals, in subtle shades of beige, peach and lavender. Entry is over a sandy bed with small patchy outcrops that you swim around until you reach the wall. A promontory juts outwards from here and is covered in really impressive, five-feet-high tube sponges, with finger sponges, whips and sea fans decorating the terrain. A bevy of bright blue basslets dance around, competing with damselfish for space. Swimming back from the outer edge through the gullies you find Nassau grouper and many filefish, boxfish, creole wrasse and angels. Back under the boat, large schools of jacks, chubbs and permit fish hang out.

↘8 East Cut	
Depth	25 m
Visibility	good to great
Currents	slight to medium
Dive type	liveaboard

On this similar wall dive, entry is over a flat-topped section of the reef, which you swim across then over some large bommies until you reach an unexpected sharp drop. The wall falls down to 40 metres or so but pausing at the rim you can find juvenile drums flitting about. Marching along the wall are some of the biggest barrel sponges you will ever see, one in particular being almost two metres in diameter. Sitting around the top rim are tiny yellow arrow crabs, as well as dramatic black and grey fans. Back up on the reef plateau are the usual suspects in terms of fish life as well as a couple of small tuna patrolling back and forth along with a small turtle.

↘9 Uno Coco	
Depth	22 m
Visibility	good to excellent
Currents	slight
Dive type	liveaboard

This dive goes under a variety of names from Uno Coco to Tres Cocos depending on how many coconut palms are growing on shore at the time. A sharp wall drops from 10 to 40 metres and is smothered in life. Dense with all sorts of corals, large sponges and crusting algaes, this is perhaps the best covered reef in the area. Huge green morays congregate in a hole and crevices are thick with gangs of lobster. In fact, almost every cranny you poke your nose into has something in it. Under the boat massive tarpon hover, ever watchful of the divers. Just above them are schools of jacks and chubbs that also seem curious about their air-breathing visitors.

Lobster and tarpon are common sights on Lighthouse Reef

Central America Dive log Belize: Lighthouse Reef

⬛10 The Aquarium

🕐	**Depth**	20 m
◑	**Visibility**	great
≋	**Currents**	slight to medium
◐	**Dive type**	liveaboard

Not dissimilar to the rest of the dives along the west of the atoll, this is another very pretty wall that drops all the way down to about 60 metres. There are lots of twists and turns along the wall, which is coated with large fans, soft corals and some very big sponges surrounded by clusters of fish. Just over the edge of the reef rim, a very friendly giant barracuda hovers, keeping completely still, while watching the divers. Also on the wall are two well-known midnight parrotfish – these guys are the largest in the parrot family and grow to 75 centimetres! Angels, boxfish, porkfish, butterflies and damsels flit among the prolific corals and sponges and there are even some tunicates. If you're watching the blue, you may spot eagle rays below and heading back to the boat you'll see the ever-present swarms of jacks, snapper and chubb shadowing the hull.

⬛11 Cathedral

🕐	**Depth**	35 m
◑	**Visibility**	excellent
≋	**Currents**	slight
◐	**Dive type**	liveaboard

Although this wall is nowhere near as pretty as some of the others at Lighthouse Reef, the topography is far more interesting, with lots of cut backs and gullies in the reef to swim through. At the bottom of the wall large lobsters hide in the crevices and at certain times of year you'll notice that the females are pregnant. Coming back up the wall and swimming through the cuts you are often met head on by large mackerel trying to get out. Back on the upper section of the reef are lots of tiny roughhead blennies poking their heads up from their holes in the rocks, flamingo tongue shells sit on sea plumes, and inside miniature caves are pairs of banded coral shrimp. The bigger pelagic fish – chubbs, jacks, snapper, creole wrasse and inquisitive great barracuda – are still hanging out under the boat but this time are joined by a tarpon. Great to watch on a safety stop.

⬛12 Tarpon Cave

🕐	**Depth**	40 m
◑	**Visibility**	excellent
≋	**Currents**	slight
◐	**Dive type**	liveaboard

This dive, on the east of Lighthouse, has more fabulous topography. Entry is over a seagrass bed at eight metres which leads across an area of sand covered in conch. At 20 metres you face a barrier formation that then rises up to 15 metres. Tunnels cut through the barrier to the reef rim, leading to the outer wall and depths well over 60 metres. Swimming into one tunnel, you'll meet a five-foot tarpon, his scales metallic silver and highly reflective, just waiting to have his photo taken. A small cave further along is dark with silversides and you can watch barracuda swoop in to feed on them. Swimming along the outer wall an eagle ray passes by below then, a few seconds later, you might see a turtle. Back up on the reef top schools of black and blue tangs go crazy in the algae. The seagrass is good for spotting stingrays as they fluff up the sand, looking for food.

⬛13 Half Moon Caye Wall

🕐	**Depth**	18 m
◑	**Visibility**	excellent
≋	**Currents**	mild
◐	**Dive type**	liveaboard

Feeling fairly similar to Tarpon Cave, this site starts on a grassy bed, a sandy bed, then passes a raised rim separating the lagoon from the sea before finally dropping down to a steep wall. It's a good end-of-day dive as you can spend time over the seagrass where there are quite a few small grey rays that are always being harassed by jacks, and several much larger southern stingrays. A baby French angelfish lives in the end of a discarded pipe and keeps a squirrelfish company. A bed of manatee grass houses masses of newborn juveniles like filefish and bandtail puffers, while baby surgeonfish shelter in coconut shells.

Queen angelfish and tiny rabbitfish on Half Moon Caye

14 The Blue Hole

🌀 **Depth**	45 m
🌓 **Visibility**	fair to good
🌊 **Currents**	none
⬤ **Dive type**	liveaboard

The Blue Hole gained celebrity status after Jacques Cousteau's Calypso expedition and the following documentary series. Sitting at the midpoint of Lighthouse Reef, it was believed to be a cave whose roof collapsed at the end of the Ice Age. Now, the deep blue, circular opening is over 300 metres across and drops to around 150 metres deep. At around 40 metres an overhanging shelf is marked by ancient stalactites. As limestone can't form beneath water, and stalactites are created by fresh water dripping through limestone rock, these are evidence that the cave was once above sea level.

This is a completely unique dive and an exhilarating experience for beginners who have rarely, if ever, been to such depths. After a thorough briefing in which guides repeatedly emphasize the depth and say things like "there's more cameras on the bottom of the Hole than in all Belize", divers are led down in a vertical line to see the stalactites. The temperature drops substantially by the time you reach 45 metres and you only get a few moments to admire the stalactites and an occasional grouper before you are told it's time to ascend again.

Apart from a few fish, the dive is rather lifeless; however, operators have picked up on the fact that the area is visited by a group of grey reef sharks and now use bait to attract them. These beautiful animals circle divers during their safety stop, hoping for further handouts.

Operators advise that many divers are highly disoriented by the depth so no matter how seasoned you are, it's sensible to stick close to your buddy and a decent carabiner (or d-clip) may be a good idea for your cameras and torches.

Into the Blue

As a relatively new diver I had heard stories about the Blue Hole. I got the opportunity to dive the site this past June. The mystery, the obscurity, the unknown that surrounds this gigantic former cave that sits off the coast of Belize had aroused my curiosity.

Then came the day of the dive. The excitement built as I donned my tank and rolled backwards off the tender into the depths. Then the enigma became a reality when all 16 of us had to descend in a large circle in unison, the DM clanging on his tank constantly to keep everyone together. "What is this?" I asked myself; "an exercise in descending to 130 feet and then ascending slowly?" Where were the sea monsters? Where were the flashing lights, or the massive surge that would carry me to unknown depths, never to be seen again?

No corals, no fish, no reef creatures. Only a few overfed, lethargic sharks and groupers waiting for the next batch of divers to descend into its depths.
Phil Tobin, diamond broker, Portland, USA

❝❞ **There's no doubt about it – this dive is a serious adrenaline rush. It's all to do with the drop to depth and, quite probably, the excitement building up to the dive as much as actually doing it.**

Central America Dive log Belize: The Blue Hole

Roatán

The largest of the Bay Islands at 58 kilometres long but less than eight wide, Roatán is also the best known and busiest island as it has an international airport. Sitting in the middle of the group, this is a great place to start a two-centre trip due to a highly developed tourism infrastructure, many good hotels and dive resorts plus a strong US influence.

The centre of the island is jungle-bound and quite lush, with hills falling steeply to the sea. The coast is ringed by palm-clad sandy beaches, riddled with tiny cayes and mangroves and studded by deep water inlets called blights. It was these that gave birth to the island's notorious history. A safe haven for boats, they were used by huge numbers of pirate ships.

Several colonial powers roamed these waters during the 16th century, their traders all fighting for possession of huge tracts of valuable hardwoods. Eventually, the traders left for more lucrative shores and Roatán was taken over by the pirates of the Caribbean including the infamous Briton, Henry Morgan (but no Johnny Depp, sadly). The pirates were incredibly well organized and built many sophisticated fortifications to defend the island. It wasn't until the 1740s that a combined Spanish army and navy offensive removed them. However, the British legacy remains in place and is evident in both the use of English and in the names of the island's towns and inhabitants.

Roatán has quite a variety of diving. A barrier reef, which sits just below the surface, rings the entire island a short way offshore. Inside this reef a protected lagoon has calm and comfortable diving, while outside, especially in the south, there are steep walls, fissures, overhangs and ledges. Northern coastal sites tend to be gentler with sloping walls and reefs, but right around the island conditions are similar.

⑮ Calvin's Crack

🕐 **Depth**	30 m
◑ **Visibility**	good
〰 **Currents**	mild
☁ **Dive type**	day boat

Rather like a game of follow the leader, this dive involves a quick drop down to the reef top plateau at about 15 metres before descending into a sharp crack in the reef. The divemaster then shepherds his group together, pauses by the reef rim and waves to an enormous green moray who is watching the morning's divers. Suddenly the leader simply drops out of sight. Divers file after him in turn, swimming through the dimly lit, narrow passageway and past gigantic, metre-wide mithrax crabs, which huddle into the cracks. A few lobsters wave a claw at the passing intruders until everyone exits from the tunnel at 27 metres. A slight current runs on the wall so you drift with it and admire the huge fan corals, which are displaying their fluffy feeding tentacles.

⑯ Valley of the Kings

🕐 **Depth**	32 m
◑ **Visibility**	good
〰 **Currents**	mild
☁ **Dive type**	day boat

This is one of the more impressive walls along the south coast as it seems to have some of the biggest corals and sponges in the area. Fan corals wave over the top of overhangs, competing for attention with azure vase sponges and amazingly long red and pink rope sponges. There are also some small black coral bushes. Winding their way through them are black and white spotted morays and a lot of the reef fish that are typical of these waters. French angelfish and boxfish are common and tend to follow divers. The relatively rare sargassam triggerfish can be spotted on occasion while there are striped snapper everywhere you look. The top of the reef here rises up to five metres in places so this can be a good snorkelling site as long as there is no current.

The inimitable longsnout seahorse on Forty Foot Wall; inside the wreck of the *Prince Albert*

⚓17 CocoView Bay and Wall

🧭 **Depth**	32 m
🔆 **Visibility**	poor to good
🌊 **Currents**	none to slight
🌀 **Dive type**	day boat

CocoView Resort sits on a tiny private caye that nestles in a shallow part of the lagoon. A channel leads from the beach to outside the reef and the lagoon has virtually been turned into a diving theme park – but don't be put off by that. This is both a great dive and snorkelling location. Just off the beach is a partly submerged kitting-up table, where you haul on your fins and then drop to your knees. A heavy chain on the sea floor leads away from the table, past partly submerged jawfish, shrimp and upside-down jellyfish to the wreck of the *Prince Albert*. This 47-metre long island freighter is upright and pretty much intact, with lots of coral growing on the structure. You can swim through the open holds and around the decks. When visibility is good you can see her entire length and, as one end is just seven metres deep, snorkellers can too. Heading off to one side, another chain leads from the bow to the fuselage of a DC3 aeroplane with pufferfish and octopus huddling in its remains. There are also two diveable walls on either side of the channel. These attract some schooling fish plus colourful rabbitfish, parrotfish and rock beauties. Divers (and snorkellers) need to be a little careful near the walls due to dive boat traffic. As you head back to shallow waters keep your eyes on the seagrass beds for flounder. Visibility in the lagoon can be poor in the rainy season, due to run-off and tides.

A juvenile spotted drum

⚓18 Forty Foot Wall

🧭 **Depth**	22 m
🔆 **Visibility**	good
🌊 **Currents**	mild
🌀 **Dive type**	day boat

Not very imaginatively named, this wall drops from about 25 feet to – you guessed it – 40 feet. The outer wall has some good sponges and soft corals with schools of snapper and spadefish. However, the big attraction here are the patches of coralline algae covering the top level of the reef. Hidden in amongst the bright green carpet are longsnout seahorses. These beautiful animals are not easy to spot though. There are also jacks, lobster, crabs and goodness knows what else, but who cares when you have just discovered one of these most beautiful of endangered creatures.

⚓19 Wreck of the Captain G

🧭 **Depth**	22 m
🔆 **Visibility**	good
🌊 **Currents**	mild
🌀 **Dive type**	day boat

Not far from French Harbour, this dive has a slightly different profile from much of the coast. The bay is shallow and slopes gently down from a few metres deep until it reaches a steeper wall. Just off the edge are the remains of a shrimping boat. She is quite broken up but the mast and rigging give the general shape. Lots of little marine animals hide in amongst the decaying remains. There is a lot of coral and sponges in the surrounding area. Large groupers, tuna, giant barracuda, turtles and plenty of schooling fish are spied as they swing past quite frequently.

🐟 Making friends with a moray

Early in our diving days we headed to Anthony's Key Resort, on Roatán. In the briefing for our daytime dive on Overheat Reef, divemaster Emilio informed us that he would be doing a controlled feeding of the two resident green morays, and that the eels might swim up to us in search of food. Don't be afraid, just put your hands in your armpits, OK?

A novice diver named Juanita from Toronto appeared to take it all in her stride. Sure enough, when we reached the bottom at 55 feet, two big, free-swimming eels were already patrolling for a handout. We settled to our knees on the sandy bottom, hands safely tucked away as instructed. Emilio pulled fish scraps from a plastic bag he carried in his pocket and the morays circled him and snapped up the pieces. Emilio quickly ran out of fish and showed the eels two open palms (the international signal for 'all gone'). But the eels were still looking hungry. And looking for more food: in BC pockets, between our legs, sniffing around our heads. It was comical (in retrospect), the sight of big, toothy eels tangled in the fins of divers wriggling out of their way with armpit-holstered hands, trying to appear calm.

This happy mayhem was interrupted for everyone at the same instant, heads turning in unison towards the direction of a gurgly scream. Juanita was bolting for the surface, a big moray having invaded her personal space. Her husband gave a powerful kick and, releasing one (and only one) hand from its under-arm shelter, stretched out and snared her ankle at the last possible moment. Having puffed all of our air, we headed for the surface as a group in an orderly fashion. You can have your thoughts about the wisdom of feeding underwater animals but don't let anybody call it 'controlled'.

David Barr, research consultant, Falcon, Western Australia

Head 30 nautical miles southwest from Roatán and you'll reach Utila, an island that is completely different in character to her bigger neighbour. Utila is as flat as Roatán is hilly and while Roatán has attained a certain level of sophistication, with its influx of tourism development, Utila retains a charming air of casual chaos.

From the moment you set foot on the airstrip (no terminal, no check-in desks, no luggage handler) you realise that this is one chilled-out little place. A favourite with long-term travellers and hikers, the small town centre has retained much of its original character. It is a rather haphazard affair with just one main road that sweeps around the bay, connecting restaurants, shops, small hotels and more dive centres than you could possibly wave your kit bag at.

Utila sits on the edge of the continental shelf so the diving is a little different to Roatán. On the south side, where the town is situated, the dives are shallow – rarely over 25 metres – but there are lots of interesting cracks and crevices along the reef walls which have created overhangs, swim throughs and sand channels to investigate. While the marine species are naturally similar to Roatán, there seems to be far more critter life. On the north side of the island, the reefs are more dramatic, with steep walls and drop-offs. However, this side is affected by weather conditions, so you may not get up there as much as you would like. It is also recognized as a whaleshark highway and there are regular sightings in the dry season.

↘20 Great Wall (Duppy Waters)

🕐 **Depth**	36 m	
◑ **Visibility**	very good	
≋ **Currents**	none to medium	
🌊 **Dive type**	day boat	

Just outside Turtle Harbour on the north of the island is one the most spectacular dives on Utila. A sharp slope descends quickly to a wall that feels like it drops off into infinity. Certainly you can't see the bottom. The slope is covered in corals and sponges and many leopard morays reside amongst them. As you go over the reef lip there are huge fan corals and giant barrel sponges reaching out into the sea. Fish hovering in the blue include jacks, creole wrasse, great barracuda and occasional turtles. Back up on the top of the reef there are plenty of juvenile fish plus grey angels, Townsend angels and damsels, and scorpionfish hiding under the soft corals. As the dive boats head back to the south coast they are often accompanied by a pod of dolphins.

↘21 Aquarium I & II

🕐 **Depth**	16 m	
◑ **Visibility**	fair to good	
≋ **Currents**	mild	
🌊 **Dive type**	day boat	

The coastal landscape on Utila's eastern end has jagged volcanic rock formations, which can be seen both above and below the waterline. The two Aquarium sites are quite shallow and great for exploring these unusual formations. Caves and overhangs have been carved by centuries of crashing waves, leaving chimneys and blowholes in the coastal strip above. Sitting in relatively calm water, you can watch the powerful wave action continuing its work. Inside the caves, if you look down, are some very interesting creatures like mantis shrimp, trunkfish and the greater soapfish. A little deeper are large garden beds of pastel-hued swaying soft corals, whips and sea plumes. Hiding amongst their fronds are flutemouths and parrotfish, banded jawfish and peacock flounders.

↘22 Ted's Point

🕐 **Depth**	23 m	
◑ **Visibility**	good	
≋ **Currents**	mild	
🌊 **Dive type**	day boat	

Just outside East Harbour on the south coast is this fantastic night dive. A sloping sand patch leads down to the remains of a small sailboat that is covered in sponges and tunicates. If you know what you're looking for you may find the very tiny, nocturnal cryptic teardrop crab sitting on a sponge. They are always there but they take some spotting! Flamingo tongue shells feed on the soft corals and neon gobies rest on sponges. There are Pederson cleaner shrimps living on their corkscrew anemone hosts and lots of other night crustaceans. Another curious find is the swollen claw mantis, a tiny chap just five or six centimetres long.

Juvenile slender filefish hiding on a whip coral; swimming through a crack on Silver Garden

N23 Halliburton Wreck

🌀	**Depth**	30 m
◑	**Visibility**	poor to good
🌊	**Currents**	mild to medium
🌀	**Dive type**	day boat

This 30-metre-long cargo ship was sunk in May 1998 to create an artificial reef. She sits upright on the seabed near the lighthouse at the edge of East Harbour and catches the tides and murk from the bay. Visibility is low but the flow of nutrients is aiding coral growth. The wreck is marked by two buoys – one is attached to the bow at 20 metres, which is a good place to start. As you descend you see new corals decorating the hold while a few large grouper hang below the bow. You can then swim around the hull or through a few openings until you reach the wheelhouse. A bicycle is locked to the rail outside and snappers hover inside unless disturbed. A giant green moray often slithers around. Finally, ascend up the second mooring line for a safety stop.

N24 Silver Garden

🌀	**Depth**	26 m
◑	**Visibility**	good
🌊	**Currents**	mild to medium
🌀	**Dive type**	day boat

The garden is really a shallow reef sitting on a sandy shelf and marked by lots of small channels. These lead down to the reef edge where a steeper drop-off reveals several stands of hard corals that are in good condition. A large school of horse-eye jacks seems to continually hang off the wall, interspersed with another school of creole wrasse – the males chasing after the females. Giant green morays lurk in the crevices in the reef and slender filefish try to camouflage themselves against seawhips. Up in the shallows are lots of juvenile fish like blennies and harlequin pipefish. This site is also a really good snorkelling area as it's calm and protected.

❖ Winds of change

When it comes to the rest of the Bay Islands, despite their charm and beauty it's hard to tell if they should be listed in a guide like this or not. Those that love Cayos Cochinos – the Hog Islands – and the larger island of Guanaja will be up in arms already, but both places fall a little behind Roatán and Utila for several reasons.

The two islands and 13 cayes that make up **Cayos Cochinos** are the closest to the mainland, 17 kilometres away, and are protected as a marine reserve. For divers, the shallow barrier reef is regarded as the macro capital of the area and is a haven for some of the rarer sea creatures in this region. In the past, Cochinos attracted the backpacker set who could stay very cheaply in the one local village – but always complained bitterly about the no-see-um population. There is now just one resort, which is highly eco-orientated, but that's about it. There is no doubt that the islands are idyllic and unspoilt and those who love them do so with a passion.

East from Roatán is the island of **Guanaja**. Christened by Christopher Columbus the 'Island of Pines', she is more mountainous and highly undeveloped. There are almost no roads, although the airport does have a tarmac runway, and very little of anything else. Most residents live in the capital, Bonacca, which is spread across two tiny cayes and completely covered by houses. When someone wants to build a new home, they erect it on stilts over the water – in front of a neighbour – and the cayes grow further out to sea, almost by the day. Guanaja also bore the full brunt of 1998's Hurricane Mitch when this humdinger of a storm swept across the Bay Islands. Most of its famous pine trees were swept away and the reefs on the southern side of the island took a battering. Despite the damage, the marine world picked itself up and is regenerating nicely. The corals may be less impressive than around the rest of the Bay Islands but you can easily spot over 100 different species of fish. However, despite the reef's will to live, business never quite recovered and the nice resort that was there eventually closed down. For several years there were just two other resorts, both somewhat rustic, but in 2007 a third opened.

If you are looking for a real getaway, Cayos Cochinos or Guanaja may well be for you. Everyone else heads for livelier Roatán and Utila.

The delightful cryptic teardrop crab is a decorator crab, but just 12-18 mm wide

Drying out

Belize

Belize City

Dive Centres

Hugh Parkey's Belize Dive Connection, T+501 (0)223 4526, belizediving.com. Day trip diving from the marina at Fort George (below) and also at Spanish Lookout Caye.

Sleeping

$$ Radisson Fort George Hotel and Marina, T+501 (0)223 3333, radisson.com/belizecity.bz. All the facilities of an international style resort with a pool and good restaurant. Conveniently located at Fort George Marina where Star Dancer is based.

$ Villa Boscardi, 6043 Manatee Drive, T+501 (0)223 1691, villaboscardi.com.

Liveaboards

Peter Hughes Star Dancer II, T+1 (1)305 669 9391, PeterHughes.com. Top-class vessel with good service from the friendly crew, great cabins, spacious dive deck, nitrox, cordon bleu meals and all drinks included in the price.

Eating

Most restaurants in Belize City are linked to hotels, although there are lots of small cafés, mostly Chinese-run. Ask your hotel reception for recommendations.

Spanish Lookout Caye

Sleeping and diving

$$ Spanish Bay Conservation & Research Center, spanishbayresort.com. T+501 (0)223 4526. Small resort near Belize City with a strong focus on marine research.

Peter Hughes Sun Dancer, Half Moon Caye and the view from the Swing Bridge in Belize City

---

Belize

Although slightly overshadowed by her neighbour's land attractions, Belize still has plenty of interesting things to do.

Belize City The former capital is divided in two by Haulover Creek: the halves are connected by the Swing Bridge, the only manually swung bridge in the world still in operation. To its north, the Fort George area includes the City Museum (US$5 entry), the National Handicrafts centre and Memorial Park. Cross south over the bridge to the commercial centre, St John's Cathedral – the oldest Anglican church in Central America – and the Baron Bliss Institute (the cultural centre).

Caye Caulker If you're not staying here, this extremely laid-back island is worth a visit. The town is just one main road and lots of sandy lanes with cafés and shops in pretty clapboard houses. In the north, there are mangroves and forests, with walking trails and good birdwatching. Water taxis from the Swing Bridge take 45 minutes and cost US$17.50 return.

Ambergris Caye Bigger and brasher than Caye Caulker, this much more developed island has a museum and cultural centre, lots of hotels, restaurants and bars. There are Maya remains dotted around but they can be hard to find. Visit Little Iguana and Rosario Cayes for birdwatching while at San Pedro Lagoon you might spot racoons and crocodiles. For nightowls, or those who like to do more than just dive, this is a good place to be based. Water taxis leave from the Swing Bridge and take about 75 minutes, US$27.50 return.

Cockscomb Basin Wildlife Sanctuary About two hours south of Belize City, in the shadow of the Maya Mountains, 100,000 acres of tropical forest rise from sea level to the summit of Victoria Peak. Originally established in 1984 to protect a large jaguar population, there are plenty of birds and beautiful flora but the chances of seeing a jaguar or any other local wild-cat, is slim. Around US$60 for a day tour.

Altún Ha Just 1 hr north of Belize City, this Maya city (Altún Ha means 'Rockstone Pond') dates from around 250 BC and was a major ceremonial and trading centre. An impressive carved jade head representing the sun god, Kinich Ahau, was found here. Day trips from US$50.

Half Moon Caye National Monument You are only likely to see the amazing birdlife on this protected island if you are on a liveaboard, see page 307.

Tikal Regarded as the most important of all the Maya archaeological sites, Tikal is just over the border in Guatemala, deep in the Petén jungle. There are dozens of stone temples and palaces, some dating from 300 BC, though the main buildings were built between AD 500 and AD 900. You can arrange a tour from Belize City or fly to Santa Elena and stay overnight in Tikal's twin town of Flores, perched on a tiny island in Lake Petén Itzá. Check out the **Tropic Air** website (tropicair.com) for day and overnight tours.

🛏	**Sleeping**	**$$$** US$150+ double room per night		**$$** US$75-150	**$** under US$75
🍴	**Eating**	**$$$** US$40+ 2-course meal, excluding drinks		**$$** US$20-40	**$** under US$20

Turneffe Atoll

Sleeping and Diving

Full-service dive resorts are located at:

$$ Blackbird Caye Resort, T+1 (1)206 463 0833, blackbirdresort.com.

$ Turneffe Flats Lodge, T+1 (1)623 298 2783, tflats.com.

Honduras

Roatán

Sleeping and diving

$$ Anthony's Key Resort, northwest coast, anthonyskey.com. One of the founding resorts with masses of activities including a dolphin encounter programme, marine research facility and many others. Meals and diving included in weekly package rates of around US$150 per day.

$$ CocoView Resort, on a small private caye half way along the south coast, T+504 455 7500, cocoviewresort.com. Club-style resort which attracts a lot of US groups. All meals and diving are included in weekly package rates of around US$130 per day. Plus the bay is definitely the best shore dive on the island.

$$ Inn of Last Resort, 5 mins from the town of West End, T+504 445 4108, innoflastresort.com. Wooden bungalows on the beach; useful for short stays.

Utila

Sleeping and diving

$$ Laguna Beach Resort, utila.com. Packages at around US$130 per night.

$$ Utila Lodge, utilalodge.com. Right in town and built on a series of jetties over the bay. Simple but nice rooms and great views at sunset. Good dive operation with an on-site school. The Shark Research Institute, also based here, runs seasonal whaleshark field trips. General packages including diving and all meals at around US$130 per night.

Honduras

The Bay Islands are not renowned for their cultural attractions despite their colourful pirate past. However, one of the most spectacular Maya sites lies at Copán, near the border with Guatemala.

Copán Ruinas One of the least known of the Maya sites, yet one of the best to visit, Copán has many exquisitely carved 'stellae', which tell tales from Maya history, and some extremely well-preserved temples.

Archaeologists are constantly discovering new sections, one of the latest being some hidden tombs. You can walk through the tunnels beneath the impressive ruins and visit the new museum where some of the more fragile finds have been displayed. Copán town is also very pretty with cobbled streets, plenty of restaurants and shops. Tours from the Bay Islands run at around US$250 for two days and one night.

Pico Bonito Cloud Forest Across from the Bay Islands, on the Honduran coast are the towering Nombre de Dios mountains. Rising to 2700 metres, they are nearly always swathed in clouds, created when cool mountain air meets warmer temperatures at the coast. Spend some time exploring the forest and spot one of the 325 known bird species. Hike through the park and, if you are lucky, see a jaguar or puma, tapir, deer or white-faced and spider monkeys. There is a splendid lodge converted from an old chocolate plantation – the cocoa pods hang over your door – and they say that big cats have been known to sit on guest's terraces.

The Lodge at Pico Bonito, picobonito.com. Rooms start at US$155 and packages are great value.

Roatán Many cruise ships dock here so there are lots of organized activities. You can go horseriding or white-water rafting, visit an iguana or butterfly farm or go sailing for a day. Tours get busy when the visiting liners disgorge their passengers.

West End For a bit of retail therapy head down to the island's small main town. It's under a mile from end to end but has plenty of restaurants and gift shops.

Carambola Nature Reserve Walk up Carambola Peak for fabulous views over the island; hike the nature trails to see orchids, growing spices and mahogany trees. Iguana Wall on the cliff side is a protected zone for iguanas and parrots.

Oak Ridge A true Caribbean fishing village, where you can imagine what life might have been like back in the pirate days. Most buildings are built over the water and the locals get about by boat.

Utila There's not a huge amount to do on Utila although there are organized hikes to see the rock formations at Iron Bound or up through the small patch of forest at Pumpkin Hill. There's an iguana breeding station, some horseback riding and seasonal whaleshark spotting. Apart from that, wander along the main road for drinks at a sunset bar or investigate the excellent handicraft shops.

Honduran parrot; looking over a Roatán lagoon at Oak Ridge; the Maya ruins at Copan.

Gone but not forgotten: although no
longer serving her original purpose,
the *Shakem* is still hard at work.
The Shakem, Quarantine Point, Grenada

ST. LUCIA

St. Vincent Passage

St. Vincent

● KINGSTOWN

ST. VINCENT AND THE GRENADINES

Mustique

Union Island

↘1 Grenada   ▶▶ p324

Caribbean Sea

Grenada

● ST. GEORGE'S

Grand Anse

True Blue Bay

Glovers Island

Atlantic Ocean

↘8

↘9

↘7

↘4   ↘6

↘3   ↘5

↘2

↘1

↘1 Fisherman's Paradise/Kapsis
↘2 Blackforest
↘3 Bianca C
↘4 Purple Rain
↘5 Whibbles
↘6 Shakem
↘7 Veronica
↘8 Happy Valley
↘9 Molinere Bay

↘2

Carriacou

GRENADA

Caribbean Sea

ST. GEORGE'S ●   Grenada

↘1 ✈

Grenada Channel

↘2 Carriacou   ▶▶ p329

Jack Adams Island

↘14   ↘15

↘12

↘13

↘10

Mabouya

Sandy Island

HILLSBOROUGH ●

TOBA

SCARBOROU

Caribbean Sea

↘11

↘10 Divers Surprise
↘11 Sister Rocks
↘12 Sharky's Hideaway
↘13 Sharky's Extension
↘14 Magic Garden
↘15 Twin Tugs

✈

Carriacou

TRINIDAD

● PORT OF SPAIN

✈

VENEZUELA

Nutmeg and cinnamon, chocolate and rum, bougainvillaea, bananas, mockingbirds, mona monkeys. The three islands that form the nation of Grenada are an assault on the senses. Tantalized by the tastes, sights and colours of the landscapes and their surrounding seas, this tiny Caribbean country is a visual feast

While all this – and more – attracts travellers to Grenada's shores, what attracts divers are the multitude of shipwrecks that lie below the surface of the shallow seas. Tales from the past linked to these sunken ships have made this a diving destination that stands apart from her near neighbours. And there is another dive feature that is unparalleled in the region, or indeed in the world: the Molinere Bay Sculpture Park. This manmade addition to the marine realm is a rare and unusual treat. Of course, there are coral reefs, but typically of the Caribbean Sea, these create a muted backdrop to the vessels that rest amongst them.

Back on dry land, terrestrial and marine vistas are complemented by a rich history and vibrant culture. Local towns, festivals and markets are unmissable and easily justify any time spent away from the sea.

BARBADOS
BRIDGETOWN

Atlantic Ocean

15 km

Grenada rating

Diving
★★★

Dive facilities
★★★

Accommodation
★★★

Down time
★★★

Value for money
★★★

Essentials

Getting there and around

Despite it having a large, modern airport, flights from other continents to Grenada are not all that frequent. Reaching the island may require a little pre-planning or flying via another Caribbean destination. There are direct flights from the UK and US with scheduled airlines such as British Airways (ba.com), Virgin (virgin-atlantic.com) and American Eagle (aa.com). Flights tend to run once or twice weekly. Various charter schedules supplement these, such as Monarch (flights.monarch.co.uk) and Air Canada (aircanada.com), while Caribbean Airlines (caribbean-airlines.com) and Air Jamaica (airjamaica.com) will get you there using connections on regional carrier LIAT (liatairline.com). From Grenada, you can fly to Carriacou with SVG Air (svgair.com) who also fly across much of the east Caribbean.

From the airport, you will need to take a taxi to your hotel. Transfers are rarely included unless you have booked a package through a tour operator. Hotels will arrange a taxi to be waiting for you though, so simply email in advance.

Travelling around Grenada isn't difficult as there is a network of small vans and mini-buses. Because these don't run to a regular schedule, many people find they end up using taxis frequently. The cost of these is comparatively high so you may want to consider car hire. Again, this is not the cheapest option but if you want to see more of the interior of these beautiful islands than you can achieve in a day trip, it is worth it.

Getting to the islands of Carriacou and Petit Martinique is easy though, with a fast and efficient inter-island ferry service run by Osprey Lines (ospreylines.com).

Local laws and customs

Grenada is an easy-going island where the influences of tourism are well noted in the area around the airport – residents refer to this as the 'tourist belt'. Normal, courteous standards of behaviour and neat dress codes are all that is required. One unusual restriction is that it is actually against the law to dress in camouflage clothing.

Carriacou is far quieter and even more laid-back than Grenada, but both islands are fairly religious with a plethora of Christian churches. Homosexuality is frowned upon, and some acts are against the law. Female travellers may also be amused (or amazed) by the chauvinistic views of the local men.

Note that there are severe penalties for any drug-related offences.

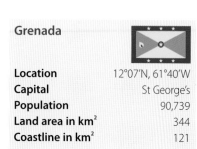

Grenada	
Location	12°07'N, 61°40'W
Capital	St George's
Population	90,739
Land area in km²	344
Coastline in km²	121

Carriacou's capital, Hillsborough

Safety

Generally, these islands are regarded as safe, although there are some tales of petty crimes. Use the safety deposit box in your room and don't go walking about at night with too much cash.

Language

Despite the islands' history of Arawak and Carib Amerindian tribes and later French colonization, English is the national language. You will also hear the locals talking to each other in a creole patois, and many place names are French, but no one will speak to you in anything but beautifully enunciated English.

Health

Medical facilities on the islands are varied, with historic hospitals and a world-renowned medical university, yet expats say that many local services are a little behind the times. The good news is that there are no specific inoculations required, nor any malaria, but there are a lot of mosquitoes so take plenty of repellent. The sun can be scorching too, yet cooling Atlantic breezes mean you may not notice. Be sure to stay hydrated (tap water is drinkable in most hotels) and well stocked chemists are easy to find.

Costs

With much of the local economy linked to the USA (the US dollar is legal tender and accepted as frequently as the East Caribbean dollar), some travellers may find these islands expensive. Thinking about budgets, regard costs as being similar to London, Sydney or San Francisco. You may not spend quite that much, but at least you will have enough cash with you. A simple meal of burger and chips will be about US$15, a fancier meal will easily triple that. Soft drinks and bottled water are pricey but the local brew, Carib, is reasonable at about US$2 a bottle. Wine too is surprisingly good value with many imported Chilean wines. In a supermarket, a decent bottle can be just US$6. As nearly all hotel rooms have a fridge, you can stock up for sunset drinks on your balcony. Alternatively, it is fairly common for hotels to offer all-inclusive packages and these can be great value, especially as there is not a huge variety of independent restaurants. Those that are may require a taxi ride to reach them. Taxi rates within the Grenada tourist belt range from US$10-20 so can add up. Friendly drivers are often willing to discount if you use them several times so always ask for a business card.

Service charges and taxes in hotels and better restaurants will add 18% to your bills. Tipping is not expected in the smaller establishments but much appreciated – add around 10% on a meal. For dive staff see page 12. Many operations ask that you leave a tip with the shop to be divided equally amongst the crew.

Tourist information → The government website can be found at grenadagrenadines.com. Or contact in the UK: T+44 208 877 4516; US: T+1 561 588 8176; Canada: T+1 416 595 1339 Dive operators are at grenadascubadivingassociation.com.

Fact file

International flights	American Airlines, Air Canada, Air Jamaica, British Airways, Caribbean Airlines, Monarch, Virgin
Departure tax	US$20
Entry	Not usually required
Internal flights	SVG Air
Ground transport	Taxis, inter-island ferries, mini-buses
Money	US$1 = 2.6 Eastern Caribbean dollars (XCD)
Language	English
Electricity	240v, plug type B (see page 16)
Time zone	GMT -4
Religion	All Christian religions are represented
Phone	Country code +1473; IDD code 11; Police 911

A bright orange seahorse on Blackforest dive site

Grenada Essentials

Dive brief

Diving

Although it formed millions of years ago, the Caribbean Sea is regarded as one of the youngest on the planet. Enclosed on three sides by the American continents, its eastern edge is denoted by a moon-shaped arc of islands. These were once gigantic mountain ranges separating a basin of land from the developing Atlantic Ocean. When sea levels rose the area flooded, forming a warm and shallow sea.

Grenada and the Grenadines sit at the very bottom of the island chain and are divided from South America by the deep water Grenada Channel. Oceanic currents and strong winds force their way into the Caribbean by passing through this channel, influencing both daily weather patterns and diving conditions.

All the islands' eastern coastlines are rugged: there are coral reefs but these are battered by the surf and rarely in good condition although larger animals can be seen when conditions allow. On the other hand, travel across to the western side of the islands and you would hardly know you were in the same place. Here, reefs drop away from delightful white sand beaches and are coated with sponges and corals.

The marine topography is a mix of sloping walls and patch reefs divided by sandy-bottomed gullies.

What makes these islands a special treat for divers are the shipwrecks. Often promoted as the Caribbean's Wreck Capital, there are plenty to explore. Some are of dubious history – cargo ships impounded on their way up from South America (no prizes for guessing the cargo) sit by small sailing yachts that came to grief on the shallow reefs during a storm. Then there is surely the Caribbean's most unique dive feature, an underwater sculpture park.

Diving is year round but scheduled according to seasons and prevailing wind patterns. Some suggest that the best time is from July to November when the water is cooler. During this period there is an event of note: it is the rainy season in Venezuela and huge quantities of fresh water flow from the delta of the Orinoco River and move northeast. Rich in nutrients, this passes through the Grenada Channel and into the Caribbean. It lasts a few weeks and is great for the marine life despite messing up the visibility for a short time.

Snorkelling

There are plenty of shallow reefs that are great for surface huggers – even for divers, very little of anything is beyond 25 metres – with several small marine reserves and the sculpture park being the best options.

Marine life

Having formed in isolation from the other parts of the world's oceans, the quantity of marine species in the Caribbean is far lower. Yet again, the currents come into play, ensuring that a continual supply of plankton feeds these young reefs and the animals that live on them. Typically of these waters, you are virtually guaranteed an encounter with a great barracuda. Large schools of creole wrasse are a given; turtles are about but always small; nurse sharks and southern stingrays are seen at times and there are just a few unusual critters like whitenose pipefish.

Vase sponges at Happy Valley

Grenada
animal
encounters

Grenada
Carriacou

barracudas
nurse sharks

Finning along a murky, sandy-bottomed channel, then suddenly stumbling upon a solitary man working at his typewriter, is a particularly strange underwater encounter. We had seen images of the sculpture park, but even they didn't quite prepare us: unusual doesn't describe it, bizarre is getting close. It may be unorthodox but it is surprisingly good fun.

Making the big decision

So many of the Caribbean islands can be regarded as similar in a lot of ways. They are all pretty and ringed by lovely turquoise water with hidden coral reefs. Access is fairly straightforward, facilities are usually good and there are dive centres all over. All that, along with the fact that the marine life is consistent no matter which one you might find the most appealing, and suddenly choosing a single destination can seem very confusing.

What makes Grenada and Carriacou stand apart from their neighbours is, without doubt, the extensive array of shipwrecks around their shores. When the conditions are right, you can explore a new one almost every day and each one will have its own unique tale to tell. Combine these two contrasting islands as a two-centre holiday and you will definitely find a Caribbean destination with a difference.

Juvenile French angelfish

Dive data

Seasons	The dry season runs from January to May. The rainy season runs from June to December which is also hurricane season
Visibility	Varies according to location and season, from 5-25 metres with an average of 20 metres
Temperatures	Air 24-30°C; water 25-29°C
Wet suit	3 mm full body suit, 5 mm in winter
Training	Courses available everywhere
Nitrox	Available in most dive centres
Deco chambers	Barbados and Trinidad

Bottom time

Grenada		**The most southerly of the Windward Islands, this independent nation includes Grenada, the largest and most populated island, and two smaller ones known as the Grenadines: Carriacou and Petit Martinique. Between these lie a scattering of smaller islands and rocky pinnacles, evidence of their volcanic origin. Mountainous, and with a range of impressive natural attractions, they were regarded for a long time as being outside the hurricane belt, until Ivan and Emily reeked havoc in 2004 and 2005 respectively.**
Grenada	▸▸ p324	The busiest, liveliest and most modern of the islands, Grenada's long and colourful history is the perfect foil for the many shallow reefs that encapsulate her shores and are home to a cluster of famed shipwrecks.
Carriacou	▸▸ p329	Retaining much more of the idealised tropical Caribbean atmosphere, this tiny island feels like a step back in time. Plus a few freshly scuttled ships are giving Grenada a run for her money.

Diversity reef area <100 km²

HARD CORALS	
	25
FISH SPECIES	
	495
ENDEMIC FISH SPECIES	
	0
FISH UNDER THREAT	
	17
PROTECTED REEFS/MARINE PARKS	
	2

All diversity figures are approximate

Grenada

An island of contrasts, Grenada swaps from being an ultra-modern young nation to a laid-back location, from a lush and green tropical paradise to rugged and weather-worn terrain, and all without blinking an eyelid. It all depends on what side of the island you are on.

Grenada measures just 18 x 34 kilometres, but the majority of its tourist facilities are based around the toe of land that extends from the southwestern corner. This is where you will find all the main landmarks of note: the capital St George's, the most famous beach on the island, Grand Anse, the international airport at Point Salines and the bays of the southern coast. Known as the tourist belt, the area is by no means an indiction of the incredibly beautiful, mountainous interior but it is where all the dives sites are.

Jutting into both the Caribbean and the Atlantic, this small area has an abundance of dive sites. Those tucked inside Grand Anse Bay and just to the north are ideal for all levels of divers. The reefs are shallow and the water is calm and protected. There are many wrecks and some of them sit at depth, but here 'deep' is easily within sport diving limits. As they say on the island, if you wanted to go any deeper you would need a shovel. Around the corner on the south coast the reefs are subject to strong ocean currents from the Atlantic so dive site visits are restricted by daily conditions.

↘1 Fisherman's Paradise/Kapsis	
🧭 **Depth**	19 m
🌓 **Visibility**	poor to fair
🌊 **Currents**	strong
🌓 **Dive type**	day boat

South west from the point of the island, this dive site sits right in the currents that flow to and from the Atlantic. The water can get choppy and the currents are rarely still. Dropping in you find a long shallow reef that leads to a small wall. You can drift along this for a while, watching the small caverns and crevices for red squirrelfish and juvenile angels until the divemaster indicates to go up and over the reef. This means you will be swimming back into the current for a while but you soon reach an elbow in the reef where there is an outboard motor covered in coral and sponges. Just around the bend are the remains of a sailing yacht, the *Kapsis*. She went down in Hurricane Ivan and is quite broken up but the shape of the hull is still distinct. The part of the wreck that attracts the most attention though is the toilet – sitting proudly on the starboard side, it is completely intact and with the seat flapping up and down in the current. A very amusing sight! After this, the dive continues to a deep archway that leads through the reef. You can swim through it, admiring the fantastic amount of snowy white soft corals that coat every surface.

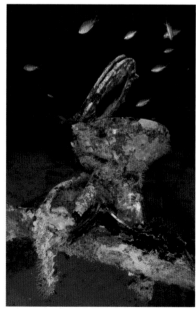

The 'talking head' on the *Kapsis*

Blackforest

Depth	26 m
Visibility	fair
Currents	slight
Dive type	day boat

One of the most indicative reefs on the outer edge of the Grand Anse bay region, Blackforest is a long, gently sloping drop that is covered in a variety of sponges, seaplumes and, of course, many black fan corals. These stand proud of the reef in rows like small trees in a young forest. It's all pretty enough and a very calm dive until you get near to the end. At about 14 metres one small area is suddenly alive with a huge lobster running about waving its antennae and several curious, free-swimming spotted moray eels. One of the local divemasters knows the location of a gigantic seahorse. It is a real beauty and heavily pregnant.

Bianca C

Depth	38 m
Visibility	poor to fair
Currents	slight
Dive type	day boat

The most famous dive on Grenada has to be the wreck of this huge, luxury cruise liner. The locals all refer to it as Grenada's *Titanic* as she had cruised into port with a full complement of guests when fire broke out. The history is quite something (see below) and you have to wonder if all her past incarnations had made her jinxed. Due to the depth, you won't see all that much of the ship but also because, as time has gone on, the vessel continues to suffer. Even sitting on the seabed, a recent storm twisted her bow, which broke away from the rest of the hull. You are also warned not to penetrate any part as she is highly unstable, with the centre of the ship now collapsing into itself. As you descend you are taken straight to the swimming pool which is quite hard to recognise. There are a few tiles not covered in silt and a couple of hand rails. It's then back up to deck level, finning along the side, which is covered in dark fans and whip corals before heading up to the fore-mast. If time allows, the dive may continue to Whibbles reef, just a short swim away.

A sharknose goby sitting on the reef at Blackforest; the *Bianca C*

🌀 A long and chequered history

Grenada's most famous wreck dive is the cruise ship, *Bianca C*, but before she came to rest beneath these waters, she had a long and chequered past. Construction of the vessel started in France in 1939. She was launched in 1944 as the *Marechal Petain*, but before she had a chance to commence her working life, was sunk by German Forces during their retreat from France. Two years later, she was raised, refitted and renamed *La Marseillaise* with her maiden voyage from Marseilles to Yokohama in 1949. A short stint as a hospital ship followed during the Suez Crisis. By 1957, she had been sold to Arosa Lines and was renamed, yet again, as the *Arosa Sky*. They kept her for just two years before economic problems forced them to sell her to the Italian Costa family who, at the time, owned one of the biggest shipping companies in the world. They refurbished her again, increased the tonnage and renamed her *Bianca C* after their daughter. She then commenced sailing from Naples to Venezuela with stops in the Caribbean. Grenada was the last port of call on the return leg.

In October 1961, the *Bianca C* left Italy on her final voyage and just ten days later was sitting at anchor in St George's harbour. In the early hours of October 22, an explosion in the boiler room caused a fire, with flames spreading quickly throughout the ship's stern. The alarm was raised and many small, local fishing vessels who had been preparing for the day ahead heard her calls. They immediately sailed out to the stricken vessel and rescued 672 of the 673 people on board: one crew member had died in the boiler room. Although there is some discrepancy on the numbers, it is said two more people died but it is a credit to the Grenadian people that there was so little loss of life.

A British Frigate, the *Londonderry*, arrived from Puerto Rico two days later to offer assistance. As the ship was still burning, the decision was made to haul her away from the port. The crew severed the anchor chain and secured a towing line. They intended to beach her in the shallows at Point Salines but this was unsuccessful, partly because the ship's rudders had become jammed by the extreme heat of the fire. She then sprung a leak and sank slowly to the seabed where she now rests.

↘4 Purple Rain

⏱	**Depth**	28 m
◐	**Visibility**	poor to fair
≋	**Currents**	slight
◒	**Dive type**	day boat

Named for the ever-present, large schools of creole wrasse, Purple Rain is a gently sloping reef. It does get a bit of current so is usually dived as drift. Dropping down to the bottom of the slope and onto the sandy seabed, you often find a couple of small turtles and then a small barracuda. Looking around, you see he has a few mates and, as the current lifts, they start zipping through the balls of baitfish that move in. Ascending up the slope, a slipper lobster appears from a tiny cave – unusual in the daytime – then a huge spiny lobster also wanders out of his hiding place. There are lots of angelfish and boxfish and the very shy redspot hawkfish.

↘5 Whibbles

⏱	**Depth**	23 m
◐	**Visibility**	poor to fair
≋	**Currents**	slight to medium
◒	**Dive type**	day boat

This lively dive lies close to Point Salines and just above the *Bianca C*. At 18 metres you meet gangs of barracudas chasing all the schools of baitfish and scads. Large trevally and even larger snappers follow them. A couple of honeycomb cowfish are having a punch-up way up in the water-column; butterflyfish cruise around the usual array of seaplumes, fans and azure vase sponges. A large swimming crab and a green moray appear from neighbouring holes in the reef. If you go very slowly, a jumping movement might catch your eye. They are very rarely seen but there are dwarf frogfish living here – they measure under 30 mm long.

↘6 Shakem

⏱	**Depth**	32 m
◐	**Visibility**	fair to good
≋	**Currents**	slight
◒	**Dive type**	day boat

One of the most popular in the area, the *Shakem* is shallow enough to be thoroughly explored. The story goes that in 2001, due to a local strike, cement had to be shipped in from Trinidad. The vessel was overloaded, her cargo shifted and she started to take in water, later sinking to her upright position on the seabed. Below the bow, the anchor is sitting on the sand with a good cover of crusting corals. Rising up the side of the hull there are young fans and soft corals coating all the surfaces. Below deck, you can see all the bags of cement tied up in stacks. There are a lot of sergeant majors inside the hold and they follow divers out, almost leading them to the crane. Stairs then lead up to the cabin and along the gangway to the stern where all the surfaces are covered in tiny white soft corals.

❝ ❞ We simply had to dive the Shakem again as on our first dive we missed the propeller – it's at the deepest point and perfectly intact.

🌀 Spice island

Grenada... Spice Island... not a first choice for a diving destination. It was an impulse holiday; booked one week and lying on Grand Anse beach the next for a much needed chill-out break with a bit of diving thrown in. The *Bianca C*, aka the Titanic of the Caribbean, is the signature dive. But, for me, the highlight was the *Shakem*, a small cargo ship sunk in 2001. Now, before I go on, I should point out I'm not a wreck girl, much preferring coral gardens with sunlight streaming through the water. I could happily sit on the seabed just watching the fish go by. But there was something about the *Shakem* that touched my sense of mystery. She doesn't have a romantic tale to tell – she sank simply by being overloaded. However, she was home to a seahorse. Shy and well camouflaged, we were less than optimistic about our chances of seeing her but luck was on our side. I sometimes wonder what happened to her. Did she ever leave the security of the Shakem in search of a mate? Who knows, but she was the first seahorse I'd ever seen and, for that reason alone, Grenada holds a special place in my heart.

Jackie Hutchings, founder, Scubadviser.com

Views of the *Veronica* (left) and *Shakem* wrecks

N7 Veronica

Depth	15 m	
Visibility	poor to fair	
Currents	slight	
Dive type	day boat	

This wreck of a coastal freighter is about 25 metres long and is sitting on a shallow reef. She originally sank off St George's but was moved when the new cruise terminal was built. The propellor is covered in small cup corals and there are more all along the port side of the hull. Leading away from the prop, the anchor chain disappears into the distance, but sadly goes too far away to investigate. Around the bow are many yellow snappers but the most interesting area has to be the central crane which is smothered in soft corals and small sponges. Inside the hold you can see some sections of engines.

N8 Happy Valley

Depth	21 m	
Visibility	poor to fair	
Currents	slight	
Dive type	day boat	

The bays running north from Molinere to Flamingo Bay are a protected zone. The shallow dives in this stretch are all very interesting, consisting of a series of small drop-offs and winding walls from about six metres down to 20. The topography is more varied than the flatter reef dives on the south side of Grand Anse, and there seems to be more life hiding in the nooks and crannies. The corals are varied too, with a lot of feathery bushes, seaplumes and huge gardens of the black seafan. There are a lot of smaller fish including both adult and juvenile French angels and lots of juvenile drums. This is a great spot for finding flamingo tongue shells laying their eggs and the very beautiful colonial anemone that grows on sponges and looks like a garden of miniature cup corals.

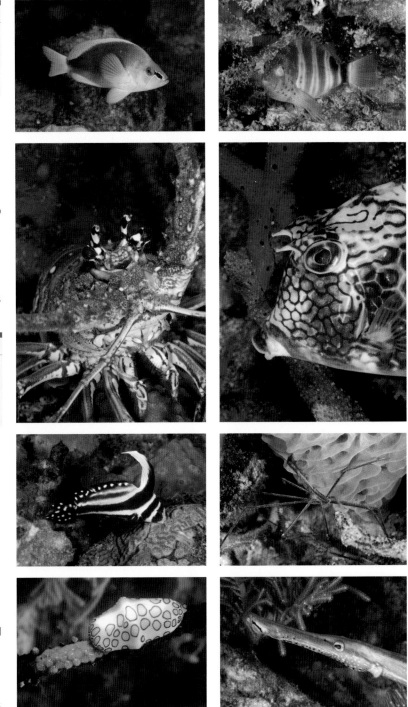

Images from Grenada, clockwise: a shy hamlet; redspot hawkfish; honeycomb cowfish; arrow crab; portrait of a flutemouth; flamingo tongue shell laying eggs; a teenage-stage drum; spiny lobster

9 Molinere Bay

🌀 **Depth**	24 m
◐ **Visibility**	poor to fair
〰 **Currents**	slight
🌊 **Dive type**	day boat

A few minutes by speedboat to the west of St George's is Grenada's most unique dive site, an underwater sculpture park. This very unusual dive is a surprise to many: perhaps because it is so unexpected, or maybe as it's something so completely different. London-based sculptor Jason de Caires Taylor created and installed the sculptures in 2006 designing each one individually to both create artificial reefs and to relate tales that are relevant to the environment, conservation and Grenada's past and local folklore. Much of the park can be explored by snorkellers as some are as shallow as five metres. The most noted sculpture is *Vicissitudes*, a ring of children from diverse ethnic backgrounds. The dive boats moor up beside this so it's very easy to see. Beyond, there is a series of long outcrops and sandy channels where more of the sculptures are hidden.

For divers, the plan is to descend to 24 metres where there is the wreck of a small sailing boat, the *Buccaneer*. She is about 20 metres long and lying on her side on a slope. There is little left of her but a good number of fish shelter inside and all the surfaces are sprouting plenty of soft and black corals. It's then time to head back up the slope and into the various sandy channels where you encounter more of the sculptures. There are 65 in total: the most quirky simply has to be the *Lost Correspondent*, while *Sienna* is by far the most emotive.

Clockwise: *Vicissitudes; the Lost Correspondent; Sienna; the Fall from grace*

Carriacou

Grenada's smaller sister sits 90 minutes by fast ferry to the north. An open channel dotted with a handful of smaller volcanic islands separates the two. Less than 20 square kilometres, this peaceful island is a contrast to her busy neighbour.

Gentle rolling hills drop to almost deserted bays with tiny wooden cottages scattered amongst the trees. The main town of Hillsborough is little more than a main road that leads off to other points yet has a surprisingly good range of facilities. But come nine o'clock at night and the island is pretty much asleep. Carriacou is a step back in time.

Her name also means 'land of reefs' and you only have to look out from shore to see these hovering beneath the surface. The water is classic Caribbean turquoise, the marine realm is healthy and some of the reef structures vary from those to the south: there are areas with huge tumbled boulders, gaping caverns and even some volcanic gases escaping like champagne bubbles from the seabed. To top it all off, there are even a few new wreck dives. Conditions are not dissimilar to those on Grenada although most dive sites are slightly more protected from the Atlantic.

◤11 Sister Rocks	
Depth	24 m
Visibility	good
Currents	mild to medium
Dive type	day boat

Two sharp-sided craggy pinnacles break the surface to the south of Hillsborough and Paradise Beach. Both are home to seabirds. Below them is, without doubt, the most dramatic dive here. There are several routes you can take to navigate around them. The western side is a slope that is completely covered in fans and corals. There are a lot of fish species feeding in the current including a resident school of barracuda. It's unusual to see, but look out for white 'snow' in and around some of the barrel sponges. This means they are spawning. Nurse sharks often take refuge under the rocks closer to the base of the pinnacles where the terrain changes to bigger boulders and crevices which reflect the land above. Other animals shelter too, like pufferfish and morays and there are many schools of small fish in the surge that washes the gaps between the islands then out to the east side.

◤10 Divers Surprise, Lighthouse	
Depth	18 m
Visibility	good
Currents	none
Dive type	day boat

A few minutes from shore is flat Sandy Island and this reef starts near the metal light beacon – more usually a perch for pelicans. There are rows of channels and gullies between the reefs which are coated in crusting corals and young hard corals. A small turtle is jammed under a ledge, and if you are really lucky you may spot a tiny opistobranch: the lettuce sea slug is an elegant and frilly little chap. There are said to be seahorses here too, but if you don't spot one of those there will be endless slender filefish hiding on the fronds of the seaplumes, some hermit crabs, lots of creole wrasse, the Shy hamlet and at least one golden moray.

The canyon leading between the Sister Rocks; a lettuce sea slug; coral clad slopes at the Sister Rocks

⑫ Sharky's Hideaway

🕐	**Depth**	23 m
◑	**Visibility**	good
🌊	**Currents**	slight
🌀	**Dive type**	day boat

This reef starts just to the north of tiny Mabouya island and continues along its western side. There are a few dives along the reef and you certainly won't get far on this one section as there is so much to see. From the first entry point you head down a slope to 23 metres. The coral growth is good with a lot of crusting hard corals. Animals living in this area include juvenile drums, coral groupers, lobsters, parrotfish and squirrelfish, morays, coral banded shrimp and masses of the tiny sharknose gobies that sit on just about every surface. The most unusual fish though is a quillfin benny – unusual in that this one displays slightly different colours and patterns to those seen in other parts of the Caribbean.

⑬ Sharky's Extension

🕐	**Depth**	13 m
◑	**Visibility**	good
🌊	**Currents**	slight
🌀	**Dive type**	day boat

Another section of the above reef, this dive focuses on exploring around the large boulders that have created many small caverns. Inside are copper sweepers, both reef and spiny lobsters and lots of small fish. At the end of the section of boulders a natural bowl in the reef heaves with waves of baitfish. Gangs of chubbs swoop in to chase them through the surge. A little further along are a series of gullies and raised reefs that are full of life – a slipper lobster, a small turtle and a school of squid compete for attention but get ignored in favour of an enormous southern stingray, which is about two metres long, and over a metre wide. Finally to round off the dive, in the next gully it's an encounter with an adult nurse shark.

⑭ Magic Garden

🕐	**Depth**	24 m
◑	**Visibility**	good
🌊	**Currents**	slight
🌀	**Dive type**	day boat

Approaching this reef from the northern side, there is the wreck of a small tug boat which lies in the sand at 20 metres. She hasn't been down for very long so, as yet, there is little coral or sponge growth on the outside of the hull but inside the small wheelhouse the fish life is phenomenal. The wheel is coated in pink sponges but you can hardly see it for the swarms of snappers and goatfish that shelter there. After a short time, it's up the nearby slope, and over the reef until you reach a shallow gully where streams of volcanic gases escape as bubbles from the sea floor. This dive then ends around the big boulders at the base of the island where Sharky's Extension starts but not before you meet up with a school of southern sennets, a small barracuda.

Nurse shark in hiding; southern stingray in the open

⚓15 Twin Tugs

⬙ **Depth**	28 m
◐ **Visibility**	good
≋ **Currents**	usually mild
⬯ **Dive type**	day boat

Two tug boats sit on the seabed north of Mabouya. Both were sunk deliberately to create dives. The slightly deeper one is the *Westsider*, which is sitting at 28 metres and is about 30 metres long. She was sunk in September 2004, but shortly afterwards Hurricane Ivan hit – the current was so strong it moved her 180 degrees around and sat her back down again. The intact propellor is inside a circular guard with the blades and surrounding hull carpeted in small pink and white soft corals. Heading up the side of the tug, the hull is also well coated in corals and small sponges. You can penetrate her to investigate the intact engine room then swim back out through a hatch to the deck. Above are swirling schools of baitfish and a solitary giant barracuda. Next, it's over to the *Boris*, just a short fin away. This tug also sits upright on the sand. She was sunk September 2007 and isn't as well covered in corals yet but is still impressive. The decks are starting to show signs of growth and you can carefully slide inside the cabin – the entry doors are very narrow – and go inside the engine room. This one is smaller and quite cramped so best just to look from outside.

❝❞ The Westsider is proof that artificial reefs really do work... all around her hull is barren seabed, but the life she has attracted in just five years is prolific.

Drying out

Most Grenada hotels are only ten minutes or so from the airport. Nearly all have a variety of room styles (often including kitchenettes) so if you are not happy with the first, ask for another. On Carriacou, guesthouses are the favoured option. Wireless internet is common and free.

Grenada
Diving
Aquanauts Grenada, T+1 473 444 1126, aquanautsgrenada.com. Located in True Blue Bay on the Atlantic coast. Large and spacious boats run by a fun, friendly multinational crew. Good onboard facilities for kit, cameras and even a toilet. Schedules planned around daily conditions. Also located in Spice Island Beach Resort.

Dive Grenada, T+1 473 444 1092, divegrenada.com. Located right on the sands of beautiful Grand Anse beach. The island's longest-established dive centre running both PADI and BSAC courses. High quality rental equipment, small groups and great personal service from the helpful British owners. Good value package deals available with the Flamboyant Hotel.

Sleeping
$$ Flamboyant Hotel, T+1 473 444 4247, flamboyant.com. Sitting at the southern end of Grand Anse beach, spacious rooms are simple but have fantastic views. Facilities include an up-tempo late-night sports bar,

pool and restaurant but you will need to be a mountain goat – the hillside location means there are a lot of steps.

$$ True Blue Bay Resort, T+1 473 443 8783, truebluebay.com. Located in a calm bay on the Atlantic coast, this peaceful resort has large, beautifully decorated rooms clustered around gardens that lead to the bay and waterfront marina. Onsite restaurant, bar, spa and watersports.

Eating
Many travellers will be on a package that includes meals at their hotel so it's no surprise that there are few independent restaurants. On the Grand Anse side, there are some behind Spiceland Mall shopping centre. These include **La Boulangerie** for café style Italian meals and **Le Château** for good value fish and local dishes. In True Blue Bay, two restaurants of note are the quiet and relaxed **De Big Fish** at the Spice Island Marina and late-night-lively **Club Bananas** a little further along the road. Both have good food and service. Keep an eye out for nutmeg ice cream – delicious.

Carriacou
Dive centres
Carriacou Silver Diving, T+1 473 443 7882, scubamax.com. A few minutes walk from the main jetty in Hillsborough, this German-owned operation runs from a charming Caribbean cottage set in lovely gardens with space to relax. Friendly and flexible owners focus on small groups, personal service and a calm atmosphere.

Sleeping
$ Ade's Dream T+1 473 443 7317, adesdream.com. Just seconds away from Carriacou Silver Diving, this friendly, family-run guest house is fantastic value. What it may lack in classy decoration it makes up for with free Wi-Fi, air-con and balconies with views over the town and beach.

Other options
For a real get-away-from-it-all option, hire a small local cottage or apartment. Down Island Villa Rentals, islandvillas.com, have options both in and out of town, or contact Carriacou Silver Diving for advice.

Eating
Hillsborough, curiously, has many eating spots for lunch, but at night, especially in low season, few remain open. **Sandisland** opposite Ade's has delicious catch of the day fish. For real class though, head back down the road to **Lyme and Dine** where Max and Claudia swap their dive kit for aprons, cooking 'European cuisine with a Caribbean twist'. A delightful restaurant with a breezy balcony overlooking their tropical gardens. US$35 for 3 courses.

Touring
Ensure you spend half a day with Mr Linky, aka Lincoln Bedeau, T+1 473 7566, who will take you around Carriacou and ensure you see and hear all the best bits of local history, around US$45 for two people.

St. George's waterfront harbour and fruit stalls in the town market

 Sleeping $$$ US$150+ double room per night $$ US$75-150 $ under US$75
Eating $$$ US$40+ 2-course meal, excluding drinks $$ US$20-40 $ under US$20

Grenada

Taking a trip to Grenada and not seeing the heart of the island would be madness. The beautiful landscapes can only be appreciated once you head well away from the southern corner. Take a day trip to get your bearings then consider hiring a car to see the rest at your leisure.

Day tours always start in the capital city of **St. George's**. The forts, churches, shops and markets tumble down steep roads to the horseshoe-shaped harbour known as the Carenage. This was once a volcanic crater. Much of the history dates back to French colonization in the 1650s but by the mid-1800s, the British were in control. The capital still shows signs of the devastating effects of Hurricane Ivan in 2004.

Heading north along the coast road, you pass through a time warp. Gone are all signs of modern development and you discover the real Grenada: hills thick with spice trees and rainforest plants are interspersed with pretty pastel houses and small towns. Tours divert inland to **Concord Falls**, then back to the coast to the town of **Gouyave**, a fishing village known for Fish Friday – a weekly festival all about eating the local catch.

On the northern tip of the island is **Sauteurs Bay**. From the clifftop above, the last remaining Carib natives jumped to their deaths in 1651 rather than be conquered by the French. The monument to them is both touching and an impressive sculpture.

Turning south, a stop is made at one of the island's most beautiful spice plantations, **Belmont Estate**. Now a thriving commercial concern, this estate was established in the late 1600s. Spices and chocolate are still cultivated using age-old methods. Don't miss the lunch here. Afterwards it's down to a rum distillery, another curious time warp. **River Rum Estate** has firmly refused to be dragged into the 21st century and is still distilling with exactly the same methods – and equipment – used in the 1700s. Taste the product and beware – this stuff is strong.

After the over indulgent assault on your senses with rum, food and spices, it's time to pass through the cooling rainforest below Mt St. Catherine, stopping for a moment at the idyllic Grand Etang Lake before heading back to town.

Carriacou

With a good mini-bus system, getting around Carriacou isn't difficult but again, it is worth taking a tour with a resident who can fill you in on the island's past and present.

Short tours start in **Hillsborough** with its banks, shops and a tiny museum before driving to **Belair** where the views from the Princess Royal Hospital over the coast can be breathtaking. In front are some age-old cannons said to be left from the days when the French were repelling the British.

The tour continues to the east, where the coast faces **Petit Martinique**. The main village is **Windward** where a group of Scottish boat builders settled in the 19th century. Even now, the boats are built in the traditional way and may take up to a year to complete. Launching one is a celebration for the whole community. Driving through the hills and back towards Hillsborough, you pass many ruins of old plantation houses and windmills. Limes and sugar were once the mainstay of island economy. To the south is nigh-on deserted Paradise Beach – the name says it all – and around Point Cistern is Tyrrel Bay, a delightful natural harbour with a marina that attracts many passing yachts.

Concord Falls; spice plantation; River Rum distillery; rush hour in Carriacou; Lyme and Dine; view from Belair

Resources

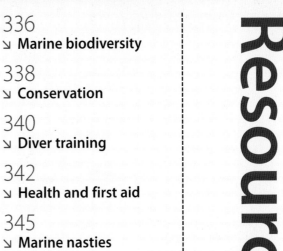

Shimmering shards: glassy sweepers, *Parapriacanthus ransonneti,* may be lacking in size, but never in numbers. *Cave 20, Zanzibar*

Marine biodiversity

When you consider that seven tenths of the planet is covered in water, it may seem curious that most divers' hit-lists are confined to the equatorial belt. But there is good reason. This is where the majority of accessible marine life resides.

All oceans are teeming with life, but many seas are too deep and too cold to encourage the development of all but the most specialized of species. These conditions also make many areas off-limits to sport diving.

The warm waters that surround the equator are known to have remained tropical for millions of years. High light levels and sun-heated waters encourage reef growth and provide time for marine species to diversify. This simple equation ensures that tropical waters are just that much richer than temperate waters. Yet nothing is ever really that simple. The world's oceans – and diving zones – are also influenced by deep water plates, ridges, submerged volcanoes and marine currents. It has been accepted for many years that the waters in the Indo-Pacific region, stretching from Madagascar in the west to the Galápagos in the east, are far richer than those of the Atlantic. However, Southeast Asia is the specific region that displays the highest levels of biodiversity.

This is due to its position in the Pacific Ocean, a geologically complex region known as the Pacific Ring of Fire: a deep water string of submerged volcanoes encircle the Pacific and were a key element in the formation of the Earth's crust and, many centuries later, resulted in an array of biologically unique island ecosystems and species.

The Coral Triangle

While past scientific research suggested that the area around the top of Indonesian Sulawesi was the Ring of Fire's epicentre, more recent studies have introduced the Coral Triangle. This is the area enclosed by Southern Indonesia, eastern Borneo, up to the Philippines, then across to Papua New Guinea and the Solomons. Studies conducted across this region have confirmed it is the global centre of marine biodiversity. Covering an area of 5.7 million km^2 (about half of the area of the United States) there are over 600 reef-building coral species (which is 75% of all species known to science) and more than 3,000 species of reef fish.

These figures vary by country with species numbers reducing the further away from the region you go. For example, in Indonesia there are around 3,400 species of fish, including 138 damselfish. Papua New Guinea has 100 damsels, but by the time you reach Fiji there are just 60. Way over in the Galápagos the

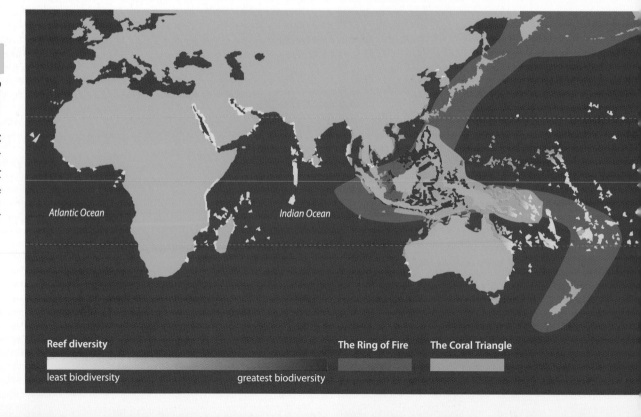

Atlantic Ocean

Indian Ocean

Reef diversity

least biodiversity   greatest biodiversity

The Ring of Fire   **The Coral Triangle**

number drops to 18, while the Caribbean has a mere 16 across its entire sea. Australia, always the exception to the rule, has the highest numbers of damsels at 142 as the continent covers tropical, temperate and cold waters.

The Indo-Pacific versus the Atlantic

Global patterns of reef and coral development started way back in the Triassic era, a mere 250 million years ago. It was during this time that the continents broke up, disconnecting certain sections of sea from others. This resulted in the Atlantic being isolated from all the other oceans so it formed reefs with distinctly different characteristics. Localised marine life was thought to be prolific in this period but a few million years later, the Ice Age kicked in and the entire Atlantic region was subjected to massive extinctions. Melting ice water flooded into the Atlantic, reducing its temperature enough to decimate the animal populations, leaving just a small refuge in the area we now know as the Caribbean.

Many of the species that had been common to all coral reefs did not survive this period and left just seven genera in common with the Indo-Pacific. Although conditions settled, species diversity never did regenerate and left this one ocean lagging behind all others.

Global reef area km²

Region	km²
PACIFIC	115,900
SOUTHEAST ASIA	91,700
INDIAN OCEAN	32,000
CARIBBEAN	20,000
RED SEA & GULF OF ADEN	17,400
ARABIAN GULF & SEA	4,200
ATLANTIC	1,600
EASTERN PACIFIC	1,600

All figures are approximate

Species diversity and discovery

The other reason for higher species diversity in the Asia-Pacific basin is the way in which ocean currents transport cold waters around the planet. The Indo-Pacific area is partly protected from arctic waters by the Russian and Alaskan land masses which allows marine life to flourish in the shallower, warmer waters, the zone where most coral reefs thrive.

This information is by no means a reason to ignore one sea or country for another. While diving in Asian waters is more likely to be a journey of discovery than it is elsewhere, new species are discovered across the world on a regular basis. Across the millenia, unique geological forces have created a variety of marine environments and many endemic species. You may not see a pygmy seahorse in the Caribbean, but you also won't see an indigo hamlet in Thailand.

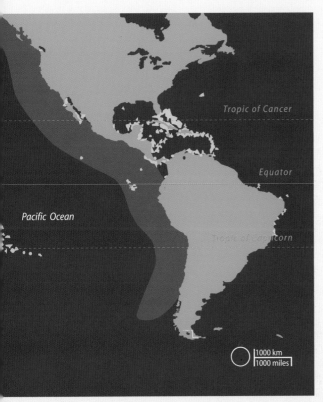

Tropic of Cancer

Equator

Pacific Ocean

Tropic of Capricorn

1000 km
1000 miles

❝❞ We feel surprise when travellers tell us of the vast dimensions of the Pyramids and other great ruins, but how utterly insignificant are the greatest of these, when compared to these mountains of stone accumulated by the agency of various minute and tender animals! This is a wonder which does not first strike the eye of the body, but, after reflection, the eye of reason.

Charles Darwin, April 12, 1836, on his theory of atoll formation.

Conservation

A few years ago, Jean-Michel Cousteau spoke on Capitol Hill: "The ocean holds 97% of Earth's water, drives climate and weather, generates more than 70% of the oxygen we breathe, absorbs carbon dioxide, supplies our fresh water through rain, provides food, and is a deep source of inspiration to our spirits."

Yet our seas are heavily endangered and coral reefs are one of the most threatened ecosystems on the planet. If destruction continues at its present rate, 70% of the world's coral reefs will disappear in a generation. And where will that leave us?

Most people (divers generally excluded) think nothing of how the fish arrives on their dinner plate, nor what happens to sewerage or the side-effects of many industries. Centuries of bad practices have led to the direct destruction of the world's coral reefs – some figures suggest that up to 30% have been lost already. Over time, few people realised they were literally killing the resource that supported them. Fishing practices, both commercial and small scale, are much to blame for the damage to many marine ecosytems. Drag-netting the ocean floor, for example, kills marine life indiscriminately while at the other end of the scale, poor local fishermen took to dropping chemicals to catch fish in greater numbers, never understanding that this kills everything, leaving nothing to support either the people or the fish. As a coral reef dies, so do other environments around it. With no reef paralleling the shore, mangrove nursery grounds become eroded and creatures that used these as a safe haven no longer can. A once protected coast is open to the ravages of weather and may well collapse into the sea. Other man-made issues like pollution simply aggravate these problems.

There is a lot of publicity about how global warming is leading to rises in sea levels, but less focus on how this impacts on coral reefs and consequently on the planet as a whole. Corals

66 99 The diving community has an important role to play in helping protect rapidly degrading coral reefs around the world. As divers, we have a personal relationship with reefs and often see firsthand the damage sustained by reef ecosystems by changing global conditions. Project AWARE provides many opportunities for individuals to participate in reef monitoring, education and conservation locally. Volunteer divers are at the core of these monitoring programmes and are natural advocates for the protection of declining underwater ecosystems.
Suzanne Pleydell, Director, Project AWARE Foundation (International)

live inside a specific temperature range (around 25-29°C) and it only takes an increase of one degree in water temperature for corals to start struggling.

Tiny individual corals feed on *zooxanthellae*, symbiotic yellow-, green- or brown-hued algaes, which live inside the corals, giving them colour and sustaining them via photosynthesis. But, as waters warm, the algae either dies, or the corals expel them, causing them to bleach. Water that is too warm also encourages the growth of harmful algae over the corals. This speeds up its demise as they block out the sun: the *zooxanthellae* cannot photosynthesise so they die, taking the corals with them. The marine realm has created an antidote to this problem – algae is usually eaten by fish, but due to overfishing, there are insufficient numbers to keep the balance. Other side-effects are seen when corals get ill and predators move in. The Crown of Thorns starfish is a typical example as these both predate on and cause coral bleaching. Their natural predators are few and the ones that do exist are depleted by overfishing as well.

Right around the world, people depend on coral reefs for foods as well as a source of income. Despite their environmental and economic importance, new research indicates that more than half of the world's coral reefs could die in less than 25 years.

Coral destruction as caused by humans – a fin or an anchor; coral bleaching caused by three Crown of Thorns starfish

Divers and conservation

A diver's role may be a comparatively small one but remember one of the first rules of diving – look, don't touch. Sadly, there are people who genuinely don't care and you have to wonder what it is they are doing if they have only gone down to destroy.

▶▶ Do not touch corals, or any living organism, as your hands can leave harmful oils and pressure can damage protective coatings allowing destructive bacteria to penetrate.

▶▶ Don't wear gloves, unless absolutely necessary, as you will be too tempted to put your hands down without thinking.

▶▶ If tough conditions dictate that you must touch the reef, a single finger is enough to give you balance, and a carefully placed reef hook does less damage than two hands.

▶▶ Don't bring anything up from the seabed, not even a shell. It may seem to be dead, but you just don't know what tiny creature has crawled inside.

▶▶ Be careful to stay above the reef, good buoyancy is vital.

▶▶ Ensure all your gauges and equipment are either hooked to your BC or tucked in a pocket.

▶▶ Watch what you do with your fins; it's easy to misjudge what is behind you.

There are many organizations dedicated to looking after our seas and the animals that live within them. Look at WWF (panda.org), Reef Check (reefcheck.org), the Marine Conservation Society (mcsuk.org), The Shark Research Institute (sharks.org) and the International Coral Reef Action Network (icran.org).

Get involved by helping to monitor reefs. Ask your dive operator about PADI's Project AWARE activities (projectaware.org) or if you have time sign up for an expedition run by a body like Coral Cay Conservation (coralcay.org) or GlobalVision International (gvi.co.uk).

🐟 A double-edged sword

Recently we dived on Zanzibar's Mnemba Atoll. We were really surprised – we hadn't expected such lovely dives. Lots of animals seen and listed in the log book, lots of images committed to the camera. Forever memories.

One day on route to a dive site on the east of the atoll, we saw boats with around 20 fishermen in each. We were a bit confused by this but our guides informed us that Mnemba is a conservation zone, meaning the waters are shared by sports people and local subsistence fishermen. The Mnemba Island Marine Conservation Area (MIMCA) officers have set guidelines on how this works: line fishing, nets of a certain size and fish traps are allowed. Spear fishing and other nets are forbidden.

After our first dive we passed the fishermen again. This time they were pulling up the nets. Much later, we returned to the beach and picked our way across the shallows to encounter them once more. We saw the dead shark first – a tiger shark. Then we saw the first manta, left on the shore awaiting its fate. Two others were being butchered a little way up the beach. The local guides asked the fishermen where the animals had been caught. They admitted they came from the Mnemba nets. More forever memories.

This type of problem isn't only limited to Zanzibar but the real tragedy there lies in the economics. Fishing methods may have been sustainable when Zanzibar had a small population, but rapid population growth means that is no longer the case. MIMCA was set up with the aim of protecting the marine life while still giving tangible benefits to the local communities. All divers and snorkellers pay $3 a day which goes to running MIMCA and back to local people for community projects.

Les Carlisle, Group Conservation Manager of &BEYOND (which owns Mnemba Island Lodge) says, "While there have been some incredible successes, this revenue is now so widely distributed that many of us wonder if it will ever have the success that was initially intended. The local people will have to change if they wish to survive. Getting them to realise this new reality is challenging but we believe it is achievable through education. Our developed world approach of saying that some must starve so we can save the environment just doesn't work. We have to take the longer more sustainable route of the locals wanting to save their own resources for their own benefit."

Diver training

For many, the underwater experience starts on holiday. There you are, snorkelling over some exotic reef but watching the divers far below and wanting to join in. So it's over to the hotel pool for a try-dive session followed by a quick resort course. For others, it can be the influence of friends at home who are so enthusiastic about their chosen pastime, they spend every waking minute talking non-stop about it. Either way, for those who discover that their blood no longer circulates without nitrogen in it, it's time to take things seriously and get qualified.

There are several ways to do this which should be considered carefully: you can train at home, abroad or even online these days, but the most important factor is to ensure that you get the best training possible from one of the world's major diving organisations. This is not a sport to cut corners over.

Training organizations

By far the largest and best known dive body is **PADI** (Professional Association of Diving Instructors, padi.com). You will see their signs right around the world, from your local dive store to resorts abroad, but they are by no means the only training organization. Other well respected international bodies include the **British Sub-Aqua Club** (BSAC, bsac.com), the **National Association of Underwater Instructors** (NAUI, naui.com) and **Scuba Schools International** (SSI, divessi.com).

Each of these has a range of comparative courses run via weekly club-style meetings, local day courses or residential courses either at home or away. All courses are well-structured, thorough and will cover the relevant concerns for each level. Courses are designed to be completed in a specific number of days and any training operation will do their best to ensure you meet that target. Before signing on the dotted line, do your research: get some recommendations, ask to meet your potential instructor then go with the company and person who makes you feel confident and relaxed within the training environment. Also bear in mind that you need to have a well-recognised certification. If your training is not internationally recognised you may find that another country will not accept your certification card and you have to start over.

Learning to dive

This should include three straightforward steps. Basic training is often called **Open Water** and builds essential skills to get you safely in the water but limits your depth and does not teach any rescue skills. An **Advanced Open Water** course will expand your knowledge and further in-water practice ensures competence in deeper water under differing conditions. Finally, take a **Rescue Diver** course. This may be included in one of the above stages but if not ensure you do it. It is important to learn how to save your own life, or someone else's, and is a vital addition to the initial training programme.

Where to learn

One option would be to go on holiday to somewhere lovely and, hopefully, qualify in warm waters under sunny skies. The downside of this is that you are giving up precious holiday time to sit in a classroom. There are several Asian hot-spots that regularly attract back-packers, gap-year travellers and those who just want to learn. Lombok's Gili islands and Thailand's Koh Tao are all well regarded and popular training destinations with PADI Open Water courses at around US$350. Bear in mind that anything much cheaper indicates that your operator may be forced to cut corners somewhere. Many rock-bottom courses do not include

Gabe conducting a try-dive session for honeymooners, Simon and Hannah, at Breezes in Zanzibar

manuals and fees. Also make sure your chosen dive school has an instructor who can speak your language.

Alternatively, you could book into a school in your home country or join a club. These will have a range of options from more relaxed week-by-week training sessions to intensive long weekend options. If these are all going to put a dent in your schedule, you could learn at your own pace with an online course (padi.com/elearning) then register with a local school for your open water dives.

When you do choose to kick off your dive training, remember that you need to be in good health and reasonably comfortable in the water – no, you don't need to be an Olympic swimmer but you should be able to swim further than from the pool edge to the swim-up bar. If you have any known medical conditions, for example asthma or diabetes, get advice from a medical professional before you start.

Continued training
At this point many people stop training, and that's fine, but the half dozen or so dives taken to get you through a course will not make you a competent diver. Practice, as they say, makes perfect so try to get in some diving on a regular basis and consider doing either some speciality or higher level courses as they will help refine your skills. Ideas are on the right.

Continued safety
Finally, every time you are back in the water remind yourself again that this is not a sport to cut corners over. It's important to be healthy when you dive, continually check the state of your equipment and always dive in a buddy pair. Listen to every dive brief carefully: the divemaster is there to ensure his divers come back safely, not just lead them around, so the information he supplies is vital to both an enjoyable dive and a safe one.

Buzz on Nautilus Explorer explaining where to find the silvertip sharks

🌑 The training ladder

There is a clear route that takes potential divers from novice to qualified, yet diving is a sport where you can, and should, keep learning. Improving your technical skills as time goes by means you will enjoy dives more, as will understanding the environment you are exploring and your impact on it.

The most interesting way to keep learning is by taking a few PADI speciality courses. Take one small course every now and then and you can build up to the ultimate non-professional accolade, Master Scuba Diver.

▸▸ Progress up through PADI Rescue Diver then concentrate on improving your own skills and levels of confidence in all situations with Deep Diver, Wreck Diver, Night Diver or even Ice Diver.

▸▸ Focus on specific interests like Digital Underwater Photographer and Underwater Videographer which will add to your camera equipment skills and can be combined with a Peak Performance Buoyancy Course which will make shooting, and diving generally, easier.

▸▸ Understanding the marine environment will also enhance your dives. Consider Coral Reef Conservation Diver, National Geographic Diver Project AWARE Specialist and Underwater Naturalist.

In addition to these great options, there are courses tailored for children: Bubblemaker can be taken at eight years old and Junior Open Water from ten. If you have family, get them involved. Or, if you want to teach there are several courses that cover instructor qualifications at varying levels, which should be augmented by plenty of in-water experience.

66 99 **Many people learn to dive while they are on holiday, just like I did. And it is a great way to learn – warm water, nice sunny days, easy conditions and no nasty distractions like work getting in the way. However, I really do like to advise people to continue their training back home. This keeps the knowledge fresh, develops skills by diving in very different environments and, of course, builds a great network of friends and professionals from local dive stores and schools.**

Deborah Sutton, Marketing Manager,
PADI International Limited

Health and first aid

There are many healthcare issues involved in being a diver and most of the "can I, can't I?" stuff will be covered by your training. The following information is for guidance only. If you are unsure about anything at all to do with how a medical condition may affect your ability to dive safely, make sure you contact a doctor with specialist dive knowledge before you go away.

Before you go

There are a couple things to take care of before you depart:

Insurance Never underestimate the necessity of good, diver-specific medical insurance. Ensure that it covers repatriation in an emergency and check the depth limitations. Many policies will only cover you up to 30 metres while others confusingly say "covered to the depth you are qualified to."

Check up If you do have any pre-existing conditions, take a quick trip down to your doctor and ensure you have both sufficient medications and information to handle your own healthcare. It may be a good idea to get a certificate clearing you to dive in order to show operators. Remember to have your teeth checked every now and then as trapped air in a cavity is a very painful thing.

Vaccinations for the tropics

With most divers heading off to at least one distant destination every year it's worth getting a full set of vaccinations then having boosters as and when necessary. Ensure you allow plenty of time to get this done in advance of your trip. For the countries listed in this guide you will require some or all of the following:

- » polio
- » hepatitis A & B
- » tetanus
- » rabies
- » typhoid
- » yellow fever

Discuss your individual requirements with your GP/practice nurse or travel clinic as you may need something more than the above.

Anti-malarials

The best way to avoid getting malaria is not to get bitten. Yes, easier said than done, but the usual advice of a repellent lotion plus covered arms and legs after dusk will help enormously. However, because you can't avoid mosquitoes in damp environments such as kitting-up areas, you may need to take anti-malarial tablets. Which one to take is where it gets more complicated and the best advice is to research via your doctor, nurse or a travel clinic but make sure you tell them you are a diver as some have side-effects such as nausea, diarrhoea and sun sensitivity. Some anti-malarials are not given to divers as they are said to cause panic or anxiety but these reports tend to be anecdotal. Good websites for current recommendations are fitfortravel.scot.nhs.uk and cdc.gov/travel.

Malaria drugs need to be taken for a period before entering an at-risk area and usually for four weeks afterwards so plan well in advance and don't forget to complete the course.

❝❞ My travel medicine kit always includes ear drying agent but I make my own. It's heaps cheaper and works just as well. Mix half rubbing alcohol and half vinegar: the vinegar helps change the pH of the ear canal to inhibit the growth of fungi which are responsible for most infections. The alcohol does the drying so if it irritates a little, reduce the quantity – this varies from person to person so it takes a bit of experimenting. The trick though is to prevent rather than treat, so if you are subject to ear problems, try this at the end of every day. And I always like to remind people that for cuts and grazes, even insect bites, there really is no substitute for a daily wash with plain old soap and fresh water.

Doctor Joann Gren, Emergency Medicine Specialist, Australia

What to take

First aid kit Most of what you will need to create a good first aid travel kit can be bought without prescription; just ask your local pharmacist to help you put together suitable items in small quantities. Consider including these items:

- » an 'anti-itch' or steroid cream (eg, hydrocortisone) for use on insect bites, rashes and skin inflammation
- » an analgesic, like paracetamol (acetaminophen) or ibuprofen
- » antihistamine tablets for mild allergic reactions
- » a small tube of antiseptic cream or antiseptic wipes
- » lots of band-aids and a small pack of sterile bandages
- » seasickness remedy
- » sinus decongestant tablets
- » rehydration sachets
- » an anti-diarrhoea drug
- » tweezers
- » an ear drying aid (eg Swim-Ear)
- » small scissors
- » latex condoms
- » and a good Swiss Army type knife.

Plus these antibiotic preparations that need to be prescribed:

- » a broad spectrum antibiotic for general infections. Discuss ciprofloxacin with your doctor as it is particularly good for marine infections
- » antibiotic drops for ear and eye infections
- » an antibiotic ointment for skin infections.

Most doctors are sympathetic to prescribing in advance if you explain why. Don't forget to get – and take – sufficient quantities of any medicines that you require on a daily basis, for instance if you are diabetic or use the contraceptive pill.

While you're there

The tropics are beautiful but they do throw up some health issues for travellers, especially those who arrive from colder climes. Here are some tips on ways to ensure your holiday isn't ruined but if in doubt always visit a local doctor. You may be reluctant to do this in some out-of-the-way village, but many doctors, even in the most remote countries, are highly trained. If you are unsure, ask a divemaster or hotel receptionist to recommend one.

Dehydration One of the most common ailments for divers. No one ever drinks enough water and being dehydrated can lead to many other problems, not least of which is the bends. Drink at least two litres of water a day. Sugary soft drinks do not aid rehydration, nor, sadly, does beer. Cramps in your feet at night is a classic indication. Use a sachet of rehydration salts to top up your levels quickly. Alternatively, add 8 level teaspoons of sugar and 1 level teaspoon of salt to 1 litre of water. Tastes foul though.

Sunburn and heat-stroke Perhaps the second most common ailment. Use factor 30 sunscreen to prevent sunburn and wear a hat while you are out on the water where there are reflected rays. Heat stroke arrives disguised as the flu (headaches, muscle aches and pains, fatigue) but with some stomach problems thrown in. If you suspect that's what you have, stay cool, drink lots of fluid and get some advice if you don't return to normal very quickly.

Mosquito bites Try not to scratch because if you do they may get infected by all the mini-nasties in seawater. Use an anti-itch cream and keep your hands in your pockets.

Seasickness Some people suffer, the rest are oblivious. If you suffer just a little, stay out in the fresh air and keep your eyes on the horizon until you get accustomed to the boat's movement. If you suffer badly, there is no doubt about it, drugs work the best. You will need to find a brand that doesn't make you drowsy and that may be a matter of trial and error. Some people swear by pressure bands, others by ginger as a natural remedy.

Ear problems Being immersed in salt water for hours at a time can cause a lot of trouble for ears. Always, always remember to clear your ears before you feel pressure, which will alleviate a lot of potential problems. However, do this gently as over-vigorous, repeated clearing can cause inflammation. People with recurring problems may want to use a steroid nasal spray a few days before a trip and continue once diving. This will cut down on inflammation caused by the normal barotrauma of diving. If your ears get sore, it may be best to rest them for a day. If you suspect you have an infection a good on-the-spot test is to press the hollow behind your ear lobe. If this is painful start the antibiotic drops.

Sinus problems Coming from cooler climates to the tropics can bring on a cold or flu-like symptoms. Many people swear by nasal decongestants as these often make equalizing easier. However, they can also wear off halfway through a dive and cause a reverse ear block, so be careful. Nothing clears sinuses as well as a good salt water sniff if it's just a case of clearing some city pollution but

anything that is very painful may indicate an infection. Again, take a day out, then start antibiotics if necessary.

Colds and flu A change in climate or the change from a busy life at home to a relaxed one somewhere nice and – wallop – you get a cold. Antibiotics will not help unless you have a specific infection so don't go swallowing the pills hoping for a miracle cure. Instead go back to mother's remedies – lots of fluid, vitamin C (oranges and lemons), keep warm and take a mild painkiller.

Allergies Many people have become intolerant to allergens such as dust mites and pollen or have food intolerances to things like wheat or tomatoes. These can cause discomfort but are not life threatening and can be easily treated with an oral antihistamine. Likewise, skin reactions to neoprene or plankton can be treated with a steroid ointment. However, if you have a serious allergy, ensure you are carrying any necessary drugs with you. Specific food allergies such as seafood or nuts are extremely dangerous, especially if you are miles offshore so carry an epi-pen with you at all times. More importantly, make sure that someone else knows where that is and what to do. Either your dive buddy or the divemaster should be fully informed of any intolerances.

Women's issues There are few women who would choose to go diving when they have their period. You can delay them by continuing the cycle of your contraceptive pill but ensure you get good advice on how long you can safely do this. If you don't take the pill but suspect that your period will come in the last few days of a trip, you can delay it for a few days by using a progesterone-only pill. Pregnancy is a little more of an issue. There is no definitive research on how a foetus might be affected by diving. Many women have dived before realizing they were pregnant with no ill effects, but is it worth the risk?

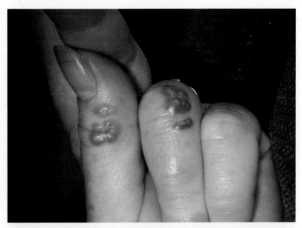

Ouch! The image above shows the effects of touching what you shouldn't. This is the result of brushing against a stinging hydroid while taking a photo, and the skin's reaction to the toxins in the hydroid.

Accidents

The Bends We are all taught about decompression sickness when training and then most of us promptly forget what we were taught. Few divers would be confident enough to cope with a buddy with a suspected bend. That's why it's imperative to dive with a recognized and trustworthy dive operation who will ensure your divemaster is able to cope. All the same, it's as well to have basic knowledge of what is going on.

Symptoms can include joint or muscle pain, dizziness, difficulty breathing, extreme fatigue, skin rashes, unconsciousness and paralysis. Treatment will depend on how severe these symptoms are so first of all ensure that the person is in no immediate danger, is warm, can breathe and has a pulse. **Then get help.** If symptoms are mild (eg, fatigue, skin rash and itching) you will probably be advised to administer 100% oxygen and a litre of fluid. If symptoms are more severe, call for assistance. You will be advised if you should administer CPR, 100% oxygen or fluids until you can reach a hyperbaric facility.

Note that CPR is designed to keep someone going until they reach a tertiary care facility and will only be of use if you can reach one in 15-20 minutes. If there is no pulse within that time, stop.

Another thing to note here is that skin bends are becoming more common. Many divemasters suspect this may be because people are stretching their bottom time by spending extended periods at shallow depths then failing to do a safety stop as their computers are still well within limits. Research is on-going in this area, but always exercise as much caution as possible.

Bruises, sprains and broken ribs It would be an amazing dive trip where someone doesn't drop a tank on their foot, slip on a wet deck or trip en route to the RIB. If you can get to a doctor do, otherwise apply the **RICE** principle… **R**est, use **I**ce on the injured area, use a **C**ompression dressing, and **E**levate it.

Olive seasnakes are venomous but are nosy rather than aggressive

Nitrogen Narcosis Not an accident as such, except that narked divers often do silly things and can have one. To reverse the effects of narcosis, ascend to a shallower depth and allow enough time on slow, controlled safety stops to recover. It may be as well to take a day off.

Severe headaches Again not an accident but may lead to one if ignored. Many people suffer from extreme headaches underwater. There are many contributing factors to this but one way to control them is to ensure you breathe constantly and gently. Try not to hold your breath – ever.

Marine creatures

No matter how careful we all are in the water there are times when the marine world takes exception to us being there:

Fish bites It may not happen often but there is the potential for an unimpressed fish to dash out and bite a diver. Triggerfish are the best known aggressors but even cute little Nemos are known to take a nip. More frequent perhaps is when poor-sighted morays emerge from a hole and chomp on a finger that's too close. In all cases, clean out the wound thoroughly with clean water or vinegar then apply an antibiotic ointment. Large bites may become infected and need antibiotics and anti-tetanus treatment. So you should keep your jabs up to date.

Venomous animals Not that you would intentionally touch anything dangerous but should you happen to get too close, use one of these basic first aid treatments then seek professional advice. The venom of some marine animals is broken down by heat and the following treatment can be used for sea urchins, crown of thorns starfish and stingrays. It will also aid, but is less effective on, stone, scorpion or lionfish, cone shells and seasnakes.

⟩ clean the wound
⟩ immerse in hot water (50°C) until pain stops (up to two hours)
⟩ apply pressure immobilization: wrap a broad, firm bandage over the bite quite tightly and extend as high as possible over the limb. Keep still, apply a splint and bind so that the limb cannot be moved.
⟩ seek advice on whether the person needs an antivenom or injection of long-acting local anaesthetic.

Snorkellers should be very careful and wear swim shoes as many toxic animals bury themselves in the sand. If you step on a ray or urchins remove obvious spines or barbs, use the hot water treatment and antiseptic creams as necessary. More commonly, fire corals, stinging hydroids and stinging plankton can be treated with acetic acid – vinegar or lemon juice – or an anaesthetic cream. Jellyfish stings can be treated this way but ensure you remove the tentacles using rubber gloves. Coral cuts are easily infected so wash the cut well with clean, soapy water or vinegar then apply an antibiotic ointment frequently. These will take a long time to heal unless you stay out of the water so you will need to repeat the treatment after each dive.

Marine nasties

Every time we dive, we descend into a realm where hidden dangers lurk in the form of unrecognized or misunderstood creatures. We are all familiar with more obvious nasties such as much-maligned sharks, seldom-aggressive barracuda and mildly stinging anemones. However, it pays to be aware of creatures you may encounter underwater that can be a less obvious threat.

Cephalopods The only nasty cephalopod is the blue-ringed octopus. Rarely aggressive, this chap spends most if his life hiding from predators. But take heed if those blue rings are flashing – this fellow harbours tetrodotoxin, one of the most deadly poisons known to man.

Corals and hydroids These fragile organisms should never be touched as they are easily damaged, but also because some will retaliate. All hard coral skeletons are made of calcium carbonate, which is hard and sharp and can cut or scratch soft skin. Some, like fire coral, also contain stinging nematocysts (a microscopic cell containing a poisoned barb) which can penetrate skin then burn or itch for some time. Swaying, fern-like hydroid clusters are seen all over reefs and are often mistaken for harmless plants. However, hydroids (or seaferns) have a sting in their 'fronds'. They contain hundreds of stinging cells in their tentacles.

Crustacea Cute as a puppy scampering about the reef floor, the mantis shrimp is deceptively dangerous. Two types are fondly described as thumbcrackers and spearchuckers depending on the shape of their modified front claws. When hunting or attacked these claws shoot out with enough power to crack a thumb or spear a hand.

Fire or Bristle Worms This caterpillar-like critter may seem innocuous and uninteresting but the ultra-fine spines can easily penetrate gloves and wetsuits. Once embedded in the skin, the spines break and cause a burning sensation, swelling or rashes. Scrubbing with pumice may help.

Fish All fish have some form of defence, even if it's just one like the razor sharp caudal blade that sits in front of the surgeonfish's tail fin. Triggerfish are perhaps the most dangerous as both titan and yellowmargined triggers are incredibly aggressive. They will chase off sea creatures and landlubbers alike when they are nesting and think nothing of nipping at a fin or an ear. Many forms of jellyfish sting, ranging from the deadly Australian box jellyfish to ones that are almost harmless. Balls of lined catfish rolling across the seabed are very entertaining; however, highly venomous, razor-sharp spines in their fins can inflict serious wounds and the venom has been known to cause death. The scorpionfish family are one of the reef's most contrasting, with some very beautiful species and some really ugly ones. They all employ the same form of defence – a ridge of venomous spines runs along their bodies which can inject varying strengths of venom into the attacker. Generally, lionfish stings are less serious than those of scorpionfish. More dangerous is the false stonefish, then the devilfish whose venom is almost as potent as the potentially deadly stonefish. Many divers confuse these species so take care to avoid them all.

Seasnakes and eels These animals suffer from a reputation they don't really deserve. Many snakes are venomous but they are mostly just curious. If a snake appears to be taking too much interest, offer it your fin to 'taste' and it will soon leave. Likewise, a moray's reputation for aggression is due to poor eyesight and the way they search for food – head poking out of a hole, mouth gaping, teeth bared. If your hand is too close they will snap, thinking it's a fish.

Sea urchins Put an unwary foot down on a sea urchin and you are unlikely to forget it. The brittle, needle-sharp spines easily penetrate skin and neoprene. The common, long-spined urchin is not toxic but others have potentially fatal poisons. Take care over those with swollen tips on the spines – these are poison sacs. The Crown of Thorns starfish is part of the same species group as sea urchins, but is better known for its ability to destroy large swathes of coral. At up to half a metre across, their thick rigid spines have sharp points. A sting has similar effects to those of sea urchins but severe cases can cause paralysis.

Shells Only a handful of shells are dangerous. These are mostly within the cone shell group which have a venom-filled, harpoon-like radula dart or tooth. Injected into prey, its venom will paralyse and is toxic enough to kill humans.

Clockwise from top left: fire coral, ball of catfish, sea urchin, cone shell, stonefish, bristleworm

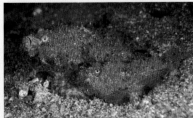

Underwater photography

There's that saying that a boat is a hole in the water you throw money into. And underwater photographers would probably say something similar about their chosen occupation. More than anything else, except perhaps tipping, this is the subject we are asked about most so here is a very brief overview.

At some point in time almost every diver is tempted to leap into the water with a camera and try to capture the excitement and emotion of their dive. However, most are disappointed with their results. Taking a good photo at 30 metres below is a completely different ball game to land photography – for two reasons: you need special equipment <u>and</u> you do need to understand about the way light changes underwater.

Cameras for underwater

It's fairly obvious that you can't take your normal camera beneath the waves: you will need either a dedicated underwater camera or a waterproof housing to keep your usual one dry. Once this was a very expensive matter but recent developments have made it all much more affordable.

If you already have a good, reasonably up-to-date camera, chances are there will be a housing available for it. Whether it's digital or film, small and compact or a top-level SLR, there is likely to be something on the market that will allow you to take it diving. Buying a housing for a camera you already own and understand means you will feel more confident using it at depth and will be saving something on the initial investment. However, if you are starting from scratch, and need to buy something new, think first about what it is you want to achieve. Do you simply want some nice little prints to show the folks back home? Then get a compact digital camera that is easy to use. However, if you are hoping to blow your best ever picture up to poster size, you will need to invest in much higher calibre equipment and that will set you back a considerable sum.

If you're not sure, consider getting a second-hand set of equipment or even hiring. You can always trade up later on, once you have learnt the ropes, worked out if you really do enjoy this rather time-consuming pastime and are willing to put in the work to maintain whatever kit you buy.

Light underwater

Next, and perhaps most importantly, you also need to have at least a basic understanding of how light changes underwater. At its simplest, light is filtered by water, so the deeper you go the darker it gets. The suns rays cannot penetrate through water in the same way they do through air. Colours also fade because the deeper you go the less red light you – and your camera – will see. The result is blue, washed out pictures.

To return light and colour to your images you will need a light source. Built-in flashes are unlikely to help much as they aren't very strong and, being mounted close to the lens, are likely to produce backscatter – reflections from particles suspended in the water. To resolve these issues you will need to add an external flash, or two. These will need to be mounted a little way from your camera so you will need arms and attachments for them. Even once you have done that, you need to be aware that flashes have their limitations too. They have to penetrate through the water, and the strength of their light reduces the further it

✪ Getting the shot

Nothing quite works like practice but these tips may help:

▶ Buy the best underwater camera you can afford. Small, throwaway cameras give throwaway photos. Underwater, you are more reliant on the quality of your equipment.

▶ As there is water between your lens and your subject, the better the quality of lens, the better the picture.

▶ Likewise, get as close as possible to your subject as the magnifying effect of water makes things appear bigger than they really are.

▶ Use a flash – or two – to return colour to the image.

▶ Research the marine environment; learn what is dangerous and what is fragile.

▶ Approach all marine creatures slowly, so as not to scare them off, and with respect. Some will retaliate if they think you are a threat.

▶ Ensure that you have good buoyancy control.

▶ Don't exceed your capabilities as a diver – always put personal safety above getting a good picture.

▶ Be courteous to other photographers and divers. If you are in a group with more than one photographer, suggest that you follow the six frame rule: on a particularly interesting subject, each person takes turns to shoot six frames then moves off, giving someone else a go. Once everyone has done so, you can always return. Never be that person who hogs a spot and ruins someone else's dive.

▶ Don't concentrate so much on what you see through the lens that you forget what is behind you (or you will miss the great white as it passes over your shoulder).

▶ A note for novice divers: no matter how excited you are to be in the water, leave the camera behind until you are truly comfortable – you can't be a good diver as well as a good photographer until you have mastered basic dive skills.

travels. If you are a long way from your subject the beam may not reach and a red fish will still appear to be blue. The most important consideration is to get as close as possible to your subject, and that is not an easy thing when most fish swim away!

The difference between film and digital

Until recently, you also needed to decide if you wanted to go with film or digital. This is much less of a heated argument these days as developments in digital technology seem to move faster than the speed of light. Despite the continual improvements, many in the professional market are still sticking with film as image quality is not limited by pixel dimensions. Debate rages as to how long this will remain true as ever more sophisticated cameras keep arriving on the market which address many of the pros and cons.

Film is also capable of handling strong and contrasting light conditions and the shutter fires in a millisecond. Only very top-end digital cameras avoid shutter lag, while compact cameras take a noticeable amount of time to focus then save the image to the card. Nearly all digital cameras struggle in very strong light, like shooting into the sun, and you can occasionally get very strangely coloured shots when the camera just can't recognize what it's looking at. For all these problems, digital enthusiasts do like to retaliate with "but I can fix all that in Photoshop!" And yes, you can fix a lot of things with image editing software, but only if your shot is nearly there: you can lighten and darken and adjust colour somewhat, but if the detail wasn't in the image file to start with, you can't easily create it. In the end, there is a lot of science behind shooting underwater, the loss of light and colour being beyond all but the best software, and many people's ability to use it. High end software is both expensive and complex so you may need to do a course to make it worth buying.

However, once you have accepted these limitations you can look at the advantages: get large storage cards and you are unlikely to run out of shots so you can take masses of images. You can also experiment a little underwater and see your results on the spot which makes it all so much easier to learn as you go.

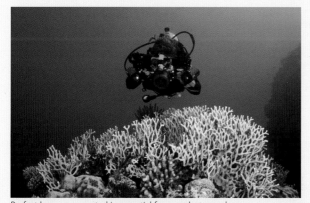

Perfect buoyancy control is essential for any photographer

❽ Camera comparisons

Many of the new breed of compact cameras can take amazing underwater shots these days. With a little effort, and providing you learn to understand and accept their limitations, you could be very happy with the results they give.

The image below left was taken on a Fuji Finepix F50D using only the integral flash. On this camera the flash is centrally located above the lens, which works well for most macro shots. A similar image taken with a Nikon D200 is on the right. It is sharper and bigger, but both are good images.

However, when it comes to shooting wide angle images you reallly will need good external strobes that will reach all the way to your subject. These images of an underwater sculpture in Grenada were taken at under ten metres deep. The left hand one was taken on the Fuji, the internal flash producing backscatter as shown by the pink dots. The right hand image was taken on the D200 with two Sea and Sea YS90s. These are mounted on either side of the lens, about 600 mm away, which avoided the backscatter and lit the subject beautifully.

Resources Underwater photography

Directory

Training and education

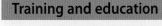

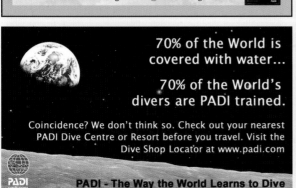

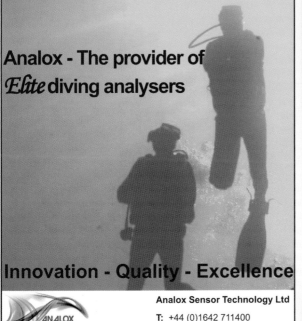

Ecuador

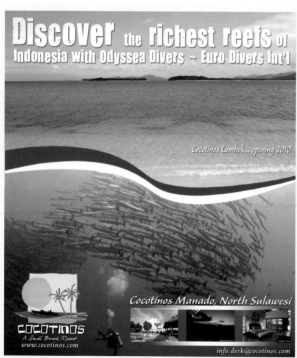

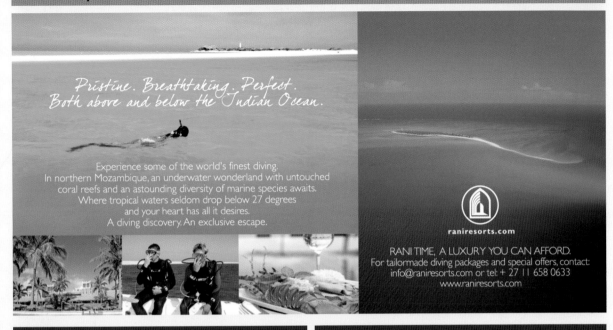
Directory

Acknowledgements

Credit where it's due

Updating Diving the World for Footprint has been a whole new voyage for us. We managed to reach a couple of places we have always wanted to see, we have seen some outstanding marine life and met lots of new people: both divers and dive professionals. As always we have to reiterate that without these people, and all our old buddies, we would never get a project like this one done. So without further ado, our continuing thanks to:

Cindi La Raia for getting us to Baja (and half of everywhere we have ever been); Tim Beard for getting us to Zanzibar and Mozambique and Alan Murphy for getting us on Air France when that other airline collapsed 48 hours before our flight!

For contributing their thoughts, being sounding boards and the best of dive buddies: Andy and Sue, Phil and Patricia, Roy and Di, Steve and Suz, Dave and Jo, Jackie and Rick, Bruce, Sue, Carole, Estelle, Mike and Sam, Spike and Clare. Thanks to Joann Gren who keeps our medical section on track and Young Skywalker, aka David Espinosa, for his continued support.

And that's not forgetting all the divers who travelled with us as we researched – the Irian Jaya, Banda and Maratua groups – nor all the people who responded to our questions, supplied a name, dropped a tip... we wish we could list you all.

For sharing their travelling tales: David Barr, Tim Beard, Bruce Brownstein, Roy Calverley, Linda Cash, Mike Caver, Lindy Chazen, Dolores Diez, Sophie and Patricio Durante, Gabriel Frankel, Joann Gren, Michelle Gaut, Jacqueline Hutchings, Sheldon Hey, Sten Johanssen, Sean Keen, Anne-Marie and Matt Kitchen-Wheeler, Sue Laing, Cindi La Raia, Gavin Macaulay, Mike and Samantha Muir, Andy Perkins, Alan Raabe, Rich Rubin, Vladimir Soto, Phil Tobin, Steve and Suzanne Turek, Peter Wincott and Inés Yturbe.

And always in memory of Larry Smith.

Many people around the world continue to be supportive, helping to ensure our memories weren't muddied and details were up to date, even when our queries had nothing to do with them.

To those who helped us with the first edition, but aren't listed here, we haven't forgotten you. The following joined the party for this edition:

Australia: Linda Cash, Dieter and Karen Gerhard, John and Linda Rumney.
Egypt: Jane Rankin, Graham Blackwell.
Fiji: Gavin Macauley and Sheldon Hey.
Galápagos: Dolores Diez, Ania Mudrewicz.
Grenada and Carriacou: Kate Fenton and the Grenada Board of Tourism; Sharon Bernstein, Max and Claudia Nagel, Gerlinde Seupel and especially Phil and Helen Saye.
Indonesia: Jonathan Cross, Andrew Lok, Andy Shorten, Annabel Thomas.
Malaysia: Vincent Chew and Michael Smith
Maldives: Anne-Marie and Matt Kitchen-Wheeler, Charlie and Ali Sabree.
Mexico: Mike Caver, Judith Fleming, Sten Johansson, Buzz Busby and the entire crew and staff of Nautilus Explorer.
Micronesia: Larry Bruton.
Mozambique: Michèle Abraham and Lindy Chazen, Marcia Baloyi and the team at Linhas Aéreas de Moçambique.
Philippines: Domingo Ramon Enerio, Rosario Afuang and the Philippines Department of Tourism, Paul O'Toole.
Tanzania: Gary Greig and Gail Arnesen, Yong Mi Janse and Fabian Huot; Paul Shepherd and Gabriel Frankel; Les Carlisle and Sarah Glen.

Bali's life would have gone into meltdown without the TLC supplied by Fiona, Kirk and Steve who helped run our lives, and hers, when we weren't there to do so ourselves. Thanks from all of us.

Finally, many thanks as ever to the entire team at Footprint but especially to Patrick Dawson, Liz Harper, Renu Sibal, Catherine Phillips, Tamsin Stirk and, as always, Alan Murphy, the non-diver who really should take time to upgrade his honorary 'C' card to a real one.

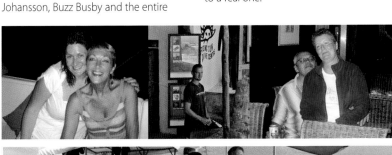

🌀 Resources

Research and reference
The following were our principal forms of reference, although there were more:

Reefbase (reefbase.org), Earthtrends (earthtrends.wri.org), The CIA World Factbook (cia.gov), Starfish (starfish.ch), The World Atlas of Coral Reefs (Spalding, Ravilious and Green)

Marine Identification
Reef Fish Identification (Allen, Steene, Humann & DeLoach); World of Water Marine Publications (Neville Coleman); IKAN Reef & Fish guides (Debelius, Kuiter, Norman, Halstead); Fishbase (fishbase.org)

Photography
Cameras Nikon F90/Nikon D200 SLRs in Sea and Sea housings; Nikonos V; Nikon Coolpix 5200 digital; Fuji Finepix F50D

Flashes Ikelite Substrobe 50's; Sea and Sea YS90 duos; Inon Z240

Lenses Nikkor 17-35 zoom, 12-24 zoom, 60mm micro, 105mm micro, 16mm, 20mm

Film Fujichrome Velvia 50 & 100 and Fujichrome Provia 100F

Suppliers Kevin Reed at Aquaphot (aquaphot.net); B&H Photo Video (bhphotovideo.com); Jon Cohen and the team at Fujifilm UK (fujifilm.co.uk)

Dive kit Amphibian Sports, London

Additional Images
Thanks to Cindi La Raia for that great portrait of us and to anyone – but especially Estelle and Phil – who ever clicked a camera then sent us a picture that has ended up on this page.

❝❞ Fish are food, not friends
Bali Tierney, London, UK

Credits

Footprint credits

Editor-in-chief: Alan Murphy
Proof reader: Tamsin Stirk
Layout and production: Beth Tierney
Picture editor: Shaun Tierney
Maps: Beth Tierney
Cover design: Robert Lunn

Managing Director: Andy Riddle
Publisher: Alan Murphy
Commercial Director: Patrick Dawson

Editorial: Sara Chare, Ria Gane, Nicola Gibbs, Jenny Haddington, Alice Jell, Felicity Laughton
Cartography: Sarah Sorensen, Kevin Feeney, Emma Bryers
Sales and marketing: Liz Harper, Hannah Bonnell
Advertising: Renu Sibal, Mike Stevens
Finance and administration: Elizabeth Taylor

Design: Mytton Williams, Bath

Photography credits

Cover images:
© Shaun Tierney/SeaFocus
Inside Images:
© SeaFocus/www.seafocus.com

Print

Manufactured in India by Replika Press Pvt Ltd

Footprint feedback

We try as hard as we can to make each Footprint guide as up to date as possible but, of course, things always change. If you want to let us know about your experiences – good, bad or ugly – then don't delay, go to www.footprintbooks.com and send in your comments.

Publishing information

Footprint Diving the World 2nd edition
© Footprint Handbooks Ltd
October 2009

ISBN 978 1 906098 76 6
CIP DATA: A catalogue record for this book is available from the British Library

® Footprint Handbooks and the Footprint mark are a registered trademark of Footprint Handbooks Ltd

Published by Footprint
6 Riverside Court, Lower Bristol Road,
Bath BA2 3DZ, UK
T +44 (0)1225 469141
F +44 (0)1225 469461
www.footprintbooks.com

Distributed in the USA by

Globe Pequot Press, Guilford, Connecticut

Disclaimer

We have, of course, tried to ensure that the facts in this guidebook are accurate. However, travellers should note that places change, owners move on, properties and companies close or are sold, and our opinions are subjective. So it is not possible to guarantee absolute accuracy or that our opinions will always coincide with yours. Travellers should obtain advice from consulates, airlines etc about travel and visa requirements before travelling. The authors and publishers do not accept responsibility for any loss, injury or inconvenience resulting from the information provided in this guidebook. This does not affect your statutory rights.

Index

Index